DATE DUE

This book has been awarded
The Adèle Mellen Prize
for its distinguished contribution to scholarship.

ASCETIC PIETY
and
WOMEN'S FAITH

Essays on Late Ancient Christianity

Elizabeth A. Clark

Studies in Women and Religion
Volume 20

The Edwin Mellen Press
Lewiston/Queenston

Library of Congress Cataloging-in-Publication

Clark, Elizabeth A. (Elizabeth Ann), 1938-
Ascetic piety and women's faith.

(Studies in women and religion ; v. 3)
Includes index.
1. Women--Religious life. 2. Asceticism--History--
Early church, ca. 30-600. I. Title. II. Series.
BV4527.C54 1986   270.2'088042   86-21828
ISBN 0-88946-529-0 (alk. paper)

This is volume 20 in the continuing series
Studies in Women and Religion
Volume 20 ISBN 0-88946-529-0
SWR Series ISBN 0-88946-549-5

All rights reserved. For information contact:
The Edwin Mellen Press   The Edwin Mellen Press
Box 450   Box 67
Lewiston, New York   Queenston, Ontario
USA 14092   L0S 1L0 CANADA

Printed in the United States of America

For

Robert Markus

with thanks

TABLE OF CONTENTS

PREFACE

The thirteen essays in this volume, written between
1977 and 1985, concern transformations both in contemporary scholarship and in late ancient Christianity. The
recent interest in social history and in women's history
has transformed the way we reconstruct the past, while
the transformations that occurred in late ancient Christianity with the conversion of the upper classes,
including numerous women, issued in a bountiful array of
literature of which this new generation of Christians
served as patrons, producers, and subjects.

For many of these devotees--Melania the Elder,
Melania the Younger, Olympias, Paula, and Demetrias, as
as well as Augustine, Ambrose, Jerome, and John
Chrysostom--a mere embrace of Christianity did not
suffice: the call was to a more rigorous religious
praxis that entailed ascetic renunciation. Thus ascetic
enthusiasm pervades much of the Christian literature of
the late fourth and early fifth centuries. The new
spirit permeates the poetry, letters, and sermons, as
well as the theological treatises, of the period. Scripture is now mined for assistance in the exaltation of
ascetic ideals.

Paradoxically, it was through such ascetic renunciation that women found new "careers" and new avenues for
patronage with its concomitant rewards. By refusing to
serve as the "cement" holding together the familial and
kinship structures of the Roman aristocracy, they

contributed to the undermining of old social mores and
the building of a new Christian society.

Yet asceticism was not so enthusiastically championed
by all Christian writers. Traditional familial values
were lauded by authors such as Faltonia Betitia Proba.
Moreover, partisans of asceticism, such as Jerome and
Augustine, often found themselves denounced as heretics
by those who believed their ascetic ardor compromised
Christian belief in the goodness of God's creation and
sexual reproduction. These are the principal themes to
be explored, illustrated, and analyzed in the essays that
follow.

The essays were originally presented to different
audiences and thus vary in scholarly style. In addition,
footnoting, capitalization, and so forth vary with the
specifications of the journals and books in which some of
the essays originally appeared. I trust that these
variations will not prove confusing to readers.

Several institutions and individuals whose assistance
was crucial in the preparation of these essays deserve
special thanks. Three grants from the National Endowment
for the Humanities provided leisure for the research and
writing of essays and books on Faltonia Betitia Proba and
Melania the Younger. The Duke University Research
Council contributed funds for editorial assistance in the
final preparation of this volume. A semester's respite
from teaching duties, arranged by my department chair,
Kalman Bland, made possible the research and writing of
"Vitiated Seeds and Holy Vessels: Augustine's Manichean
Past." The invitation to deliver three lectures at
Wichita State University as the 1982 Ransom-Butler
lecturer gave impetus to the writing of several of the
essays on women. Various sessions of the American
Academy of Religion, the American Society of Church

History, the Byzantine Studies Conference, the Oxford
International Conference on Patristic Studies, the
Society of Biblical Literature, and the 1985 Conference
on Images of the Feminine in Gnosticism heard original
versions of many of the essays. I thank the institutions
and my fellow scholars who provided me with time, inspiration, and a forum for these endeavors.

Many individuals have assisted me in my research for
these essays. Among those who deserve special mention
are Kalman Bland, Peter Brown, Alan Cameron, Ann Wharton
Epstein, Robert Gregg, Sidney Griffith, Dennis Groh,
David Halperin, Diane Hatch, Cynthia Herrup, Paula
Fredriksen Landes, Robert Markus, Ann Matter, Roland
Murphy, Elaine Pagels, John Schütz, Karen Torjesen,
Robert Wilken, and Orval Wintermute. Library staffs at
Duke, Dumbarton Oaks, and Mary Washington College were
more than ordinarily helpful. Present and former Duke
graduate students Jay Geller, Amy-Jill Levine, Blake
Leyerle, Teresa Shaw, and Maureen Tilley provided
research and editorial assistance. I especially thank
Teresa Shaw for her proofreading, and Shelia Walker for
her typing, of a difficult manuscript. My thanks also go
to Herbert Richardson, editor of Edwin Mellen Press, who
invited me to prepare this volume for publication.

I wish to acknowledge the kind permission given by
the editors or publishers of the following journals,
volumes, or presses to reprint articles or chapters that
originally appeared elsewhere:

Anglican Theological Review ("Ascetic Renunciation
    and Feminine Advancement: A Paradox of Late
    Ancient Christianity")

Byzantinische Forschungen ("Authority and Humility:
    A Conflict of Values in Fourth-Century Female
    Monasticism")

Church History ("Claims on the Bones of Saint
Stephen: The Partisans of Melania and Eudocia"
and "John Chrysostom and the Subintroductae")
Cistercian Publications, publishers of *Studia
Patristica* XVIII ("Piety, Propaganda, and
Politics in the *Life of Melania the Younger*")
Edwin Mellen Press, publishers of John Chrysostom,
On Virginity; Against Remarriage; translation
by Sally Rieger Shore ("Introduction")
Pergamon Press, publishers of *Studia Patristica* XVII
("The Virgilian *Cento* of Faltonia Betitia Proba")
Union Theological Seminary, publishers of Union
Papers No. 1 ("The State and Future of
Historical Theology: Patristic Studies")
Vergilius ("Jesus as Hero in the Vergilian *Cento*
of Faltonia Betitia Proba"; I also thank the
co-author of this article, Diane Hatch, for
permission to reprint it).

In addition, I wish to thank Edwin Mellen Press for
allowing concurrent publication of "Heresy, Asceticism,
Adam and Eve: Interpretations of Genesis 1-3 in the
Later Latin Fathers" (also to appear in *Intrigue in the
Garden: Genesis 1-3 in the History of Interpretation*
edited by Gregory Robbins).   I thank Fortress Press for
allowing a concurrent publication of "Vitiated Seeds and
Holy Vessels: Augustine's Manichean Past" (also to
appear in *Images of the Feminine in Gnosticism*, edited by
Karen King).   "Devil's Gateway and Bride of Christ:
Women in the Early Christian World" will also be included
in the forthcoming volume, *Gender and Cultural Contexts:
Feminist Reconstructions*, edited by Jean O'Barr.

Last, this volume is dedicated to Robert Markus,
whose scholarship on late antiquity has enriched many of

us, and whose sympathetic encouragement has brightened some of the dimmer moments in the years during which these essays were composed.

Elizabeth A. Clark
Duke University

August 1986

ABBREVIATIONS

Aen.	*Aeneid*
AnalBoll	*Analecta Bollandiana*
AthR	*Anglican Theological Review*
CCL	Corpus Christianorum, Series Latina
CF	*Classical Folia*
ChH	*Church History*
CIL	*Corpus Inscriptionum Latinarum*
CJ	*Classical Journal*
C&M	*Classica et Medievalia*
CSEL	Corpus Scriptorum Ecclesiasticorum Latinorum
CTh	*Codex Theodosianus*
DACL	*Dictionnaire d'Archéologie Chrétienne et de Liturgie*
Ep., Epist.; Epp.	Epistle, Epistles
Evth	*Evangelische Theologie*
GCS	Die Griechischen Christlichen Schriftsteller der ersten drei Jahrhunderte
G&R	*Greece and Rome*
JbAC	*Jahrbuch für Antike und Christentum*
JRS	*Journal of Roman Studies*
JThS	*Journal of Theological Studies*
MGH	*Monumenta Germaniae Historica*
MGH, AA	*Monumenta Germaniae Historica, Auctores Antiquissimi*
PG	Migne, Patrologia Graeca
PL	Migne, Patrologia Latina
PL Supp	Patrologia Latina, Supplementa

PVS	*Proceedings of the Virgil Society*
RAug	*Recherches Augustiniennes*
RBén	*Revue Bénédictine*
REA	*Revue des Etudes Anciennes*
REL	*Revue des Etudes Latines*
SC	Sources Chrétiennes
SIFC	*Studi Italiani di Filologia Classica*
ST	Studi e testi
TU	Texte und Untersuchungen zur Geschichte der altchristlichen Literatur
VChr	*Vigiliae Christianae*
ZKircheng	*Zeitschrift für Kirchengeschichte*
ZNW	*Zeitschrift für die Neutestamentliche Wissenschaft*

ASCETIC PIETY
and
WOMEN'S FAITH

Essays on Late Ancient Christianity

INTRODUCTION

THE STATE AND FUTURE OF HISTORICAL THEOLOGY: PATRISTIC STUDIES

In Memory of Wilhelm Pauck (1901-1981): Memorial Notices, Liturgical Pieces, Essays and Addresses, edited by David W. Lotz. Union Papers No. 2 (New York: Union Theological Seminary, 1982), pp. 46-56.

What is the present state and probable future of historical theology in the field of patristics? The question can be succinctly answered: less theology, more history. The past two decades have witnessed a shift away from the inclusion of patristics as a sub-field of theology, and all signs point to a continuation of this trend. The shift from a theological to an historical emphasis in patristics can be correlated with two phenomena affecting all present scholarship on Christianity.

First, the former domination of Christian studies by neo-orthodox theology has subsided and that subsidence, I venture, would have pleased the man we honor here, Wilhelm Pauck. Pauck warrants inclusion in the ranks of the minor prophets, for already in 1954, ruing the Barthian dominance of historical scholarship, he looked to the day when the confessional theologies then so popular would be "viewed as impossible because of their neglect of the historical dimensions of the Christian faith."[1] These were his words at the time of his inauguration as professor of church history at Union

3

Theological Seminary. Three years later he voiced the
same concern: "What we need is historical understanding,
not theosophy. The churches have more need of a Harnack
than a Barth."[2] To Harnack's importance for current
historical studies I shall return; for now, Pauck's success at prognostication should be heralded.

A second and related phenomenon affecting patristics
is its transfer from the seminary to the university. In
the university, there is little place for piety to in-
trude, to claim itself as the *telos* of Christian
scholarship. Christian studies may indeed constitute
only a fraction of the university religion department's
course offerings and in no way are seen as *apologiae* for
the faith. In the university setting, it matters not if
the results of scholarly investigation are discomforting
to traditional Christian religiosity. Just as in the
nineteenth and early twentieth centuries New Testament
scholarship was wrenched from the service of the church,
so now patristic studies have cast off their former
ecclesiastical moorings. Thus patristics is no longer
a discipline devoted primarily to the investigation of
dogmatic developments in and for themselves; rather, it
finds its new home amidst studies of the late ancient
world, commanding attention as one among many cultural
phenomena of late antiquity. Patristic scholars soon
realized that they must become more sensitive to the
political, social, economic, religious, and cultural
movements of the period. They had to look more carefully
at the work of archeologists, classicists, art historians, numismatists, and papyrologists in order to do
their own work; in fact, they sometimes needed to become
archeologists, numismatists, and so forth, themselves,
And the move to the university also made clear that
patristics scholars needed to learn much from the social

science disciplines as well as from the humanities. As
they learned, they put fresh questions to the texts in
place of the traditional--and sometimes tired--ones
Christian dogmatics had asked for centuries. Their
reading and scholarly investigations introduced them to
strange new worlds.

A nice illustration of the point is afforded by a
glance at the bibliographies and footnotes of Peter
Brown's recent works. They indicate in an illuminating
manner what an inventive scholar of the early Christian
era might be reading today. To be sure, the books on
dogma are still there, but what else do we find? First
of all, the type of literature commonly read by classicists and ancient historians: *Onomastic Studies in the
Early Christian Inscriptions of Roman Carthage; Manpower
Shortage and the Fate of the Roman Empire in the West;
Porphyrius the Charioteer;* "The Ceiling Paintings in
Trier and Illusionism in Constantinian Painting." But
beyond these, we note other works that only a few, if
any, earlier patristics scholars would have read for
professional edification: *On Shame and the Search for
Identity; Purity and Danger; Spirit Mediumship and
Society in Africa.* We are here in a different world, an
exciting world--but one for which most scholars of early
Christianity received no specific training. Hence they
have been thrust again into the role of students; probably the best thing that could happen to *any* scholar!

To locate more precisely the shifts in the world of
patristic studies, we might take as a foil that prince
of church historians so dear to Wilhelm Pauck, Adolf von
Harnack. And a superb foil Harnack provides, for as a
liberal historian he was concerned to note the ever-
changing quality of Christianity in all its relations
with culture.[3] Political, social, economic influences

could not be discounted in the formation of Christian
dogma, Harnack insisted, over against others of his
time. He sharply criticized as "unscientific" the
notion that dogma simply "unfolded itself." His view
was that dogma had its history "in the individual living
man and nowhere else."[4] He called on scholars to take
that notion seriously, to look at "the actual conditions
in which believing and intelligent men have been
placed."[5] Thus, in using Harnack as a foil, we erect no
straw man who will topple at the first blow.

A difference immediately evident between the present
generation of patristics scholars and Harnack is an
ideological one. Despite Harnack's concern for political
influences on dogma, Hegelian idealism colored his
approach to early Christianity. Thus Harnack, envision-
ing the *Geist* at work in human history,[6] spoke of the
"progressive concretion of the spirit."[7] Although
Marxists have not swamped the field of patristics, there
is nonetheless today a greater emphasis on the ways in
which material processes shaped early Christian theology,
much as they shaped other ideologies. Even if scholars
may not be entirely comfortable with Marx's and Engels'
slogan, "Life is not determined by consciousness, but
consciousness by life,"[8] they are perhaps *more* comfortable with it than they are with Harnack's "progressive
concretion of the spirit." That relative difference of
ease is reflected in the works now considered essential
reading for the patristics scholar. Such classics as
the works on late ancient economic and social issues by
Mikhail Rostovtzeff[9] and A.H.M. Jones,[10] for example,
are now supplemented by more technical studies, such as
Richard Duncan-Jones' *The Economy of the Roman Empire:
Quantitative Studies*[11] and Peter Garnsey's *Social Status
and Legal Privilege in the Roman Empire.*[12] Among

American scholars, Robert Grant has been influential in
relating ancient political, economic, and social history
to patristic scholarship, as is especially evidenced by
his *Early Christianity and Society: Seven Studies*.[13]

But the change in ideological perspective isn't all.
The passing of the decades has given us a wealth of
material not available to Harnack. Scholars today, of
course, possess critical editions of many patristic texts
published since Harnack's time. (Consider, for example,
the state of Gregory of Nyssa's writings before the critical work of Werner Jaeger and his colleagues.[14]) The
older series of critical editions that were begun in
Harnack's era, such as *Texte und Untersuchungen zur
Geschichte der altchristlichen Literatur* and *Patrologia
Orientalis*, have been joined by newer ones: *Corpus
Christianorum*, *Sources Chrétiennes*, *Oxford Early Christian Texts*, and the new *Corpus Patristicum Hispanum*.
And twentieth-century translations have made patristic
primary source material available for classroom use.

Likewise, the uncovering of hitherto unknown Gnostic
materials, particularly the Manichean and Nag Hammadi
documents, would have delighted Harnack, whose interest
in Gnosticism remained keen from his graduate-school days
to his final work on Marcion.[15] But the famous
Harnackian dictum on Gnosticism, that it was "the acute
secularizing or hellenizing of Christianity, with the
rejection of the Old Testament,"[16] is now seen to require
extensive modification, if not outright rejection, given
the hot debates on pre-Christian, extra-Christian, and
Jewish Gnosticism.

Without doubt, the discussion of Gnosticism has
dominated the past two decades of patristic scholarship.
A cursory glance at the titles of articles in the patristics journal *Vigiliae Christianiae* during the 1970s gives
the impression that more of them were devoted to

Gnosticism than to any other single topic of research, and the 1978 International Conference on Gnosticism at Yale demonstrated that the work of previous decades had hardly exhausted the field. A new generation of scholars has arisen to join the ranks of Hans Jonas and Gilles Quispel: for example, Klaus Koschorke,[17] Bentley Layton,[18] Birger Pearson,[19] and Pheme Perkins.[20] So complex and technical have Gnostic studies become that it was a pleasant surprise to register the immense popular success that awaited Elaine Pagels' *The Gnostic Gospels*.[21] It is clear that both the editing of patristic texts and recent "finds" have given us much new material on which to work.

In addition, the past two decades have seen discussion of topics that have been with us for centuries, but are now being investigated anew. One such topic is heresy. Here the seminal work was Walter Bauer's *Rechtgläubigkeit und Ketzerei im ältesten Christentum*, published in English in 1971 as *Orthodoxy and Heresy in Earliest Christianity*.[22] The book was provocative in several respects. First of all, there was its sheer unsettling effect upon those who had accepted the church fathers' claim that "orthodoxy" was chronologically prior to "heresy." As Bauer showed, in some early Christian centers such as Edessa, "heresy" was the earliest form of Christianity we know.

Since the publication of Bauer's book, there has been a mushrooming of work on heresy, quite apart from the interest in Gnosticism. Monophysites have received attention from W.H.C. Frend,[23] Jacques Jarry,[24] Roberta Chesnut,[25] and Robin Darling.[26] Priscillian has been studied by Henry Chadwick.[27] Nestorian texts have been edited and commented on by Luise Abramowski and Alan Goodman, among others.[28] Arianism has also proved a

fertile field for scholars, with recent contributions by
Manlio Simonetti,[29] Thomas Kopecek,[30] Rudolf Lorenz,[31]
and Robert Gregg and Dennis Groh.[32] As for the Donatists, they have received ample study in the past three
decades: in English, there has been Frend's book, *The
Donatist Church*,[33] but there are other important works
on the subject by Hans-Joachim Diesner,[34] Jean-Paul
Brisson[35] and the excellent study by Emin Tengström.[36]

Bauer's book also served to stimulate another tendency of modern patristic scholarship: to focus on
particular geographical centers of Christianity, an
enterprise that inevitably brought to light the diversity
of early Christian communities. The older chronological
and dogmatic approaches had little helped us to understand the variations in Christian belief and practice
that might be present from city to city, province to
province. One product of the new interest in particular
cities was the American Academy of Religion's working
group on The Social World of Early Christianity that for
several years devoted itself to the study of Antioch.
Two members of that group, Wayne Meeks and Robert Wilken,
have enriched our knowledge of that city in their *Jews
and Christians in Antioch in the First Four Centuries of
the Common Era*.[37] As might have been expected, the investigation of particular centers meant that archeological research was of increasing importance to the
patristics scholar. We may still have much to learn,
for example, about the city of Origen and Eusebius,
Caesarea, from the archeological work proceeding there.[38]
Indeed, Palestine in general is becoming an area of
archeological interest for patristics as well as for
Biblical scholars.[39]

Another development, reflected in Bauer's concentration on Edessa, has been a widening recognition that the

Greek and Roman boundaries of patristic studies have
been too narrow; we have neglected such areas of early
Christian development as Syria and Armenia. Arthur
Vööbus' work in collecting, editing, and interpreting
Syriac texts deserves special mention.[40] And the new
generation of Syriac scholars, including Roberta Ches-
nut,[41] Robert Murray,[42] Sebastian Brock,[43] Micheline
Albert,[44] and Sidney Griffith,[45] among others, ensures
that the field will continue to flourish. Entire con-
ferences are now devoted to topics such as "East of
Byzantium: Syria and Armenia in the Formative Period."[46]
Such emphases remind those trained only in Greek and
Latin that the early Christian world encompassed the
Orontes as well as the Tiber.

Lastly, there has been of late an interest in topics
and approaches that some would claim are stimulated by
recent political and social concerns, especially as
those have been manifested in America. Women's studies
is a case in point. To be sure, there have been in
decades past studies pertaining to women in the early
Christian era. The difference between past and present
lies in the current widespread interest in the subject,
and in the desire to move the subject from the periphery
to a more central place in the scholarship on the early
Christian era. The Gnostic material has excited much
interest in this respect,[47] and our understanding of the
Gnostic sects may be modified as we learn more about
their theologies and practices in relation to women.
The "orthodox" women are emerging in their own right as
well, with attention now directed to Macrina, Olympias,
the Melanias, Jerome's circle, and so on.[48] Investigations of the social world of early Christianity will
undoubtedly take more account in the future of these
women, the realizations of any ecclesiastical fund-
raiser's dream.

Also perhaps sparked by social events of our time is
the changed approach to the study of the Fathers: there
is a noticeable tendency toward "debunking."   In recent
discussions of heresy, for example, we find a manifest
sympathy with the supposed heretics and a suspicion of
the orthodox Fathers.   Far from receiving special favor,
the latter have been called high-handed, if not outrightly criminal, in their discouragement (indeed oblitera-
tion) of their opponents.   This tendency was noted by
Patrick Henry in a paper delivered at the 1979 Oxford
Patristics Conference.   Henry wrote,

> We tend to see everything in terms of power
> struggles, manipulations, negotiations, lobby-
> ings, trade-offs, compromises, revolutions
> ....And recent experience, at least in the
> United States, has given us a very jaundiced
> view of those who come out on top in politi-
> cal contests.   We instinctively assume that
> those who have risen to the top have done so
> by hook, crook, chicanery, deception (or for
> sure, 'trimming'), corruption....And in the
> early Church, the Fathers are, for the most
> part, those who come out on top.   Given our
> assumptions their very identity as Fathers
> puts them on trial.[49]

Although the heavy concentration of recent scholarship on
the heretics has been criticized, I would argue that we
do not appreciate the richness of the patristic era unless we give equal voice to those who lost out in the
evolution of mainstream Christianity, and unless we note
with some care the methods by which those now called
saints of the church won the day.   Although we may feel
sympathy for the heretics because they were the "under-
dogs," the shift in attitude is also attributable to the

new secular environment in which patristic studies
flourish. Our subjects, no longer treated as sacrosanct,
may have rude questions put to them, the answers to which
may not cast favorable light on the heroes of yore. But
then, sleuthing in history is like sleuthing elsewhere:
dark corners are illuminated, skeletons in closets rat-
tled.

Harnack, in a different context, expressed himself
in a way appropriate to this topic: "We study history,"
he wrote, "in order to intervene in the course of history
and we have a right and duty to do so....To intervene in
history--this means that we must reject the past when it
reaches into the present only to block us."[50] Given his
concern for the utility of scholarship for future cultural endeavors, Harnack might not have been entirely
alarmed at the present direction of patristic studies.

There have been many other fascinating investigations
of the patristic period of late--studies, for example,
of the ancient church historians, especially Eusebius;[51]
of patristic exegesis;[52] of the influence of classical
forms on Christian writing;[53] of Judaism and its relation to early Christianity.[54] There have been magnificent biographies of Augustine[55] and of Origen[56] that will
instruct any future student of the early Christian era.
None of these endeavors should be slighted. The sheer
abundance of subjects that could be here mentioned is
itself a clear indication that patristics scholarship is
being reborn. Inevitably we feel the teething pains, no
doubt to be followed by the adolescent rebellion, but
someday we shall surely see much of the recent scholarship on the Fathers--and the "Mothers"--of the early
Christian era find a welcome home in the academic study
of late antiquity.

NOTES

[1]Wilhelm Pauck, "Adolf von Harnack's Interpretation of Church History," in *The Heritage of the Reformation,* rev. ed. (Glencoe, Ill.: The Free Press of Glencoe, 1961), p. 350.

[2]Wilhelm Pauck, "A Brief Criticism of Barth's *Dogmatics,*" in *Heritage,* p. 358.

[3]Wilhelm Pauck, "An Exposition and Criticism of Liberalism," in *Heritage,* pp. 314-15; *Harnack and Troeltsch: Two Historical Theologians* (New York: Oxford University Press, 1968), p. 28.

[4]Adolf Harnack, *History of Dogma,* tr. Neil Buchanan from the 3rd German ed. (Boston: Roberts Brothers, 1897), I, 12.

[5]Ibid., I, 13.

[6]Adolf Harnack, "Was hat die Historie an fester Erkenntnis zur Deutung der Weltgeschehens zu bieten?" *Erforschtes und Erlebtes* (= *Reden und Aufsätze,* n.f. 4) (Giessen: Alfred Töpelmann, 1923), pp. 187ff.

[7]Adolf Harnack, "Über die Sicherheit und die Grenzen geschichtlicher Erkenntnis," *Erforschtes und Erlebtes,* p. 5; translation of the phrase "fortschreitende Objektivierung des Geistes" is Pauck's, *Heritage,* p. 339.

[8]Karl Marx and Friedrich Engels, *The German Ideology,* Parts I and II, ed. R. Pascal (London: International Publishers, 1939), p. 15.

[9]M.I. Rostovtzeff, *Social and Economic History of the Roman Empire,* 2nd. ed. rev. (Oxford: Clarendon Press, 1957).

[10]A.H.M. Jones, *The Later Roman Empire, 284-602,* 2 vols. (Norman, Ok.: University of Oklahoma Press, 1964); *The Roman Economy,* ed. P.A. Brunt (Totowa, N.J.: Rowman

and Littlefield, 1974); Jones, J.R. Martindale, and J. Morris, eds., *The Prosopography of the Later Roman Empire*, Vol. I: *A.D. 260-395* (Cambridge: Cambridge University Press, 1971).

[11]Cambridge: Cambridge University Press, 1974.

[12]Oxford: Clarendon Press, 1970.

[13]San Francisco: Harper & Row, 1977.

[14]Werner Jaeger, *et al.*, *Gregorii Nysseni Opera* (Berlin: Weidmann, 1921-   ).

[15]Adolf Harnack, *Marcion: Das Evangelium von fremden Gott* (Leipzig: J.C. Hinrichs Verlag, 1923).

[16]Harnack, *History of Dogma*, I, 226.

[17]Klaus Koschorke, *Hippolyt's Ketzerbekämpfung und Polemik gegen die Gnostiker* (Wiesbaden: O. Harrassowitz, 1975); *Die Polemik der Gnostiker gegen das kirchliche Christentum*. Nag Hammadi Studies 12 (Leiden: Brill, 1978).

[18]Bentley Layton, ed. and tr., *The Gnostic Treatise on Resurrection from Nag Hammadi*. Harvard Dissertations in Religion 12 (Missoula, Mont.: Scholars Press, 1979).

[19]Birger A. Pearson, *The Pneumatikos-Psychikos Terminology in I Corinthians: A Study in the Theology of the Corinthian Opponents of Paul and Its Relation to Gnosticism*. SBL Dissertation Series 12 (Missoula, Mont.: SBL for the Nag Hammadi Seminar, 1973); "Jewish Haggadic Traditions in *The Testimony of Truth* from Nag Hammadi (CG IX, 3)," in *Religious Syncretism in Antiquity: Essays in Conversation with Geo Widengren*, ed. Birger A. Pearson. American Academy of Religion Series on Formative Contemporary Thinkers 1 (Missoula, Mont.: Scholars Press, 1975).

[20]Pheme Perkins, *The Gnostic Dialogue: The Early Church and the Crisis of Gnosticism* (New York: Paulist Press, 1980).

[21]New York: Random House, 1979.

[22]Tübingen: Mohr/Siebeck, 1934; ET of 2nd German ed., ed. Robert A. Kraft and Gerhard Krodel, tr. Philadelphia Seminar on Christian Origins (Philadelphia: Fortress Press, 1971).

[23]W.H.C. Frend, *The Rise of the Monophysite Movement* (Cambridge: Cambridge University Press, 1972).

[24]Jacques Jarry, *Hérésies et factions dans l'Empire Byzantin du IV*^{e} *au VII*^{e} *siècle.* Recherches d'archéologie, de philologie, et d'histoire 14 (Cairo: L'Institut français d'archéologie orientale, 1968).

[25]Roberta C. Chesnut, *Three Monophysite Christologies: Severus of Antioch, Philoxenus of Mabbug and Jacob of Sarug* (London: Oxford University Press, 1976).

[26]Robin Darling, *Religious Leadership in Sixth-Century Syria: Monophysite Piety and Political Philosophy in Severus of Antioch* (New York: The Edwin Mellen Press, forthcoming).

[27]Henry Chadwick, *Priscillian of Avila. The Occult and the Charismatic in the Early Church* (Oxford: Clarendon Press, 1976).

[28]Luise Abramowski, ed., *Untersuchungen zum Liber Heraclidis des Nestorius.* Corpus Scriptorum Christianorum Orientalium 242 (Louvain: Secrétariat du Corpus SCO, 1963); Luise Abramowski and Alan E. Goodman, eds., *A Nestorian Collection of Christological Texts*, 2 vols. (Cambridge: Cambridge University Press, 1972).

[29]Manlio Simonetti, *La crisi ariana del IV secolo.* Studia Ephemeridis "Augustinianum" 11 (Rome: Institutum Patristicum "Augustinianum," 1975).

[30]Thomas A. Kopecek, *A History of Neo-Arianism*, 2 vols. Patristic Monograph Series 8 (Cambridge, Mass.: Philadelphia Patristic Foundation, Ltd., 1979).

[31]Rudolf Lorenz, *Arius judaizans? Untersuchungen zur dogmengeschichtlichen Einordnung des Arius.* Forschungen zur Kirchen-und Dogmengeschichte 31 (Göttingen: Vandenhoeck & Ruprecht, 1979).

[32]Robert C. Gregg and Dennis E. Groh, *Early Arianism: A View of Salvation* (Philadelphia: Fortress Press, 1981).

[33]Oxford: Clarendon Press, 1952.

[34]Hans-Joachim Diesner, *Kirche und Staat im spätrömischen Reich* (Berlin: Evangelische Verlaganstalt, 1964).

[35]Jean-Paul Brisson, *Autonomisme et Christianisme dans l'Afrique romaine de Septime Sévère à l'invasion vandale* (Paris: Editions E. de Boccard, 1958).

[36]Emin Tengström, *Donatisten und Katholiken. Soziale, wirtschaftliche und politische Aspekte einer nordafrikanischen Kirchenspaltung* (Göteborg: Elanders Boktryckerei Aktiebolag, 1964).

[37]SBL Sources for Biblical Study 13 (Missoula, Mont.: Scholars Press, 1978).

[38]Lee I. Levine, *Roman Caesarea. An Archeological-Topographical Study*, Qedem 2, Monographs of the Institute of Archaeology of the Hebrew University of Jerusalem (Jerusalem: "Avha" Cooperative Press, 1975) and *Caesarea Under Roman Rule* (Leiden: Brill, 1975); Robert J. Bull and D. Larrimore Holland, eds., *The Joint Expedition to Caesarea Maritima*, vol. I, BASOR Supplemental Studies 19 (Missoula, Mont.: Scholars Press, 1975).

[39]See, for example, Robert C. Gregg, *Romans, Jews, and Christians in the Golan (Third through Seventh Centuries)*, forthcoming.

[40]Arthur Vööbus, *Syriac and Arabic Documents Regarding Legislation Relative to Syrian Asceticism* (Stockholm: Estonian Theological Society in Exile, 1960); *History of Asceticism in the Syrian Orient*. Corpus Scriptorum Christianorum Orientalium 184, 197 (Louvain: Secrétariat du Corpus SCO, 1958-1960); *Syrische Kanonessammlungen: ein Beitrag zur Quellenkunde*. Corpus Scriptorum Christianorum Orientalium 307, 317 (Louvain: Secrétariat du Corpus SCO, 1970), and many others.

[41]Roberta C. Chesnut, *Three Monophysite Christologies* (see n. 25 above).

Introduction 17

[42]Robert Murray, *Symbols of Church and Kingdom: A Study in Early Syriac Tradition* (London: Cambridge University Press, 1975).

[43]Sebastian P. Brock, ed., *The Syriac Version of the Pseudo-Nonnos Mythological Scholia.* University of Cambridge Oriental Publications 20 (Cambridge: Cambridge University Press, 1971).

[44]Micheline Albert, ed. and tr., *Jacques de Saroug, Homélies contre les Juifs.* Patrologia Orientalis 38, 1 (Turnhout: Brepols, 1976).

[45]Sidney H. Griffith, "Chapter Ten of the *Scholion*: Theodore bar Kônî's Apology for Christianity," *Orientalia Christiana Periodica* 47 (1981) 158-188; "Theodore bar Kônî's *Scholion*: A Nestorian *Summa Contra Gentiles* from the First Abbasid Century," in *East of Byzantium: Syria and Armenia in the Formative Period* (Washington, D.C.: Dumbarton Oaks Publications, 1982); "Ephraem, the Deacon of Edessa, and the Church of the Empire," *Diakonia. Studies in Honor of Robert T. Meyer* (Washington, D.C.: Catholic University of America Press, 1986), pp. 22-52.

[46]Dumbarton Oaks Conference, Washington, D.C., May 9-11, 1980.

[47]For example, material in Elaine Pagels, *The Gnostic Gospels* (see above, n. 21).

[48]Rosemary Ruether, "Misogynism and Virginal Feminism in the Fathers of the Church," in *Religion and Sexism: Images of Women in the Jewish and Christian Traditions* (New York: Simon and Schuster, 1974); "Mothers of the Church: Ascetic Women in the Late Patristic Age," in *Women of Spirit: Female Leadership in the Jewish and Christian Traditions*, ed. Rosemary Ruether and Eleanor McLaughlin (New York: Simon and Schuster, 1979); Anne Yarbrough, "Christianization in the Fourth Century: The Example of Roman Women," *Church History* 45 (1976) 149-165; Elizabeth A. Clark, *Jerome, Chrysostom and Friends: Essays and Translations.* Studies in Women and Religion 2 (New York: The Edwin Mellen Press, 1979); *The Golden Bough, The Oaken Cross: The Virgilian Cento of Faltonia Betitia Proba.* AAR Texts and Translations 5 (Chico, Cal.: Scholars Press, 1981) (with Diane F. Hatch); *The Life of Melania the Younger;*

Introduction, Translation, Commentary (New York: The
Edwin Mellen Press, 1984).

[49]Patrick Henry, "Why is Contemporary Scholarship
So Enamored of Ancient Heretics?," typescript, pp. 5-6.

[50]Adolf Harnack, "Über die Sicherheit," p. 7 (see
above, n. 7), tr. in Pauck, *Heritage*, p. 340.

[51]Glen F. Chesnut, *The First Christian Histories.
Eusebius, Socrates, Sozomen, Theodoret and Evagrius*
(Paris: Beauchesne, 1977); Harold A. Drake, *In Praise
of Constantine: A Historical Study and New Translation
of Eusebius' Tricennial Orations.* University of
California Classical Studies 15 (Berkeley: University
of California Press, 1976); Robert M. Grant, *Eusebius
as Church Historian* (Oxford: Clarendon Press, 1980);
Timothy Barnes, *Constantine and Eusebius* (Cambridge,
Mass.: Harvard University Press, 1981).

[52]Rowan A. Greer, *The Captain of Our Salvation: A
Study in the Patristic Exegesis of Hebrews.* Beiträge
zur Geschichte der biblischen Exegese 15 (Tübingen:
J.C.B. Mohr, 1973); Maurice Wiles, *The Divine Apostle:
The Interpretation of St. Paul's Epistles in the Early
Church* (Cambridge: Cambridge University Press, 1967);
T.E. Pollard, *Johannine Christology and the Early
Church.* Society for New Testament Studies Monograph
Series 13 (Cambridge: Cambridge University Press,
1970); Peter J. Gorday, *Principles of Patristic Exegesis
in Origen, John Chrysostom and Augustine* (New York:
The Edwin Mellen Press, 1983).

[53]Robert D. Sider, *Ancient Rhetoric and the Art of
Tertullian* (London: Oxford University Press, 1971);
Robert C. Gregg, *Consolation Philosophy: Greek and
Christian Paideia in Basil and the Two Gregories.*
Patristic Monograph Series 3 (Cambridge, Mass.: Phila-
delphia Patristic Foundation, 1975); Patricia Cox,
Biography in Late Antiquity: A Quest for the Holy Man
(Berkeley: University of California Press, 1983).

[54]Robert L. Wilken, *Judaism and the Early Christian
Mind: A Study of Cyril of Alexandria's Exegesis and
Theology* (New Haven: Yale University Press, 1971);
N.R.M. De Lange, *Origen and the Jews: Studies in*

Jewish-Christian Relations in Third-Century Palestine.
University of Cambridge Oriental Publications 25 (Cambridge: Cambridge University Press, 1976).

[55]Peter Brown, *Augustine of Hippo: A Biography* (Berkeley: University of California Press, 1967).

[56]Pierre Nautin, *Origène: sa vie et son oeuvre.* Christianisme antique 1 (Paris: Beauchesne, 1977).

PART I

WOMEN IN LATE ANCIENT CHRISTIANITY

DEVIL'S GATEWAY AND BRIDE OF CHRIST: WOMEN IN THE EARLY CHRISTIAN WORLD

Ransom - Butler Lectures
Wichita State University (1982)

The materials out of which this paper is constructed might well promote despair among many feminist scholars. In the first place, the sources are exclusively literary--and to make matters worse, the literature is written *by* men *about* women. The literature, moreover, is so propagandistic and rhetorical that the attempt to extract historical information from it might seem futile. Far from hearing women's voices directly, we might reasonably question whether the male voices we hear can sound an authentic note. Thus, these sources, penned by church leaders whose views on women are barriers enough to a sympathetic reading, were constrained within contemporary literary conventions that seem to hide rather than reveal the full humanity of their subjects.

In addition, the women who served as the subjects of the church fathers' literary endeavors were from an elite class. Indeed, we can confidently assert that their social status and wealth contributed significantly to their selection as literary subjects. Although archeology, inscriptions, and (for Egypt) papyri lend limited assistance to uncovering "ordinary" women's lives in the early Christian era, extended portraits of women

almost exclusively concern those whose real estate holdings were scattered throughout a half-dozen provinces of
the Roman Empire and whose annual income could have supported hundreds, probably thousands, of people.[1]

Yet discouragement occasioned by the sources is not
the dominant motif of this paper, for women in early
Christianity have been the subject of much lively writing
in recent years. Spurred by the feminist movement of the
past two decades, scholars with a raised consciousness of
women's issues turned to the old sources with new eyes.
Following a pattern we now recognize as typical in
feminist scholarship, they first raised up for inspection
the misogyny so prevalent in the writings of the church
fathers.[2] Although this project is by no means complete,
given the enormous corpus of patristic literature, a
second task soon took precedence: to uncover the lives
of actual women in early Christianity. Here a monumental
task of historical reconstruction awaited them, since the
meagre materials pertaining to women had to be fleshed
out and interpreted in light of scholarship on late
antiquity in its social, economic, legal, literary,
medical, philosophical, and educational dimensions, a
task for which traditional theological education had not
prepared them. Although older generations of male
scholars had sometimes claimed that women's status was
elevated by Christian ideology, few attempts had been
made to detail the limits of that ideology or to uncover
its economic and social correlates. The paper that follows will encompass both stages of historical research:
although the church fathers' misogyny will be amply
illustrated, the detailing of women's lives in ancient
Christianity will receive attention as well.

I turn now to the problem suggested by the title of
my paper: the dual evaluation of woman by the church

fathers as the "devil's gateway" and the "bride of
Christ." The fathers' alternate condemnation and exaltation of the female sex is both striking and baffling.
Their extreme ambivalence on the topic of womanhood has
led some modern commentators to assert that women made
progress in the early Christian centuries, and others,
looking at different evidence, to conclude that they re-
gressed. In this instance, both sides are right--
depending on which groups of women they focus. To illustrate how women both "won" and "lost" is my present task.

First, listen to the voices of the church fathers
themselves. Listen to the early third-century North
African church father Tertullian harangue a female
audience in his treatise, "On the Dress of Women." He
exhorts Christian women to dress simply and modestly, and
justifies his exhortation in these words:

If such strong faith remained on earth, as
strong as the reward of faith expected in
heaven, not one of you, dearest sisters, from
the time she acknowledged the living God and
learned about herself, that is, about the
condition of women, would have desired a more
charming dress, not to speak of a more brilliant one. She would rather go about in
cheap clothes and strive for an appearance
characterized by neglect. She would carry
herself around like Eve, mourning and peni-
tent, that she might more fully expiate by
each garment of penitence that which she
acquired from Eve--I mean the degradation of
the first sin and the hatefulness of human
perdition. "In pains and anxieties you bring
forth children, woman, and your inclination
is for your husband, and he rules over you"

(Gen. 3:16)--and you know not that you are
also an Eve?

God's judgment lives on in our age: the
guilt necessarily lives on as well. *You* are
the devil's gateway: *you* are the unsealer
of that forbidden tree: *you* are the first
forsaker of the divine law; *you* are the one
who persuaded him whom the devil was not
brave enough to approach; *you* so lightly
crushed the image of God, the man Adam; because of *your* punishment, that is, death,
even the Son of God had to die. And you
think to adorn yourself beyond your "tunic
of skins?" (Gen. 3:21)[3]

Or again, listen to the words of John Chrysostom,
bishop of Constantinople at the close of the fourth century. In the following passage, he warns male ascetics
who have renounced sexual activity of the dangers that
await them, the effeminacy into which they will sink,
if they share a residence with a woman similarly vowed to
celibacy. In his description of the feminine characteristics that will rub off on the man who attempts to live
in such a situation, he compares this disgrace to the
taming of a corageous lion:

Just as someone captures a proud and fiercely-
glaring lion, then shears his mane, breaks his
teeth, clips his claws, and renders him a disgraceful and ridiculous specimen, so that this
fearsome and unassailable creature, whose very
roaring causes everyone to tremble, is easily
conquered even by children, so these women
make all the men they capture easy for the
devil to overcome. They render them softer,
more hot-headed, shameful, mindless, irascible,

insolent, importunate, ignoble, crude, servile,
niggardly, reckless, nonsensical, and to sum it
all up, the women take all their corrupting
feminine customs and stamp them into the souls
of these men.[4]
And yet, the fathers who utter such vituperations
also lavish praise on women. The fourth-century church
father Jerome had numerous female friends whom he frequently lauded. Sensitive to the fact that his male
contemporaries might ridicule his praises, he defended
his practice by an appeal to the New Testament:

> An unbelieving reader might perhaps laugh
> at me for laboring so long over the praises
> of the ladies. He will rather condemn himself
> for pride than us for foolishness if he will
> ponder how the holy women who were companions
> of our Lord and Savior ministered to him from
> their own substance (Lk. 8:1-3), how the three
> Marys stood before the cross (John 19:25) and
> how especially Mary Magdalene, who received
> the name "tower" (Magdala) from the zeal and
> ardor of her faith, was first worthy to see
> Christ rising, even before the apostles (John
> 20:11-18). For we judge moral excellences
> not by people's sex, but by their quality
> of spirit....[5]

The very man who claimed that women turn men into cowardly lions, John Chrysostom, had a close female friend and
confidante, Olympias, whose merits he constantly sang in
his seventeen extant letters to her. In the anonymous
Life of Olympias, her many virtues are described:

> No place, no country, no desert, no island, no
> distant setting, remained without a share in
> the benevolence of this famous woman; rather,

she furnished the churches with liturgical
offerings and helped the monasteries and convents, the beggars, the prisoners, and those
in exile; quite simply, she distributed her
alms over the entire inhabited world, And
the blessed Olympias herself burst the supreme
limit in her almsgiving and her humility, so
that nothing can be found greater than what
she did. She had a life without vanity, an
appearance without pretence, character without
affectation, a face without adornment; she
kept watch without sleeping, she had an
immaterial body, a mind without vainglory,
intelligence without conceit, an untroubled
heart, an artless spirit, charity without
limits, unbounded generosity, contemptible
clothing, immeasurable self-control, recti-
tude of thought, undying hope in God, ineffable
almsgiving; she was the ornament of all the
humble and was in addition worthily honored
by the most holy patriarch John.[6]

Most interesting of all is the elevation of female
martyrs and ascetics to the rank of "brides of Christ."
A notable text that exploits this image is Jerome's letter to the adolescent heiress Eustochium, who had
recently taken a vow of virginity. In his lengthy
epistle to Eustochium praising her decision for the celibate life and warning her of the pitfalls she must now
avoid, Jerome over and again rings the theme that she is
to be "the bride of Christ." He opens his letter with
the words of Psalm 45, "Forget your own people and your
father's house, and the King [here meaning Jesus] will
desire your beauty."[7] Since Eustochium is now the Lord's
bride, Jerome feels constrained to address her as "Lady."[8]

He reminds the girl's mother, his friend Paula, that she is now the "mother-in-law of God."[9] Throughout the letter, Jerome depicts Eustochium and her fiancé Jesus as swooning lovers, and often borrows the erotic language of the Song of Songs to sing this epithalamium that, para-doxically, celebrates sexual renunciation.[10] At the letter's conclusion, Jerome imagines Eustochium flying to heaven, where she is greeted by Jesus her Spouse. Eustochium, now united with her betrothed, cries to him in the words of Song of Songs, "Many waters cannot quench love, neither can the floods drown it."[11]

How are we to account for the evaluation of the female sex as both devil's gateway and bride of Christ? How are we to account for the chilling negativity of some descriptions, given the praise of women's piety and steadfastness in others? The answer is three-fold.

First, the church fathers inherited the literary traditions of classical paganism, of ancient Israel, and of primitive Christianity, which did not always accord the female sex the rights and dignity we today deem appropriate. Although virtuous wives, learned mothers, and brave heroines all can be found in the pages of classical literature, we also have such works as Juvenal's *Sixth Satire*, which in 661 lines catalogues the depravities, infidelities, cruelties, avarice, lies, extravagance, superstition, and murderous designs of wives. There is also the famous poem of Semonides in which the poet compares women to dogs, weasels, asses, monkeys and other animals, and concludes that women are the greatest evil Zeus made.[12] Such proverbs as these passed down in the Greek tradition: "There are only two days on which a woman can refresh you: on the day of marriage and when she is buried";[13] The grasshopper is to be praised as happy, since their females have no

voices";[14] "O Zeus, what need is there to abuse women?
It would be enough if you only said the word 'woman.'"[15]
The literature of pagan antiquity contributed its share
to the misogyny of later Western culture.

Although the Hebrew tradition did not portray women
in general so negatively, female villains nonetheless
lurk in the pages of Scripture: the names of Jezebel and
Delilah became virtual synonymns for the treachery and
deceit some church fathers thought characteristic of
women. The Wisdom tradition of Hebrew Scripture, as
well, was replete with images of "dangerous women," such
as the "Madam Folly" of Proverbs 5 and the "loose women"
young Hebrew men were warned to shun if they wished to
escape "the Pit" of destruction.[16] And surveying the
prophetic literature, we might wonder *why* the standard
metaphor of the Hebrew prophets for Israel's apostasy was
that of an unfaithful *woman.*[17]

Yet--and most interestingly--the canonical Hebrew
Scriptures never so much as repeated, much less
developed, the one story exploited by later Christians to
restrict women's activities: the tale of Eve and the
serpent in the Garden of Eden. The church fathers would
not have accepted Carol Meyers' interpretation of the
text,[18] for as early as the New Testament itself, Genesis
3 was singled out as *the* Old Testament passage most useful in rationalizing women's secondary status. I Timothy
2:11-15 provides our most explicit testimony:

> Let a woman learn in silence with all submis-
> siveness. I permit no woman to teach or to
> have authority over men; she is to keep silent.
> For Adam was formed first, then Eve; and Adam
> was not deceived, but the woman was deceived
> and became a transgressor. Yet woman will be
> saved through bearing children, if she

continues in faith and love and holiness,
with modesty.
As is evident, the author of I Timothy rests his case not
only on Genesis 3; he also appeals to the creation story
in Genesis 2, in which Eve is created second, after Adam
(unlike the Genesis 1 rendition of creation, in which
man and woman are created simultaneously). Church
fathers cited these verses over and again to justify
woman's subordinate role. The church fathers believed
the apostle Paul himself to have written the book of
I Timothy (a view rejected by Biblical scholars today),
giving added authority to these words.

The "subjection" of women to which I Timothy refers
concerns the penalty God placed on Eve for her role in
the first sin, as described in the traditional English
translation of Genesis 3:16: "I will greatly multiply
your pain in childbearing; in pain you shall bring forth
children, yet your desire shall be for your husband, and
he shall rule over you." John Chrysostom, writing in the
late fourth century, comments on these verses. Eve must
accept servitude, he asserts; she must allow herself to
be governed by a man and acknowledge her husband as a
lord, since she did not bear her liberty well when she
had it.[19] He claims, "When she misused her power, and
although created as a helper was found to be treacherous
and to have ruined everything,"[20] then God's words of
condemnation fell upon her.

For Chrysostom, the implications for the present are
that no woman may teach. "Why not?" Chrysostom asks
rhetorically, and answers his own question: "Because she
taught Adam once and for all, and taught him badly....
She exerted her authority once, and exerted it badly....
Therefore let her descend from the professor's chair!
Those who know not how to teach, let them learn. If they

do not want to learn, but rather want to teach, they
destroy both themselves and those who learn from them."[21]

Without doubt, the most important conclusion the
church fathers drew from the prohibition of women as
"teachers" was that they were to be denied access to the
priesthood. The female sex must "step aside" from the
weighty task of caring for souls, Chrysostom intones in
his treatise *On the Priesthood*, for "the divine law has
shut women out from the ministerial office," however much
they may desire it.[22] That I Corinthians 14:34 prohibits
women from even "speaking" in church was taken as another
indication that God's Word did not countenance women as
preachers.[23]

In a fourth-century church order called the *Apostolic
Constitutions*, yet another reason is given why women cannot be priests: Jesus nowhere sent out women to preach,
despite a large female following that included his mother
and sisters.[24] The author writes thus:

And if in what came earlier we did not
allow women to teach, how can we assent to
their being priests, which is contrary to
nature? For this is an error of Gentile
atheism to ordain women as priests to the
goddesses; it is not in the dispensation of
Christ. And more, had it been necessary for
women to baptize, certainly the Lord would
have also been baptized by his own mother,
not by John, or when he sent us as well to
baptize, he would have sent women with them
for this purpose. But now, nowhere, neither
by command nor in writing did he transmit
this, since he knew the order of nature and
the fittingness of things, being the Creator
of nature and the Legislator of the
arrangement.[25]

The limitation of women's roles in patristic Christianity could thus be justified by an appeal to Biblical
texts that upheld woman's subordinate status at creation,
her guilt for the original sin, and the dangers women
posed for men. Such readings of the Bible were only
reinforced by misogynous views derived from the classical
pagan tradition. The weight of ancient traditions was
thus one factor that prompted the church fathers to
denigrate the worth of women in general and to counsel
limits on their roles.

A second reason why early Christian attitudes toward
women and their roles in the church often appear negative
can be categorized as "socio-historical." In the era of
Christianity's precarious establishment, a variety of
schismatic and heretical sects abounded, Christian by
their own proclamation, but beyond the pale in the
opinion of the Catholic church fathers. Since the "mainstream" church was in competition with these sects for
adherents, it distressed orthodox churchmen that women
found these groups appealing.[26] Although the fathers
blame female attraction to these sects on women's weak-
mindedness and propensity to be led astray, it is not
without interest that women appear to have been more
readily accepted as religious leaders in the schismatic
and heretical sects than they were in Catholic orthodoxy.
Two examples of religious groups that gave women more
opportunity for leadership than did Catholic Christianity
will here suffice: Montanism and Gnosticism (an
"umbrella" term for a wide variety of sects flourishing in
the patristic era that offered to their enlightened
adherents an escape from the evils of the material world
and the celestial tyrants who governed it).

Montanism was a charismatic movement that proclaimed
the imminence of the Kingdom of God, an enthusiasm that

most Christians had abandoned by the mid-second century,
when Montanism arose. Believers should prepare for the
Kingdom's arrival by a life of disciplined renunciation,
taught Montanus, the sect's founder. The Montanists
believed that the Holy Spirit directly inspired their
views and they highly esteemed prophecy in the name of
the Holy Spirit. Women sat in the highest ranks of the
movement, a phenomenon characteristic of spiritualistic
movements throughout Christian history. Montanus
included in his immediate circle two female prophetesses,
Priscilla and Maximilla, believed by the Montanists to be
direct vehicles for the Holy Spirit's revelations.[27]
(Priscilla, for example, had a vision in which Christ
appeared to her as a *female* to announce the descent of
the heavenly Jerusalem.[28]) A scandalized church writer
asserts that the Montanists even "magnified these females
above the Apostles and every gift of Grace, so that some
of them go so far as to say that there is in them something more than in Christ."[29] Moreover, church authorities report that Montanist women taught and prophesied
publicly, indeed, baptized and celebrated the Eucharist.
The women apparently appealed to Galatians 3:28 (in
Christ Jesus "there is neither male nor female") and to
the Biblical tradition of prophetesses for Scriptural
support.[30] Despite the fathers' many criticisms of
Montanism, they nonetheless conceded that this schismatic
group was perfectly orthodox in its doctrine of God and
its confession of Christ.[31]

The same could not be affirmed, however, of the
various Gnostic sects: the church fathers unanimously
condemned the Gnostic depictions of God and Christ. One
aspect of Gnostic theology particularly reprehensible to
the fathers was the Gnostic propensity to picture the
Godhead as including female elements and powers, such as

Grace, Thought, and Wisdom. Those Gnostics whose understanding of God approximated orthodox Christianity's
might call on "the Father, the *Mother*, and the Son,"[32]
thus offering praise to a Trinity with an explicitly
female element.

Likewise, Gnostic Scriptures included episodes in
which the female disciples of Jesus, especially Mary
Magdalene, receive higher status as Christian leaders
than they do in Matthew, Mark, Luke, and John. Thus a
Gnostic gospel entitled "The Gospel of Mary" singles out
Mary Magdalene as the recipient of special and private
teaching by Jesus, a point that enrages the hot-tempered
Peter who doubts the validity of her revelation.[33]

Women found expanded roles for themselves in some
Gnostic sects more readily than in orthodox Catholicism.
The Gnostic leader Marcus encouraged his female followers
to view themselves as prophets. When he initiated a woman
into the sect, it is reputed that he said to her, "Be-
hold, Grace has come upon you; open your mouth and
prophesy."[34] Even worse in the eyes of the church
fathers was Marcus' allowing women to serve as co-priests
with him.[35] The heretic Marcion was reputed to have
allowed women to baptize.[36] And the Carpocratian sect of
Gnostics boasted a famous woman teacher, Marcellina, who
journeyed to Rome as a representative of her movement.[37]

Orthodox churchmen reserved strong curses and condem-
nations for such practices. Tertullian, with whose view
of woman as the "devil's gateway" we began, described a
woman who led a Gnostic congregation in North Africa as
a "viper."[38] In his treatise *On the Prescription of
Heretics* (meaning the Gnostics), Tertullian further
excoriates women as leaders of Gnostic sects. He writes:
"These heretical women--how bold they are! They have no
modesty; they are audacious enough to teach, to engage in

argument, to perform exorcisms, to undertake cures, and
maybe even to baptize."[39]

How are we to explain the greater access to religious
leadership allowed Gnostic women? Elaine Pagels suggests
that the prominence Gnostics gave to the feminine element
within the Godhead was the decisive determinant;[40] she
here sees theology as the legitimation of a more liberal
social organization.[41] Other scholars question her
interpretation. They note that the Gnostic evaluation of
the female divinities is ambiguous at best,[42] and hence
provides questionable support for Gnostic women's
expanded leadership roles. Some of Pagels' critics
attempt to offer other explanations. The Egyptian prove-
nance of Gnosticism has been mentioned as a possible
determining factor, for in Egypt women enjoyed more legal
rights than in other areas of the Mediterranean world.[43]
Still another possible explanation for the prominence of
women's leadership in Gnostic sects rests on the supposition that Gnostics came from a wealthy and educated
section of the population;[44] if the supposition is
correct, Gnostic women leaders may have received offices
on the basis of their social and economic status. Whatever the precise reasons for the Gnostics' allowance of
women religious leaders, such women leaders are firmly
attested.

Over against the Gnostic allowance of women as
religious leaders, orthodox Christianity upheld an ethic
called by the New Testament scholar Gerd Theissen
(borrowing from Ernst Troeltsch) "love-patriarchalism."
In place of genuine equal rights and equal roles for
women, mainstream Christianity preached an ethic of
equality for all people--but one that was to be evidenced
only "in Christ," not in the real world. Theissen
writes, "In the political and social realm, class-specific

differences were essentially accepted, affirmed, even
religiously legitimated."[45]   That in Jesus Christ there
was no "male and female," as Paul put it,[46] was *not*
translated into the bettering of women's position in the
social-historical arena, as it was by the Gnostic and
Montanists sects.

In the second and third centuries, the Christian
church was engaged in the quest of its own "self-
definition."[47]   Striving to define itself over against
non-Christians without and dissenters within, the church
drew firm lines, precise boundaries, between itself and
these heretical and schismatic movements. Its desire
for differentiation was all the stronger since the sects
so often claimed that *they* possessed the correct understanding of Christian truth. To demarcate the boundaries
between "us" and "them," the church fathers singled out
for attack various features of the sects' allegedly mis-
guided teaching and practice, such as the leadership
roles of Gnostic women. Over against the blasphemies and
permissiveness of the sects, no orthodox Catholic woman
should teach, preach, baptize, exorcize, offer the
Eucharist, or prophesy. Thus the mainstream church's
limitation of women's roles can be understood in part as
an aspect of its quest for self-definition.

The third reason for the church's limitation of
women's roles may well have been the most important: for
men, women were inextricably linked with sexuality,
marriage, and procreation. Although many women today reject an identity that focuses on their sexual and
reproductive capacities, we can nonetheless argue that
women would be esteemed for their childbearing role (if
for nothing else) in societies that placed a high value
on reproduction, such as ancient Israel. But it was
inevitable that when increasingly ascetic currents came

to dominate Christianity, women as the symbols of
sexuality and procreation would be accordingly denigrated.

The New Testament itself provides fuel for the
ascetic fire. The Gospels represent Jesus as unmarried
and report he taught that those who become eunuchs for
the sake of the Kingdom of Heaven were blessed;[48] that
feeling lust in one's heart is as wicked as actually committing adultery;[49] that in the resurrection, there will
be no marrying or giving in marriage.[50] Sentiments such
as these were taken by later generations of Christians to
mean that celibate living was an ideal recommended by
Jesus himself to which people should aspire.

I Corinthians 7 serves to strengthen the ascetic
resolve. There the only reason Paul gives for marriage
is that it tamps down "the temptation to immorality";
those who are "aflame with passion" are advised to marry.
Given that "the form of the earth is passing away," Paul
thinks that Christians might better abstain from marriage
with all its attendant responsibilities and "worldly
troubles." Paul acknowledges that not everyone had his
gift for celibacy, but he nonetheless wishes that all
might have it. Marriage, he implies, is for those too
weak to control their sexual desires. It promotes an
"anxiety about worldly affairs." In contrast, those who
remain single are able to expend their energies upon
"the affairs of the Lord, how to be holy in body and
spirit." Whether Paul would have given the same advice
if he had foreseen that "the form of the world" was not
to pass away is a moot question. Once Paul's letters
were enshrined as Holy Scripture, Christians believed
that his opinions were meant to hold for all time.

Marriage and reproduction could not be completely
denigrated by the church fathers, however, for the church

wished to praise the goodness of God's creation and the
human body over against some Gnostics who claimed that
both the world and our bodies were the products of an
evil creator or unfortunate accidents.[51] For some of
them, reproduction was simply the nasty trick by which an
evil creator had lured humans into becoming the agents
for the further dispersal of spiritual particles amidst
the gross material body and its animal passion. Faced
with such a stark condemnation of reproduction, the
church fathers felt compelled to recall God's first command to Adam and Eve in Genesis 1:28: "Be fruitful,
multiply, fill the earth and subdue it."

That the fathers' championing of Genesis 1:28 was
less than enthusiastic we can infer from a cursory
examination of that most laudatory of all early Christian treatises on marriage, Clement of Alexandria's,
written around 200 A.D.[52] The work is intended to refute
Gnostic views of marriage and reproduction, and to demonstrate how orthodox Christian teaching differed from
them.

In his survey of Gnostic teaching on marriage,
Clement makes clear that Gnostics who live celibate lives
are wrongly motivated;[53] they live ascetically because
they hate the created order.[54] Clement agrees with them
only to the extent that "to attain the knowledge of God
is impossible for those who are still under the control
of their passions."[55] Wishing to praise marriage,
Clement feels compelled to explain why Jesus didn't
marry; among the reasons he presents are that Jesus had
his own bride, the church, and in any case, did not need
a "helpmeet," since he was God on earth.[56] Clement com-
piled a list of Biblical characters who married, and in
his enthusiasm to sanction marriage, even included
Paul![57] Clement concludes that marriage is an acceptable

form of Christian life if, and only if, it is undertaken
for the purpose of begetting children with a "chaste and
controlled will."[58] He generously grants that it is
possible to serve the Lord in marriage, as well as in
celibacy[59] (one such service the partners render is to
"suffer with each other and 'bear one another's bur-
dens'"[60]). And if any further proof is needed that
reproduction is good, Christians are reminded that Jesus
himself was truly born.[61] Clement's is surely a very
modest encouragement of marriage.

     Later church fathers repeat his arguments and add
some of their own. To Augustine, the church owes the
view that the blessings of marriage include not just offspring and a control for lust, but also the sacramental
bonding of the partners.[62] Hence marriage is given a
religious status: the partners are united in a relationship like Christ's to the church,[63] and neither childlessness nor infidelity can rupture it. Augustine's
stress on the sanctity of marriage is partly occasioned
(as is Clement's) by his desire to combat the alleged
excesses of the ascetic movement, with its lightly-veiled
suspicion of first marriage and its outright condemnation
of second marriage.

     We can gage this rising tide of asceticism in early
Christianity by several measures. One is the increasing
attention given to the Virgin Mary. From the second
century on, her status as *perpetual* virgin was
increasingly stressed: Mary was not involved in sexual
relations *after* the birth of Jesus any more than she had
been before. The "documentation" (if we may call it
that) for this view is provided by an apocryphal Gospel,
the *Protevangelium of James*, which graphically offers
physiological "proof" that Mary remained a virgin despite
Jesus' birth (a woman attendant who doubted that a virgin

had brought forth "made the test" and was punished by God
for her unbelief).[64] Of course, the lauding of Mary's
perpetual virginity raised some problems for Scriptural
interpretation, for the New Testament in numerous places
mentions the brothers and sisters of Jesus. That problem
did not daunt the great exegete of the fourth century,
Jerome; in his classic treatise, *Against Helvidius*, he
explains that the alleged siblings of Jesus were in truth
not blood-brothers and sisters, but relatives;[65] the word
"brother," he argues, is often used metaphorically in
Scripture, just as Joseph is called the "father" of
Jesus.[66] The point of Jerome's exegesis, of course, is
to praise Christian virginity in general and that of Mary
in particular.

A second such measure of growing ascetic concern lies
in the attacks on remarriage from the late second century
on. To be sure, Paul had written in I Corinthians 7 that
he thought widows would be happier if they did not
remarry,[67] but he, no more than the later author of
I Timothy who actively counseled the remarriage of
widows,[68] could have imagined the wholesale onslaught
against second marriage that arose after his time.

Thus Tertullian, writing around 200 A.D., affirms
that second marriage "resembles sexual defilement."[69] He
mocks those Christians who confess that because the end
of the world is at hand, we should take no thought for
the morrow, yet are anxious for their posterity and the
fate of their inheritances.[70] From Tertullian's vantage
point, their expressed concerns are simply "pretexts with
which we color the insatiable desire of the flesh"[71]--
that is, those who wish to remarry are trying to excuse
sexual indulgence. According to John Chrysostom, widows
have no plausible justification for remarrying: they
cannot even claim inexperience, having once been through

the horrors of matrimony and childbearing.[72]   He concludes that they must be either suffering from amnesia
about the conditions of marriage, be craving worldly
glory, or be governed by sexual lust.[73]

Jerome advises a young widow named Furia not to return to what he calls the "vomit" of marriage. He mocks
her desire for children: "Do you fear the extinction of
the Furian line if you do not present your father with
some little fellow to crawl upon his chest and drool down
his neck?"[74] He concludes his letter with the sobering
exhortation, "Think everyday that you must die, and you
will never think of marrying again."[75] Such denunciations of second marriage, when coupled with the
exaltation of Mary's perpetual virginity, reveal that the
values of early Christianity were undergoing a sharp
transformation from the praise of motherhood and wifely
virtue we find both in the Old Testament and in many
Latin documents.[76]

An irony of early Christian history is that the
ascetic movement, which had so many features denigrating
of women and marriage, became *the* movement that, more
than any other, provided "liberation" of a sort for
Christian women. *If* they could surmount their identification with sexual and reproductive functioning, women
were allowed freedoms and roles they otherwise would not
have been granted. I do *not* posit that most women
consciously chose the ascetic life as an "escape" from
marriage. Nonetheless, their renunciations, motivated by
religious concerns, served to liberate them from the
traditional bonds of marriage. The advantages they received in adopting asceticism were practical as well as
theoretical.[77]

In the fourth century, asceticism flowered. Indeed,
our sources indicate that by the end of the third

century, women were taking to the Egyptian desert to live
as hermits;[78] in the first half of the fourth century,
communal monasteries were established there for women.[79]
Asceticism for women became popular in the West a few
decades later: the 350s and 360s saw the adoption of
"house asceticism" by noble Roman women, and in the 370s
and 380s, they left home and homeland to found monasteries in Palestine. In the decades thereafter,
monasticism spread all over the Mediterranean world.
What advantages did this new way of life offer?

First, in the eyes of our male authors, asceticism
allowed women to overcome the negative qualities associated with femaleness: lightmindedness, vanity,
frivolity, and lack of intelligence were suddenly and
miraculously overcome by women who undertook an ascetic
program. Once these women swept away the old world of
property, husbands, and children, they were inducted
into a new status that elevated them above the deficien-
cies of the female condition. Sometimes they are said
to have become "men"; at other times they are said to
have become "angels." As Jerome phrased it, once a woman
prefers Jesus Christ to a husband and babies, "she will
cease to be a woman and will be called a man."[80] She was
now considered a man's equal, not his inferior.[81] To
those women who undertook the ascetic life, Jerome quoted
Paul's words, that in Christ Jesus "there is no male and
female," as an emblem of their new-found equality.[82]
Once we recover from the shock of the fathers' andro-
centric bias, we can see that they affirmed in the most
positive terms of their culture (viz., terms of "male-
ness") that female ascetics had shed those negative
characteristics which, to their minds, marked out women.

To be sure, the overcoming of the alleged deficien-
cies of femaleness was also manifest in earlier

Christianity, namely, in martyrdom. Female martyrs are
consistently called "virile," possessors of "manly
spirit."[83] According to the fourth-century Latin church-
man Ambrose, for example, Agnes, reputed to be a victim
of the emperor Diocletian's persecution earlier in the
century, is said to have risen "above nature,"[84] by which
he means the "nature" of her sex, as well as "human
nature" more generally. In his rhetorical rendition of
Agnes' martyrdom, he claims that she was "undaunted by
the bloody hands of executioners, unmoved by the heavy
dragging of the creaking chains." Although girls of her
age (namely, twelve), customarily cannot tolerate even a
glare from their parents, and shriek when pricked by a
needle,[85] Ambrose asserts that Agnes surpassed her sex as
well as her age in bravery. He celebrates her:

> What terror the executioner struck to make
> her afraid, what flatteries to persuade her!
> How many longed that she might come to them in
> marriage! But she replied, "It would be a
> wrong to my Spouse [i.e., Jesus] to anticipate
> some man's pleasing me. The One who first
> chose me for Himself shall receive me. For
> what, o murderer, do you delay? Let this body
> be destroyed, a body that can be loved by eyes
> of men I do not want." She stood, she prayed,
> she bent her neck. You could perceive the
> executioner tremble, as if he himself had been
> sentenced; the hand of the murderer shook,
> his face paled as he feared another's peril,
> when the girl did not fear her own. Thus you
> have in one victim a twofold martyrdom, of
> modesty and of piety: she both remained a
> virgin and acquired martyrdom.[86]

Likewise, the decidedly unfemale characteristics
displayed by the North African woman Vibia Perpetua,
martyred probably in the year 203 A.D., are vividly portrayed in the account of her martyrdom. On the day
before Perpetua was to fight the beasts, she had a vision
in which she was led to the arena. In her own words,
she tells how in the vision an Egyptian was brought out
to fight her. She reports, "I was stripped and I was
made a man." She triumphs over her opponent whom, upon
waking, she realized had been the Devil.[87] That to fight
in the arena as one condemned to martyrdom might make one
"manly" is here most graphically asserted.

Once the era of the Roman persecutions was over, however, martyrdom no longer offered a way for Christian
women to demonstrate their "manliness." Asceticism was
now judged to be the new arena in which a woman could
exhibit her "manly courage." (The phrase is almost a
tautology in Greek, since the very word for courage,
andreia, indicates its masculine association.) The
church fathers frequently asserted that asceticism was a
new form of martyrdom, one in which we could be martyred
daily. Jerome, in *Epistle* 130, addressed to a teenage
heiress, Demetrias, who had abandoned her plans for
marriage at the eleventh hour and taken a vow of
perpetual virginity, imagines the timid young woman sum-
moning up courage to announce her change of plans to her
family. He pictures her saying:

> What is to become of you, Demetrias? Why
> do you tremble so to defend your chastity?
> This situation demands candor and courage! If
> in a time of peace you are so afraid, what
> would you do if you were suffering martyrdom?
> If you cannot endure a scowl from your family,
> how could you bear the persecutors' tribunals?

If the examples of men do not challenge you,
be encouraged and take confidence from the
blessed martyr Agnes who overcame both youth
and tyranny, who by her martyrdom won the
victor's crown for the name of chastity.[88]
Thus the courage of an earlier woman stood as a model for
the new "martyrs" of the post-persecution era, the
ascetics.

Removed from the category of "womanhood" and its
attendant complications by ascetic devotion, females
would learn (according to the fathers) that asceticism
offered them unprecedented freedom: freedom from the
domestic problems occasioned by slaves, money, in-laws,
sick children, marital suspicion and jealousy, not to
speak of the verbal abuse and physical blows to which the
church writers attest many wives were subjected.[89]
Ascetic women were exempt from the curse of Genesis 3:16.
As Jerome put it:

When Jesus was crowned with thorns, bore our
sins and suffered for us, it was to make the
roses of virginity and the lilies of chastity
grow for us out of the brambles and briers
that have formed the lot of women since the
day when it was said to Eve, "in sorrow you
shall bring forth children, and your desire
shall be for your husband, and he shall rule
over you."[90]

Jesus' overcoming of original sin is here interpreted
strictly as the advent of asceticism. For women, Eve's
curse was undone through the adoption of the virginal
profession.

For some ascetic women, another practical advantage
of this way of life was the freedom to pursue friendships
with the opposite sex. It is of interest that both

Jerome and John Chrysostom, whose denigrating comments
regarding women and marriage we noted earlier, cultivated
circles of female ascetics with whom they maintained
lifetime bonds of devotion.   In fact, some of their contemporaries thought their relations with women were a bit
overly close, and used that charge to discredit them.[91]
In these circles of friendship, scholarly pursuits were
undertaken.   Indeed, Jerome's circle in Rome can best be
described as a late ancient coed study group.   He and his
female friends investigated Scripture, and many of his
treatises and letters respond to the detailed questions
posed by these ascetic friends.   Some of them even
learned Hebrew so that they could better appreciate the
Old Testament.[92]   When we consider how rare was the
knowledge of Hebrew among *male* churchmen of the fourth
century, their accomplishment is truly astounding.

   Although the fathers disapproved of women speaking in
public, we hear that some of these female ascetics
carried on public debates.   Marcella, one of Jerome's
circle, is called by him the foremost student of Scripture in Rome after he departed the city.   Jerome
testifies that members of the clergy sought her out, so
highly did they regard her.   (The fact that she credited
her answers to male authorities so as not to appear to be
in violation of New Testament injunctions against women
teaching is a quaint touch Jerome adds to his encomium.)
Marcella is also represented as engaging in public debate
during the Origenist   controversy in Rome.[93]

   Opportunities for travel in the form of pilgrimages
to Egypt, the home of the desert fathers, and to Palestine, the locale of the Holy Places of Biblical fame, also
enriched the lives of ascetic women.   For matrons, trips
about the Mediterranean unaccompanied by fathers or husbands would not have been sanctioned.   Yet when the

travel was called pilgrimage, not only was it acceptable
for female ascetics, it was laudable. One of the rare
pieces of ancient Christian literature written by a woman
is the account of the nun Egeria who, in the later fourth
century, took a pilgrimage to the Holy Land and Asia
Minor.[94] That her journey was one long marvel to her is
abundantly evident from her chronicle, a travel diary
that she composed for her sister nuns back home. Her
excitement shines through her less than elegant prose as
we follow her ascending Mount Sinai; viewing the spot
upon which Lot's wife turned into a pillar of salt (now
submerged in the Dead Sea, Egeria regretfully reports);
journeying to Edessa, where she heard read the correspondence between Jesus and King Abgar, and to the
impressive shrine of St. Thecla in Isauria; and last,
reverencing the sacred places in the Holy Land associated
with Jesus' life and death.

Another such account of a female's pilgrimage to the
Holy Places is Jerome's memorial of his friend Paula that
details her visit to the desert fathers in Egypt and the
holy sites of Biblical fame.[95] Such a tour involved a
veritable course in Biblical geography. Paula saw, among
other things, Cornelius' house in Caesarea, the valley
where Joshua told the sun to stand still, the Bethlehem
grotto where Jesus was born, and the cave in which Lot
slept with his daughters--the latter provided an occasion
for Paula to exhort the maidens with her against the
dangers of drinking wine. She also crossed the Egyptian
desert with "manly courage," Jerome reports, in order to
visit the desert fathers; in doing so, she discounted
"her sex and the weakness of her frame."[96] Thus
pilgrimage provided to ascetic women increased opportunities for travel and on-site instruction.

A last and important contribution of asceticism was
that it allowed some women to hold positions of religious
leadership, even though orthodox Christian women were not
to be ordained to the priesthood. Although Romans 16
calls Phoebe a *diakonos*, a deacon, and I Timothy 5 refers
to a group in the church called "the widows," it remains
unclear whether these titles meant the same in the
earliest decades of Christianity as they did later. We
know from patristic literature that the widows were a
class of women devoted to prayer, but their office seems
to have died out in the course of the fourth century. To
replace them arose the deaconesses, vowed to the celibate
life, who assisted with various liturgical functions
involving women.[97] According to the Council of Chalcedon
in 451 A.D., deaconesses were to be forty years old before they received office.[98] In Eastern Christendom, if
not in Western, they underwent a genuine ordination to
their posts,[99] unlike virgins and widows. We are
fortunate to possess the prayer that was used in the
ordination service for deaconesses:

> O eternal God, the Father of our lord
> Jesus Christ, the Creator of man and of woman,
> who did fill with the Spirit Miriam, Deborah,
> Anna and Huldah, who did not deem unworthy that
> your only-begotten Son should be born of a
> woman, who also in the tent of witness and in
> the Temple ordained women as keepers of your
> holy gates: now look upon this your servant
> who is being ordained as a deaconess, and
> give her the Holy Spirit, and purify her
> from any defilement of the flesh and spirit
> (II Cor. 7:1), so that she may worthily
> accomplish the work entrusted to her and to
> your glory and the praise of your Christ,

with whom to you and to the Holy Spirit be
glory and adoration forever. Amen![100]
The deaconesses did not teach publicly in the church or
baptize, but apparently they engaged in some private
teaching of women. The fourth-century *Apostolic Constitutions* explains the deaconesses' mission: since the
bishop could not send deacons to women's households without giving rise to scandalous rumors amid the pagan
community and hence discrediting the church, deaconesses
were sent.[101] Probably they engaged in preparing women
to become baptismal candidates. Deaconesses must have
been essential participants in the baptism ceremony, for
in baptism, the candidates were anointed with oil on
various points of their bodies and since it was not
considered appropriate for the male officiant to anoint
any portion of a woman's body below the forehead, the
deaconess carried out this task.[102] With time, the
office of deaconess died out, subsumed in that of the
nun. Yet in the ascetic heyday of the fourth and fifth
centuries, we hear of many deaconesses.

A number of celibate women were also able to found and
direct women's monasteries. In some cases, an ascetic
bloodbrother appears to have inspired the establishment
of the women's monastery. Thus Pachomius, founder of
Egyptian communal monasticism, is said to have created
a monastery for his sister to head.[103] Likewise, both
Augustine and Caesarius of Arles wrote monastic *Rules* for
convents of which their sisters had assumed leadership.[104] In other cases, the women themselves undertook
the founding of monasteries. These were women of wealth
who achieved their status as monastic superiors because
they financed a monastery's construction. Into this
latter category falls Chrysostom's friend Olympias (also
ordained a deaconess, although she was under-age),[105] who

founded one of the first, perhaps *the* first, monastery
for women in Constantinople.[106]   Her *Life* reports that
about 250 women enrolled in her monastery, located next
to the Great Cathedral of the city.[107]   In addition, we
know that Jerome's friend Paula founded, funded, and became the superior of a monastery for women in Bethlehem.[108]   Similarly, Melania the Elder, in the late 370s
or early 380s, built monasteries for men and for women
on the Mount of Olives,[109] as her granddaughter, Melania
the Younger, was to do several decades later.[110]
Although the sources pertaining to these monasteries tell
us much more about the women's piety, humility, and
other Christian virtues than they do about the leadership
they exerted as heads of monastic establishments, we
nonetheless have firm testimony to the fact of the
women's governance of monasteries as well as to the sis-
terly support they gave each other in the communal life.

In these several ways, then, asceticism provided new
opportunities for women in the patristic era. The
"progress" achieved by Christian women in this period is
firmly linked to the ascetic program. For matrons, on
the other hand, the traditional injunctions to subser-
vience, submissiveness, and silence prevailed; to them,
early Christianity brought no significant amelioration
of status. The fourth-century Latin bishop Ambrose
compares the lot of married women with ascetic ones in
the following manner:

> The marriage bond is not then to be shunned
> as though it were sinful, but rather declined
> as being a galling burden. For the law binds
> the wife to bear children in labor and in
> sorrow, and is in subjection to her husband, for
> he is lord over her. So, then, the married
> woman, but not the widow, is subject to labor

and pain in bringing forth children, and she
only that is married, not she that is a virgin, is under the power of her husband. The
virgin is free from all these things, who has
vowed her affection to the Word of God, who
awaits the Spouse of blessing with her lamp
burning with the light of a good will. And
so she is moved by counsels, not bound by
chains.[111]

Although the literary sources tell us little about
married or non-elite women, celibate women, especially
celibate elites, receive more attention than is sometimes
assumed. As religious and monastic leaders, students
of literature, pilgrims, and patrons, they prefigure the
women of later centuries whose lives are being uncovered
by feminist scholarship of our era.

NOTES

[1]For Olympias' holdings, see the *Life of Olympias*, 5; for Melania the Younger's, see the *Life of Melania the Younger*, 7, 11, 14, 18, 20; and Palladius, *Lausiac History*, 61. According to the Latin version of Melania the Younger's *Life* (15), her annual income was about 1700 pounds of gold (=120,000 gold *solidi*). Although it is risky to estimate what 1700 pounds of gold could buy in 400 A.D., we have Gregory the Great's calculation from about two hundred years later that 80 pounds of gold would have been sufficient to support 3000 nuns for a year (Paul the Deacon, *Life of St. Gregory the Great*, II, 27), Melania's annual income may "translate" to be as high as $123 million.

[2]The foremost example is probably Rosemary Radford Ruether's "Misogynism and Virginal Feminism in the Fathers of the Church," *Religion and Sexism: Images of Woman in the Jewish and Christian Traditions*, ed. Rosemary R. Ruether (New York: Simon and Schuster, 1974), pp. 150-183.

[3]Tertullian, *On the Dress of Women*, I, 1, 1-2.

[4]John Chrysostom, *Instruction and Refutation Directed Against Those Men Cohabiting With Virgins*, 11.

[5]Jerome, *Ep.* 127, 5.

[6]*Life of Olympias*, 13.

[7]Jerome, *Ep.* 22, 1.

[8]*Ibid.*, 2.

[9]*Ibid.*, 20.

[10]*Ibid.*, 1; 25.

[11]*Ibid.*, 41.

[12]Semonides, frag. 7 (*Anthologia Lyrica Graeca*, ed.
E. Diehl [Leipzig: Teubner, 1925], I, 3, 52-59).

[13]Hipponax of Ephesus, in Stobaeus, *Florilegium* 68, 8
(*Ioannis Stobaei Anthologium*, ed. O. Hense [Berlin:
Weidmann, 1958], II, 515).

[14]Xenarchus, frag. 14 (*Comicorum Atticorum Fragmenta*,
ed. T. Kock [Leipzig: Teubner, 1880-88], II, 473).

[15]Carcinus, frag. 3 (*Tragicorum Graecorum Fragmenta*,
ed. B. Snell [Göttingen: Vandenhoeck and Ruprecht,
1971], I, 213).

[16]Proverbs 9:13-18.

[17]Ezekiel 16; Hosea 1-3.

[18]See Carol Meyers, "Recovering Eve: Biblical Woman
Without Post-Biblical Dogma," in *Feminist Theory and the
Disciplines*, ed. Jean F. O'Barr (forthcoming).

[19]John Chrysostom, *Discourse 4 on Genesis*, 1.

[20]John Chrysostom, *Homily 26 on I Corinthians*, 2.

[21]John Chrysostom, *Discourse 4 on Genesis*, 1.

[22]John Chrysostom, *On the Priesthood*, II, 2.

[23]*Ibid.*, III, 9.

[24]*Apostolic Constitutions*, III, 6.

[25]*Ibid.*, III, 9.

[26]For a fascinating analysis of how the author of the
Pastoral Epistles attempted to keep women from deserting
to heretical groups, see Jouette Bassler, "The Widows'
Tale: A Fresh Look at I Tim. 5:3-16," *Journal of Biblical Literature* 103 (1984), 23-41.

[27]Hippolytus, *Refutation*, VIII, 12; Eusebius, *Church
History*, V, 16.

[28]Epiphanius, *Heresies*, 49, 1.

[29]Hippolytus, *Refutation*, VIII, 12.

[30]Didymus the Blind, *On the Trinity*, III, 41, 3; Cyprian, *Ep.* 75, 10; Epiphanius, *Heresies*, 49, 2.

[31]Hippolytus, *Refutation*, VIII, 19.

[32]*Apocryphon of John*, 2, 9-14 (*The Nag Hammadi Library*, ed. J.M. Robinson [San Francisco: Harper & Row, 1981], p. 99).

[33]*Gospel of Mary* (trans. in R.M. Grant, *Gnosticism; A Sourcebook of Heretical Writings From the Early Christian Period* [New York: Harper and Brothers, 1961], pp. 65-68).

[34]Irenaeus, *Against Heresies*, I, 13, 3-4.

[35]Hippolytus, *Refutation*, VI, 35; Irenaeus, *Against Heresies*, I, 13, 1-2.

[36]Epiphanius, *Heresies*, 42, 4.

[37]Irenaeus, *Against Heresies*, I, 25, 6.

[38]Tertullian, *On Baptism*, 1.

[39]Tertullian, *On the Prescription of Heretics*, 41.

[40]Elaine Pagels, *The Gnostic Gospels* (New York: Random House, 1979), pp. 59, 66.

[41]Pagels, *Gnostic Gospels*, p. 164 n. 1; Pagels herself concedes that theology was not always the prime determinant for the sects' social practices, for neither the Marcionites nor the Montanists had divine female principles, yet allowed larger roles to women.

[42]Elisabeth Schüssler Fiorenza, "Word, Spirit and Power: Women in Early Christian Communities," in *Women of Spirit: Female Leadership in the Jewish And Christian Traditions*, ed. Rosemary Ruether and Eleanor McLaughlin (New York: Simon and Schuster, 1979), p. 50; Raoul Mortley, *Womanhood: The Feminine in Ancient Hellenism, Christianity and Islam* (Sydney: Delacroix, 1981), pp. 59, 55, 62.

[43]Mortley, *Womanhood*, pp. 61-62.

[44]Kurt Rudolph, "Das Problem Einer Soziologie und 'Sozialen Verortung' der Gnosis," *Kairos* 19 (1977), 36-39; on the intellectual status of Gnostics, see Hans G.

Kippenberg, "Versuch Einer Soziologischen Verortung des
Antiken Gnostizismus," *Numen* 19 (1970), 225. Pagels suggests that the move to equality found support "primarily
in rich or what we would call bohemian circles" (*Gnostic
Gospels*, p. 63). For the prominence of rich women among
the supporters of Pelagius, see Peter Brown, "The Patrons
of Pelagius: The Roman Aristocracy Between East and
West," *Journal of Theological Studies*, n.s., 21 (1970),
56-72 (reprinted in *Religion and Society in the Age of
Saint Augustine* [New York: Harper & Row, 1972], pp. 208-
226). For the centrality of wealthy women to the
Priscillianists, see Henry Chadwick, *Priscillian of
Avila: The Occult and the Charismatic in the Early
Church* (Oxford: Clarendon Press, 1976), pp. 20, 37-40,
144.

[45]Gerd Theissen, "Social Stratification in the Corin-
thian Community," in *The Social Setting of Pauline
Christianity*, trans. John Schütz (Philadelphia: Fortress
Press, 1982), p. 109; see E. Troeltsch, *The Social
Teaching of the Christian Churches*, trans. D. Wyon (New
York: Macmillan, 1931), I, 79.

[46]Galatians 3:28.

[47]See the essays in E.P. Sanders, ed., *Jewish and
Christian Self-Definition, Vol. I: The Shaping of Chris-
tianity in the Second and Third Centuries* (Philadelphia:
Fortress Press, 1980).

[48]Matthew 19:12.

[49]Matthew 5:27.

[50]Mark 12:25 = Matthew 22:30 = Luke 20:35-36.

[51]See references in chapters 8-10 of Hans Jonas, *The
Gnostic Religion. The Message of the Alien God and the
Beginnings of Christianity*, 2nd ed. rev. (Boston: Beacon
Press, 1963).

[52]Clement's "On Marriage" (=*Miscellanies* III) is
translated in *Alexandrian Christianity* (ed. J.E.L.
Oulton and H. Chadwick [Philadelphia: Westminster,
1954], pp. 40-92).

[53]Clement, *Miscellanies*, III, 1, 4.

[54]*Ibid.*, 3, 12.

[55]*Ibid.*, 5, 43.

[56]*Ibid.*, 6, 49.

[57]*Ibid.*, 6, 52-53.

[58]*Ibid.*, 7, 58; 11, 71.

[59]*Ibid.*, 12, 79.

[60]*Ibid.*, 1, 4.

[61]*Ibid.*, 17, 102.

[62]Augustine, *City of God*, XIV, 23.

[63]Augustine, *On Marriage and Concupiscence*, I, 17, 19; 10, 11.

[64]*Protevangelium of James* 19-20 (in *New Testament Apocrypha*, ed. W. Schneemelcher, trans. A.J.B. Higgins et al. [Philadelphia: Westminster Press, 1963-1966], I, 384-385).

[65]Jerome, *Against Helvidius*, 16-17; 19.

[66]*Ibid.*, 18.

[67]I Corinthians 7:39-40.

[68]I Timothy 5:11-14.

[69]Tertullian, *Exhortation to Chastity*, 9, 1.

[70]*Ibid.*, 9, 5; 12, 1; 12, 3; 12, 4.

[71]*Ibid.*, 12, 1.

[72]John Chrysostom, *On Not Marrying Again*, 1.

[73]*Ibid.*

[74]Jerome, *Ep.* 54, 4, 2.

[75]*Ibid.*, 18, 3.

[76]An analysis of cultural models in transition helps us to spot the conflict that was destined to arise when the new ascetic model for female living confronted the older reproductive one. Naomi Quinn of Duke University's

Anthropology Department claims that such shifts in
ideology are not simply reflective of economic conditions. Her claim seems appropriate to the present case,
for there is nothing in the economic circumstances, nar-
rowly construed, of many female ascetics to explain their
rapid and enthusiastic desertion of traditional ideas.

[77]The rationale given their cause sounds similar to
that of contemporary separatist feminists, who claim that
women's subordination stems from their association with
sexuality and reproduction, and who thus create separate
women's organizations to free themselves from male domination. For a summary of the separatist position, see
Alison M. Jagger, *Feminist Politics and Human Nature*
(Totowa, N.J.: Rowman & Allanheld, 1983), pp. 103, 105,
267; Alice Echols, "The Taming of the Id: Feminist
Sexual Politics, 1968-83," in Carole S. Vance, ed.,
Pleasure and Danger: Exploring Female Sexuality (Boston:
Routledge & Kegan Paul, 1984), pp. 55, 58.

[78]Athanasius, *Life of Antony*, 3.

[79]*Life of Pachomius*, 5 (Pachomius founds the women's
monastery for his sister).

[80]Jerome, *Commentary on the Epistle to the Ephesians*,
III (Eph. 5:28) (PL 23, 533).

[81]Jerome, *Ep.* 71, 3, 3.

[82]Jerome, *Ep.* 75, 2, 2.

[83]E.g., John Chrysostom, *On S. Pelagia*, 2; *On S.
Drosis*, 3; *On the Maccabees*, 1, 3; *On Saints Bernice and
Prosdoce*, 4.

[84]Ambrose, *On Virgins*, I, 2, 5.

[85]*Ibid.*, 2, 7.

[86]*Ibid.*, 2, 8-9.

[87]*Martyrdom of Perpetua and Felicitas*, 10.

[88]Jerome, *Ep.* 130, 5.

[89]Augustine, *Confessions*, IX, 9; John Chrysostom, *On
Virginity*, 40.

[90]Jerome, *Ep.* 130, 8.

[91]Jerome, *Ep.* 45; on John Chrysostom, see Photius, *Bibliotheca*, cod. LIX (PG 47, 198): among the charges leveled against Chrysostom was that he saw women alone.

[92]Jerome, *Epp.* 39, 1, 2-3; 108, 26, 3.

[93]Jerome, *Ep.* 127, 9-10.

[94]Translation by John Wilkinson, *Egeria's Travel's* (London: SPCK, 1971).

[95]Jerome, *Ep.* 108, 7-14.

[96]*Ibid.*, 14.

[97]For a traditional view of the question, see Roger Gryson, *The Ministry of Women in the Early Church*, tr. J. Laporte and M.L. Hall (Collegeville, Minn.: Liturgical Press, 1980). For a less traditional view, see the forthcoming book of Karen Jo Torjesen, *Women's Leadership in Early Christianity*.

[98]Canon 15, Council of Chalcedon.

[99]*Apostolic Constitutions*, III, 15; VIII, 19.

[100]*Ibid.*, VIII, 20.

[101]*Ibid.*, III, 15.

[102]*Ibid.*

[103]*Life of Pachomius*, 5.

[104]Augustine, *Ep.* 211; Caesarius of Arles, *Rules for the Holy Virgins*.

[105]*Life of Olympias*, 3-6; Palladius, *Dialogue*, 56; 60.

[106]Raymond Janin, *La Géographie ecclesiastique de l'empire byzantine*. I:3: *Les Eglises et les monastères* (Paris: Institut français d'études byzantines, 1953), pp. 395-6.

[107]*Life of Olympias*, 6.

[108]Jerome, *Ep.* 108, 20.

[109]Palladius, *Lausiac History*, 46; 54; Paulinus of Nola, *Ep*. 29, 10.

[110]*The Life of Melania the Younger*, 41; 49.

[111]Ambrose, *Concerning Widows*, 81.

PIETY, PROPAGANDA, AND POLITICS IN THE
LIFE OF MELANIA THE YOUNGER

Studia Patristica XVIII /2: Papers of the
1983 Oxford Patristics Conference (1986)

The *Vita Melaniae Junioris* constitutes one of the
earliest and fullest *Lives* of women saints in the
Christian tradition. Yet since Melania was not widely
celebrated in the calendar of the western church, and
since full Greek and Latin texts of her *Vita* were discovered and published only within the last century,[1] she
is less well-known than she deserves.

Melania's story can be rapidly summarized: born in
about 385 A.D.[2] to Valerius Publicola (son of Melania the
Elder) and his wife Albina, Roman Christian aristocrats,
Melania at the age of thirteen was married to her seven-
teen-year-old cousin, Valerius Pinianus. Although
Melania begged her young bridegroom to adopt the ascetic
life, he refused to consider the issue until they had
produced two children to inherit their vast fortune.
When both of their infant offspring died, Melania ex-
tracted a vow of celibacy from Pinian. Yet it was not
until the death of her father, who had opposed her
ascetic renunciation, that Melania was truly free to
embrace her preferred mode of life. The problems involved in the liquidation of the couple's extensive
property and the disposal of their fortune occupy a significant portion of the *Vita*: to them I shall return.

Fleeing the Gothic advance on Rome, Melania, Pinian, and Albina decamped for a period in Sicily, suffered near-shipwreck during a storm at sea, and settled on one of their North African estates, near Thagaste, where they lived for seven years. During her North African sojourn, Melania founded monasteries for men and women, concerning which she received advice from Augustine, Alypius, and Aurelius of Carthage. In about 417 A.D., the trio left for Palestine, stopping in Egypt en route to visit Cyril of Alexandria.

Once in Palestine, they lived first at the cells attached to the Church of the Holy Sepulcher. Melania and Pinian then made a return trip to Egypt in order to visit the desert saints, to whom they dispersed funds acquired through the recent sale of their Spanish properties. Only after the death of Melania's mother (probably in 431 A.D.) did Melania construct a monastery on the Mount of Olives to house ninety women. After Pinian's death and a four-year period of mourning, she undertook in 435 or 436 the building of another monastery for monks who provided the chanting for the Churches of the Ascension and the Eleona.

Scarcely had Melania finished the construction of the men's monastery when she received an invitation from her uncle Volusian to join him in Constantinople, where he had been sent by the Western court to complete arrangements for the marriage of the Western emperor Valentinian III and the Eastern princess Eudoxia. According to the *Vita*, Melania saw the proposed trip as an opportunity to attempt once more the conversion of her still-pagan uncle. (Augustine's earlier efforts to convert Volusian and his circle had failed: both Augustine's letters and the *City of God*, dedicated to their mutual friend Marcellinus, detail his attempts.)[3] As we might expect, Volusian was converted on his deathbed.

Melania's journey to Constantinople and her sojourn
at the Theodosian court constitute one of the more
interesting episodes of the *Vita*. Melania impressed the
court with her anti-Nestorian speeches, and won the
affection of the empress Eudocia, who journeyed the next
year to Jerusalem to visit her as well as the Holy
Places. While Eudocia was in Jerusalem, Melania dedicated the martyrium she had constructed after her return
from Constantinople. On December 31, 439 A.D., having
celebrated Christmas in Bethlehem and the Feast of St.
Stephen in Jerusalem, Melania died, entrusting her
monasteries to her faithful priest and companion, the
presumed author of the *Vita*. The *Vita Melaniae Junioris*
also contains much information pertaining to the
heroine's ascetic and religious practices, intellectual
interests, speeches to her nuns, battles with the Devil,
and devotion to the saints and to relics.

Although the document exhibits many of the same concerns as other late ancient and early medieval *Vitae*, it
is distinguished from them in several respects. For
example, the *Vita* is remarkably restrained in the number
and types of miracles it attributes to its heroine: only
three in the Greek *Vita* (four in the Latin), all involving not-too-spectacular cures. These are rehearsed only
in a brief section at the end of the *Vita* and by no means
constitute a central feature of the account. Yet like
other hagiographical works, such as the *Life of Antony*,
the *Vita Melaniae Junioris* makes its subject an exemplar
of theological orthodoxy[4] in a way that she most likely
was not: another point to which I shall return. Moreover, although *Lives* of saints conventionally stress
their hero or heroine's ascetic renunciations, Melania's
Vita is distinguished by the extreme quality *both* of
her asceticism *and* of her renunciation: there are few

other saints in Christian history, I suppose, who had as
much to renounce as Melania did.

It is, in fact, Melania's very wealth and aristocratic status that make the *Vita* of perhaps more interest
for late ancient social history than for hagiography.
By virtue of her wealth and social position, Melania was
connected with figures of major political and religious
importance: Theodosius II, Eudocia, Serena (wife of
Stilicho and mother-in-law of Honorius), Augustine, Cyril
of Alexandria, Paulinus of Nola, Palladius, and Proclus
of Constantinople. Through our knowledge of them, we
have a means to "check," in effect, a few details of the
Vita. By comparison of our sources, we can to some extent uncover the "historical Melania the Younger,"
whereas we cannot always glean such alternate perspectives on other saints' lives. What we learn from this
comparative investigation is that the *Vita* conceals as
much as it reveals: at times, it must do so deliberate-
ly. Thus the *Vita Melaniae Junioris* is not just a simple narrative of a holy woman, meant for the edification
of Christian readers; it is also *Tendenzliteratur*, designed to present Melania as a paragon of orthodoxy and
a hater of heretics, in this unlike the Melania we know
from other sources.

No doubt the tendentious quality of the *Vita Melaniae
Junioris* stems in part from the theological predilections
of its author, and to him we must first turn. Given the
earlier raging disagreement among scholars over whether
the original *Vita* was composed in Greek or in Latin,[5] it
is surprising to discover that all modern commentators
agree on the identity of the anonymous author: Gerontius. The first indications regarding authorship are
supplied by the text itself: the writer makes clear
that he was the priest who spent many years at Melania's

side. Unworthy as he claims he is, he was nonetheless
favored by the saint, whom he considers a spiritual
mother.[6]

Early in the eighteenth century, Lenain de Tillemont
posited that the *Vita* had been composed by a monk in
Melania's Jerusalem monastery.[7] The monk was later
identified as Gerontius,[8] and outside sources have cor-
roborated his identity. Cyril of Scythopolis reports
that Gerontius assumed the direction of Melania's monasteries for forty-five years after her death and that he
died during the reign of the emperor Zeno[9] (A.D. 474-
491). In Cyril's *Life of St. Euthymius*, Gerontius is
described as an ardent Monophysite who was sent on an
embassy to convince the desert monk Euthymius that
Chalcedonian doctrine was heretical, but who could not
overcome Euthymius' impassioned defense of Chalcedon.
While the other delegate, Elpidius, was won to Euthymius'
side, Gerontius steadfastly held to his Monophysite
opinions.[10] Gerontius remained a Monophysite to the end.
He was finally driven from his monastery for his heretical views, forced to wander in the desert, and died outside the Catholic communion.[11]

The *Life of Peter the Iberian* also affirms that
Gerontius was an avid anti-Chalcedonian. It reports
that Gerontius broke with Juvenal, bishop of Jerusalem,
over the latter's assent to the Chalcedonian formula:
Gerontius compared Juvenal to Judas, the betrayer of
Jesus.[12] Probably it is safe to infer that Gerontius was
among those monks who clamored to have Juvenal deposed as
bishop of Jerusalem and replaced by the anti-Chalcedonian
Theodosius, a partisan of Dioscorus of Alexandria. In
Cyril of Scythopolis' *Life of St. Euthymius*, we indeed
learn that it was the heterodox bishop Theodosius who
sent Gerontius to the embassy to convince Euthymius of

Chalcedon's error.[13] It is an attractive hypothesis
that the Monophysite Theodosius, who held the episcopal
chair of Jerusalem for twenty months in 452-453 A.D.
before Juvenal's return,[14] was the recipient of the Greek
version of the *Vita Melaniae Junioris*.

Gerontius' purpose in composing the *Vita* appears to
have been twofold. First, he was eager to celebrate the
magnitude of Melania's renunciations, and to this end he
stressed her extreme wealth and aristocratic connections,
which then set the account of her asceticism in high
relief. Second, he wished to present his heroine as a
model of orthodoxy who endeavored to win heretics and
pagans to the orthodox Christian cause. That Gerontius
so portrayed Melania may have had more to do with his
own championing of Monophysitism than the actual theological leanings and personal associations of Melania
warranted.

First, Melania's ascetic piety. According to Gerontius, from childhood on, Melania yearned for the ascetic
life. She attempted to flee her marriage, and was
restrained only by "holy men" who reminded her of Paul's
words, "Wife, how do you know if you will save your
husband?"[15] (here taken to mean a husband's conversion
to asceticism, not simply to Christianity). Melania's
concern for chastity continued after Pinian's vow of
celibacy: she counselled (and bribed) young people to
retain their virginity and to shun "filthy pleasures."[16]
From an early age, she refused to bathe and wore rough
clothing underneath her silken dress.[17] As she advanced
in her asceticism, she lengthened the duration of her
fasts to five days a week (and would have fasted on
Easter as well, if not restrained by her mother), slept
in sackcloth, and in a box so constructed that she could
neither stretch out nor turn over.[18] The *Vita* claims

that, during her years in Jerusalem, she spent Lent in a
small cell on Olivet, and when her sackcloth was shaken
out at Easter, it emitted lice.[19]

Melania's most spectacular renunciations, however,
and those that by her own confession proved the greatest
temptation, were concerned with wealth. The problems
Melania and Pinian faced in their journey from riches to
rags involved the dispersal of their annual discretionary
income, the liquidation of their enormous estates scattered throughout the empire, and the sale or manumission
of their slaves.

Although the Greek and Latin *Vitae* differ on whether
the income mentioned was Melania's or Pinian's, they
agree that the figure was 120,000 pieces of gold and that
this excluded money derived from the spouse's property.[20]
Assuming the "pieces of gold" mean gold *solidi*, the income amounts to 1666 pounds of gold annually.[21] This
figure poses a problem, however, for the *Vita* portrays
Melania as the richest woman in Rome (not even the
emperor's mother-in-law could afford her Roman mansion)[22], yet we know from Olympiodorus that the richest
senators accrued about 4000 pounds of gold annually, and
that senators of moderate wealth, between 1000 and 1500
pounds.[23] If we posit that Melania and Pinian *each* had
about 1700 pounds of gold annually, that figure would
indeed boost them to the level of the richest senators.
Yet even if we imagine them to be only average among
senators in their wealth, their fortune was still vast.
Symmachus, for example, is considered by Olympiodorus to
have been only in the middle ranks of senatorial
wealth,[24] yet we know that he owned nineteen houses and
estates,[25] and spent two thousand pounds of gold on the
games he sponsored for his son's praetorship.[26] Thus
even a middle level of senatorial wealth would have been

vast by contemporary standards, certainly by the standards of university professors. Since at the time of
Gregory the Great, eighty pounds of gold was deemed sufficient to support 3000 nuns for one year,[27] we can
readily calculate that 1666 pounds of gold a year was
more than enough to provide a magnificently luxurious
lifestyle for one person, even taking into account fluc-
tuating gold values and the abstemious diets of Gregory's
refugee nuns.

Once Melania and Pinian began their renunciations,
their money was dispersed across the Roman empire, both
east and west, for charitable and religious causes. It
was also used to build and support monasteries in North
Africa and Jerusalem. From their mansion on the Coelian
Hill in Rome, however, they received next to nothing:
unable to sell it at the time of Alaric's advance, it
was burned during the sack of Rome.[28] The ruins of the
palace have been uncovered and identified from inscriptions and a lamp found therein.[29] Its original splendor
can at least be imagined from the colonnaded porticos,
statues, mosaic pavements, and fountains found in the
course of the excavations.[30]

The Roman mansion, however, was only one of Melania
and Pinian's properties. They owned an estate in the
suburbs,[31] a villa on the seacoast, perhaps in
Campania,[32] an estate in Sicily,[33] and property in Spain,
Africa, Mauretania, Britain, Numidia, Aquitania, and
Gaul.[34] From the Latin *Vita*, we learn that their estate
near Thagaste, where they fled from the Gothic invasion,
was larger than the town itself, had a bath, and was
inhabited by numerous artisans who worked in gold, silver, and copper.[35] This piece of information shows that
the family's income was derived not just from agricul-
ture, but also from manufacture. Although neither *Vita*

reveals the total number of slaves Melania owned,
Palladius in the *Lausiac History* claims that she freed
eight thousand of her slaves at the beginning of her
renunciations, when she was still in Rome.[36] Despite
our lack of figures, we can readily calculate that the
number of slaves they owned bespoke great wealth: John
Chrysostom reports that a man who owned between one and
two thousand slaves was rich.[37]

The dispersal of this vast property was a special
problem for the couple, since neither had reached legal
majority (age twenty-five) when they began their renunciations. A special dispensation, the *venia aetatis*,
was required for minors to dispose of their property,
but family members could still block the dispensation
by arguing that the young person was given to prodigality
or suffered from mental derangement,[38] as Melania's
relatives might have had reason to claim (in fact, the
Vita reports that all of her senatorial relatives opposed
the sale of her property).[39] It took the threat of a
slave revolt, on the occasion that Melania's slaves
learned they were to be sold, to prompt her and Pinian
to seek assistance from the authorities.[40] Going
straight to the top, they petitioned Serena, mother-in-
law of Honorius and wife of Stilicho, in late 407 or
early 408 (the date can be determined from Serena's comment in the *Vita* that she had seen Melania in all her
worldly glory four years earlier, and we know that Serena
was in Rome in January 404 for the celebration of the
sixth consulship of Honorius).[41] According to the *Vita*,
Serena used her influence with Honorius to extract from
him a decree enjoining public officials in the provinces
where Melania had property to sell it and remit the
proceeds to her.[42]

The *Vita* provides another interesting datum related
to the family's exodus from Rome: an unnamed city prefect, described as "a very ardent pagan," attempted along
with the Senate to confiscate Melania and Pinian's property for the public treasury. However, Gerontius
reports, the prefect felt the hand of "God's Providence":
just then, the Roman people rioted during a bread
shortage, the prefect was killed in the riot, and the
couple's property was preserved, for the moment, intact.[43] The fact that Melania and Pinian, as members of
the senatorial class, would have had to apply to this
city prefect for a *venia aetatis* in order to sell their
real estate raises the interesting possibility, not
addressed in the *Vita*, that the prefect was alerted to
their wish for a property sale by their application for
such a dispensation.

We are fortunately aided in our interpretation of
this event by sources other than the *Vita*. From them
we learn that Stilicho, who realized the military weakness of Rome, wished to pacify Alaric, but that the
Senate, of a more war-mongering temper, consistently refused Alaric's demands for gold, silver, and precious
goods, or acquiesced to them only in part. Stilicho's
concessive attitude toward Alaric, when coupled with the
rumor that he wished to raise his own son to the Eastern
throne, led to his execution on August 22, 408. Later
that year or early in 409, on the pretext that Stilicho's
widow Serena was in collaboration with Alaric, the Senate
had her strangled. Stilicho's friends had their property
confiscated; Zosimus adds that some of them were tortured
and executed.[44]

Famine and plague beset Rome; Alaric continued to
press his demands. Zosimus and Sozomen both report that
the city prefect, Gabinus Barbarus Pompeianus--our

unnamed city prefect of the *Vita*--suggested that Etrus-
can rituals be performed to ward off the Gothic danger.
He even had the connivance of Pope Innocent I in his
plan, but when it transpired that the rites had to be
performed in public with the participation of the Senate,
"no one dared."[45]

It has been proposed by Alexander Demandt and
Guntram Brummer that Serena's intervention to help liqui-
date Melania's property, without consulting the Senate,
was a central reason for her downfall: it dampened the
hopes of Rome's senators who wished to lay claim to
Melania's property, probably to help raise the money
demanded by Alaric. Furthermore, they posit, Melania
may have been in danger after Serena's execution because
of their association with her. Demandt and Brummer argue
that since it was contrary to Roman law to confiscate
personal property unless a criminal charge had been
raised against its owner, some charge was needed if
Melania and Pinian's property was to be appropriated.
They posit that the charge probably used by Pompeianus
was the couple's association with Serena.[46] This hypothesis, although attractive, cannot be proved from the
sources, which give only sketchy mention of Serena's
execution, while the *Vita Melaniae* tells nothing of a
charge being raised against its heroine because of her
association with Serena. Although it may well be that
the Senate and Pompeianus hungrily eyed Melania's property as a source of money to pacify Alaric, and that
Melania's exodus from Rome was connected with the downfall of her highly placed protector, Serena, the precise
thesis of Demandt and Brummer is impossible to prove.

What we *can* affirm is that Gerontius wished to use
Melania's connection with Serena and the Western court
to highlight her importance. Even though she had

renounced her wealth and status for a life of impoverished asceticism, she could still mingle with royalty on a
near-equal basis and expect to receive their intervention
and protection. Gerontius likewise stresses Melania's
enthusiastic reception at the Eastern court in Constantinople: she has daily conversations with the royal
women, "edifies" Theodosius II himself, and becomes the
beloved "spiritual mother" of the empress Eudocia,[47] who
visits her in Jerusalem and attends the dedication of
her martyrium on the Mount of Olives.[48] The point of
such emphasis, of course, is to prove that renunciation
does not detract from the importance of the ascetic
devotee. Female aristocrats who undertake the ascetic
life are here shown to be even more influential in their
renunciation than they would have been had they remained
devoted wives and mothers of the next generation of
prefects and consuls. Melania thus provides a near-
perfect example of propaganda for the ascetic cause for
aristocratic women.

     But Gerontius has another purpose as well: to pre-
sent Melania as an exemplar of orthodox Christianity,
worthy of emulation by all the faithful; in his prologue,
he recounts her "ardor for the orthodox faith, an ardor
hotter than fire."[49] Yet what constituted "orthodoxy"
in the fifth century was not so easily ascertained in
the midst of the doctrinal struggles of the day: those
who ended on the winning side of the debate were not the
only ones who thought themselves orthodox, as Gerontius
himself well exemplifies, who remained convinced to the
end that he, a Monophysite, was a partisan of Christian
truth.[50]

     The *Vitae* of saints composed in this period, more-
over, are notoriously open to doctrinal manipulation on
the part of their authors, whatever the dogmatic views

held by the subjects of such accounts may have been.
Thus the *Life of Antony*, for example, is not simply the
biography of an Egyptian ascetic, but Athanasius' *amicus*
brief for Nicene Christianity;[51] the *Historia Monachorum*
is not an innocent collection of monkish lore, but
"gentle propaganda" for the Origenist cause.[52] Although
the *Life of Melania the Younger* represents its heroine
as a hunter of heretics, herself completely dissociated
from heretical taint, Gerontius has perhaps manipulated
his evidence, for the "historical" Melania the Younger,
as revealed in other sources, was closely involved with
heretical currents of her time. Just as he, a Monophysite, deemed himself the proclaimer of Christian
truth, so he paints his heroine, who in truth flirted
with heresy, in shades of high orthodoxy.

First, let us recall who Melania the Younger was:
the granddaughter of Melania the Elder, deeply implicated
in the Origenist controversy through her association with
Rufinus, prime translator of Origenist materials into
Latin; from her own avid reading of Origen's works; from
her friendship with men branded as Origenists, such as
Evagrius Ponticus and Palladius; and through her support
of the Tall Brothers, who fled the Nitrian desert at the
time of Theophilus of Alexandria's attack on Origenism
in 399-400 A.D.[53] As the Origenist controversy heated
up in Palestine during the course of that year, Melania
the Elder took the opportunity to leave for the West.[54]
What we learn from Palladius--but not from the *Vita
Melaniae Junioris*--is that a prime reason for the grandmother's return at this time was to prevent her granddaughter from being "completely ruined by evil teaching
or heresy or bad living."[55] Surely Palladius has something specific in mind. We can piece the situation
together from various sources.

Origenism had become a *cause célèbre* not only in
Egypt and Palestine: Rome, too, had caught fire, with
pro- and anti-Origenist factions raging.[56]   The pro-
Origenist group was associated with Rufinus, the antis
with Jerome's circle.   Pope Anastasius, who assumed
office at the end of 399, condemned Origenism,[57] and his
impulse to do so came at least in part from Jerome's
friends in Rome.   Jerome's admirer Marcella, whom Jerome
praised for her public activity against Origenism, was
in the front line of attack.[58]   In his *Apologia ad
Hieronymum*, Rufinus complained about a "certain matron"
who had stirred up accusations against him by circulating
false copies of his translations:[59]   surely this was
Marcella.   E.D. Hunt suggested, and his suggestion seems
entirely correct, that what Melania the Elder hoped to
save her granddaughter from was falling into the hands
of the anti-Origen, pro-Jerome faction in Rome.[60]   In
this goal she was apparently successful, for the younger
Melania remained friendly with men whom Jerome considered
Origenists.   She sheltered Palladius in her home when he
came on a delegation to Rome in 404 A.D.,[61] and remained
on excellent terms with Paulinus of Nola,[62] whom Jerome
never won for his camp.

The *Vita Melaniae* tells nothing of these incidents;
one could never guess from the work that Melania and
Pinian were so beloved by Rufinus that the latter could
refer to Pinian as "amantissimus filius noster," and
planned to translate Origen's *Homilies on Deuteronomy*
for him.[63]   But the *Vita* does reveal that Melania the
Younger was a special partisan of *apatheia*, the very
quality that Jerome had earlier singled out as the hallmark of Origenist teaching.[64]   Gerontius reports that
Melania strove to shape her life to conform to "angelic
apatheia."[65]   In addition, he repeats a story she told

that (he says) she heard from an old saint, the point of
which was that to be a true disciple, one must become as
impervious to feeling as a statue when it is beaten.[66]
In this context, it is helpful to recall that it was
Rufinus who translated into Latin Evagrius Ponticus'
treatise on *apatheia*.[67] We would never know from the
Vita Melaniae Junioris, however, that Origenism had ever
figured in the life of its heroine.

   To some observers of the period, Origenist teaching
had found a dangerous successor in Pelagianism. Points
of similarity between the two theologies seemed obvious:
Pelagius' alleged teaching on the possibility of sinlessness, for example, could be understood as a new version
of Origenist *apatheia*.[68] That Rufinus could be seen as
a bridge between the two movements is suggested by the
fact that his translation of Origen's *Commentary on
Romans* was heavily used by Pelagius.[69] Yet the association of Melania's group with Pelagianism was not just
indirect. We know that she, Pinian, and Albina actually
met with Pelagius in Palestine in 418 A.D. They wrote
to Augustine in that year reporting that Pelagius had,
in their presence, condemned propositions labelled
"Pelagian." Perhaps Melania thought that this report
would be enough to restore Pelagius to Augustine's good
favor; if so, she was mistaken. Augustine replied in *De
gratia Christi* that their attempt to rehabilitate
Pelagius was not satisfactory.[70]

   Others in Melania's circle were also friends with
Pelagius and Pelagians. Paulinus of Nola, for example,
was a friend of Pelagius; in 417 A.D., Augustine wrote
to Paulinus to express the hope that the relationship
between himself and Pelagius had been terminated.[71]
Paulinus was also friends with Aemilius, the bishop of
Beneventum, who presided at the marriage of Julian of

Eclanum,[72] later to be a prime Pelagian opponent of
Augustine; to celebrate the marriage, Paulinus himself
composed an *epithalamium* that urged the couple to adopt
a life of chastity.[73] We also know that Pinian's good
friend Timasius, who served as emissary between Pinian
and Augustine during the near-ordination of Pinian at
Hippo,[74] was an acknowledged disciple of Pelagius.[75]
Melania's uncle Volusian, moreover, while he was a prefect of Rome, dragged his feet at uprooting Pelagianism
from that city.[75] Peter Brown has argued, very sugges-
tively, that Augustine's reluctance to tackle Pelagius
outrightly by name until 415 A.D. had to do with the
presence in North Africa of this highly placed group of
Roman refugees.[77] Throughout their seven years near
Thagaste, they made stunning contributions to the North
African church,[78] a good enough reason for their theological predilections not to be too rudely handled.

A third theologically questionable association of
Melania was with the Donatists. The Latin version of
the *Vita*, though not the Greek, bluntly reports that on
Melania's vast estate near Thagaste, larger than the
town itself, there were two bishops in residence, one
for "those of our faith" and one for "the heretics."[79]
Given the time (410 A.D. and thereafter) and the place
(North Africa), the reference surely is to the schismatic
Donatists. That a large property owner would tolerate
the presence of a Donatist bishop on his estate is not
surprising. As Emin Tengström has argued in *Donatisten
und Katholiken*, it was in the best interests of the
estate owners to placate their agricultural workers on
religious matters, for the workers had a propensity to
flee when repression reared its head, and owners had to
pay taxes on their land whether or not their workers remained productive.[80]

Melania had already experienced one slave uprising
on her estate near Rome, an uprising that had taken the
intervention of Serena and Honorius to settle. On the
occasion of that slave rebellion, Melania is represented
in the *Vita* as saying to Pinian,

Perhaps it is an opportune time for us
to see the empress. For if our slaves
who are nearby have rebelled against us
in this way, what do you think those outside the cities will do to us, I mean
those in Spain, Campania, Sicily, Africa,
Mauretania, Britain, and the other
lands?[81]

What indeed? Apparently Melania prevented further
unrest by allowing the Donatists on her North African
estate to have their own church without interference.
We know that in 409 A.D., a rumor had circulated in North
Africa that amnesty was being granted to Donatists, a
rumor Augustine was quick to quell;[82] Melania's arrival
in Africa occurred shortly after the circulation of this
story, which may have encouraged her to believe that
harboring Donatists was permissible. A few years later,
she would have a further reason for not disturbing the
Donatist sympathies of her workers: her uncle's friend
Marcellinus would be executed in 413 A.D. in the after-
math of Donatist repression in North Africa.[83]

In the Greek version of the *Vita*, evidence pertaining
to Donatism does not emerge--nor, for that matter, *any*
evidence that would link Melania with heresy or schism.
She is orthodoxy personified, a fighter of heretics. She
is careful to associate with bishops who are noted for
their "doctrine."[84] She lectures her nuns on guarding
"the holy and orthodox faith."[85] She resolutely attempts
to convert "Samaritans, pagans, and heretics,"[86] a

reference perhaps designed to bring her activities into
accord with the wording of Theodosius II's decree of
January 438 A.D., *De Judaeis, Samaritanis, Haereticis,
et Paganis.*[87] In fact, the most important pagan Melania
converted was her uncle Volusian, probably a year before
the Theodosian decree. And the *Vita* reveals that
Melania's efforts to convert Volusian were not entirely
free of threats involving imperial intervention.[88]

As for heretics, Gerontius reports that in Melania's
zeal for orthodoxy, she attempted to convert anyone even
suspected of heresy, and if she failed in her effort,
she refused that person's donation for the poor.[89] When
Melania journeyed to Constantinople, Gerontius represents
her as there taking up cudgels against Nestorianism, a
point not specifically mentioned in the Latin version of
the *Vita*. She leads anti-Nestorian discussions among
wives of senators and men noted for their learning.[90]
Theodosius himself is said to have been "edified" by
her religious teaching.[91]

Moreover, the high praise lavished on bishop Proclus
of Constantinople in the *Vita*[92] takes on added meaning
when we recall his anti-Nestorian bias. Proclus' letters
and sermons testify to his high regard for Mary as the
theotokos and to his campaign against Nestorianism;[93]
Nestorius himself singled out Proclus for special criticism.[94] From Proclus' perspective, the Nestorians were
"new Jews," whose teaching reduced Christ to a mere man.[95]
Thus Melania's anti-Nestorian proclivities no doubt contributed to her high regard for the anti-Nestorian
bishop of Constantinople.

Pelagianism is a more minor target in the *Vita*.
Gerontius is careful to have Melania ascribe her miracles
not to her own power, but to God's agency.[96] When once
she was asked to work a cure, she replied, "Since I am a

sinner, I am not capable of doing this."[97]   She confessed
that if she ever imagined herself to be good, she
immediately recognized the thought as one of the Devil's
traps.[98]   Gerontius also reports a prayer the empress
Eudocia uttered, on the theme that God rewards us not
according to our merits, but simply through his benevolence and the intercession of the saints.[99]

   The editor of the Latin *Vita*, however, includes one
interesting episode in more detail than does the editor
of the Greek version: a report of Melania's miraculous
cure of a pregnant woman whose fetus had died within her
before birth.   In the Greek version, by Melania's prayer
and action, the fetus is expelled and the woman saved.[100]
The Latin version, in addition to describing in grim detail the surgeon's procedures in cutting away bits of the
fetus, has Melania deliver a speech that sounds suspiciously as if it were designed to rebut the Pelagian
accusation that the doctrine of original sin implied that
childbearing was sinful.   According to Gerontius, Melania
commented to the assembled group that, as God has made
human fetuses, the process cannot be deemed "filthy";
only sin is "filthy" and "abominable."   Bodily parts
which God has created cannot be so, she asserted, for by
the procreative process were born patriarchs, prophets,
apostles, and other saints.[101]   Melania is thus represented as admitting our human sinfulness but denying
that childbearing involves sin.   She did not attribute
her miraculous cure on this occasion to her own powers,
but to the virtues of the saints.[102]   The story as told
in the Latin *Vita* fits well into the debate over original
sin, marriage, and childbearing that had occurred not
many years earlier between Pelagians and Augustinians.

   Most important of all, and impossible to overlook,
the *Vita Melaniae Junioris* does not even once mention the

name of Melania the Elder.[103] There is no mention of
the details that we know of the elder Melania's life
reported in Palladius' *Lausiac History* and other sources:
especially is there no mention of Palladius' claim that
she served as the chief inspiration for her granddaughter, Melania the Younger, in her ascetic renunciation.[104]
Nor do we hear in the *Vita* about the voyage Melania the
Elder made back to Rome, after years in Jerusalem, "as
an old woman of sixty," to rescue her now-married granddaughter from "bad teaching or heresy or bad living."[105]
And despite the fact that Melania the Younger's monasteries receive ample attention in the *Vita*, her grandmother's monastic foundations on Olivet--one for men and
one for women--go completely unmentioned. Strikingly,
even when Gerontius cites a passage from the *Lausiac
History* that included a reference to the elder Melania,
he omits this line from his citation.

The citation appears in Chapter 1 of the *Vita*:
Melania the Younger there begs Pinian to practice chastity with her. She asks that if he cannot because of
"the burning passion of youth," that he leave her body
"free," in return for which she will give him all her
possessions. Thus will she fulfill her religious
goal.[106] In Palladius' account of this speech, Melania's
reason for her ascetic desire is that she wished to
inherit "the zeal of my grandmother whose name I
bear."[107] Although Gerontius' use of this passage from
the *Lausiac History* served as a central case in the argument between Mariano Rampolla and Cuthbert Butler over
the original language of the *Vita*,[108] neither they nor
others have noted the line that the *Vita* omits, the
specific reference to Melania the Elder. The omission
is all the more striking if we imagine, as both Rampolla
and Butler did, that the author of the *Vita* had the text

of the *Lausiac History* before him.[109]   This omission,
when coupled with the silence regarding the elder Melania
throughout the *Vita*, leads us to suspect a tendentious
motive. The fame of Melania the Elder among Christians
in late antiquity was such (Paulinus claims that
"volumes" were written about her)[110] that her absence
from her granddaughter's *Vita* must be a deliberate move,
in fact, a *damnatio memoriae*.[111] That Gerontius was not
averse to employing this technique, we know by an admission he makes in the Latin *Vita*: when speaking of the
city prefect who attempted to confiscate Melania and
Pinian's property, Gerontius tells his readers that he
will not report the man's name: "praefectus...cuius
etiam minime nomen recordor...."[112]

The same castigation to silence perhaps explains why
the Elder Melania's monasteries in Jerusalem receive no
mention in the *Vita*. Other explanations for the omission
have, indeed, been posited. G.D. Gordini, for example,
suggests that either the monasteries had disappeared by
the time of Melania the Younger's sojourn in Palestine,
or they had passed into the control of "Easterners."[113]
Either explanation is of course possible. Yet we know
from Palladius that Melania the Elder endowed her monasteries,[114] which would suggest that there were funds to
support them for at least some years after her death in
about 410 A.D. Second, the explanation that Melania the
Younger would not have wished to join a monastic community with "Eastern" practices assumes (with Rampolla)
that Melania the Younger's monasteries were decisively
"Western," a view I have criticized and qualified elsewhere.[115] Conceivably the younger Melania simply wanted
to have her *own* monastery, on which she could bestow her
largesse and serve as patron. Yet a further motive might
be that the grandmother's association with "heresy" had
made her monasteries suspect.

One further incident in the *Vita* perhaps pertains to
Melania the Elder. Gerontius relates in chapter 28 an
event that provoked his heroine to wrath. Once during
the recitation of the *anaphora*, Gerontius inadvertently in-
furiated Melania by including the name of someone who
had been suspected of heresy. The person is not named,
but is described as a foreigner to Palestine, "a certain
woman of high status" who had settled at the Holy Places
some time earlier and had finished her life there.
Melania the Younger was so angry at Gerontius' inclusion
of this name that she threatened never again to attend
the liturgy: hearing the name once was once too much
for her.[116] Could this highly born foreign woman in
Palestine who had fallen under suspicion of heresy be
Melania's own grandmother? We know of nobody else who
so fits the description.[117]

The thesis seems to us plausible that the excision
of Melania the Elder from the text was deliberate on the
author's part. The woman who, according to Palladius,
provided the model and inspiration for her young granddaughter's renunciation has become a non-person, and the
only plausible reason for this appears to relate to the
dogmatic suspicions adhering to Melania the Elder's name.

The animus against Melania the Elder may also in
part explain the marked antagonism running throughout
the text toward her son, Valerius Publicola, who, according to Gerontius, posed the major obstacle to Melania
the Younger's adoption of asceticism.[118] We are told in
the *Vita* that "the Devil" led Valerius Publicola astray
to the point where he considered disinheriting Melania;
he is said to have "persecuted" the couple in their quest
for ascetic renunciation.[119] On his deathbed, Valerius
Publicola repented his "sin" of attempting to prevent
Melania's renunciation.[120]

The picture of Valerius Publicola given in the *Vita* is not entirely in keeping with that presented in other sources. Palladius, for example, reports that Publicola and other members of the elder Melania's family provided the funds that enabled her to make "donations to churches, monasteries, guests, and prisons."[121] Paulinus of Nola affirms that although Publicola had not adopted the ascetic life as his mother had wished, he was "rich through works"; he inwardly espoused Christian humility even though he still wore worldly clothing. His sense of religious duty, according to Paulinus, was "striking": he was as devoted to Christ as he was beloved by Paulinus himself.[122]

Now the contrary pictures of Publicola in the *Vita* and in the writings of Paulinus and Palladius may simply reflect the differing perspectives of the authors. We have no reason to doubt that Valerius Publicola provided generously for Christian causes, that as a wealthy lay-man, his contributions were entirely in accord with what churchmen and ascetic leaders (such as Palladius and Paulinus) might hope them to be. But there is also no reason to doubt that (as the *Vita* reports) he may have balked when his daughter, perhaps his only heir, attempted to flee her marriage, renounce childbearing (thus depriving him of descendants), and disperse the vast family inheritance. Having spent much of his own childhood as a virtual orphan because of his mother's ascetic enthusiasm (she abandoned him in Rome when he was a young boy and left for a career of ascetic devotion in the East), Valerius Publicola may well have wished his daughter to adopt a mode of life in which Christian concern was not divorced from the usual societal expectations for aristocratic maidens.

But a second hypothesis may be posed concerning the
Vita's hostility to Publicola: the very fact of his
association with Melania the Elder, his mother, may have
damaged him in the author's eyes.   As C.P. Hammond has
suggested, and his suggestion seems entirely plausible,
the exaggerated picture of the enmity prevailing between
Melania the Younger and her relations "is caused partly
by a desire to exalt Melania herself at the expense of
her family, partly by a fear of the taint of heresy"[123]
such as clung to the reputation of her grandmother.   To
be sure emphasizing parental opposition heightens
Melania the Younger's heroism and thus can be understood
as a typical hagiographical device,[124] but we suspect
that the denigration of Valerius Publicola may have
something to do with the text's total disregard for
Melania's paternal grandmother.

That heretics could be the most avid of heretic-
hunters is not unknown in Christian history: Nestorius
furnishes the outstanding case in point.[125]   The author
of the *Vita Melaniae Junioris*, himself unorthodox, later
an outcast for his ardent Monophysitism, so pictures
Melania as to divorce her from all association with
heretics and heretical movements.   Since evidence from
outside the *Vita* indicates that Melania was not in truth
so doctrinally pure, we may reasonably conclude that the
Vita Melaniae Junioris is not free of tendentious,
indeed, propagandistic, qualities.

NOTES

[1]Latin text, discovered in 1884 but not published
until 1905, by Mario Rampolla del Tindaro, *Santa Melania
Guiniore, senatrice Romana: documenti contemporei e note*
(Roma: Tipografia Vaticana, 1905). Greek text discovered
by the Bollandists in 1900, published in 1903: Hippolyte
Delehaye, "S. Melaniae Junioris. Acta Graeca," *Analecta
Bollandiana* 22 (1903), 5-50. The Greek text used here is
that given in Denys Gorce, *Vie de Sainte Mélanie. Texte
grec, introduction, traduction et notes*. Sources
Chrétiennes 90 (Paris: Les Editions du Cerf, 1962).
English translation of the *Vita* and commentary in Elizabeth A. Clark, *The Life of Melania the Younger. Introduction, Translation and Commentary*. Studies in Women
and Religion 14 (New York/Toronto: The Edwin Mellen
Press, 1984).

[2]The traditional date given was 383 A.D., but this
was calculated from a dating of Melania's father's death
which is now considered too early. Based on a revised
chronology of the letters of Paulinus of Nola and Augustine, Valerius Publicola's death is now dated two or
three years later, to 406 or 407 A.D. Since Melania is
said to have been twenty when she began her renunciations, and this occurred at the time of her father's
death, her birth date should be moved up to about 385 A.D.

[3]See Augustine's Epistles 135-138. For the dedication of the *City of God* to Marcellinus, see *De civitate
Dei* I, praefatio (CCL 47, 1).

[4]See Robert C. Gregg and Dennis E. Groh, *Early
Arianism: A View of Salvation* (Philadelphia: Fortress
Press, 1981), ch. 4, for a discussion of how Athanasius
makes Antony a spokesman for Nicene orthodoxy.

[5]Priority of the Latin championed by Rampolla;
priority of the Greek argued by Adhémar d'Alès, "Les Deux
Vies de Sainte Mélanie le Jeune," *Analecta Bollandiana*
25 (1906), 401-450.

[6]*Vita*, prologus; 68 (Gorce, pp. 126, 266).

[7]Louis Sebastian Lenain de Tillemont, *Mémoires pour servir à l'histoire ecclésiastique des six premiers siècles* (Paris: Charles Robustel, 1709), XIV, 233.

[8]Carolus deSmedt, "Vita Sanctae Melaniae Junioris," *Analecta Bollandiana* 8 (1899), 17.

[9]Cyril of Scythopolis, *Vita S. Euthymii* 45 (Schwartz, p. 67); *Vita S. Theodosii* (Schwartz, p. 239).

[10]Cyril of Scythopolis, *Vita S. Euthymii* 27 (Schwartz, pp. 42-44).

[11]*Ibid.*, 45 (Schwartz, p. 67).

[12]*Vita Petri Hiberii* (Raabe, p. 32, Syriac; p. 36, German).

[13]Cyril of Scythopolis, *Vita S. Euthymii* 27 (Schwartz, p. 42).

[14]On Theodosius, see Evagrius Scholasticus, *Historia Ecclesiastica* II, 5 (Bidez and Parmentier, p. 52); Zacharias Rhetor, *Historica Ecclesiastica* III, 3-5 (Brooks, pp. 156-159 Syriac; pp. 107-109 Latin); *Vita Petri Hiberii* (Raabe, pp. 52, 57 Syriac; pp. 53, 58 German); Cyril of Scythopolis, *Vita S. Euthymii* 27 (Schwartz, pp. 41-45).

[15]*Vita* 1; 4 (Gorce, pp. 130, 132, 134); I Cor. 7;16.

[16]*Vita* 29 (Gorce, pp. 182, 184).

[17]*Vita* 2; 4 (Gorce, pp. 132, 134).

[18]*Vita* 22; 24; 25; 32 (Gorce, pp. 172, 174, 176, 178, 188).

[19]*Vita* 40 (Gorce, p. 204).

[20]Greek and Latin *Vitae* 15 (Gorce, p. 156; Rampolla, p. 11).

[21]72 *solidi* = 1 pound of gold.

[22]*Vita* 14 (Gorce, pp. 154, 156).

[23]Olympiodorus, frag. 44, in Photius, *Bibliotheca* 80 (PG 103, 280).

[24]*Ibid.*

[25]Otto Seeck's count, *Q. Aurelii Symmachi Quae Supersunt.* MGH, AA VI (Berlin: Weidmann, 1883), pp. xlv-xlvi.

[26]Olympiodorus, frag. 44, in Photius, *Bibliotheca* 80 (PG 103, 280).

[27]Paul the Deacon, *Vita S. Gregorii Magni* II, 27 (PL 75, 97).

[28]*Vita* 14 (Gorce, p. 156).

[29]See G.B. deRossi, "La casa dei Valerii sul Celio et il monastero di S. Erasmo," *Studi e Documenti di Storia e Diritto* 7 (1886), 235-243; Guiseppe Gatti, "La casa celimontana dei Valerii e il monastero di S. Erasmo," *Bullettino della Commissione Archeologica Communale di Roma* 30 (1902), esp. 148-149; Guiseppe Bovini, *Monumenti figurati paleocristiani conservati a Firenze nelle raccolte pubbliche e negli edifici di culto* (Città del Vaticano: Pontificio Istituto di Archeologia Cristiana, 1950), pp. 8-13; Antonio M. Colini, *Storia e topographia del Celio nell' antichita* (Roma: Tipographia Poliglotta Vaticana, 1944), pp. 253-258; and all *CIL* references therein.

[30]Rampolla, *Melania*, p. 170; Colini, *Storia*, pp. 255-256.

[31]*Vita* 7 (Gorce, p. 140).

[32]*Vita* 18 (cf. 11) (Gorce, pp. 162, 146).

[33]*Vita* 11; 19 (Gorce, pp. 146, 166).

[34]*Vita* 11; 20 (Gorce, pp. 146, 168); Palladius, *Historia Lausiaca* 61 (Butler, p. 156).

[35]Latin *Vita* 21 (Rampolla, p. 14).

[36]Palladius, *Historia Lausiaca* 61 (Butler, p. 156).

[37]John Chrysostom, *Hom. 63 in Matt.*, 4 (PG 58, 608).

[38]*Vita* 8 (Gorce, p. 140); *Codex Theodosianus* II, 17, 1 (Mommsen, pp. 102-104); *Codex Justinianus* II, 44 (45),

1-2 (Krueger, p. 114); Gaius, in *Digesta Iustiniani
Augusti* XXVII, 10, 1; 3 (Mommsen, I, 812); Ulpian, *Liber
singularis regularum* 12 (Krueger, p. 17); Justinian,
Institutiones I, 23, 3 (Moyle, I, 160-161).

[39]*Vita* 12 (Gorce, p. 152).

[40]*Vita* 10-11 (Gorce, pp. 144, 146, 148).

[41]*Vita* 12 (Gorce, pp. 148, 150); Claudian, *Panegyri-
cus de sexto consulatu Honorii Augusti*, esp. 11. 578ff.
and 640ff.

[42]*Vita* 12 (Gorce, p. 152).

[43]*Vita* 19 (Gorce, p. 166).

[44]Sources: Zosimus V, 26-49; Sozomen, *Historia
Ecclesiastica* VIII, 25; IX, 4; 6; Olympiodorus, frag. 5;
9; Orosius, *Historia adversum Paganos* VII, 38.

[45]Zosimus, V, 41 (CSHB 30, 305); Sozomen, *Historia
Ecclesiastica* IX, 6, 3 (GCS 50, 398) (other pagan
rituals).

[46]Alexander Demandt and Guntram Brummer, "Der Prozess
gegen Serena im Jahre 408 n. Chr.," *Historia* 26 (1977),
479-502.

[47]*Vita* 56; 58 (Gorce, pp. 238, 242).

[48]*Vita* 58-59 (Gorce, pp. 240, 242, 244, 246).

[49]Greek *Vita*, prologus (Gorce, p. 126); the editor of
the Latin *Vita* claims in the prologue that Melania
affirmed "the unity of the Trinity" (Rampolla, p. 4).

[50]See above, pp. 65-66.

[51]Gregg and Groh, *Early Arianism*, ch. 4.

[52]C.P. Hammond, "The Last Ten Years of Rufinus' Life
and the Date of His Move South from Aquileia," *Journal of
Theological Studies*, n.s. 28 (1977), pp. 395, 397;
Jerome, *Ep.* 133, 3 (CSEL 56, 246).

[53]See E.D. Hunt, "Palladius of Helenopolis: A Party
and Its Supporters in the Church of the Late Fourth Century," *Journal of Theological Studies*, n.s. 24 (1973),
472-473; E. Schwartz, "Palladiana," *Zeitschrift für die*

Neutestamentliche Wissenschaft 37 (1937), 169-174;
Charles Pietri, "Esquisse de conclusion: l'aristocratie
chrétienne entre Jean de Constantinople et Augustin
d' Hippone," *Jean Chrysostome et Augustin: actes du
colloque de Chantilly* 22-24 Septembre 1974, ed. Charles
Kannengiesser, Théologie Historique 35 (Paris: Editions
Beauchesne, 1975), pp. 294, 300; Antoine Guillaumont, *Les
'Kephalaia Gnostica'* d'Evagre le Pontique et l'histoire
de l'Origénisme chez les Grecs et chez les Syriens.
Patristica Sorbonensia 5 (Paris: Editions du Seuil,
1962), pp. 47, 57, 64; Maurice Villain, "Rufin d'
Aquilée--La Querelle autour d'Origène," *Recherches de
Science Religieuse* 27 (1937), 5-37, 165-195; Francis X.
Murphy, *Rufinus of Aquileia (345-411). His Life and
Works.* The Catholic University of America Studies in
Medieval History, n.s. 6 (Washington, D.C.: Catholic
University of America Press, 1945), pp. 126-131. For
primary source material on Theophilus' attack on the Tall
Brothers and their flight, see Sozomen, *Historia Ecclesi-
astica* VIII, 12-13 (GCS 50, 364-367) and Palladius,
Dialogus de Vita S. Joannis Chrysostomi, 6-7 (Coleman-
Norton, pp. 37-42). On Melania's reading of Origen, see
Palladius, *Historia Lausiaca* 55 (Butler, p. 149), a
passage now thought to pertain to Melania the Elder.

[54]Melania the Elder returned West in the last weeks
of 399 or early in 400; see Nicole Moine, "Melaniana,"
Recherches Augustiniennes 15 (1980), 27. For the Tall
Brothers' flight from Palestine to Constantinople, see
the letter of Theophilus in Jerome, *Ep.* 90, 2 (CSEL 55,
144); Schwartz, "Palladiana," p. 174; Hunt, "Palladius,"
p. 473.

[55]Palladius, *Historia Lausiaca* 54 (Butler, p. 146).

[56]For discussion, see Charles Pietri, *Roma Christiana. Recherches sur l'église de Rome, son organisation,
sa politique, son idéologie de Miltiade à Sixte III (311-
440)* (Roma: Ecole Française de Rome, 1976), pp. 435,
448-450.

[57]Anastasius, *Epistola ad Simplicianum Mediolanensem*
1-2 (PL 22, 722-774).

[58]Jerome, *Ep.* 127, 9-10 (CSEL 54, 152-153); Murphy,
Rufinus, pp. 126-127.

[59]Rufinus, *Apologium contra Hieronymum* I, 19 (CCL 20,
53); Murphy, *Rufinus,* pp. 129-131, 134; Hammond, "The
Last Ten Years," p. 385.

[60]Hunt, "Palladius," pp. 477-478.

[61]Palladius, *Historia Lausiaca* 61 (Butler, p. 157).

[62]Paulinus of Nola, *Ep.* 29, 12 (CSEL 29, 258-259);
Carmen 21, 198-307, 836-840 (CSEL 30, 164-168, 185).
Recall that Melania was on her way to see Paulinus on her
flight from Rome when she was blown off course (*Vita* 19
[Gorce, p. 166]).

[63]Rufinus, *Prologus in Omelias Origenis super Numeros*
(CCL 20, 285).

[64]Jerome, *Ep.* 133, 3 (CSEL 56, 246); so stressed by
Guillaumont, *Les 'Kephalaia Gnostica'*, p. 67.

[65]*Vita* 70 (Gorce, p. 270).

[66]*Vita* 44 (Gorce, p. 212); for suggestions as to
possible sources for the story, see Rampolla, *Melania*,
p. 233 n. 30.

[67]Jerome, *Ep.* 133, 3 (CSEL 56, 246). According to
Guillaumont, the reference is to Evagrius' *Practicos* (*Les
'Kephalaia Gnostica'*, p. 67).

[68]For a discussion of the evidence, see Robert F.
Evans, *Pelagius: Inquiries and Reappraisals* (New York:
Seabury Press, 1968), pp. 17, 20-23.

[69]See Evans, *Pelagius*, p. 19.

[70]Augustine, *De Gratia Christi* I, 1-2 (PL 44, 359-
361); also see Hammond, "The Last Ten Years," p. 422.

[71]Augustine, *Ep.* 186, 1, 1; 1, 3; 12, 39 (CSEL 57,
45, 47, 78).

[72]On Aemilius and the wedding, see P.G. Walsh, *The
Poems of Paulinus of Nola*. Ancient Christian Writers 40
(New York/Ramsey, N.J.: Newman Press, 1975), pp. 399
n. 1, 402 n. 47. Aemilius was among the bishops sent to
Constantinople from the West in late 405 or early 406 to
address the matter of John Chrysostom's exile (Palladius,
Dialogus de Vita S. Joannis Chrysostomi 4 [Coleman-Norton,
p. 22]); thus Aemilius is another link between Melania's
circle and Chrysostom. See Rampolla, *Melania*, pp. 194-
195; Pietri, *Roma Christiana*, pp. 1321-1322, 1324; Peter
Brown, "The Patrons of Pelagius: The Roman Aristocracy
between East and West," in Brown, *Religion and Society*

in the Age of Saint Augustine (New York: Harper and Row,
1972), pp. 214-215.

[73]Paulinus of Nola, *Carmen* 25, esp. 11. 231-236 (CSEL
30, 245).

[74]Augustine, *Ep.* 126, 6 (CSEL 44, 12).

[75]*Ibid.*; *De Natura et Gratia* I, 1 (PL 44, 247);
Pietri, "Esquisse," pp. 302-303.

[76]*Decretum Constantinii Imperatoris et Edictum* (PL
45, 1750-1751; PL 56, 499-500).

[77]Brown, "The Patrons of Pelagius," in *Religion and
Society*, pp. 217-218.

[78]*Vita* 20-22 (Gorce, pp. 168, 170, 172).

[79]Latin *Vita* 21 (Rampolla, p. 14). That a Donatist
bishop is meant is also assumed by Paul Allard, "Une
Grande Fortune romaine an cinquième siècle," *Revue des
Questions Historiques* 81 (1907), 11; Georges Goyau,
Sainte Mélanie (383-439) (Paris: J. Gabala, 1909), p. 9;
and Henri Leclerq, "Mélanie la Jeune (Sainte)," *Dictionnaire d'Archéologie Chrétienne et de Liturgie* XI, 213.

[80]Emin Tengström, *Donatisten und Katholiken.
Soziale, wirtschaftliche und politische Aspekte einer
nordafrikanischen Kirchenspaltung* (Götteborg: Elanders
Boktryckerei Aktiebolag, 1964), pp. 135-138.

[81]*Vita* 11 (Gorce, p. 146).

[82]Augustine, *Ep.* 105, 2, 6 (CSEL 34, 599).

[83]Orosius, *Historia adversum Paganos* VII, 42, 16-17
(CSEL 5, 558-559); Augustine, *Ep.* 151, 4-8 (CSEL 44, 384-
389).   Also see Madeleine Moreau, "Le Dossier Marcellinus
dans la correspondance de Saint Augustin," *Recherches
Augustiniennes* 9 (1973), 93-102.

[84]*Vita* 36 (Gorce, p. 194).

[85]*Vita* 43 (Gorce, p. 210).

[86]*Vita* 29 (Gorce, p. 184).

[87]Theodosius II, *Novella* 3 (Mommsen, II, 7-10).

[88]*Vita* 53 (Gorce, p. 232).

[89]*Vita* 27 (Gorce, p. 180).

[90]*Vita* 54 (Gorce, p. 232).

[91]*Vita* 56 (Gorce, p. 238).

[92]*Vita* 53 (Gorce, p. 232).

[93]See Proclus' sermon "De Laudibus S. Mariae" (PG 65, 680-692) and his "Letter to the Armenians," (*Ep.* 2) (PG 65, 856-873).

[94]In a sermon translated by Marius Mercator (*Collectio Palatina* 23; ACO I, 5, 44), Nestorius, after speaking of the disturbances stirred up in the city, reminds his audience that Paul (in Titus 1:9) writes that a bishop must adhere to true doctrine, so that he can move his hearers and refute objectors--but Paul did not mean that a bishop had the right to wound those who disagreed with him.

[95]Proclus, *Ep.* 2, 13-14 (PG 65, 869, 872).

[96]*Vita* 60; 61 (Gorce, pp. 246, 248, 250).

[97]*Vita* 60 (Gorce, p. 248).

[98]*Vita* 62 (Gorce, p. 250).

[99]Latin *Vita* 59 (Rampolla, p. 33).

[100]Greek *Vita* 61 (Gorce, pp. 248, 250).

[101]Latin *Vita* 61 (Rampolla, p. 34): "Nihil enim foedum aut immundum Deus fecit in homine, sed omnia membra consequentia creavit: solum enim peccatum immundum est et abominabile; nam membra immunda esse non possunt quae Dominus creavit, unde nati sunt patriarchae, prophetae et apostoli et ceteri sancti."

[102]In both Greek and Latin *Vitae* 61 (Gorce, p. 250; Rampolla, p. 35).

[103]Noted also by Gorce, *Vie*, pp. 180-181 n. 3, and Nicole Moine, "Mélanie la Jeune (Sainte)," *Dictionnaire de Spiritualité* X, 960.

[104]Palladius, *Historia Lausiaca* 61 (Butler, p. 155).

[105]Palladius, *Historia Lausiaca* 54 (Butler, p. 146).

[106]*Vita* 1 (Gorce, pp. 130, 132).

[107]Palladius, *Historia Lausiaca* 61 (Butler, p. 155).

[108]Rampolla, *Melania*, p. lxiv; E.C. Butler, "Cardinal Rampolla's Melania the Younger," *Journal of Theological Studies* 7 (1906), 631.

[109]Rampolla, *Melania*, pp. lxvii-lxviii; Butler, "Cardinal Rampolla's Melania," p. 631.

[110]Paulinus of Nola, *Ep.* 29, 6 (CSEL 29, 251).

[111]Gorce agrees: *Vie*, p. 35.

[112]Latin *Vita* 34 (Rampolla, p. 18).

[113]Gian Domenico Gordini, "Il monachesimo romano in Palestina nel IV secolo," in *Saint Martin et son temps*. Studia Anselmiana 46 (Rome: Herder, 1961), p. 90.

[114]Palladius, *Historia Lausiaca* 54 (Butler, p. 148): money was left to provide for the monastery.

[115]Clark, "Commentary," *The Life of Melania the Younger*, pp. 119-129.

[116]*Vita* 28 (Gorce, pp. 180, 182).

[117]An hypothesis independently proposed, but supported by Moine, "Melaniana," pp. 73-74. This interpretation depends on taking the phrase that the woman was "in communion with us, the orthodox" (*Vita* 28 [Gorce, p. 182]) to mean not that she was taking part in services with Melania and Gerontius on Olivet, but merely that she considered herself part of the orthodox communion; or, conceivably, that she had earlier communed with Melania (if the woman were Melania the Elder, possibly during her trip West in 400 A.D.). The Latin version (Rampolla, p. 16) reads, "Communicabat autem et nobiscum, fictam fidens habens," which sounds as if the woman were actually taking the Eucharist in the company of Melania.

[118]*Vita* 1; 6; 7; 12 (Gorce, pp. 130, 136, 138, 150).

[119]*Vita* 12 (Gorce, p. 150).

[120]Greek *Vita* 7 (Gorce, p. 138); Latin *Vita* 12 (Rampolla, p. 10).

[121]Palladius, *Historia Lausiaca* 54 (Butler, p. 146).

[122]Paulinus of Nola, *Ep.* 45, 2-3 (CSEL 29, 381-382).

[123]Hammond, "The Last Ten Years," p. 380 n. 3.

[124]Moine, "Melaniana," p. 57.

[125]Socrates Scholasticus, *Historia Ecclesiastica* VII, 29 (Hussey, II, 799).

CLAIMS ON THE BONES OF SAINT STEPHEN: THE PARTISANS OF MELANIA AND EUDOCIA

Church History 51 (1982), 141-156

As Peter Brown has so eloquently described in *The Cult of the Saints: Its Rise and Function in Latin Christianity*, bones became an avenue to power in late antiquity.[1] Wealthy Christians who could lay claim to the bodies of the holy dead gained status through their willingness to share the *gratia* thus acquired with those lacking relics of their own; Paulinus of Nola, proprietor of Saint Felix's remains, affords an illuminating example.[2] Patronage was restyled, Brown argues, as the royal, priestly, or monastic controllers of bones became the intermediaries through whom the saints' generosities were bestowed on sinful humans.[3] Yet cooperation was not always the dominant spirit in the dispensing of *gratia*: relics could provide new opportunities for competition, as is dramatically illustrated by a rivalry confused and perhaps forever obfuscated by contradictory texts. The rivals are the heiress-turned-ascetic Melania the Younger and the empress Eudocia, wife of Theodosius II. The bones are Stephen's.

Although Stephen was depicted in Acts 7 as the first Christian martyr, he was nonetheless a relative late-comer to the world of cultic exaltation. We are fortunate to possess a detailed account describing his debut.[4] In December of 415 A.D., as Bishop John of Jerusalem

labored with fellow ecclesiastics at Diospolis (Lydda)
over the thorny questions of Pelagianism,[5] a Palestinian
priest named Lucian was receiving supernatural nightly
visitations. Lucian tells us in his account, our source
that relates the finding of Stephen's bones, that the
nocturnal visitor identified himself as Gamaliel, no
longer a Pharisaic teacher but a baptized Christian.[6]
Gamaliel instructed Lucian to alert Bishop John, for he
would soon reveal to them the location of Stephen's body,
which he himself had retrieved after the stoning and had
buried on family property near the town of Caphargamala.[7]
Lucian's recalcitrance having been overcome, an excava-
tion was organized at the spot Gamaliel indicated.[8] As
the diggers neared the tomb, the air became so suffused
with fragrance that Lucian believed he had entered paradise. Instantly, 73 people were healed. Demons fled,
hemorrhages ceased, fevers subsided, and many other
miracles occurred, "too many to enumerate." The relics
of Stephen then were carried to the church of Sion for
deposition,[9] the church that until 335 A.D. had served
as the episcopal headquarters of Jerusalem.[10]

The bones, as well as the story, traveled rapidly:
not all of Stephen found rest in the church of Sion.[11]
Lucian himself appropriated some of the remains, which
he gave to Avitus, a Spanish refugee priest in Palestine.
Avitus in turn sent them and a Latin translation of
Lucian's tale to Bishop Balchonius of Braga; bones and
letter were to be delivered to Paulus Orosius, returning
to the West after the council of Diospolis.[12] Whether
the relics reached their destination in Braga has been
doubted, for they shortly appeared on the island of
Minorca and at Uzalis in North Africa.[13] On Minorca
their power converted Jews.[14] At Uzalis, the bishop,
Evodius, described the many miracles they effected,

including the cure of the noblewoman Megetia, whose jaw
had been dislocated by intense nausea during her preg-
nancy.[15] Augustine's sermons and treatises, as well as
the last book of the *City of God*, bear witness to the
cult of Stephen in North Africa.[16] Inscriptional evidence from the area also testifies to the popularity of
the protomartyr.[17]

Whether Stephen's bones found their way to Constantinople with similar speed is debatable.[18] Although the
ninth-century historian Theophanes reports that in the 420s
the bishop of Jerusalem repaid the munificence of Theodosius II and his virgin sister Pulcheria by dispatching
the right hand of Stephen to Constantinople, no contemporary record of this *translatio* exists.[19] The silence of
such historians as Sozomen, who admired Pulcheria and took a
lively interest in relics, is difficult to explain if the
event occurred as Theophanes relates. However, contemporary
sources do not dispute two other points regarding the
imperial family's association with the bones of Stephen, namely,
that some of them were brought by the empress Eudocia
from Palestine to Constantinople in 439 and were deposited
in Pulcheria's church of Saint Lawrence and that in June
of 460 a basilica to Stephen which Eudocia had erected in
Palestine was dedicated.[20] The evidence pertaining to
Eudocia's association with Stephen's bones further suggests that rivalry for prestige could be based on possession of his holy remains. One such set of claims
constitutes the subject of this essay.

The two major sources for this investigation are the
Life of Melania the Younger and the *Life of Peter the
Iberian*. Their testimony is supplemented by the evidence
of Byzantine historians and hagiographers. Critical
editions of the *Life of Melania* were published at the
beginning of the twentieth century.[21] It has for its
subject a Roman heiress who with her young husband and

mother fled the devastation of Alaric's invasion. Their
wanderings throughout the Mediterranean world and her
establishment of monasteries for men and women on the
Mount of Olives provide a fascinating chapter of late
ancient social history. The *Life of Melania* was in all
likelihood composed by Gerontius, a priest in constant
attendance upon Melania in Jerusalem and the inheritor
of the directorship of her monasteries.[22] From contemporary sources we learn that Gerontius was a rabid
Monophysite who persistently refused to unite with the
Chalcedonians. His Monophysite sympathies were revealed clearly in his disdain for Juvenal, bishop of
Jerusalem, whom he considered a second Judas for his
betrayal of Christian truth at Chalcedon, that is, for
his endorsement of the council's creed.[23] Gerontius
eventually was expelled from his own monastery and died,
late in the fifth century, outside the Catholic communion.[24] The original text of the *Life of Melania*
probably was composed in Greek.[25] It most likely can be
assigned to the period 450-455 A.D.[26] Whether it was
written before or after Chalcedon remains problematic:
although d'Alès favors a date prior to the council (or,
at the very least, before Juvenal's ouster in 452
A.D.),[27] the stony silence surrounding the bishop in the
text may suggest that the *Life of Melania* was composed
later than October 451.[28]

The second source, the *Life of Peter the Iberian,*
concerns a Georgian prince whose Syriac biography became
known only late in the nineteenth century.[29] Nabarnugios,
as the prince was called in his native tongue, spent his
adolescence as a hostage at the Theodosian court. His
protracted association with Eudocia in Constantinople no
doubt accounts for the devotion he and his biographer
accord her.[30] Despite his esteem for the empress,
Nabarnugios escaped with a friend to Jerusalem, where

they were welcomed by Melania, probably in 438,[31] and
entered the monastery she had constructed for men on the
Mount of Olives. The *Life* reports that Gerontius himself was responsible for supplying the prince with both
a suitably Christian name (Peter) and the monastic habit
he so enthusiastically adopted.[32] Peter later was ordained bishop of Maiouma, the port city of Gaza, by
Theodosius, a Monophysite who briefly served as bishop
of Jerusalem.[33] Through Eudocia's intervention, Peter
avoided the imperial punishment meted out to Bishop
Theodosius' supporters after the latter's downfall.
Nonetheless, Peter wandered in exile throughout Egypt
and Arabia for years.[34] His biographer, John Rufus,
also the author of the *Plerophoria*,[35] shared Peter's
Monophysite sympathies as well as his cloister.[36] John
Rufus composed the *Life* at the end of the fifth century,
after Peter's death in 491.[37]

Palestinian Monophysitism included among its adherents not only Gerontius and John Rufus, but Eudocia
herself. The empress was instrumental in replacing
Juvenal of Jerusalem with the aforesaid Theodosius, who
reigned as bishop for about 20 months until imperial
troops were sent to reestablish Juvenal on his episcopal
throne in 453.[38] Eudocia so came to abhor the Catholic
faith that the persuasions of the saint Simeon Stylites
and the abbot Euthymius were required to win her for
Chalcedon in late 455 or 456.[39] In addition to fostering
her Monophysite leanings, Eudocia's Palestinian sojourn
had made her a devotee of Saint Stephen. Indeed, the
two texts under consideration reveal that Melania and
Eudocia were engaged in a rivalry centered on the relics
of the protomartyr.

Despite the fact that the *Life of Melania* insists
that its heroine so divested herself of her fortune that
she, her husband Pinian (with whom she had taken a vow

of chastity), and her mother Albina considered enrolling
themselves on the lists of the church's poor when they
first arrived in Jerusalem, she nonetheless had the
means to command possession of relics of the prophet
Zechariah, the Forty Martyrs of Sebaste, and Stephen for
her monasteries.[40] Of the many points on which Gerontius
remains silent, the source of Melania's relic supply is
one. He states in chapter 48 of the *Life* that she owned
these relics, but he never tells where she acquired them.

However, the *Life of Melania* does provide information about the buildings Melania constructed to house
her new treasures. Their first home was an oratory she
built especially for them in the women's monastery on
Olivet.[41] The monastery itself had been erected only
after her mother's death, an event that occurred probably
in 431.[42] The deposition of relics in the oratory must
have taken place within the year, for Pinian is still in
evidence, and he died in late 431 or 432.[43] In about
435, before her journey to Constantinople, Melania built
a monastery for men near the spot where Christians believed Jesus had last stood on earth before his Ascension.[44] Upon her return from the eastern capital, she
constructed a martyrium in or near the men's monastery
to ensure that prayers would be offered there on her behalf after her own demise.[45] It was in this martyrium
that Melania planned to deposit relics just at the time
she learned of Eudocia's visit to Palestine in 438.[46] A
later chapter of the *Life* discloses that the martyrium
of the men's monastery housed the relics of Stephen, so
these presumably were the ones to be honored in the 438
deposition.[47] Since the text previously stated that
Melania had some of Stephen's remains in the women's
monastery, one must assume that either she removed all
of his relics from the women's to the men's monastery,
divided them between the two, or acquired a fresh supply,

an assumption the text does not warrant. We do know
that the relics of some martyrs remained in the women's
cloister, since Melania asks to be placed close to them
as she is dying.[48]

Melania's path intersects with Eudocia's at the very
time she completed the martyrium for the men's monastery
and was about to deposit her relics of Stephen there.
According to Socrates' *Church History*, the emperor Theodosius, in gratitude for the blessings God had showered
on him, sent Eudocia to Jerusalem. Socrates adds that
the empress earlier had taken a vow to visit Palestine
if she should live to see the marriage of her daughter.[49]
That event transpired in October of 437.[50] So Eudocia
set out, laden with expensive presents for the churches
of Jerusalem.[51] Socrates reports that she adorned the
cities en route both going and coming.[52] Evagrius adds
that she was a particular success at Antioch, where she
gave a public address citing Homer and was honored by a
statue erected for her.[53] Of the motivation for the
trip, Evagrius pleads ignorance but states that he
thought other accounts were not true to the facts.[54] Was
Evagrius, or were other historians, hinting that intra-
familial relations at the Theodosian court were already
strained?[55]

On the other hand, the *Life of Melania* reports that
Eudocia's trip had a twofold purpose: to visit both the
Holy Places and Melania herself, who Eudocia thought of
as a spiritual mother.[56] According to this text, their
friendship was of recent origin, dating back only to
Melania's just-completed trip to Constantinople.[57] There
she had helped convert her pagan uncle Volusian, the
ex-prefect of Rome, who was visiting the eastern capital
for the wedding of Eudocia's and Theodosius' daughter
Eudoxia to Valentinian III.[58] The Greek version of the

Life in fact represents Volusian as staying in an
imperial residence, attended in his illness by Eudocia's
(or Eudoxia's) nurse.[59]

The *Life of Melania* makes much of the friendship
that developed between Melania and the empresses at that
time. It portrays the imperial women as benefiting from
Melania's edifying presence.[60] They enjoyed hours of
conversation, much of which pertained to religion. The
Greek *Life* reports that Melania talked theology "from
dawn to dusk"; specifically, she argued against Nestorianism.[61] Given Eudocia's support of Monophysitism at
mid-century, Melania's anti-Nestorian arguments perhaps
found a welcome audience.[62] At the end of her sojourn
in Constantinople, she begged that Theodosius allow
Eudocia to visit her in Palestine.[63] Thus a visit to
Melania is represented as a central motive for Eudocia's
trip.

Shortly after Melania finished the martyrium of the
men's monastery, she learned that Eudocia was en route
to Jerusalem and had already arrived at Antioch.[64] That
Melania was not earlier apprised of Eudocia's visit and
was thrown into confusion by the news (should she or
should she not go out to meet the empress?) weakens
Rampolla's claim that Eudocia made the trip primarily to
see Melania.[65]

In the version of their encounter provided by the
Life of Melania, Melania left her ascetic seclusion to
meet Eudocia at Sidon, where for several days Melania
stayed at the martyrium of Saint Phocas.[66] Given the
political overtones of their reunion, it is perhaps
significant that Gerontius informs us that this martyrium
was said to be on the spot where, when Jesus at first
refused to heal her daughter, the Canaanite woman replied
that "even the dogs eat the crumbs that fall from their

masters' table."[67] Mention of this biblical episode
serves to remind the reader of Melania's characteristic
humility and sets the stage for a new manifestation of
her self-effacement in her reunion with the Augusta of
the East.

Melania, however, here has no monopoly on humility:
Gerontius is at pains to emphasize that the desire to
appear humble was even more pronounced on the part of
the empress, who received Melania "with every honor."
Eudocia admitted that she had hoped to be "worthy" to
see Melania and confessed that it was a glory for her
"to honor the woman who had so purely glorified the
heavenly king."[68] The empress' one request was that she
might be present at the ceremony in which the holy relics
(here unspecified) would be deposited in Melania's new
martyrium.[69] As is revealed later, the relics of Stephen
are the ones housed there.[70] Nothing in either the
Greek or the Latin versions of the *Life of Melania* suggests that Eudocia knew about the proposed deposition
ahead of time or took any special part in the ceremony.
Nor is there mention of any bishop officiating.

An incident connected with the deposition that receives ample though confused testimony is the injury of
Eudocia's foot.[71] Although the two versions of the *Life
of Melania* provide varied accounts of where and when the
accident occurred, they both make clear that such an
injury did take place and that prayers pertaining to
Eudocia's recovery were offered in the church of the
Anastasis.[72] In the Latin version of the *Life*, Eudocia
is represented as entering the Anastasis and praying,
"I thank you, Lord, for deeming me worthy to visit, not
because of merit, but because of your benevolence and
the intervention of your holy martyrs and your handmaid
Melania."[73] Eudocia, having been cured, returned to

Constantinople, accompanied as far as Caesarea by
Melania.[74]

According to Gerontius' treatise, the production was
entirely Melania's. On her own initiative, she had
built a new martyrium in which to house the relics of
Stephen and had arranged for a ceremony of deposition.
Eudocia's role was minimal: she merely requested permission to attend the ceremony, attended, and hurt her
foot. Her association with Melania here serves the same
function as the introduction of Serena earlier in the
account, namely, to demonstrate that Melania mingled with
royalty and was honored by them as a saintly woman whom
even empresses would do well to emulate.[75]

The matter might rest there, with the reader awed by
Melania's importance and edified by her humility, if
other evidence did not suggest that we are dealing with
a battle joined over who owned Stephen's relics, who
built the churches erected in his honor, and who officiated at the deposition ceremony.

On the issue of ownership, for example, take the information furnished by the inscription reported in 1889
from the church of Saint Stephen at Zapharambolou
(ancient Euchaïta or Theodoroupolis). The inscription
ostensibly was composed by Eudocia on her way home from
Jerusalem.[76] It relates that the empress gave to the
church a foot of Saint Stephen, "which I received as a
gift," and that the relic was presented because Stephen
had cured Eudocia of the pain she, Stephen's "pitiable
friend," had suffered in her left knee and foot.[77] This
explanation clearly refers to the accident in Jerusalem.
Although the authenticity of the inscription has been
doubted, we have strong evidence that Eudocia did have
relics of Stephen in her possession after her Jerusalem
sojourn.[78] Marcellinus' blunt report in his *Chronicle*

for 439 A.D. states that Eudocia returned to Constantinople bearing "beatissimi Stephani martyris reliquias"
that were deposited, probably later, in a church
Pulcheria built to honor Saint Lawrence.[79] Had Eudocia
acquired relics of Stephen in return for the expensive
gifts she is said to have brought to the bishop of
Jerusalem?[80] Eudocia now appears as a co-owner of the
bones of Saint Stephen.

That impression is not simply supported but expanded
in the *Life of Peter the Iberian*. Eudocia is here shown
orchestrating the deposition of Stephen's relics. She
constructs a "beautiful church" to the martyr "outside
the northern gates" of Jerusalem in which to house
Stephen's remains.[81] In addition, she invites Cyril of
Alexandria to preside over the deposition of Stephen's
relics and to consecrate her church. Cyril is delighted
to oblige. He officiates at the deposition of Stephen's
relics on the fifteenth of May. The events connected
with Melania pale in significance. On the sixteenth of
May, at Melania's request, Cyril presides at a deposition
of the less important relics of the Forty Martyrs of
Sebaste and the Persian Martyrs in a "small church" on
Olivet.[82] This small church is of course Melania's
martyrium, but John Rufus states that Eudocia, not
Melania, was responsible for its construction: an
inscription on the wall of the martyrium testifies to the
fact, he comments.[83]

John Rufus' account, so different from Gerontius',
is worthy of note in the following respects: (1) Cyril
of Alexandria is present to officiate at Eudocia's request; (2) Eudocia has already, that is, by 438 A.D.,
constructed a church to Stephen outside the walls of
Jerusalem; (3) Eudocia, not Melania, is responsible for
the construction of the martyrium on the Mount of Olives;

(4) while Eudocia possesses the relics of Stephen,
Melania has remains of only the Forty Martyrs and the
Persian Martyrs, none of Stephen. What are we to make
of these discrepancies?

The first issue is the presence of Cyril of Alexandria. Cyril's involvement with Eudocia in Jerusalem is
possible, even plausible, but not demonstrable. Cyril
was in Jerusalem at some point during the late 430s or
440; he wrote a letter mentioning his sojourn in Aelia.[84]
Internal evidence provided by the letter led F.-M. Abel
to date it to 440 A.D.[85] However, the epistle itself
mentions nothing about Eudocia or the deposition of
relics; it merely establishes Cyril's presence in the
city. Further, although the *Chronicle* of John of Nikiou
mentions that Theodosius requested Cyril to accompany
Eudocia to Jerusalem, it does not speak of Cyril's participation in any ceremonies connected with Eudocia
there.[86] Neither source can be used to demonstrate the
claim that Cyril officiated at the deposition of
Stephen's relics. In fact, both are suspect. Paulus
Peeters has concluded, "it is impossible for us to see
in the intervention of Saint Cyril anything else than a
Monophysite invention, for the purpose of putting Peter
in personal relationship with the great doctor whose
name the anti-Chalcedonians wished to claim for themselves."[87]

Those who accept the testimony of Cyril's presence
at the deposition ceremonies must account for why Cyril
is not so mentioned in the *Life of Melania*. F.-M. Abel
has proposed the following explanation: if the *Life of
Melania* was composed for Dioscorus of Alexandria, as
Adhémar d'Alès suggested, it would not have been appropriate to mention Cyril, since Dioscorus had been charged
with extorting Cyril's estate from his inheritors.[88]

Under the circumstances, it would have been impolitic
for Gerontius to exalt the former bishop.[89]
However, Abel's thesis is damaged by an earlier
reference to Cyril in the *Life of Melania*. Even though
Gerontius is noticeably silent about Cyril later in his
account, he does comment that Melania, Pinian, and Albina
stopped in Alexandria on their way from North Africa to
Jerusalem; there they were received by Cyril "in a manner
worthy of his holiness."[90] If Abel's thesis were correct, would not this favorable reference to Cyril have
been omitted? Once again, the grounds for historical
certainty are weak, but suspicions of propagandistic
partisanship are strengthened.

The bishop one should expect to find officiating at
the deposition ceremony is Juvenal of Jerusalem, but in
fact the two sources equally ignore him. Juvenal is not
mentioned anywhere by name in the *Life of Melania*.[91]
And in the *Life of Peter the Iberian* he is described in
another context as a traitor like Judas, whom the saintly Peter flees.[92] The silence of the accounts is
probably attributable to the Monophysite loyalties of
the authors. Although in the 430s Juvenal had been a
partisan of Cyril and in fact had been a leader of the
pro-Eutychian faction at Ephesus in 449, his about-face
at Chalcedon enraged many Palestinian Christians.[93] Most
likely, at the time Gerontius wrote, either events were
in progress to depose Juvenal or that event had already
occurred: Gerontius may well have been among the monks
who clamored for Juvenal's removal and the elevation of
the Monophysite Theodosius.[94] John Rufus, a confirmed
Monophysite who wrote his account some decades later,
would not be any more favorably inclined to Juvenal than
was Gerontius.

A second issue of conflict between these accounts is whose church or martyrium was being dedicated in 438. The *Life of Melania* mentions only a martyrium Melania had erected, where the relics she owned were to be placed. But in the *Life of Peter the Iberian*, Eudocia was responsible for constructing a "beautiful church" outside the northern gates of the city, and it was there that Stephen's relics were deposited. By reporting that Eudocia had built a basilica to Stephen that was ready to be dedicated by 438, John Rufus highlights the empress' devotion to Stephen and indirectly minimizes the importance of Melania's martyrium. How probable is it that the basilica could have been constructed by 438? Surely it was not completed during Eudocia's brief stay in Jerusalem. She was in Constantinople for her daughter's wedding on 29 October 437 and was back home in 439.[95]

M.-J. Lagrange posits that Eudocia may have built a small shrine for martyrs on the site where the future church was to be raised and that this was the structure in which the relics of Stephen were deposited in 438.[96] But then one must ask why Stephen's sacred relics would be deposited in an unfinished building that would be under construction for another two decades? As Simeon Vailhé expressed the objection, "Decorum and respect work against this explanation."[97]

A different explanation has been proposed by F.-M. Abel: that Juvenal during his visit in 431 to Constantinople interested Eudocia in financing the construction of a church for Saint Stephen and that the project was near enough completion to hold a deposition ceremony when Eudocia arrived in 438.[98] (This church would then be the one Melania visited on Stephen's feast day, 26 December 439.)[99] Abel posits that in the late 450s, after having returned to Catholic orthodoxy, Eudocia

embellished or perhaps rebuilt part of the basilica, and
a second dedication of the church took place in 460, the
dedication attested by Cyril of Scythopolis.[100] Abel
argues further that Eudocia's basilica is the same one mentioned by Pseudo-Basil of Seleucia, although Pseudo-
Basil attributes the construction of the church to
Juvenal of Jerusalem.[101] Abel asserts that we are not
obliged to imagine that this was a church other than
Eudocia's; different writers simply ascribed the erection of that church to the person they wished to place
in the limelight.[102] Such is Abel's reconstruction of
events.

The historical evidence strongly suggests that there
was a church or martyrium to Stephen in Jerusalem before
the mid-fifth century, yet these two texts are in conflict. All divergences are perhaps best understood as
relating to the diverse purposes of their authors, who
wished to claim the glories of Stephen for their own
candidates, or, at the very least, not to assign them to
rival claimants.

A third problem presented by the two accounts concerns the identity of the person responsible for
constructing the martyrium for Stephen on the Mount of
Olives: Melania or Eudocia. The *Life of Melania* suggests that the martyrium was ready for a deposition
ceremony at the time Eudocia arrived in Jerusalem.[103]
This notion does not preclude the hypothesis that Eudocia
might have given Melania funds for the martyrium's construction while Melania was visiting in Constantinople,
but there is no evidence for that conjecture in either
Life. The *Life of Peter the Iberian* relates not only
that Eudocia built the martyrium, but also that she en-
graved an inscription on its wall testifying to her
patronage. There is no reference to such an inscription

or to such patronage in the *Life of Melania*. Again, the
sources are in conflict, and there is no other evidence
to help decide the case.

Lastly, and most importantly, the *Life of Peter the
Iberian* has removed from Melania's possession the relics
of Stephen. It is only in Eudocia's church that
Stephen's relics are laid to rest. According to this
text, Melania has in her possession merely the relics of
the Forty Martyrs of Sebaste and those of the Persian
Martyrs. Denying Melania possession of Stephen's relics
is the surest sign that these texts are engaged in polite
warfare: polite, to be sure, because John Rufus is eager
to praise Melania as a holy woman.[104] He credits her
and Pinian with the upbringing of his fellow Monophysite,
Gerontius.[105] Most important of all, John Rufus pictures
Melania extending the right hand of Christian fellowship
to Peter upon his arrival at Jerusalem and welcoming him
to her monastery.[106] In all these ways, Melania is not
to be faulted by the author of the *Life of Peter the
Iberian*. Yet for John Rufus, Melania is no match for
the Monophysite empress. To the latter belongs the
power and the glory--and the relics of Stephen. Bones
have become the symbols around which contests, whether
historical or literary, for prestige are waged. Juvenal
cannot emerge in the forefront, given the Monophysite
predilections of John Rufus and Gerontius. Nonetheless,
leaving aside the question of Juvenal, the authors of
the two accounts have divided loyalties. For Gerontius,
Melania always held first rank; for Peter the Iberian,
Eudocia did. And the two authors affirm their heroines'
relative statuses by associating them with the relics of
Stephen or by depriving them of that association.

Even in death, the rivalry remained. In October
460, Eudocia was buried in the tomb she had constructed

for herself next to Stephen's basilica.[107] Although
her sister-in-law and rival Pulcheria deposited the
relics of Stephen that Eudocia had brought home to
Constantinople in her own church of Saint Lawrence and
would live on in history as the heroine of Chalcedon,
Eudocia would rest in the company of other relics of
Stephen, the most holy of the Christian dead.[108] Stephen
had admonished the early Christians that "the Most High
does not dwell in houses made with hands."[109] Nonetheless, Eudocia, as she built her own tomb, could take
comfort in the fact that she would lie near Stephen's
house in death.

As for Melania, we do not know the precise location
of her burial. Conceivably, she found *refrigerium* next
to the relics of Stephen as well, those she had honored
on Olivet. Gerontius, however, imagines higher glories
for her. Not only does he portray Melania in her dying
hours beseeching the martyrs whose relics she had
revered to show compassion to her and asking them to be
her ambassadors to God,[110] he also depicts her entering
heaven. There Melania is greeted by angels, prophets,
apostles, and lastly, by "the holy martyrs, whose memory
she had glorified and whose combats she had voluntarily
endured," who joyfully throng to greet her.[111] In the
contest for exaltation through association with the
church's honored dead, it would be difficult to judge
whether Melania or Eudocia was the winner.

NOTES

[1]Peter Brown, *The Cult of the Saints: Its Rise and Function in Latin Christianity* (Chicago 1981).

[2]For Paulinus' devotion to Felix, see Paulinus of Nola, *Carmina* 12-16, 18-21, 23, 26-29 (*Corpus Scriptorum Ecclesiasticorum Latinorum* 30. 42-81, 96-186, 194-206, 246-306), and Brown, pp. 53-57, 59-60, 64.

[3]Brown, pp. 33, 38.

[4]Lucian, *Epistola ad omnem ecclesiam, de revelatione corporis Stephani martyris* (trans. Avitus in Migne, PL 41. 807-818). The critical edition of the text is by S. Vanderlinden, "Revelatio Sancti Stephani," *Revue des Etudes Byzantines* 4 (1946): 178-217. On the texts of the two recensions of the letter, see Henri Leclercq, "Etienne (Martyre et Sépulchre de Saint)," *Dictionnaire d'archéologie chrétienne et de liturgie* 5, pt. 1, cols. 631-635 (hereafter cited as DACL).

[5]J.D. Mansi, *Sacrorum Conciliorum Nova et Amplissima Collectio* (Florence, 1759-), 4:311-320.

[6]Lucian, *De revelatione* 3 (Migne, PL 41.809). Acts 5:33-39; 22:3.

[7]Lucian, *De revelatione* 3 (Migne, PL 41.809).

[8]Ibid. 4-5 (Migne, PL 41.811).

[9]Ibid. 8 (Migne, PL 41.815).

[10]F.-M. Abel, "Jérusalem," DACL 7.2320-2321.

[11]The power of the saint did not diminish with the division of the corpse. As Hippolyte Delehaye has expressed it, "Et il fait remarquer ailleurs que, quoique les corps des martyrs soient divisés et dispensés en plusieurs tombeaux, la grâce qui y est attachée reste entière" (*Les Origines du culte des martyrs*, Subsidia Hagiographica 20, 2d ed. rev. [Brussels 1933], p. 62).

[12]Gennadius, *Liber de scriptoribus ecclesiasticis* 23, 46-48 (Migne, PL 58.1081, 1084-1085). The text of Avitus' letter is in Vanderlinden, pp. 188-189; and in Migne, PL 41.805-808.

[13]Vanderlinden, p. 179.

[14]Severus, *Epistola Severi ad omnem ecclesiam* (Migne, PL 41.821-834).

[15]Evodius, *De miraculis Sancti Stephani Protomartyis* 2.1-9 (Migne, PL 41.843-848).

[16]Augustine, *Tractatus 120 in Joannis Evangelium* 4 (Migne, PL 35.1954); idem, *Sermo* 318.1 (Migne, PL 38.1437-1438). The texts indicate by their language ("*modo*," "*nuper*") that the *inventio* was recent. Augustine's *Sermons* 314-319 concern Stephen. See also idem, *De civitate Dei* 22.8 (Migne, PL 41.766-771). A convent in Carthage had some bones of Stephen, according to Pseudo-Prosper, *Liber de promissionibus et praedictionibus Dei* 4, 6, 9 (Migne, PL 51.842).

[17]For North African inscriptions relating to the cult of Stephen, see Paul Monceaux, *Enquête sur l'épigraphie chrétienne d'Afrique*, vol. 4, *Martyrs et reliques* (Paris, 1907), inscriptions 228 (perhaps from the convent mentioned by Pseudo-Prosper), 229, 245, 274, 303, 306.

[18]Anastasius' account (Migne, PL 41.817-822), claiming the bones arrived during Constantine's reign, has been doubted. Marie-Joseph Lagrange, *Saint Etienne et son sanctuaire à Jérusalem* (Paris, 1894), p. 54, n. 1, calls it "une pièce apocryphe." John Wortley, "The Trier Ivory Reconsidered," *Greek, Roman, and Byzantine Studies* 21 (1980): 385-386, claims it is a legend alluding to a later period.

[19]Theophanes, *Chronographia*, a.m. 5920, (deBoor, 1:86-87). Theophanes gives the date as 428 A.D. For a correction to 421, see Kenneth G. Holum and Gary Vikan, "The Trier Ivory, *Adventus* Ceremonial, and the Relics of St. Stephen," *Dumbarton Oaks Papers* 33 (1979): 119, 128; and Kenneth G. Holum, "Pulcheria's Crusade A.D. 421-22 and the Ideology of Imperial Victory," *Greek, Roman, and Byzantine Studies* 18 (1977): 163, n. 46.

[20]On the empress' having brought the bones to
Constantinople, see below, pp. 104-105. On the erection
and dedication of the Palestinian basilica, see Cyril of
Scythopolis, *Vita S. Euthymii* 35 (Schwartz, p. 54). The
church was thereafter commented on by Antoninus Martyr,
Perambulatio locorum sanctorum 25 (Tobler, 1:105);
Theodosius, *De terra sancta* 10 (Tobler, 1:66); Evagrius,
Historia Ecclesiae 1.22 (Bidez and Parmentier, p. 32).
In the late nineteenth century, its ruins were discovered
and excavated, for a summary, see Hugues Vincent and
F.-M. Abel, *Jérusalem: Recherches de topographie,
d'archéologie et d'histoire*, vol. 2, *Jérusalem nouvelle*
(Paris, 1926), fasc. 4. 766-767.

[21]The definitive corrected Latin and Greek texts were
first published by Mariano Rampolla del Tindaro, *Santa
Melania Giuniore, senatrice romana: Documenti contemporei
e note* (Rome 1905), improving on the earlier Greek text
in Migne, PL 116.753-794, and on the Bollandists' text
in *Analecta Bollandiana* 22 (1903): 5-50. The modern
edition of the Greek text by Denys Gorce, *Vie de Sainte
Mélanie*, Sources Chrétiennes 90 (Paris 1962), is used
throughout this essay.

[22]Long before modern scholars became interested in
the *Vita Melaniae*, Lenain de Tillemont, *Mémoires pour
servir à l'histoire ecclésiastique des six premiers
siècles* (Paris 1709), 14:251-252, suggested Gerontius
as its author. Of more recent scholars, C. DeSmedt,
"Vita Sanctae Melaniae Junioris," *Analecta Bollandiana*
8 (1889): 7, appears to be the first to identify Gerontius as the author. Also see *Vita Melaniae* 65, 68
(Gorce, pp. 262, 264, 266).

[23]Cyril of Scythopolis, *Vita S. Euthymii* 45, 27
(Schwartz, pp. 67, 42-44).

[24]Cyril of Scythopolis, *Vita S. Sabae* 30 (Schwartz,
p. 115).

[25]For the arguments, see Adhémar d'Alès, "Les Deux
Vies de Sainte Mélanie la Jeune," *Analecta Bollandiana*
25 (1906): 401-450. Compare Rampolla, pp. lxviii-lxx,
who assigns prior status to the Latin version.

[26]D'Alès, p. 430. Slightly over a decade would have
elapsed since Melania's death in 439.

[27]Ibid., pp. 446, 449.

[28]See below, p. 107. Ernest Honigmann, "Juvenal of Jerusalem," *Dumbarton Oaks Papers* 5 (1950): 228, appears to favor the post-Chalcedonian date. On the contrary, d'Alès, p. 446, favors a date before Juvenal's removal in 452. D'Alès believes the Latin version of the *Life of Melania* might contain a reference to Chalcedon (chap. 44), a sign of its possibly later composition than the Greek version (d'Alès, p. 449). Vincent and Abel, fasc. 4.748, attribute the omission of Juvenal's name at the deposition as a sign that Eudocia wished him to stay in the background. F.-M. Abel, "Saint Cyrille d'Alexandrie dans ses rapports avec la Palestine," *Kyrilliana* (Cairo 1947), p. 225, n. 50, might favor a post-Chalcedonian date.

[29]*Vita Petri Hiberi*, in *Petrus der Iberer: Ein Charakterbild zur Kirchen- und Sitten-geschichte des Fünften Jahrhunderts*, ed. and trans. Richard Raabe (Leipzig 1895).

[30]*Vita Petri Hiberi* 48 (Raabe, p. 49).

[31]Paul Devos, "Quand Pierre l'Ibère vint-il à Jérusalem?," *Analecta Bollandiana* 86 (1968): 338, 345, 347. If Kenneth G. Holum's dating is correct, Melania did not arrive back in Jerusalem until Easter week 438. See Kenneth G. Holum, *Theodosian Empresses: Women and Imperial Dominion in Late Antiquity* (Berkeley, 1982), chap. 5, n. 39. Peter would have come to Melania's monastery between then and May 438, for he supposedly was present when Eudocia visited Melania. See *Vita Petri Hiberi* 33 (Raabe, p. 37).

[32]Ibid., 32 (Raabe, p. 36).

[33]Ibid., 53-55 (Raabe, 54-56); Evagrius, *Historia Ecclesiae* 2.5 (Bidez and Parmentier, p. 52); Zacharias Rhetor, *Historia Ecclesiastica* 3.4 (Brooks, p. 108 for Latin, p. 158 for Syriac). See also Devos, p. 350.

[34]For Eudocia's protection of Peter, see Zacharias Rhetor, *Historia Ecclesiastica* 3.5, 7 (Brooks, pp. 109, 110 for Latin, pp. 159, 160 for Syriac). For Peter's exile, see *Vita Petri Hiberi* 57-97 (Raabe, pp. 58-96).

[35]See Eduard Schwartz, *Johannes Rufus, ein mono-physitischer Schriftsteller* (Heidelberg 1912), pp. 9-12.

[36]Raabe, p. 9. For typical Monophysite sentiments, see John Rufus, *Plerophoria* 3, 19, 42, 79 (trans. F. Nau, *Patrologia Orientalis* 8 [1912]: 14-15, 38-39, 93, 135-136), and *Vita Petri Hiberi* 32, 133, 134 (Raabe, pp. 36, 122-123).

[37]Raabe, pp. 9-10. See Devos, p. 349, for a correction of E. Schwartz's date of 489 for Peter's death.

[38]Theophanes, *Chronographia*, a.m. 5945 (deBoor, p. 107); John of Nikiou, *Chronicon* 87 (ed. H. Zotenberg, *Notices et extraits des manuscrits de la Bibliothèque Nationale* 24, pt. 1 [Paris 1883], p. 473); Nicephorus Callistus, *Ecclesiastica Historia* 15.9 (Migne, PG 147.29-34); Cyril of Scythopolis, *Vita S. Euthymii* 27, 30 (Schwartz, pp. 41, 47); Honigmann, pp. 251, 252-256; F. Nau, "Résumé du monographies syriaques," *Revue de l'Orient Chrétien* 19 (1914): 133.

[39]Or she came to abhor those who espoused the Catholic faith, namely, Pulcheria. See Holum, *Theodosian Empresses*, chap. 7; Paul Goubert, "Le Rôle de Sainte Pulchérie et l'eunuque Chrysaphios," in *Das Konzil von Chalkedon: Geschichte und Gegenwart*, ed. Aloys Grill-meier and Heinrich Bacht, 3 vols. (Würzburg 1954), 1: 304. On the persuasions of the saint and the abbot, see Cyril of Scythopolis, *Vita S. Euthymii* 30 (Schwartz, pp. 47-49); Nicephorus Callistus, *Ecclesiastica Historia* 15.13 (Migne, PG 147.40-41).

[40]On the vow of chastity, see *Vita Melaniae* 6 (Gorce, p. 136). On their poverty, see ibid., 35 (Gorce, p. 194). For the finding of the relics of Zechariah, see Sozomen, *Historia Ecclesiastica* 9.17 (Bidez and Hansen, pp. 407-408). One of Eudocia's poetic compositions was on Zechariah; see Photius, *Bibliotheca*, codices 183-184 (Migne, PG 103.536-537). For Melania's earlier devotion to the remains of Saint Lawrence, see *Vita Melaniae* 5 (Gorce, p. 134). The Forty Martyrs of Sebaste were soldiers martyred in Cappadocia or Armenia under Licinius; the *passio* is given in Oskar von Gebhardt, *Acta Martyrum Selecta* (Berlin 1902), pp. 166-181. Pulcheria is credited with discovering the remains of the Forty for Constantinople and providing them with a proper resting

place: see *Chronicon Paschale*, a. 451 (Dindorf, 1:590);
Marcellinus, *Chronicon*, a. 451 (Mommsen, pp. 83-84);
Sozomen, *Historia Ecclesiastica* 9.2 (Bidez and Hansen,
pp. 392-394). That the feast of the Forty was already
celebrated in Constantinople when Nestorius was bishop
is revealed by John Rufus, *Plerophoria* 1 (Nau, pp. 11-12).

[41]*Vita Melaniae* 48 (Gorce, p. 218). The oratory of
the women's monastery is called a *martyrium* in the Latin
version of the *Vita*, chap. 66 (Rampolla, p. 38).

[42]*Vita Melaniae* 41 (Gorce, p. 204). On the date of
her mother's death, see Gorce, p. 205, n. 5.

[43]*Vita Melaniae* 48-49 (Gorce, pp. 218, 220). On the
date of Pinian's death, see Gorce, p. 220, n. 2.

[44]The traditional dating of the trip to the end of
436 and early 437 is found in Rampolla, pp. 230, 253,
xl-xlii; and in Gorce, pp. 44 and 224, n. 1. It has been
challenged by Holum; see n. 31 above. On the monastery
for men, see *Vita Melaniae* 49 (Gorce, pp. 220-222).

[45]*Vita Melaniae* 57 (Gorce, p. 240).

[46]Ibid., 58 (Gorce, p. 240).

[47]Ibid., 64 (Gorce, p. 258).

[48]Ibid., 65 (Gorce, p. 262). The dying Melania tells
the nuns while she is in their convent that she wants to
be carried into the oratory so as to be near the martyrs.
In the Latin *Vita* 66 (Rampolla, p. 38), Melania asks her
priest (Gerontius) to enter the martyrium that adjoined
her cell to offer the oblation.

[49]Socrates, *Ecclesiastica Historia* 7.47 (Hussey, 2:
838); John of Nikiou, *Chronicon* 87 (Zotenberg, p. 470).

[50]Socrates, *Ecclesiastica Historia* 7.44 (Hussey, 2:
832-833, has the wrong date); Marcellinus, *Chronicon*,
a. 437 (Mommsen, p. 79); *Chronicon Paschale*, a.437
(Dindorf, 1: 582).

[51]Socrates, *Ecclesiastica Historia* 7.47 (Hussey, 2:
838). Concerning the cross Eudocia took for the church
of the Ascension, see John Rufus, *Plerophoria* 11 (Nau,
p. 27).

[52]Socrates, *Ecclesiastica Historica* 7.47 (Hussey, 2: 838).

[53]Evagrius, *Historica Ecclesiae* 1.20 (Bidez and Parmentier, pp. 28-29).

[54]Ibid., 1.21 (Bidez and Parmentier, p. 29).

[55]When relations reached the breaking point in the early 440s, Eudocia left for Palestine, never to return to Constantinople. Her absence from the ceremony for the deposition of John Chrysostom's remains in January 438 may point in the direction of her disfavor. Theodoret, *Historia Ecclesiastica* 5.36 (Parmentier, p. 339). For a perceptive discussion of the power politics at work in the relations of Pulcheria and Eudocia, see Holum, *Theodosian Empresses*, especially chap. 4; and idem, "Pulcheria's Crusade," pp. 169-170. An alternate hypothesis is that Eudocia may have left already for Palestine; her visit in Antioch and other cities might account for the length of time it took her to reach her destination. For the deposition ceremony, see also Proclus, *Oratio* 20 (Migne, PG 65.827-834); Socrates, *Ecclesiastica Historia* 7.45 (Hussey, 2: 834); Marcellinus, *Chronicon*, a.438.2 (Mommsen, p. 79).

[56]*Vita Melaniae* 58 (Gorce, p. 242); Rampolla, p. 239.

[57]*Vita Melaniae* 56 (Gorce, p. 238); see n. 31 above.

[58]*Vita Melaniae* 50 (Gorce, p. 224). On Volusian, see André Chastagnol, "Le Sénateur Volusien et la conversion d'une famille de l'aristocratie romaine au Bas-Empire," *Revue des Études Anciennes* 58 (1956): 241-253. On Augustine's efforts in 412 to win Volusian, then proconsul of Africa, for Christianity, see Augustine, *Epp.* 132 and 137; for Volusian to Augustine, *Ep.* 135; and for Marcellinus' involvement, *Epp.* 136 and 138.

[59]*Vita Melaniae* 55 (Gorce, p. 236). The names Eudocia and Eudoxia are sometimes confused in the two versions of the *Vita*.

[60]Ibid., 56 (Gorce, p. 238).

[61]Ibid., 54 (Gorce, p. 232).

[62]Cyril of Scythopolis, *Vita S. Euthymii* 30 (Schwartz, pp. 47-49); Nicephorus Callistus, *Ecclesiastica Historia* 15.13 (Migne, PG 147.40-41); John of Nikiou, *Chronicon* 87 (Zotenberg, pp. 473-474). Perhaps the mention of the specifically anti-Nestorian tone of Melania's instruction was an addition either by the author of the text, a Monophysite, or by the transcriber of the Greek text; the Latin *Vita* omits it. Melania died before the Monophysite controversy reached its peak.

[63]*Vita Melaniae* 56 (Gorce, p. 238).

[64]Ibid., 57, 58 (Gorce, p. 240).

[65]Ibid., 58 (Gorce, pp. 240, 242). Compare Rampolla, p. 239.

[66]For this obscure saint, see the panegyric of Asterius of Amasea (Migne, PG 40.300-313), and C. Van de Vorst and Paulus Peeters, "Saint Phocas," *Analecta Bollandiana* 30 (1911): 252-295. *Vita Petri Hiberi* 106-109 (Raabe, p. 101-102) mentions the relics of Phocas as associated with the Sidon area.

[67]Matthew 15:27; *Vita Melaniae* 58 (Gorce, p. 242).

[68]Ibid., 58 (Gorce, p. 244).

[69]Ibid.

[70]Ibid., 64 (Gorce, p. 258; Rampolla, p. 37).

[71]Ibid., 59 (Gorce, p. 244; Rampolla, p. 33). The texts are unclear as to whether the incident happened on Olivet or elsewhere. In addition, the Latin text makes the Anastasis and Melania's martyrium sound like one and the same place. See Gorce, p. 245, n. 2; Rampolla, pp. 239-240.

[72]*Vita Melaniae* 59 (Gorce, p. 244; Rampolla, p. 33). Eudocia may have been staying at or near the Anastasis. See Vincent and Abel, p. 192, for a description of quarters for pilgrims at the church. Eudocia's association with the church of the Anastasis is commemorated in an inscription taken from an unknown church in Constantinople. It represents her as worshipping at the tomb

of the one who "died as man but lives as God," namely at the sepulchre of Jesus in the Anastasis. *Epigrammatum Anthologia Palatina* 1.105 (ed. Frederic Dübner, 3 vols. [Paris 1864], 1: 12).

[73]The anti-Pelagian touch is found only in the Latin version of *Vita Melaniae* 59 (Rampolla, p. 33).

[74]Ibid., 59 (Gorce, p. 244).

[75]Ibid., 11-13 (Gorce, pp. 146-154).

[76]G. Doublet, "Inscriptions de Paphlagonie," *Bulletin de Correspondance Hellénique* 13 (1889): 295.

[77]Ibid., p. 294.

[78]The abbreviations of the empress' name and the date are considered suspect. Ibid., p. 295; Rampolla, p. 240.

[79]Marcellinus, *Chronicon*, a. 439.2 (Mommsen, p. 80); see also Theophanes, *Chronographia*, a.m. 5945 (deBoor, 1: 106); Nicephorus Callistus, *Ecclesiastica Historia* 15.14 (Migne, PG 147.41). The evidence is uncertain as to the date the church was built: Raymond Janin says only "by 450" in *Le Géographie ecclésiastique de l'Empire Byzantin*, vol. 1.3, *Les Eglises et les monastères*, 2d ed. (Paris 1969), pp. 301-302. Holum, *Theodosian Empresses*, chap. 6, postulates that Pulcheria built the church in the early 440s when she was in retirement in the Hebdomen palace. The church was located in a district called "Pulcheriana" after Pulcheria's numerous foundations there. See Jean Papadopulos, "L'Eglise de Saint Laurent et les Pulchériana," *Studi Bizantini* 2 (1927): 59-60.

[80]Socrates, *Ecclesiastica Historia* 7.47 (Hussey, 2: 838); Evagrius, *Historia Ecclesiae* 1.21 (Bidez and Parmentier, p. 29). For the cross she took for the church of the Ascension, see John Rufus, *Plerophoria* 11 (Nau, p. 105). Eudocia also returned home with Barsauma's cloak; see Nau, "Résumé," p. 117.

[81]*Vita Petri Hiberi* 33 (Raabe, p. 37).

[82]Peter the Iberian possessed relics of the Persian Martyrs. Ibid., 17, 18-19, 22, 23 (Raabe, pp. 25-26,

28, 29). In all likelihood, the bones of the Persian Martyrs deposited on Olivet were the ones Peter had brought with him to Jerusalem. Ibid., 32-33 (Raabe, p. 37).

[83]Ibid., 33 (Raabe, p. 37).

[84]Cyril, *Ep.* 70 (Migne, PG 77.341).

[85]Abel, "Saint Cyrille," p. 222. Abel thinks the official mentioned was appointed to carry messages between Theodosius in Constantinople and Eudocia in Palestine; as he passed through Antioch, the messenger was asked to take a petition to Cyril in Palestine (p. 244).

[86]John of Nikiou, *Chronicon* 87 (Zotenberg, p. 470).

[87]Paulus Peeters, review of "Le Lieu du martyre de Saint Etienne" by M.-J. Lagrange, in *Analecta Bollandiana* 24 (1905): 137.

[88]D'Alès, p. 449. In the prologue to the *Vita Melaniae*, the recipient of the account is called a "holy priest" and "your holiness" (Gorce, pp. 124, 126). For Abel's explanation, see Abel, "Saint Cyrille," p. 225, n. 50. On Dioscorus' persecution of Cyril's inheritors, see the letter of one of the nephews, Athanasius, to the Synod of Chalcedon, in Mansi, *Sacrorum Conciliorum*, 6.1021-1028; also see Liberatus, *Breviarium* 10 (Migne, PL 68.992), and Goubert, pp. 309-311.

[89]Abel, "Saint Cyrille," p. 225, n. 50.

[90]*Vita Melaniae* 34 (Gorce, p. 190).

[91]At the scene of Melania's death, someone present is called simply "the bishop." Ibid., 67 (Gorce, p. 264). Since the person is praised as *theophilestatos*, Juvenal's claim to be this unidentified person is open to doubt. In Codex Parisinus 1553, fol. 286-301, the bishop mentioned is called the bishop of Eleutheropolis, who arrives with his clergy (see Migne, PG 116.792; and n. 28 above). However, Honigmann, p. 228, n. 23, thinks the person is Juvenal.

[92]*Vita Petri Hiberi* 32, 52 (Raabe, pp. 36, 53).

[93]For a discussion of the evidence, see Honigmann, p. 242.

[94]*Vita Petri Hiberi* 52 (Raabe, p. 53). It was the Palestinian monks and clergy who drove Juvenal from his see.

[95]On the wedding date, see Marcellinus, *Chronicon*, a. 437 (Mommsen, p. 79); *Chronicon Paschale*, a. 437 (Dindorf, 1: 582). On the date of her return, see Marcellinus, *Chronicon*, a.439.2 (Mommsen, p. 82).

[96]M.-J. Lagrange, "Le Lieu du martyre de Saint Etienne," *Revue Biblique*, n.s. 1 (1904): 468-471; considered by Leclercq, "Etienne," DACL 5, pt. 1, col. 651.

[97]Simeon Vailhé, "Les Monastères et les églises Saint-Etienne à Jérusalem," *Echos d'Orient* 8 (1905): 85. See also Leclerq, "Etienne," DACL 5, pt. 1, col. 670; Paulus Peeters, review of Lagrange's "Le Lieu," 136-137. Vailhé assumes that the relics of Stephen deposited were those from Sion, not ones Eudocia owned personally.

[98]Vincent and Abel, fasc. 4.747-748.

[99]Ibid., fasc. 4.748; Gerontius, *Vita Melaniae* 64 (Gorce, p. 254). John Rufus, *Plerophoria* 79 (Nau, pp. 135-136), provides evidence that there was a martyrium to Saint Stephen and Saint John in Jerusalem before Chalcedon.

[100]Vincent and Abel, fasc. 4.749-750; Cyril of Scythopolis, *Vita S. Euthymii* 35 (Schwartz, p. 54). Among those who argue that the church was not dedicated until Eudocia's return to orthodoxy is Lagrange, *Saint Etienne*, p. 69.

[101]Pseudo-Basil, *Homilia* 41 (Migne, PG 85.469).

[102]Vincent and Abel, fasc. 4.748. Honigmann, pp. 226-227, wishes to distinguish the church of Juvenal mentioned by Pseudo-Basil (Migne, PG 85.469) from the church Juvenal and Eudocia undertook together, the church that was dedicated on 15 June 460.

[103]*Vita Melaniae* 57 (Gorce, p. 240).

[104]*Vita Petri Hiberi* 29 (Raabe, p. 34).

[105]Ibid., 31 (Raabe, p. 35).

[106]Ibid., 27-28 (Raabe, pp. 32-33).

[107]Antoninus Martyr, *Perambulatio* 25 (Tobler, 1: 105); Evagrius, *Historia Ecclesiae* 1.22 (Bidez and Parmentier, p. 32). For other relics in Eudocia's church, see L. Robert, M.N. Tod, and E. Ziebarth, eds., *Supplementum Epigraphicum Graecum*, vol. 8, *Palaestina* (Lyons 1937), inscription 192, p. 28.

[108]On Pulcheria, see Goubert; see also Eduard Schwartz, "Die Kaiserin Pulcherie auf der Synod von Chalkedon," *Festgabe für Adolf Jülicher* (Tübingen 1927), pp. 203-212. To the Monophysites, Pulcheria's support of Chalcedon was a sign she was unfaithful to her religion. See John Rufus, *Plerophoria* 3 (Nau, pp. 14-15). John of Nikiou, *Chronicon* 87 (Zotenberg, p. 471), calls Pulcheria "perverse," a covert supporter of Flavian.

[109]Acts 7:48.

[110]Gerontius, *Vita Melaniae* 64 (Gorce, pp. 258, 260).

[111]Ibid., 70 (Gorce, p. 270).

FALTONIA BETITIA PROBA AND HER VIRGILIAN POEM: THE CHRISTIAN MATRON AS ARTIST

Ransom-Butler Lectures,
Wichita State University (1982)

Although the Church Fathers lauded individual women
who chose the paths of martyrdom or asceticism, they also
condemned females-in-general for a host of evils, indeed,
for the very entrance of evil to the world. Thus it is
not surprising that many of *our* contemporaries have
yearned to unearth early Christian letters and treatises
written by women in the hope that they would reveal an
estimate of the female sex different from that of their
male counterparts. While I sympathize entirely with the
enterprise, the results of the search have not been
heartening. Yet the very lack of literature written by
women in antiquity suggests that Faltonia Betitia Proba's
poem might interest an audience larger than scholars of
late antiquity alone, for it is one of the rare documents
of early Christianity composed by a woman.

Why have so few scholars heretofore shown interest in
Proba's poem? The quest to uncover ancient literature
composed by women is recent, undoubtedly stimulated by
the contemporary women's movement. Beyond this observa-
tion, we note that many classical scholars of the older
school did not deem early Christian literature, with its
sometimes less than elegant style, worthy of serious
attention. Most important, the poetic form Proba chose,

the cento, appeared contemptible to classicists who
valued the beauty of Virgilian Latin. Some explication
of the cento form may illuminate their disdain.

To compose a cento, one pieced together lines or
parts of lines from earlier works to create a new meaning: the word "cento" itself is thought originally to
have meant a "patchwork cloak."[1] Those who wrote in
Greek used Homer as the source for their centos.
Although Homeric centos existed before the Christian era,
Latin centos were not written until the second century
A.D.[2] Of the Latin authors whose lines were most frequently borrowed for the composition of centos, Virgil is
notable. Since children encountered Virgil's poems in
elementary school and their influence on the educated
public remained long after school days were over, cento
writers found them an obvious source for phrases. The
earliest Latin centos were not on Christian themes; indeed, most of them concerned the tales of classical
mythology.[3] Proba was one of the first writers to use
Virgilian verses for a Christian purpose, and others of
her era followed suit.[4]

Through centos, educated Christians of the fourth and
fifth centuries A.D. could appropriate the elegance and
power of Virgilian verse for their new, Christian purposes. Yet the writing of centos posed many problems for
Christians: not only did they face grammatical difficulties regarding gender, number, case and agreement; there
was the larger question of how words originally describing bloody warfare and pagan deities could be borrowed to
express an ethic of peace and a monotheistic religion.
Since the amalgamation of pagan and Christian sentiment
did not always produce an aesthetically pleasing result,
modern commentators have often denigrated the artistic
activity involved in cento composition. As one critic

put it, the ancient popularity of cento writing can only
be attributed to "the general poverty of ideas of the
period....The idea of such 'Centos' could only have arisen
among people who had learnt Virgil mechanically and did
not know of any better use to which to put all these
verses with which they had loaded their brains."[5] A more
generous estimate is possible: some might even find
admirable the Christian centoists' desire to express "the
new doctrine with an art equal to antiquity."[6]

Writing a Latin cento, Proba uses Virgil's *Ecologues,*
Georgics, and *Aeneid* as her sources. Since she borrows
heavily from the *Aeneid* in her depiction of episodes from
Jesus' life, a reflection on how the adventures of the
prototypical Roman hero could be appropriated to relate
the story of Jesus' life may here be helpful. According
to Virgil, Aeneas' destiny after Troy's defeat by the
Greeks is to lead a contingent of Trojan followers to a
region of Italy where, through the intermarriage of
Trojans and Latins, the Roman race will be created.
Aeneas is a hero in pursuit of a new realm which he must
first find; he must then defeat the native Latins who
resist his claims to settle there. The goal of much
longer range, though no less the fruit of Aeneas' success, is the evolution of the Romans in accord with
Divine Providence to be masters of the world, whose
efforts to establish civilized values amid a peaceful
regimen are foretold and acclaimed by Jupiter himself.
The Romans, heirs of Aeneas, are thus the gods' chosen
people.

Yet many are the struggles Aeneas must surmount in
order to achieve his divinely-ordained goal: the wrath
of deities such as Juno, who try to thwart him at every
turn; his own discouragement and despair; and his passion
for the Carthaginian queen Dido, who seeks to prevent him

from leaving her realm for Italy. In his descent to the
underworld in Book VI, Aeneas learns of the promised
greatness of Rome and foresees its heroes in the centuries to come. Here he becomes a convert to Roman destiny
and ascends to the world spiritually reborn, purified,
and fully committed to the larger purpose of Roman destiny. He thus completes his quest, from which he had
occasionally faltered, pressing on despite life's
obstacles.

   Many features of Aeneas' characterization could be
used by Proba to portray the Christian hero, Jesus. Both
Aeneas and Jesus were alleged to have one divine and one
human parent; both exemplify moral prowess; both exhibit
compassion for suffering humans and undertake a mission
to overcome that suffering. Through Aeneas, as through
Jesus, a better world is promised to all persons who will
devote their energies to its realization: Proba could
easily transform Aeneas' ideal of founding the Roman
state into Christ's mission of establishing the Kingdom
of God. Thus the project of appropriating lines from
Virgil's *Aeneid* to create a new, Christian poem is perhaps not so inane as it first appears. With this
argument, some critics who have mocked the construction
of centos may be in part pacified.

   What do we know about the poem's author? If we were
left merely with the evidence provided by the cento itself, we could say only that Proba had earlier written
a poem on war she now as a Christian regretted (the
sentiment of regret may be a clue to Proba's fairly
recent conversion to Christianity).[7] From a few scanty
notices left by writers of the late patristic and
medieval periods, we know more: she was married, she had
two sons, and her poem on war had treated Magnentius'
rebellion against Constantius II in 353 A.D.[8] Her

Virgilian cento was thus composed later than 353, but
how much later remains a subject of dispute, with the
late 350s or early 360s the favored time range.[9] From
inscriptional and other evidence, we gather that Proba
was a member of the illustrious *gens Petronii*, and that
a near relative (her father?) had been consul and prefect
of Rome in the 320s and early 330s.[10] Her husband,
Clodius Celsinus Adelphius, was also of aristocratic
background; he held the office of a provincial governor,
and later, of proconsul and prefect of Rome.[11] Proba's
two sons assumed the offices customary for young men of
their rank as they matured:[12] indeed, only because the
men of Proba's family achieved public fame and hence had
their names recorded in inscriptions do we know these few
details about her.

Although scholars have disputed the precise dating of
Proba's cento, one attractive theory posits that it was
written in response to the pagan emperor Julian's decree
forbidding Christian teachers to explicate classical
texts to students.[13] In his attempt to thwart the spread
of Christianity, Julian insisted that proper education
required the instructor's "mental health," a condition
from which professors who taught one thing (the pagan
classics) while believing another (the Christian Gospel)
were automatically debarred.[14] The decree, issued in
362, must have elicited at least momentary concern among
Christians--although only momentary, for Julian died soon
thereafter and the decree was rescinded with the return
of Christian emperors to the throne. We know, however,
that a few Christians attempted to circumvent the decree
by casting Biblical stories into the forms of epic,
comedy, odes, and other genres, so that Christian
students could learn the teachings of their faith in the
trappings of classical style.[15] Since all education was

based on the Greek and Latin classics, and the assumption
of a man's career depended upon such an education,
rigorous Christians pondered how to educate their children without exposing them to the adventures of Jupiter
or the sins of adulteresses and murderers.

Proba's *Cento* may thus have been a response both to
Julian's decree and to the larger question of proper education for Christian children. By piecing together lines
of Virgil so that they sang of Christ rather than of
arms, horses, and wars,[16] Proba provided a pedagogic tool
for young Christians: we know that her *Cento* was widely
used for educational purposes in late antiquity and the
Middle Ages.[17] Children could learn their Virgil, but
Virgil so transformed that he sang "Christ's sacred
duties,"[18] as Proba puts it. Thus if the thesis that
relates the composition of the *Cento* to Julian's decree
is correct, we can posit something about both its date
(namely, 362 A.D. or soon thereafter) and the uses to
which it was put.

Proba's poem does not, of course, in 694 lines concern itself with the entire Bible: it concentrates on
the stories of creation and Fall in Genesis 1-3, and on
selected episodes of Jesus' life as depicted in the
Gospels, with heavy stress on the birth and infancy narratives and on the final events of Jesus' life. The
Cento is introduced by a catalog of the woes and wars
that Proba had depicted in her earlier poem. Now,
however, as a Christian she seeks inspiration from God
for the theme of her *Cento*: "That Virgil put to verse
Christ's sacred duties let me tell."[19] Proba here
affirms that Virgil, when correctly understood, testifies
to Jesus. Although this opinion is dubious as an historical argument, most early Christians believed that both
the Old Testament and the best pagan writing had in
veiled ways predicted the coming of the Messiah, Jesus.

Proba begins her story of creation in Biblical
fashion: "*Principio*," "in the beginning." She narrates
how God the Father established the heaven and earth, the
sun, moon, stars, divided light from darkness, distinguished the seasons one from another. The last act of
creation is of human beings, as in Genesis 1. However,
in her description of human creation, Proba abandons
Genesis 1 for Genesis 2 with its account of Eve's creation from Adam's rib. Proba's rendition is worth quoting
in full:

He [God] pulled plump clay and gave it shape
By kneading on the spot the fertile ground,
Its soil quickened from the year's first months.
And now--so suddenly--the image of
Such holiness! Man's new shape went forth,
Handsome at first beyond comparison,
Resembling God in countenance and shoulders--
Man, whose mind and intellect a greater God
Influences, and so sends forth to greater tasks.
For man a match is sought; but from so large
A throng none dared approach the Man; none dared
Be named helpmeet to his new realm.
Without delay, at once God gave untroubled
Rest throughout the young man's limbs,
And made his eyes close in pleasant sleep.
And now in the middle course of shady night,
The Almighty Sire laid the ribs and entrails bare.
One of these ribs he plucked apart from
The well-knit joints of youthful Adam's side,
And suddenly arose a wondrous gift--
Imposing proof--and shone in brilliant light;
Woman, a virgin she, unparalleled
In figure and in comely breasts, now ready
For a husband, ready now for wedlock.

For him, a boundless quaking breaks his sleep;
He calls his bones and limbs his wedded wife.
Dazed by the Will divine he took and clasped
Her hand in his, folded his arms around her.[20]

God then addresses the couple he has created, informing
them, "This is your home, this is your native land." He
adds, "On this I put no end, nor hour of destiny: Dominion without end have I bestowed," the famous line from
Aeneid I, 279, in which is revealed to Aeneas the destiny
of the future Romans.[21] The Garden in which Adam and Eve
are placed is described by Proba in terms taken from
Virgil's lines pertaining to mankind's Golden Age,[22] when
nature brought forth her bounty with little assistance
from human beings. God instructs the pair about the
fateful tree and adds an admonition not contained in the
Genesis account: God warns Adam with one word, "Woman,"
and counsels him, "Let no creature's passion get the best
of you, if glory from the godly fields, befitting you,
awaits."[23]

After a colorful description of the natural glories
of Eden, Proba introduces the serpent who cleverly suggests to Eve that something is lacking from her and
Adam's otherwise blissful existence: if she but feast on
the forbidden tree, she will perceive the missing elements. They eat, and

New light
Of understanding straightway dazed their eyes;
Yet quickly, frightened by their sudden
    sightedness,
They veiled their bodies under branching
    clothes of leaves.[24]

As in Genesis 3, Adam attempts to blame the sin on Eve
and exonerate himself. God places the penalties of hard
work and death on the humans, and a curse on the serpent,

but--interestingly enough--the curse of female subjection
is not mentioned among the penalties God prescribes.
With the couple's expulsion from Eden, the Golden Age has
come to an end.

Proba briefly relates Noah's experiments with viti-
culture, Cain's murder of Abel, the Great Flood, and the
Exodus from Egypt, before she turns to her "greater
task," as she calls it, the recital of Gospel stories.
We hear of the virgin birth and the infancy of Jesus,
much of which Proba borrows from Matthew's account. With
"time's fulfillment," Jesus assumes his public ministry,
is baptized by John and commissioned by God to "govern
your subjects with authority,"[25] just as Aeneas was.
Proba here interrupts the narration to report her own
conversion to Christianity and her baptism. Returning to
the Gospels, she describes Jesus' temptation by the devil
in the form of a serpent and recounts her version of the
Sermon on the Mount, which bears only slight resemblance
to Matthew 5-7. Proba also includes the Gospel episodes
of Jesus and the rich young man, the storm at sea and
Jesus' walk on the waters, the triumphal entry into Jerusalem, the cleansing of the Temple, the Last Supper,
trial, crucifixion, empty tomb, resurrection, and ascension. She concludes her poem with two pious hopes: that
her husband and descendants will continue to perform the
Christian rites, will "keep the faith," and that Jesus
will "draw near his devotees."[26]

To return to our opening theme: given the scarcity
of early Christian writers who were women, does Proba's
poem reveal an assessment of femaleness different from
that provided by her male counterparts? The evidence, I
think, is mixed--disappointingly mixed, if we had hoped
to ascribe to Proba a "higher consciousness." On the
positive side, we note that the first description of Eve

is not at all pejorative: she is called a "wondrous
gift" who shines "in brilliant light."[27] God's purpose
in creating humans, Proba writes, is so that he would
have someone to "rule the lands," and the fact that the
verb is in the plural (*tenerent*) could be interpreted to
mean that Proba wished to include Eve along with Adam as
one to whom dominion over the earth was given.[28] Moreover, Eve is not subjected to Adam as the punishment for
her role in the original sin: her punishment, death, is
exactly the same as his. This one feature sets Proba's
poem apart from the sentiments of the Church Fathers, who
dwell endlessly on Eve's condemnation as the justification for women's secondary status. When we turn to the
scenes of Jesus' birth and infancy, we note that Mary's
role is supreme: she does not need Joseph to protect her
and Jesus. In addition, Proba's depiction of Mary tends
to exalt maternity; her words provide a pleasing contrast
to those of the Church Fathers who denigrated childbearing and saved their praise for women choosing the
virginal life.

But much can be said on the negative side as well.
That at creation Adam experiences a "boundless quaking"
could be interpreted as a presage of the unhappy events
to come. And when Proba portrays God's instruction to
the couple not to touch the forbidden tree, she introduces a theme absent from the Genesis account: the
warning to Adam about "woman." Shortly before Eve eats
the fruit and offers it to Adam, she is called "hapless"
(*infelix*), "vowed to future ruin," and is said to be "the
cause of such great sin."[29] When Eve offers the fruit to
Adam, Proba claims that she has risen to "greater madness."[30] Indeed, the language used to depict Eve
throughout the episode in the Garden is heavy with associations connoting madness, frenzy, rage. Last, when God

condemns Eve, He calls her "most remorseless wife,"
(*saevissima coniunx*), "the origin and cause of all these
ills"; she is "lost" (*perdita*) and does "not perceive
what dangers stand about" her from now on.[31]
Turning to the New Testament section of the poem, we
note that Proba's tender depiction of the Christchild's
mother is the one and only reference to a particular
woman in her entire rendition of Jesus' life. Proba's
failure to include any other Gospel episode pertaining to
a woman shows that her poem concentrates less on women
than do the Evangelists' accounts. Certainly she might
have used the stories of Mary and Martha, the woman taken
in adultery, the Samaritan woman at the well, the raising
of Jairus' daughter, the healing of the woman with an
issue of blood, or those pertaining to Mary Magdalene.
Moreover, in rendering the story of Jesus' resurrection,
Proba fails to include the evidence of the Gospels that
Jesus' first resurrection appearance was to a woman or
women.[32]
Likewise Proba's account of Eve: although she does
not subject Eve to Adam as does Genesis 3, she nonetheless omits all material from Genesis 1 on the simultaneous creation of the sexes and the creation of both man
and woman in God's image. Indeed, Proba assigns the
image of God only to Adam (Adam resembles God "in countenance and shoulders"[33]); Eve is nowhere included in the
"resemblance" to God. To be sure, the view that only
Adam was in God's image was espoused by some Church
Fathers, who used as their Biblical justification the
words of Paul in I Corinthians 11:7 that man "is the
image and glory of God; but woman is the glory of man."
The exclusion of women from participation in God's image
was taken by these Church Fathers as further testimony
to the secondary status of females, and Proba contributes

to this view by her failure to include Eve in the "resemblance" that man shared with God. Proba thus elaborates upon the Biblical materials in ways that render woman's status worse than it actually is in the Bible. Yet the largest share of responsibility for these omissions and failures must rest with Proba's sources.

To begin, Proba worked with Biblical texts that had long been set: there was no way to avoid the fact that the author of Genesis 3 represents the woman as the first to be tempted and as responsible for giving the fruit to Adam. Although *our* contemporaries might claim that Eve is portrayed as exhibiting both more curiosity and more initiative than Adam, traits that we deem praiseworthy, early Christian writers did not so judge the account. Eve's curiosity, like Pandora's, was taken to be a peculiarly female vice. With good reason, Genesis 3 has been labeled the central destructive myth of western culture as far as influence on women's status is concerned.[34] The nineteenth-century feminist, Elizabeth Cady Stanton, proposed a solution to the problem: discard Genesis 3 and be rid of much destructive ideology. As she put it,

> Take the snake, the fruit-tree and the woman
> from the tableau, and we have no fall, no
> frowning Judge, no Inferno, no everlasting
> punishment--hence no need of a Savior. Thus
> the bottom falls out of the whole Christian
> theology. Here is the reason why in all the
> Biblical researches and higher criticisms, the
> scholars never touch the position of women.[35]

But if Genesis 3 is not to be expunged from the pages of Scripture--and surely Proba along with countless Christians through the ages would not have it expunged--then we must acknowledge that the Bible itself contains the

lines that make woman the first perpetrator of sin. Although Paul in Romans 5 does not even mention Eve, but
assigns the blame for the sin to Adam ("sin came into the
world through one man"),[36] in II Corinthians 11:3 he
speaks of Eve's being led astray. A few decades later,
Paul's followers were claiming that Eve's responsibility
for the sin was the reason why women should not teach or
have authority over men. As the author of I Timothy 2
writes, "For Adam was formed first, then Eve; and Adam
was not deceived, but the woman was deceived and became
a transgressor." The Church Fathers in commenting on the
original sin followed the interpretation of I Timothy
that the woman was to be assigned the heavier blame.
Although Proba adopts their interpretation, she receives
support from the words of Genesis 3 that describe the
first step into evil as taken by the woman, not by the
man.

A second source for Proba's less-than-generous
assessment of Eve stems from her use of Virgil's poetry.
That Virgil saw women as exemplifying passion, disorder,
and madness seems evident from his poems and has been
explicitly argued in a dissertation by Grace West.[37] The
sexual impulse in general was dangerous, thought Virgil.
Passionate love leads several of his characters astray:
Dido is the case in point, but also recall the tale of
Orpheus and Eurydice in *Georgics IV*. Virgil extends his
critique of sexual passion to the animal kingdom: one
feature of the behavior of bees that he found singularly
attractive was that they did not (he thought) engage in
sexual activities and thus were able to preserve the
order, stability, and cohesion of their tiny empire far
better than humans who were plagued by raging lust.[38]
And women in Virgil's poetry seem especially subject to
irrational and wicked behavior. The passages Proba

appropriates from Virgil to describe Eve and her sinful
act resonate with such assumptions.

For example, when Proba designates Eve an "impious
wife," she borrows the phrase from a passage in the
Aeneid referring to Clytemnestra's murder of Agamemnon.[39] The "boundless quaking" that disturbs Adam's
sleep before Eve is plucked from his side are words derived from Virgil's account of the Fury Allecto's attack
upon Turnus while he slept.[40] When Proba has God warn
Adam about the dangers of women, her words are borrowed
from a line in *Georgics III* in which Virgil advises
farmers to keep their male and female cattle separate,
for the female, he says, "wastes the strength" of the
male, inflames him with her presence, causes him to forget the peaceful groves, and impels him to ferocious
contests with the other males.[41] Such, Virgil thinks,
are the dangers that the female of the species presents.

Moreover, the words depicting the madness and frenzy
of Eve are taken from passages in Virgil that represent
women as singularly prone to irrational acts. When Proba
writes of Eve that by her "sinful deed she rose to
greater madness," her words are derived from Virgil's
account of Amata's being plunged into a maddened frenzy
as she was driven by the Fury Allecto to thwart the gods'
plans for the marriage of Lavinia and Aeneas.[42] A second
reference to Eve's "madness" is taken from Virgil's description of Dido's self-immolation,[43] as is her line
that speaks of Eve's "guile and disastrous sin."[44] The
"doom" of Eve is also depicted in lines taken from the
tale of Eurydice, who, in fleeing unwanted advances,
failed to note the approach of a lethal serpent.[45] Thus
there is ample evidence that Virgilian verses relating
to female evil or ill-fate were prominent in Proba's mind
when she described the first woman of Genesis. Proba's

depiction of Eve owes much to Virgil's traditional
assumptions about women.

If anything is revealed about Proba in her *Cento*, it
is not her special interest in women, but rather her
class identification. Proba's place as a member of the
Roman aristocracy is abundantly clear. First, the very
fact that Proba could write a cento at all, composed
entirely out of Virgilian lines, speaks much about her
education and hence her class. She, like aristocratic
males of her era, was thoroughly familiar with the works
of the greatest Latin poet, Virgil. Indeed, what we
infer about Proba's literary training accords well with
our admittedly limited knowledge of women's education in
late antiquity. Certainly women's education had
developed considerably since the time of the Greek writer
Xenophon, whose upper-class brides were so untutored that
even the modest principles of household organization
might baffle them unless they were granted intelligent
direction by their husbands.[46] According to Henri
Marrou, the Hellenistic era initiated changes in women's
education that were long-lasting; he cites evidence for
co-education and for secondary education programs for
girls even before the dawn of the Roman Empire.[47] From
Latin literature, we gather that within the social
classes there described (namely the upper and middle),
boys and girls studied together.[48] Although aristocratic
women did not enjoy higher philosophical study, or the
rhetorical training accorded young men destined for public service, they did receive literary educations. It is
thus revealing to note in Jerome's letters to women the
numerous references to Virgil, Persius, Terence,
Quintilian, Cicero, Horace, and others—and Jerome writes
as if he expects the female recipients to catch his allusions. Probably they did, for these women were often

bilingual in Greek and some of them even studied
Hebrew.[49] Thus there is every reason to think that
Proba's comprehensive knowledge of Virgil must bespeak
the fine literary education that was provided for daughters of the Roman aristocracy.

Yet evidence exists within Proba's poem for her
interest in "class" issues. For example, by Proba's
time, a prominent feature of Christian devotion was the
renunciation of riches. Does this theme appear in
Proba's poem? No. There is no evidence whatsoever in
the *Cento* that the aristocrat Proba believed that Christian commitment summoned one to abandon possessions or
donate them to the church. In this respect, Proba's
values, such as we can reconstruct them from her *Cento*,
are not those of the Christian ascetics.

To be sure, Proba strongly condemns selfishness:
greed was one of the primary evils, she thought, that
afflicted human life from the time of Cain's fratri-
cide.[50] She enjoins her readers to share their goods
with kin,[51] but does not mention the indigent. Those who
sit tight on buried gold, who do not share with relatives,
she affirms, are the sort of people who will end up in
Hell.[52] Yet when Proba picks which Biblical scenes pertaining to Jesus' infancy she will relate, it is
Matthew's wealthy magi bringing precious gifts who
appear,[53] not the humble shepherds of Luke's account.
And Proba has Jesus rather subtly sanction class distinctions when she puts these words in his mouth, "Whatever
wealth exists/For each," men should joyously call upon
their common God.[54] Most interesting is line 477 of the
Cento, a fabrication on Proba's part that has no parallel
in the Gospels: to the list of topics Jesus addresses in
the Sermon on the Mount, Proba adds a reference to
clients. Proba has Jesus say that those who "cozen a

client in entangling snare" will suffer the pangs of
damnation later on.[55] The verse is revealing of Proba's
social class in which the patron's support of clients
was an expected duty of his or her rank.

Last, in Proba's treatment of the story of the rich
young man, Jesus nowhere commands the youth to sell his
goods for the sake of the poor. He urges the youth merely to "learn...contempt for wealth,"[56] an innocent-enough
injunction that could easily be reconciled with the
actual possession of riches. As in the Gospel story, the
rich young man in Proba's poem turns away in despair--but
here we rather wonder why, since he was not ordered to
sell his goods or adopt a life of ascetic renunciation.
In ways such as these, Proba appears as a representative
of her class, exhibiting more resemblances to men of her
own rank than she does to females as a group.

A second way in which Proba's non-ascetic interests
are revealed lies in her concern for home, husband, and
children. Her social and domestic values seem to be
those cherished by Roman aristocrats of all ages: filial
piety and marital devotion. We may not incorrectly imagine her as a model of traditional Roman matronhood.
Despite the greater freedoms enjoyed by women in the
Roman imperial period,[57] the exemplary wife and mother
lived on in legend even in Proba's time.[58] About women's
emancipation in the Roman Empire, an historian of late
antiquity has written, "There is perhaps nothing more
striking in the social history of Rome than the inveter-
ate conservatism of Roman sentiment in the face of accomplished change."[59] Yet whatever advances women had
gained in society at large, Christians upheld an ideal of
wifely modesty more in keeping with the ancient Roman
standard. Despite rapid social changes occurring in the
later Empire, the aristocratic family retained its

traditional functions.[60] For Christian as well as pagan
aristocrats, marriage continued to be understood almost
exclusively from the point of view of familial and
societal interests,[61] that is, the continuation of the
family line and property. Proba's poem suggests that she
embraced many of the values upheld by the Roman nobility
of an earlier era. To be sure, asceticism had not yet
won the day at the time when she composed her *Cento* in
the late 350s or early 360s; nonetheless, we may imagine
that she might have been among those who were shocked to
hear of aristocratic women abandoning their homes and
children, such as Jerome's friend, Paula, and Melania the
Elder did a decade or two later.

    Far from exalting the ascetic life, there is not a
single verse in the 694 lines of Proba's *Cento* that hints
she believed asceticism to be the superior mode of Christian living. Nowhere does she present either Jesus or
Mary as a model for the Christian celibate; it is rather
Mary's maternity she stresses. Proba's concern that the
Christian adopt correct domestic virtues is revealed both
in her frequent use of Virgilian lines which in their
original context reflected those values and in her own
explicitly stated version of Christian teaching. The
earlier sections of the *Cento* reveal these interests
plainly. Thus the very notion of parricide fills her
with horror.[62] Domestic themes occupy her mind, too:
she emphasizes the "marriage" of Adam and Eve[63] and the
bliss they enjoyed before their Fall.[64] The first
fratricide--Cain of Abel--she denounces with a shudder,[65]
and rues that this monstrous crime became more prevalent
as the Age of Iron emerged.[66]

    When we turn to the section of the poem devoted to
Gospel themes, we find that the story of Jesus' infancy
and Herod's massacre of the innocents occupies a

considerable portion of the text, perhaps a reflection of
Proba's own maternal interests. Her rendition of Herod's
slaughter and Mary's escape with her baby are worth
citing in full:

> Then shouts and strident squalling,
> The sobbing breath of babes in arms crescendoed.
> Corpses of sons lay strewn before their parents'
> Eyes, flung at the doorway. But the mother,
> With good reason spurred to terror at
> Such plaintive sobs, ferrying her child
> Upon her breast, escaped the violent mob,
> And made her way again to the full mangers.
> And here, beneath the pitching, lowly roof,
> She began to nurse her son, her full paps
> Milking to his tender lips. Here, child,
> Your cradle will be the first to pour
> Out blossoms in profusion, just for you;
> And mixed with cheerful sow's bread everywhere
> Will be the earth; and bit by bit the Egyptian bean
> Will overflow with delicate acanthus.[67]

Notable in this rendition of the tale from Matthew's
Gospel are two points. First, Joseph is nowhere evident
in the scene. It is Mary alone who comprehends the situation, plans the escape, and takes action. She is at the
center of events and no male figure detracts from her
importance. The theme of Mary's nursing the infant Jesus
is Proba's own touch, a passage unprecedented in any of
the canonical Gospels--but one that obviously emphasizes
maternity.

A second point, and one of religious interest, is
that Proba's description of the Christchild's cradle,
with the blossoms in profusion, the sow's bread, the
Egyptian bean, and the acanthus are borrowed directly
from Virgil's Fourth *Eclogue*,[68] a poem that was understood

by Christians to predict the coming of the Christ. Virgil's *nova progenies*, the "offspring now new" of his
Fourth *Eclogue*, who would usher in a new Golden Age for
Rome, was readily adapted by Christian readers to refer
to Jesus.[69] The bliss that Virgil believed the boy would
bring to the world was ascribed by Proba to Jesus. Virgil's claim that the Age of Iron would cease with the
child's development is parallel to Proba's testimony
throughout her poem that the coming of Jesus has brought
salvation to sinners such as herself. Thus the scene of
Herod's massacre, as rendered by Proba, reveals both a
maternal sympathy and a consciousness that the Virgilian
lines she borrowed for her portrayal would convey
Messianic overtones to Christian readers.

According to Proba, Jesus' teaching during his adult
ministry also stressed devotion to family. Proba has him
recommend sharing with kin as a central Christian virtue.
Striking one's parents will result in eternal punishment
for the offender, Proba's Christ warns.[70] In his advice
to the rich youth, Jesus counsels that he not forsake a
brother, and remarks, "Let chaste home/ Preserve its
sense of modesty,"[71] words of Proba's own invention,
foreign to the Gospel accounts. Thus we have good reason
to argue that the ostensibly Christian values that Proba
recommends in her poem are in actuality the traditional
Roman ones of respect for parents and kin, sanctity of
home, and marital chastity.

We can also focus on the Virgilian sources Proba
appropriated in order to demonstrate the numerous times
she used verses derived from Virgilian episodes manifesting those traditional Roman virtues. It is probably not
accidental that such lines came to her mind as she
searched for suitable Virgilian verses with which to
express her Christian message: the values expressed
therein were ones she, too, wished to honor.

Without doubt, the chief manifestation of filial
piety in the *Aeneid* occurs in the scenes of Aeneas'
dramatic rescue of his father Anchises from the doomed
city of Troy, his grief at Anchises' death, his institu-
tion of offerings and funeral games in honor of his
father, and his emotion-filled reunion with Anchises in
the underworld. Proba, we posit, found these scenes
especially memorable, for she utilized them frequently
to convey her new Christian beliefs. Thus she uses ten
times the lines in which Aeneas tries to persuade his
elderly father to leave Troy;[72] on five occasions alone
does she borrow lines derived from the scene in which the
hair of Aeneas' son Iulus catches fire as an omen from
the gods, an omen that convinces Anchises to leave the
city with Aeneas.[73] Examples from other scenes pertaining to Aeneas' filial devotion to his father could be
multiplied.

Proba's interest in Virgilian scenes pertaining to
children also seems evident throughout her *Cento*, for she
appropriates lines from them a disproportionate number of
times: Evander's grief at the death of his only child
Pallas;[74] episodes regarding Iulus/Ascanius (especially
Dido's love for the child);[75] scenes describing Camilla
(especially the lines that depict Camilla's father rescuing her as an infant,[76] lines that Proba borrows for
the massacre of the innocents scene)[77] are all prominent.

Likewise prominent are lines from Virgilian episodes
that depicted marital devotion: Dido's love for the now-
dead husband of her youth, Sychaeus;[78] Andromache's
devotion to Hector;[79] Creusa's devotion to Aeneas--are
all borrowed on numerous occasions by Proba in the creation of her poem. Most significantly, Creusa's greeting
to her husband Aeneas, "Sweet husband," is used by Proba
in the closing lines of her poem as a tribute to her own

husband, Adelphius.[80] Thus the domestic and marital
values of classical Rome lived on in Proba's *Cento*. No
abandonment of children and husbands, no haircloth
shirts, no adoption of voluntary indigence are recommended in its lines.

In fact, various features of Proba's *Cento* could be
taken to support the argument that Proba composed the
poem for her own sons. Three such features have already
been noted: that the episodes depicted in the *Cento* involve males almost exclusively; that many scenes are
composed from lines that originally depicted Virgilian
episodes pertaining to young men and boys, such as
Aeneas' son; and that Jesus' teaching is recast so that
it has special relevance to upperclass males who must
learn the proper moral code of responsibility for clients
and kinfolk.

A fourth and hitherto unmentioned factor may be added
to the others: that Jesus throughout the *Cento* is depicted more as an epic hero than as a "suffering servant."
Jesus' impressively masculine appearance is frequently
mentioned, in a manner foreign to the Gospels: his thunderous voice, "towering shanks," and "height and breadth
of shoulder" all receive comment.[81] In addition, Jesus'
refusal to allow his honor to be violated without
reprisal is far more characteristic of epic heroes than
of his portrayal in the New Testament. In the crucifixion scene sketched by Proba, Jesus lashes out at his
persecutors in words absent from Scripture:

What makes you tie these bonds?
Has overweening racial pride possessed you?
Some day, for wrongs committed, you will pay
With punishment unlike this one to me.[82]

Such a depiction of the angry Jesus who does not take insult lightly illustrates Proba's attempt to cast Jesus

in the mold of a classical hero. As such, he would provide an attractive model for young men who were learning
what "honor" meant to Romans. Although we cannot prove
that Proba wrote the poem as a contribution to her own
sons' education--indeed, no evidence exists that allows
us to do so--, we can safely assert, at a minimum, that
Rome's aristocratic young men would have made a natural
audience for the *Cento*.

We must here remember Proba's precise situation in
early Christian history: she lived after the age when
martyrdom was the route to Christian glory, yet just before the flowering of female asceticism. In the late
fourth century, asceticism became the new path to Christian glory for females: there, as in martyrdom, they
could show that they were the equals of men in overcoming
the temptations and the biological needs of the body.
Among the Roman aristocracy, asceticism came into its own
a decade or two after the time Proba composed her poem.
To be sure, a few female aristocrats such as Jerome's
friend Marcella had already, in the 350s or early 360s,[83]
secluded themselves in their Roman palaces to adopt a
life of extreme renunciation, but the golden years of
asceticism did not arrive in Rome until the 370s and
380s, when traditional Romans were shocked to see women
of the leading families abandon their children and journey the high seas to Palestine where they established
monasteries for women. Proba, by virtue of her chronology, missed that--although her great-great-granddaughter
Demetrias forsook plans for marriage at the eleventh hour
and was congratulated by Jerome for her espousal of perpetual virginity.[84] Whether Proba herself would have
taken the route of virginal renunciation had it been
offered to her, can be doubted: the devotion to children, and the open reference to her "husband sweet"

(*dulcis coniunx*)[85] in the *Cento* suggest that the roles of
wife and mother were pleasing to her. Yet because Proba
opted for home and family, when those about her were on
the verge of casting them off, means that later generations were left something exceedingly rare: a piece of
early Christian literature written not by a theologian,
a priest, or a monk, but by a female layperson.

NOTES

[1]*Oxford Classical Dictionary*, ed. N.G.H. Hammond and
H.N. Scullard, 2nd ed. (Oxford, 1970), p. 220. For possible derivations of the word, see Filippo Ermini, *Il
centone di Proba e la poesie centonaria latina* (Rome,
1909), pp. 19-21.

[2]Ermini, *Centone*, pp. 23-24.

[3]*Ibid.*, pp. 42ff.

[4]Texts in Carolus Schenkl, ed., *Cento Vergilianus de
laudibus Christi. Poetae Christiani Minores*, CSEL 16
(Vienna, 1888). An English translation of and commentary on
Proba's *Cento* can be found in Elizabeth A. Clark and
Diane F. Hatch, *The Golden Bough, The Oaken Cross: The
Virgilian Cento of Faltonia Betitia Proba*. AAR Texts and
Translations Series 5 (Chico, Cal., 1981). All citations
of the *Cento* in this essay are taken from this transla-
tion.

[5]Domenico Comparetti, *Vergil in the Middle Ages*, tr.
E.F.M. Benecke (1908; rpt. ed., Hamden, Conn., 1966),
p. 53.

[6]Ermini, *Centone*, p. 161.

[7]*Cento* 1-28.

[8]Isidore of Seville, *De viris illustribus* 22 (18);
De originibus I, 39, 26; see also B. de Montfaucon,
Diarium Italicum (Paris, 1702), p. 36.

[9]Ermini, *Centone*, pp. 13, 58; A.G. Amatucci, *Storia
della letteratura latina* (Bari, 1929), p. 147; Maria
Cacioli, "Adattamenti semantici e sintattici nel centone
virgiliano di Proba," *Studi Italiani di Filologi
Classica*, n.s. 41 (1969), 196-197; Mario Bonario,
"Appunti per la storia della tradizione virgiliana nel IV
secolo," in *Vergiliana: Recherches sur Virgile*, ed. H.
Bardon and R. Verdière (London, 1971), p. 39; R.A.

Markus, "Paganism, Christianity, and the Latin Classics
in Fourth Century," in *Latin Literature of the Fourth
Century*, ed. J.W. Binns (London, Boston, 1974), p. 3.

[10]A.H.M. Jones, J.R. Martindale, and J. Morris, *The
Prosopography of the Later Roman Empire, Vol. I: A.D.
260-395* (Cambridge, 1971), pp. 1144, 733-734.

[11]M.T.W. Arnheim, *The Senatorial Aristocracy in the
Later Roman Empire* (Oxford, 1972), pp. 114-115: *CIL* IX,
1576 (discussed in Ermini, *Centone*, p. 9); *stemma* in
Ermini, *Centone*, p. 9; Jones, *Prosopography*, I, 192-193.

[12]See Ermini, *Centone*, pp. 9-10; Jones, *Prosopography*, I, 1144, 640-642, 49.

[13]Amatucci, *Storia*, p. 147. The edict is discussed
by Julian in his *Ep.* 36 (42 Hertlein).

[14]Julian, *Ep.* 36, 422 A-B.

[15]Sozomen, *Church History* V, 18.

[16]*Cento* 48.

[17]Amatucci, *Storia*, p. 147; Comparetti, *Vergil*, p.
29; Ermini, *Centone*, pp. 20ff.

[18]*Cento* 23.

[19]*Cento* 23.

[20]*Cento* 116-135.

[21]*Cento* 143.

[22]*Cento* 144-147; lines from *Eclogue* IV, 40; *Georgics*
IV, 208; *Aeneid* IX, 610-611.

[23]*Cento* 154-155.

[24]*Cento* 206-209.

[25]*Cento* 380, 409 (cf. *Aeneid* VI, 851).

[26]*Cento* 689-694.

[27]*Cento* 129-130.

[28]*Cento* 113.

[29]*Cento* 200; 202.

[30]*Cento* 203.

[31]*Cento* 263-265.

[32]Matthew 28; Mark 16; Luke 24; John 20.

[33]*Cento* 120.

[34]Mary Daly, *Beyond God the Father: Toward a Philosophy of Women's Liberation* (Boston, 1973), p. 47.

[35]Elizabeth Cady Stanton, letter to the editor, *The Critic* (New York) March 28, 1896, p. 219.

[36]Romans 5:12.

[37]Grace S. West, "Women in Vergil's Aeneid," Ph.D. diss., University of California at Los Angeles, 1975.

[38]*Georgics* IV, 197-202; see Charles Segal, "Orpheus and the Fourth *Georgic*: Vergil on Nature and Civilization," *American Journal of Philology* 87 (1966), 310-311.

[39]*Cento* 171; *Aeneid* XI, 267.

[40]*Cento* 133; *Aeneid* VII, 458.

[41]*Cento* 154-155; *Georgics* III, 21ff.

[42]*Aeneid* VII, 386; *Cento* 203.

[43]*Aeneid* V, 6; *Cento* 212.

[44]*Cento* 238; *Aeneid* IV, 563.

[45]*Cento* 239; *Georgics* IV, 458.

[46]Xenophon, *Oeconomicus* VII, 4-IX.

[47]H.I. Marrou, *A History of Education in Antiquity*, trans. George Lamb (New York, 1964), p. 141.

[48]Marrou, *History*, pp. 202, 302.

[49]Ovid, *Tristia* II, 369-370; Martial, *Epigrams* VIII, 3, 16.

[50]*Cento* 301; 305-306.

[51] *Cento* 475-481,

[52] *Cento* 305-306; 475-481.

[53] *Cento* 352ff.

[54] *Cento* 470-471.

[55] *Cento* 477.

[56] *Cento* 522.

[57] J.P.V.D. Balsdon, *Roman Women: Their History and Habits* (London, 1962), pp. 14-15, 45, 179-180, 217, 219; Sarah Pomeroy, *Goddesses, Whores, Wives, and Slaves: Women in Classical Antiquity* (New York, 1975), ch. 8.

[58] See Pomeroy, *Goddesses*, pp. 149-150.

[59] Samuel Dill, *Roman Society from Nero to Marcus Aurelius* (London, 1905), p. 78.

[60] Jean Dumortier, "Le Mariage dans les milieux chrétiens d'Antioche et de Byzance d'après Saint Jean Chrysostome," *Lettres d'Humanité* 6 (1947), 162.

[61] Bernard Grillet, "Introduction générale," *Jean Chrysostome, La Virginité*. SC 125 (Paris, 1966), pp. 32 and 63, n. 1.

[62] *Cento* 4.

[63] *Cento* 132-135.

[64] *Cento* 139-147.

[65] *Cento* 287.

[66] *Cento* 303-304.

[67] *Cento* 369-379.

[68] *Eclogue* IV, 18; 23; 20; 19; 28; 20.

[69] See Pierre Courcelle, "Les Exégèses chrétiennes de la Quatrième Eclogue," *Revue des Etudes Anciennes* 59 (1957), 294-296.

[70] *Cento* 477-478.

[71]*Cento* 524; 526.

[72]*Aeneid* II, 634ff.

[73]*Aeneid* II, 680-700.

[74]*Aeneid* VIII, 514; 552; XI, 158.

[75]*Aeneid* I, 664-722.

[76]*Aeneid* XI, 550; 541; 544.

[77]*Cento* 373-374.

[78]See Clark and Hatch, *Golden Bough*, pp. 117-118 for references.

[79]*Ibid.*

[80]*Ibid.*

[81]*Cento* 573; 556; 462.

[82]*Cento* 621-623.

[83]Jerome, *Ep.* 127.

[84]Jerome, *Ep.* 130.

[85]*Cento* 693.

JESUS AS HERO IN THE VERGILIAN
CENTO OF FALTONIA BETITIA PROBA
(with Diane F. Hatch)

Vergilius 27 (1981), 31-39

Among the many works of literature from late antiquity all but forgotten in our time is Faltonia Betitia
Proba's poem on the creation of the world and the life
of Jesus. Perhaps composed in response to Julian's decree of 362 A.D. forbidding Christian teachers to offer
instruction on the pagan classics,[1] the 694-line *Cento
Vergilianus de laudibus Christi*[2] stands near the beginning of the Christian Latin poetic tradition.[3] The
earliest Latin poem to focus on the opening chapters of
Genesis, Proba's *Cento* is thus the first in a succession
of poems devoted to the themes of Creation and Fall.[4]
Both Proba's sex and her aristocratic background suggest
interesting topics for the investigations of social historians.[5] It is the *form* of her poem, however, that here
captures our attention.

Proba, to be sure, did not invent the cento; Homeric
centos existed before the Christian era.[6] The first
Latin centos we know of appear at the end of the second
century A.D.[7] and are devoted primarily to mythological
themes.[8] Proba, however, was one of the first to employ
Vergil's works for a Christian purpose, and others followed suit: we have centos from the fourth and fifth
centuries called *Versus ad gratiam Domini*, *De Verbi*

incarnatione, and *De Ecclesia.*[9] The serious purpose of
the Christian centos is noteworthy and contrasts sharply
with the triviality of such productions as Ausonius'
cento on weddings, which the poet himself labels "ludi-
crous" (*ridenda*).[10] Although the cento is an oddity
foreign to modern taste and has, in fact, been severely
condemned as illustrating late antiquity's "poverty of
ideas,"[11] centos were indeed popular in Proba's day.
And it is precisely the *form* of Proba's poem that prompts
questions of its content: because her portrayal of Jesus
is constructed largely from lines of the *Aeneid,* we must
ask how the Vergilian derivations affect the Christian
subject matter. Most particularly, we ask to what extent
and in what ways Proba's portrayal of Jesus is colored
by the classical understanding of the heroic ideal.

The question is difficult to answer. We remain
ignorant of Proba's poetic intention and must argue from
textual evidence alone. Yet because the hero to whom
she would have turned as her exemplar, Aeneas, differed
in important respects from his Homeric predecessors, she
had at hand a heroic model more adaptable to Christian
purposes. Whether or not Aeneas fully realized the new
heroic virtue of *humanitas* has been fiercely debated;[12]
early Christian theologians as well as modern critics
have been quick to indict him for his proclivity to
bloodshed.[13] Despite their denunciations, some elements
in Vergil's portrayal of his hero, such as Aeneas' quest
for a goal transcending his personal happiness, his ini-
tiation of a realm in which "dominion without end"[14]
would prevail, and the aura of divinity that surrounds
him,[15] could be readily adapted to a depiction of Jesus.
Further, some features of Jesus' life as described in the
Gospels typify the paradigmatic hero.[16] For example,
his birth from a virgin mother and a divine father

(Aeneas' mother was a goddess, his father   a mortal),
his narrow brush with death in infancy, his battling a
power of evil (the story of the temptation), and his
early death are all characteristic of the heroic pattern.
Although Proba emphasizes these features of Jesus' life
in recounting Gospel scenes,[17] she does not stop there.
Far from limiting her account to the material found in
the New Testament, Proba elaborates upon it, and in so
doing, portrays Jesus after the fashion of the classical
hero.

Proba's poem, although epic in tone, is Christian,
not pagan. Several years earlier, probably before her
conversion to Christianity, she had composed a poem on
the uprising of Magnentius against Constantius II.[18]
She tells us in her *Cento* that in the earlier poem she
sang of "horses, arms of men, their wars,"[19] a play on
the opening line of the *Aeneid*, but that now she re-
nounces her fascination with pagan themes and aims
instead to relate Biblical narratives. Yet the manner
in which Proba announces her retraction indicates that
she is "christianizing" the epic convention. Whereas
classical authors invoke the Muses at the beginning of
their poems, Proba proclaims that she will no longer
"lead the Muses from Aonian peak."[20] She will instead
call upon God to unloose his Spirit into her heart so
that she may find Christian inspiration:[21] she prays to
God, "Make straight my mind."[22] The Castalian fount of
which pagan poets spoke becomes, for Proba, the baptismal
waters from which she emerged, ready to begin her new,
Christian song.[23] The poem and invocation give a sense
of her lofty purpose:

> From her earliest time, leaders had broken sacred
> Vows of peace--poor men, caught up in a fatal
> Greed for power. And I have catalogued

The different slayings, monarchs' cruel wars,
And battle lines made up of hostile
Relatives. I sang of famous shields,
Their honor cheapened by a parent's blood,
And trophies captured from no enemy;
Bloodstained parades of triumph "fame" had won,
And cities orphaned of so many citizens,
So many times. I do confess. It is
Enough to bring these errors back to mind.
Now, God almighty, accept my sacred
Song, I pray; unloose the utterance
Of your eternal, sevenfold Spirit, and so
Unlock the inmost sanctum of my heart
That I may find all mysteries within
My power to relate--I, Proba, prophetess.
No longer do I care to seek the ambrosial
Drink, nor does it please to lead the Muses
From Aonian peak; no vain misunderstanding
Should persuade me that rocks talk
Or to pursue as themes the laureled tripods,
The empty vows and brawling deities
Of noblemen, and defeated household gods.
It is not my task, indeed, to publicize
My fame on the strength of words, thereby
To seek some small acclaim from human favor.
But wet from the Castalian fount have I,
In imitation of the blessed, and thirsting,
Drunk the offerings of the holy day.
And here shall I begin my song. Be present,
God, make straight my power of mind!
That Virgil put to verse Christ's sacred duties
Let me tell.[24]

Such a christianizing of classical conventions, a commonplace of fourth-century Christian Latin poetry,[25] is
significant for our investigation because it alerts us
at the beginning of the *Cento* that Proba probably intended her poem to parallel, in certain respects, the
masterpieces of her pagan predecessors. It comes as no
surprise, then, to find her embellishing the Gospel accounts in ways that bring Jesus into greater conformity
with the heroic tales of classical literature, to discover her explicitly calling Jesus a "hero"[26] and speaking of the *pietas* he achieved.[27]

  If Proba's *Cento* was composed in response to Julian's
decree forbidding Christian teachers to give instruction
in the pagan classics, as has been suggested,[28] it is
not unreasonable to imagine that Proba had further motivation for wishing to portray Jesus as the embodiment of
the heroic virtues: namely, to offer a rejoinder to the
distinctly unheroic, indeed most uncomplimentary picture
of Jesus that emerged in the vitriolic writings of that
emperor.[29] Julian calumniates Jesus (whom he refers to
as "the corpse")[30] both in the *Caesares* and *Contra
Galilaeos*. In the former work, Jesus is represented as
welcoming hardened criminals to his cause without de-
manding that they reform; if they continue to commit
grave sins after baptism, they need only smite their
chests and all will be forgiven.[31] In *Contra Galilaeos*,
Jesus is depicted as a morally weak and miserable human
being,[32] whose teachings prompt bloodshed within
families.[33] Further, Christians do not even know if
Jesus taught how to live a holy life.[34] As for his
deeds, Jesus did nothing worth hearing about--he performed some minor healings and exorcisms scarcely worthy
of mention.[35] Jesus' record of heroic action in Julian's
rendition is flatly weak. No charismatic orator, Jesus

was incapable of convincing even his friends and relatives to adopt his teaching.[36] To sum up, the Christian
religion, Julian claims, is identical with impiety,
atheotētos, from which only Hellenic wisdom could rescue
its deluded devotees.[37]

Proba may indeed have been motivated to portray
Jesus as a hero in response to Julian's assessment of
Jesus' character as unheroic: the hypothesis is an intriguing one, although, we admit, ultimately undemon-
strable, given our ignorance of Proba's familiarity with
contemporary Greek literature[38] and of the poem's precise date.[39] But whether or not Proba specifically
shaped her poem as a response to Julian, she clearly
casts Jesus in the heroic mold. She accomplishes this
in three decisive ways.

First, Proba comments frequently on Jesus' physical
appearance: in her rendition of his biography, he has a
magnificent and commanding presence. When we recall the
Gospels' total absence of comment on this topic and the
early Christian predilection to view Jesus as the Suffering Servant of Isaiah 52-53, whose "appearance was so
marred beyond human semblance," who "had no beauty or
comeliness that we should look at him," we immediately
grasp what a striking change Proba has here effected.
In Jesus' first public appearance after his baptism and
temptation, Proba tells us that his impressive appearance
led crowds to gape; persons of both sexes run to stare
at him.[40] They admire his face, his stride, even his
voice[41]--and of his booming, thunderous voice we hear
again in the scene of the cleansing of the Temple.[42]
So majestic is Jesus with his "height and breadth of
shoulder"[43] that the crowds do not merely follow him,
they mob him in a "deafening din,"[44] Proba writes in her
prelude to the Sermon on the Mount.

Jesus' physical prowess and regal appearance also
receive special attention in another scene, the walk
upon the waters, which Proba combines with the pericope
of the storm at sea. The disciples, here called
"sailors,"[45] cower frightened in their boat, imagining
their imminent deaths.[46] Suddenly they glimpse Jesus
coming to them across the water. He approaches: "Light
as the light winds/ And swifter than the lightning's
branching bolts/ He sought the leaning waves."[47] The
disciples are said to "recognize their King and his
strong right hand" (*dextram potentem*).[48] Jesus strides
through the waves, not letting "the ocean wet his towering shanks,"[49] a line that in its original context
referred to the blinded giant Polyphemus, stumbling
through the sea in an attempt to locate Aeneas' men:[50]
Proba has turned the mock-heroic into the heroic. Reach-
ing the boat, Jesus climbs aboard, and his weight is such
that the ship "groans" when he seats himself, just as
Charon's skiff groaned when the hero Aeneas boarded it
to cross the Styx.[51] In her rendition of the storm at
sea Proba depicts a true hero, mighty in strength, bringing leadership and solace to his troubled men.

Second, Proba reconstructs the crucifixion scene as
a dramatic episode in which she presents a Jesus different from the Gospels' sacrificial Lamb of God. Although
Jesus, in Proba's rendition, had already told the disciples at the Last Supper, "For the sake of many/ Shall one
life be given"[52] (a line we might imagine portended his
willing sacrifice), his behavior on the cross speaks
otherwise. Jesus does not go meekly to his death in the
Cento. He seizes the occasion to lash out at his persecutors with these words: "What makes you tie/ These
bonds? Has overweening racial pride possessed you?/ Some
day, for wrongs committed, you will pay/ With punishment

unlike this one to me."[53] There is no incentive in any
Gospel for Proba to fabricate such a speech. What would
inspire her to place such words on Jesus' lips?

One characteristic of the classical hero is that he
does not permit his honor or his person to be violated
without reprisal. Whatever the risk, wrath is a heroic
prerogative. Although *pius* Aeneas appears less bellicose
and more tender of heart than Homer's heroes, even he is
moved to vengeful rage on several occasions, the most
notable of which occur in Book 10, after Pallas' death,
and at the end of the epic. When he spots on Turnus the
war belt Turnus had stripped from the slain youth Pallas,
Aeneas flies into a rage.[54] Despite Turnus' plea for
mercy with regard to his father's grief, an appeal we
might have thought would sway his opponent,[55] Aeneas,
aflame with wrath, sinks his sword into Turnus' chest.[56]
That is the blunt conclusion of Vergil's epic. There is
no note of forgiveness, only one of revenge. Although
Aeneas' deed has been, if not excused, at least explained
on the grounds of political expediency,[57] it assuredly is
not in accord with the gospel of "turn the other cheek."
And in Proba's poem, we posit, Jesus' condemnation of his
persecutors from the cross is more in keeping with
Aeneas' vengeful action than it is with the Christian
preaching of love for enemies. This scene, when taken
in conjunction with two others--that of Jesus' temptation, in which he angrily addresses the tempter-snake as
perfide and *periture*,[58] and that of the cleansing of the
Temple, in which, as in the New Testament, he vents his
rage at the moneychangers[59] has led Ilona Opelt to conclude, "Proba's Christus ist kein liebender, sondern
ein zürnender Gott."[60]

A third way in which Proba invites the reader to
compare Jesus with Vergil's hero lies in her

appropriation of lines describing the mission of Aeneas
and his Roman descendants to depict the divine task assigned Jesus and, more explicitly, to represent him as
the embodiment of *pietas*. The glories that Vergil saw
coming to fruition in the Augustan Empire, Proba trans-
fers to the Kingdom of God. No educated contemporary
could have missed her reassignment of some of the
Aeneid's most famous lines. Jesus is called "the
founder of/ A godly race" (*divinae stirpis origo*), words
originally describing Vergil's hero.[61] Jesus is the man
"whose might would take possession of the world," a line
adapted from the prophecy to Latinus that he will acquire
a foreign son-in-law (namely, Aeneas) whose descendants
will rule the earth.[62] Just as Aeneas learns in his
visit to the underworld that the second king of the
Romans will be "sent for dominion" (*missus in imperium*),
so does God assign this task to Jesus in Proba's poem.[63]
At Jesus' baptism, God instructs him in the very words
Vergil used to foretell the future Roman glory of which
Aeneas would be the originator:

> Listen, my Son,
> I bear you witness: in whatever place
> The rising and setting sun surveys the sea,
> Either side, from East to West--happy
> At your offerings made complete, you shall
> Behold all regions turned and rûled
> Beneath your feet. Govern your subjects with
> Authority....[64]

Here Proba has skillfully transferred the divinely ordained mission of Aeneas and the Roman State to Jesus'
establishment of the Kingdom of God.

If Jesus in his fulfillment of that mission recalls
Aeneas but goes beyond him, he presents a stark contrast
with Adam. Although it is to Adam that Proba has God

announce, "dominion without end have I bestowed" (the
famous line from the *Aeneid* predicting Rome's illustrious
future),[65] she like other Christians believed that Adam
had failed miserably in carrying out his divinely-
appointed task. From the time of Paul, Christians had
compared the first man Adam, "the man of dust," with
whom sin and death had entered the world, to "the last
Adam," Jesus, who overcame both.[66] Proba adds a new
dimension to this comparison by shaping its central feature as the clash between the *impius* and the *pius* man.
Although Adam and Eve were created with the possibility
of enjoying "dominion without end," as a result of the
Fall they became *profani* and were cast out from their
paradisaical home.[67]

Jesus, by contrast, both teaches *pietas* and embodies
it. He challenges his listeners to "pursue the better,"[68] to make themselves "worthy of God,"[69] to respect
the ties of kin and friendship.[70] He also provides the
decisive image of *pietas* from the time of his birth--
when, in Proba's words, *fides* was made plain[71]--to that
of his resurrection, when he informs the disciples that
pietas "has fought the rugged journey through and won."[72]
That Proba considers *pietas* the foundation of Christianity is also evident in the closing lines of the
Cento, as she entreats her *dulcis coniunx* to join her in
winning merit through *pietas*, and prays that their descendants may "keep the Faith"[73] that she and Adelphius
hold dear. Proba's stress on *pietas* as the cornerstone
of the Christian life, embodied in its founder, cannot
but call to the minds of her audience the Virgilian hero
for whom *pius* was the distinctive epithet.[74] It also
provides a sharp retort to pagans like Julian who
habitually accused the Christians of *dussebeia,
atheotēta, asebeia.*[75]

Proba's Jesus, we conclude, undoubtedly displays
heroic traits. Other commentators have noted how difficult it was for later Christian poets to depict the
warrior hero as a Christian.[76] Proba's task was different: to imbue the Christ with heroic virtues. In so
doing, she diverged from the Gospel traditions, but gave
to her readers a portrait of a divine man who would have
commended Aeneas' *pietas*. Hence we have in Proba's *Cento*
not the "christianization of the hero," but the "heroiza-
tion of the Christ."

NOTES

[1]For Julian's decree, see *Epist.* 36 (42 Hertlein).
A.G. Amatucci, *Storia della letteratura latina* (Bari
1929) 147, thinks that Proba composed her cento in response to the decree. See also Caterina Cariddi, *Il
centone di Proba Petronia* (Naples 1971) 18. While scholars have hesitated to assign Proba's cento a precise
date, most favor one around 360 A.D., within a range of
354-370. See Filippo Ermini, *Il centone di Proba e la
poesia centonaria latina* (Rome 1909) 13 (about 360 A.D.);
58 (between 360-370); Maria Cacioli, "Adattamenti semantici e sintattici nel centone virgiliano di Proba," *SIFC*
41, n.s. 1 (1969) 196-97 (after 353); Mario Bonario,
"Appunti per la storia della tradizione virgiliana nel
IV Secolo," in *Vergiliana: Recherches sur Virgile*, ed.
N. Bardon and R. Verdière (Leiden 1971) 39 (between 353-
366). R.A. Markus, "Paganism, Christianity and the Latin
Classics in the Fourth Century," *Latin Literature in the
Fourth Century*, ed. J.W. Binns (London and Boston 1974)
3, argues for a date in the 350s.

[2]Carolus Schenkl, ed., *Poetae Christianae Minores.
Corpus Scriptorum Ecclesiasticorum Latinorum* 16 (Vindo-
bonae 1888). For a translation of, and commentary on,
Proba's *Cento*, see Elizabeth A. Clark and Diane F. Hatch,
*The Golden Bough, the Oaken Cross: the Virgilian Cento
of Faltonia Betitia Proba*. American Academy of Religion
Texts and Translations 5 (Chico, California 1981).
The *Cento* was composed after an earlier poem, the subject
of which (the rebellion of Magnentius) dates it to 353
A.D. or later.

[3]Commodian's place as the earliest Christian poet
writing in Latin has been challenged: see Pierre
Courcelle, "Commodien et les invasions du Ve siècle"
REL 24 (1946) 239-46, and Jean-Paul Brisson, *Autonomisme
et Christianisme dans l'Afrique Romaine* (Paris 1958)
390-91. The debate continues; for further opinions concerning the problem, see Berthold Altaner and Alfred
Stuiber, *Patrologie: Leben, Schriften und Lehre der
Kirchenväter*, 8th ed. (Freiburg, Basel, and Vienna 1978)

182. Juvencus, writing ca. 330 A.D., therefore stands
as the first Christian Latin poet. A critical edition
of his *Evangeliorum Libri* can be found in CSEL 24.

[4]Cyprian of Gaul (CSEL 23); Avitus (*Monumenta Ger-
maniae Historica, Auctores Antiquissimi*, 6.2); Marius
Victor (CSEL 16); Hilary of Arles (CSEL 23); Dracontius
(MGH 14); Sedulius (CSEL 10); see also Stanislas Gamber,
*Le livre de la 'Genese' dans la poésie latine au Vme
siècle* (Paris 1899) chap. 1. Milton's *Paradise Lost*
deservedly remains the most famous example of a poem
concerned with the Creation and Fall.

[5]We know very little about Proba. From Isidore of
Seville, *De viris illustribus* 22 (18) (PL 83, 1093) and
De orig. 1.39.26 (PL 82, 121); from a note on a medieval
codex (see B. de Montfaucon, *Diarium Italicum* [Paris
1702] 36), and the prosopography of her male relatives
(see A.H.M. Jones, J.R. Martindale and J. Morris, *The
Prosopography of the Later Roman Empire*, vol. 1: A.D.
260-395 [Cambridge 1971] 1144) we learn that Proba was a
member of the illustrious Petronii who married Clodius
Celsinus Adelphius, prefect of Rome in 351. They had
two sons, Clodius Hermogenianus Olybrius and Faltonius
Probus Alypius, both of whom had distinguished careers
and served as prefects of Rome. Also see Clark and
Hatch (above, note 2), chaps. 1-2.

[6]Ermini (above, note 1) 23-24. Tertullian, writing
about 200 A.D., also mentions the Homeric centos (*On the
Prescription of Heretics* 39.5). For an Homeric cento
ascribed to Valentinus, found in Irenaeus' *Against
Heresies*, see Robert L. Wilken, "The Homeric Cento in
Irenaeus' *Adversus Haeresus* I, 9, 4," VChr 21 (1967) 25-
33. For possible Pythagorean influence on Valentinus'
cento, see Jérome Carcopino, *De Pythagore aux Apôtres*
(Paris 1956) 189-202.

[7]Ermini (above, note 1) 23.

[8]Narcissus, Europa, Procne and Philomela are
examples, and Hosidius Geta's *Medea* is one of the more
notable centos of the era. See the Latin text and English
translation in Joseph J. Mooney, *Hosidius Geta's Tragedy
"Medea": A Vergilian Cento* (Birmingham 1919). See
Ermini (above, note 1) 42ff. for a list of topics for
centos.

[9]The texts of these Christian centos can be found in
Schenkl, CSEL 16, 609-27. There is also a Greek cento
composed out of the plays of Euripides on the passion of
Christ (*Christus patiens*); it has been attributed, probably falsely, to Gregory of Nazianzus. See André
Tuilier, *Grégoire de Nazianze: La Passion du Christ*.
SC 149 (Paris 1969), for a discussion of the authorship
(11-18), as well as for the text and translation of the
cento.

[10]Ausonius, *Cento nuptialis*, trans. H.G. Evelyn-White
(London 1919) (Loeb Classical Library, I, 373, 375).

[11]Domenico Comparetti, *Vergil in the Middle Ages*,
trans. E.F.M. Benecke (Hamden, Conn. 1966; reprint of
2d ed. 1931) 53.

[12]Supporters of Aeneas' quest for *humanitas* include,
among many others, Richard Heinze, *Virgils Epische
Technik* (Stuttgart 1976; reprint of 3d ed. 1915) 271-80;
George Howe, "The Development of the Character of Aeneas,"
CJ 26 (1930) 185; C.M. Bowra, "Aeneas and the Stoic
Ideal," G&R 3 (1933-34) 11, 14, 19; Viktor Pöschl, *The
Art of Vergil: Image and Symbol in the Aeneid*, trans.
Gerda Seligson (Ann Arbor 1962) especially 18, 53-58;
Brooks Otis, *Virgil: A Study in Civilized Poetry*
(Oxford 1964) 91, 222-23, 311, 348, 381-82; G. Karl
Galinsky, *Aeneas, Sicily and Rome* (Princeton 1969) chap.
1. For qualifications, see Galinsky; Gunnar Carlson,
"The Hero and Fate in Virgil's *Aeneid*," *Eranos* 43 (1945)
131-34; and Brian Morris, "Virgil and the Heroic Ideal,"
PVS 9 (1967-70) 32-33.

[13]See Michael C.J. Putnam, *The Poetry of the Aeneid:
Four Studies in Imaginative Unity and Design* (Cambridge
1965) 157, 192-93; also John R. Wilson, "Action and
Emotion in Aeneas," G&R 2d ser. 16 (1969) 72-75. A
strong tradition prevailed that, far from being a hero,
Aeneas was in fact a villain, a traitor to Troy. For a
summary of the evidence, see Galinsky (above, note 12);
Meyer Reinhold, "The Unhero Aeneas," C&M 27 (1966) 195-
207; for the church fathers' criticisms, see Tertullian,
To the Heathen 2.9; Lactantius, *Div. Inst.* 5.10; Orosius,
History Against the Pagans 1.18.1.

[14]*Aen.* 1.279.

[15]*Aen.* 1.588-89.

[16]See such works as Jan DeVries, *Heroic Song and Heroic Legend*, trans. B.J. Timmer (London 1963) 211-16; Lord Raglan, *The Hero: A Study in Tradition, Myth and Drama* (New York 1937) 179-90; Ludwig Bieler, *Theios anēr: Das Bild des "Göttlichen Menschen" in Spätanike und Frühchristentum*; reprint of 1935-36 ed. (Darmstadt 1967) 1.24-134; C.M. Bowra, "The Hero," in *The Hero in Literature*, ed. Victor Brombert (Greenwich, Conn. 1969) 22-26.

[17]On Jesus' virginal mother and divine father, see *Cento* 341, 345, 349; 23 lines of the *Cento* are devoted to the story of Herod's massacre (357-79); 27 lines recount Jesus' overcoming of the tempter-serpent (429-55). We regret that space does not permit us to quote from the Latin text at length, although we shall do so where feasible.

[18]*Cento* 3-8. See B. de Montfaucon (above, note 5) 36.

[19]*Cento* 48: *semper equos atque arma virum pugnasque canebam*; see also *Aen.* 9.777.

[20]*Cento* 14: *nec libet Aonio de vertice ducere Musas*.

[21]*Cento* 9-12.

[22]*Cento* 22: *hinc canere incipiam. praesens, deus, erige mentem*.

[23]*Cento* 20-22.

[24]*Cento* 1-23.

[25]Another example is furnished by Paulinus of Nola, *Carmen* 15.26f. See the discussions in Charles Witke, *Numen Litterarum: The Old and the New in Latin Poetry from Constantine to Gregory the Great* (Leiden 1971) chap. 2; Christine Mohrmann, "La langue et le style de la poésie chrétienne," REL 25 (1947) 280-97; A. Hudson-Williams, "Virgil and the Christian Latin Poets," PVS 6 (1966-67) 11-21.

[26]*Cento* 518: *atque huic responsum paucis ita reddidit heros*.

[27]*Cento* 664: *vicit iter durum pietas et vivida virtus.*

[28]See note 1 above.

[29]The authors wish to thank Professor Barry Baldwin, University of Calgary, for calling their attention to this point.

[30]*Contra Galilaeos* 335 B.

[31]*Caesares* 336 A-B.

[32]*Contra Galilaeos* frag. 4.

[33]Ibid., frag. 6.

[34]Ibid., 205 E.

[35]Ibid., 191 E.

[36]Ibid., 213 B.

[37]Ibid., 229 D.

[38]We know nothing of her reading, although it is usually assumed that aristocratic women of this era could read Greek. See Jerome, *Epist.* 107.9 and 12. See also Elizabeth A. Clark, *Jerome, Chrysostom, and Friends: Essays and Translations* (New York 1979) 74-75, and Henri Marrou, *A History of Education in Antiquity,* trans. George Lamb (New York 1964) 202, 302, 369.

[39]See note 1 above on the dating of the *Cento.*

[40]*Cento* 384-86. The lines are taken from *Aen.* 7.812-14, where the female warrior Camilla is described before her admirers.

[41]*Cento* 387: *qui vultus vocisque sonus uel gressus eunti est!*

[42]*Cento* 572-73:
> *horrescit visu subito insonuitque flagello significatque manu et magno simul intonat ore.*

[43]*Cento* 461-62:
...*medium nam plurima turba
hunc habet atque umeris extantem suspicit
altis.*

[44]*Cento* 459-61.

[45]*Cento* 544: *qualia multa mari nautae patiuntur in
alto.*

[46]*Cento* 540-44.

[47]*Cento* 547-48:
*par leuibus ventis et fulminis ocior alis
prona petit maria et pelago decurrit aperto.*

[48]*Cento* 550.

[49]*Cento* 556: *necdum fluctu latera ardua tinxit.*

[50]*Aen.* 3.655.

[51]*Cento* 559; *Aen.* 6.413.

[52]*Cento* 598: *unum pro multis dabitur caput.*

[53]*Cento* 621-23.

[54]*Aen.* 12.940-47.

[55]*Aen.* 12.932-35.

[56]*Aen.* 12.946-51.

[57]See, for example, Mario A. Di Cesare, *The Altar
and the City: A Reading of Vergil's Aeneid* (New York
1974) 237-38.

[58]*Cento* 448, 451:
*dissimulare etiam sperasti, perfide serpens?
quo periture ruis maioraque viribus audes?*

[59]In words used by Dido to express her outrage at
Aeneas' impending desertion of her in *Aen.* 4.595; see
Cento 574-75.

[60]Ilona Opelt, "Der zürnende Christus im Cento der
Proba," JbAC 7 (1954) 114.

[61]*Cento* 347; *Aen.* 12.166.

[62]*Cento* 345; *Aen,* 7,258.

[63]*Cento* 348; *Aen,* 6.812.

[64]*Cento* 406-09; *Aen.* 7,97, 100-01; 6,851.

[65]*Cento* 143; *Aen.* 1,279.

[66]Romans 5:12-21; I Corinthians 15:21-22, 45-49.

[67]*Cento* 213: *continuo invadit: 'procul, o procul este profani.'*

[68]*Cento* 471: *communemque vocate deum. meliora sequamur....*

[69]*Cento* 522-23:
      *disce, puer, contemnere opes et te quoque dignum
      finge deo, et quae sit poteris cognoscere virtus.*

[70]*Cento* 524-25:
      *da dextram misero et fratrem ne desere frater,
      si iungi hospitio properat, coniuge volentem.*

[71]*Cento* 354: *tum vero manifesta fides....*

[72]*Cento* 664: *vicit iter durum pietas et vivida virtus.*

[73]*Cento* 693-94:
      *...et si pietate meremur,
      hac casti maneant in religione nepotes.*

[74]If *pietas* is, as R.D. Williams defines it, "an attitude of responsibility towards gods and men, an attitude which may involve the subjugation of individual passions...to the demands of duty" (*The Aeneid of Virgil, Books I-VI* [London 1972] xxiii), it is not a quality shared by Homer's heroes but is a distinctively Virgilian qualification.

[75]See, for example, Julian, *Fragmentum Epistolae* 305 C, 305 D; *Misopogon* 357 D, 363 A; *Epist.* 41.436 B,

438 C; *Epist.* 47.435 B. For recent treatments of
Julian's anti-Christian sentiments, see William G. Malley,
*Hellenism and Christianity: The Conflict Between Hellenic
and Christian Wisdom in the Contra Galilaeos of Julian
the Apostate and the Contra Julianum of St. Cyril of
Alexandria.* Analecta Gregoriana 210 (Rome 1978); and
G.W. Bowersack, *Julian the Apostate* (London 1978) 83-84;
see also Johannes Geffcken, *The Last Days of Greco-Roman
Paganism,* trans. Sabine MacCormack; trans. of the 1929
German rev. ed. (Amsterdam, New York and Oxford 1978)
136-58.

[76] See, for example, Dennis M. Kratz, "Ruodlieb:
Christian Epic Hero," CF 27 (1973) 252-66.

PART II

ASCETICISM AND SEXUALITY

ASCETIC RENUNCIATION AND FEMININE ADVANCEMENT: A PARADOX OF LATE ANCIENT CHRISTIANITY

Anglican Theological Review
63 (1981), 240-257

"Many that are first will be last, and the last first"[1]: Jesus' words transvaluating classical notions of status were interpreted anew by the fourth and fifth-century partisans of Christian asceticism in the West. Describing the ascetic renunciation of Latin aristocrats, they claimed that those who had been first in "the world" were also first in the ranks of ascetic heroism. Although both sexes vied in the contest for exaltation-by-humiliation, women who converted from the secular to the "angelic" life won especially extravagant praise.[2] They were more honored as ascetics than they were as the mothers, wives, and daughters of the senatorial aristocracy. Not only did bishops and monks throng to meet them;[3] empresses, on their golden thrones,[4] begged them to converse. Nobles gathered dirt from their feet and clothing, "...crimson silk and gilded trappings playing servant to old black rags."[5] Jerome's congratulation to the adolescent heiress Demetrias on her vow of virginity illustrates the point precisely. He writes:

> All the African churches leaped in
> exultation....All the islands between

Africa and Italy were full of the
news....Then Italy shed her mourning
garments and the half-ruined walls of
Rome regained in part their former
splendor....The news spread to Eastern
shores and the cities of the interior
discerned this triumph of Christian
glory....Had you married, one province
would have known you; as Christ's virgin, you have been heard of by the
whole world.[6]

What are we to make of such accolades? They were
undoubtedly designed not merely to exalt their subjects
to an even loftier status than they had formerly enjoyed; they were also weapons of warfare against the
prevalent opinion that monasticism in and of itself degraded aristocrats of either sex. Jerome himself
reports how "strange, ignominious, and debasing" the
ascetic life was considered by many Roman nobles.[7]
Ambrose repeats the sentiments of "the foremost citizens"
at the news of Paulinus' renunciation: "It is unbear-
able that a man of such a family, such a lineage, such
talent, endowed with such great eloquence, should re-
tire from the senate and break the succession of a
noble house."[8] Monks were thought to resemble beasts:
Eunapius compares them to swine; Libanius, to ele-
phants.[9] Rutilius Namatianus complains of the "light-
fleeing" monks whose teachings metamorphose young men
from good families.[10] And Salvian of Marseilles expresses shock that a reputedly Christian population believes that an ascetic profession is socially debasing,
that "when a man changes his garb, he immediately
changes his rank."[11]

It was not merely the shabby dress, unkempt hair,[12] or unpleasant odor[13] of those who had renounced the world that constituted the offense: there were the larger social problems of money diverted from family inheritances, and of eligible women refusing to serve as the social cement binding noble families in marriage. Cries that once-married people who adopted ascetic practices were "robbing their children" could be expected, as could the disappointment of parents whose daughters declared for perpetual celibacy, or the schemes of brothers to prevent alienation of family property.[14] When even Christian emperors enacted legislation to prevent fortunes from leaving the upper classes,[15] we know that the problem was deemed significant. In the face of such opposition, we can better understand the motivation behind Jerome's plea that, upon a declaration of asceticism, Christians should divest themselves totally and immediately of their goods,[16] lest they fall into the sin of Ananias and Sapphira, holding back that which had been promised to the Lord:[17] such injunctions bespeak an anxiety that the ties of the world might prove too binding for the prospective ascetic's determination to follow Jesus' counsel of perfection, "Sell all and give to the poor."[18]

Two lines of retort were developed by churchmen who suspected that the complaining kin of such ascetics were, in Jerome's phrase, thinking less of the latters' souls and more of their own bellies.[19] First, they advocated practical measures: ascetics must divorce themselves from family relationships. Although their argument appealed to Jesus' words, "Who are my mother and my brothers?"[20], it was not primarily motivated by a desire to follow the indigent son of a Galilean

carpenter whose social status bore little resemblance
to that of the Anicii and the Ceionii. Nor was the
cutting off of affectional relations in and for itself
the central issue, although *apatheia* was much praised
in some quarters.[21] Rather, when a wide variety of
Western and Eastern fathers warn that the pull of kin
is in truth prompted by the devil and thus to be avoided, the concern most directly underlying their fear is
that families tend to involve people in problems of the
material world, property, inheritances.[22] As Basil of
Caesarea put it, association with one's "fleshly relatives" might make a would-be ascetic's heart "return to
Egypt."[23] And in the case of those lacking legal
authority to disregard their relatives' commands,[24] the
hand of God was thought to intervene, bringing ill-fate
to those who so blasphemously attempted to dampen the
young ascetic's enthusiasm. Eustochium's aunt
Praetextata, who misguidedly tried to alter her niece's
somber garb and simple coiffure, speedily expired after
an angel threatened her in a dream.[25] Likewise, Ambrose
implies that providence arranged the death of a recal-
citrant father who hindered his daughter's adoption of
the ascetic life.[26] By such examples, the literary ad-
vocates of asceticism encouraged their protégées to cut
themselves off from their kin--although the goal was
nearly impossible of literal fulfillment by the aristocratic ascetics of late Latin antiquity, since so many
of them were related to each other.[27]

     Christian writers also argued a second line, of
considerable rhetorical appeal, against those who feared that the ascetic life was degrading for one of elevated station: far from representing a decline in
status, they claimed, the monastic life was truly "en-
nobling." No matter how long their lineages or how

bulging their coffers, the adoption of monastic practices made prospective ascetics even more "aristocratic."
Thus Pammachius, "the glory of the Furian line," who
put on his monkish garb while still a Roman senator, was
called by Jerome the "noblest" of monks, "great among
the great, leader among leaders," "the first of monks in
the first city of the world." By his renunciation he had
become "more wealthy and famous than before."[28] Marcella, descended from consuls, had found "true nobility" as
a chaste Christian widow.[29] Both Paula and Demetrias,
of noble families, became "nobler still" by their holiness.[30] As for Melania the Elder, we learn from Paulinus
of Nola that she was elevated above her consular grand-
fathers by "despising mere fleshly nobility."[31] The
spiritual ennoblement of the wealthy who renounced their
riches for Christ provided in addition an edifying contrast to the shocking behavior of the lowly who used the
church to better their social position.[32] Those who had
been first in the world could rest assured that they were
still first in the Kingdom.

Nor were such words regarding the worldly nobility of
these ascetics empty: the aristocratic status of early
Western ascetics is well-known and was reflected in the
style of monasticism they developed.[33] Although early
Eastern monasticism boasted a few practitioners stemming
from wealth or noble birth,[34] most desert fathers were of
humble background, if we judge correctly from the evidence. This conclusion is derived not only from overt
comments about the menial occupations in which they or
or their parents had engaged,[35] but also from the fact
that some of them could not read at all, or could not
read Greek and Latin,[36] a sure sign of their lack of culture and hence class. By contrast, the initiators of
Western asceticism—Jerome, Paulinus, Ambrose, Sulpicius

Severus, John Cassian, Paula, Marcella, the two
Melanias--were of higher social status, and their rank
colored the type of monasticism they developed.

A careful look at the sources pertaining to these
aristocratic ascetics reveals striking similarities in
the monastic styles of the men and the women: their man-
ners of life were indeed far more alike than they would
have been had these men and women not made their renunciations. In particular, the freedom the women enjoyed
and the assertive behavior permitted them would have been
curtailed had they been transformed into Christian
matrons: the church upheld traditional ideas regarding
married women.[37] In many respects, the patristic asser-
tion that ascetic women were "virile" is based on an
accurate representation of the concrete conditions of
their lives, conditions that resembled the men's.[38] To
document that claim, an appeal is made to two important
features of the asceticism practiced by Latin male aristocrats that are also found in the habits of their female
counterparts.

First, the ascetic style cultivated by these men was
"house monasticism." Like Roman nobles of old, they were
urbanites who retreated to their country estates when
city affairs proved harassing.[39] Augustine saw this type
of monasticism practiced in Milan and Rome during his
Italian sojourn, and Possidius implies that Augustine
himself lived in this manner when he first returned to
Thagaste.[40] The desert father Serapion was also introduced to ascetics in Rome who had retired into a life of
seclusion amid the bustle of the city.[41] Paulinus lived
on property he owned after his decision for the ascetic
life,[42] as did Sulpicius Severus, to whom Paulinus wrote,
"You are a host in your house so that your home may be a
hospice."[43] Jerome's correspondent Rusticus also lived

at home, and his friend Pammachius, who continued to
carry out his senatorial duties after his ascetic decision, retained his Roman holdings.[44] Ownership of property was not, then, absolutely condemned, if one adopted
the correct attitude toward it, namely, not allowing oneself to be mentally captive to wealth.[45]

   We have before us a genteel form of asceticism. No
long-haired, wandering eccentrics, the subject of mockery
among Western authors,[46] these aristocrats practiced
their renunciation in polite retreat, exchanging the
letters that were the hallmark of cultivated society,[47]
making simple meals palatable to their senatorial
tastes,[48] writing verse,[49] worrying about the fate of
vintage wines harvested from their estates abroad.[50]
Their manner of life as ascetics differed not totally
from that of their secular days.

   A second notable feature of the men's monastic practice was the absence of physical labor. Paulinus, Pammachius, Sulpicius Severus, and others, had never labored
in "the world"; in the monastic life--despite their
rhetorical tributes to the beauty of work[51]--their daily
routine consisted mainly of worship, study, writing, and
contemplation. Melania the Younger's husband Pinian, who
joined her in ascetic renunciation, devoted his time to
"reading, gardening, and solemn conferences."[52] John
Cassian, founder of monasteries at Marseilles, regretted
that his monks would not accept the pattern of labor set
by the desert fathers,[53] and Martin of Tours expressly
favored contemplation over work for his monks.[54] Indeed,
a study of the early monastic *Rules* for men demonstrates
how those from wealthy backgrounds were gradually included in the category of "sick and infirm" so that lighter
activities (Augustine recommends administrative duties)
could be assigned them in accordance with the words of

Acts 4:35, that "distribution was made to each as any had
need."[55] As Augustine warned in his treatise *On the Work
of Monks*, in which he excuses those ascetics raised in
luxury from the more gruelling sorts of labor, "...in
this Christian campaign for piety, the rich are not
humiliated so that the poor may be raised to *superbia*."[56]
The absence of physical labor in their lives, so different from the ideal of the earlier Eastern ascetics,
accords well with the genteel renunciation they had made.

The ascetic pattern of the women is similar to the
men's in both respects. First, the setting of "familial
monasticism" was even more prominent among these ascetic
females than among the males; perhaps we simply have more
information about them. Marcella lived at home in ascetic renunciation, as did Paula before her departure for
the East, Melania the Younger both in Italy and in Jerusalem, and the Roman widow Lea.[57] Early in her ascetic
career, Ambrose's sister Marcellina lived in the family
home at Rome.[58] Sulpicius Severus praises a virgin who
refused to see Martin of Tours when he passed by "the
small piece of property on which she had confined herself
in modesty for several years."[59] In 393, a church
council at Hippo recommended "home asceticism" for virgins *if* they were under the careful eyes of their
parents.[60]

The qualification of the council's recommendation--
"if"--shows that the appropriateness of house asceticism
for women had been called into question; certain difficulties unique to women could arise when a woman lived by
herself or with her family. Indeed, the subject meets
with considerable ambivalence on the part of ascetic
enthusiasts like Jerome. Early in his writing career,
Jerome warned Eustochium against virgins who had their
own property and were "honored by all": are such women

even virgins, he asks suspiciously?[61] Although two years
later, in 386, he urged Marcella to abandon Rome for
Palestine (like Abraham she should flee country and kin),
he tempers his ardor for her leaving: after all, the
Kingdom is within and holy men live everywhere.[62] And by
405, he is advising a virgin in Gaul to stay at home with
her mother, not to leave the family household: if she
lived in her mother's womb, why not in her house?[63]

No doubt Jerome's belated encouragement of familial
asceticism resulted from his years of experience with the
problems, indeed, the outright dangers, of other ascetic
life-styles for women. Of course, it would be ideal if
all ascetic women would live under the discipline of
Paula's convent, but since he could not coerce every
ascetically-inclined woman into the cenobium (although
waywardness might occur there, too),[64] the second best
option was for her to stay at home.

Certainly living at home was vastly preferable, in
the church's judgment, to the notorious and prevalent
practice of "spiritual marriage" in which a man and a
woman, both dedicated to chastity, shared the same
house.[65] According to our sources, the woman, when criticized, often argued that she needed the man as protector and household manager.[66] But, our ecclesiastical
authors retort, in addition to the scandal syneisaktism
provoked, a major disadvantage of the arrangement was
that the woman sacrificed her freedom.[67] As Jerome put
it, the man rules the household, allots the servants
their tasks, and controls the expenditures;[68] women are
just as much "enslaved" by the arrangement as they are
within marriage itself.[69] The point is an important one:
if the ascetic life is designed to bring freedom to
women, "spiritual marriage" failed to achieve that goal.

But could women have freedom even within their
familial households? The attainment of ascetic freedom
might prove difficult, given the family obligations of
these ancient aristocrats. Thus while Marcella's mother,
Albina, lived with her, Marcella encountered maternal
resistance to her adoption of ascetic renunciation, and
this despite Jerome's honied words concerning Albina's
spirituality. Albina pressured Marcella to marry a
wealthy old suitor; Marcella refused. And to Marcella's
disappointment, her mother gave part of their fortune to
her brother's family, already rich, rather than to the
poor or the church.[70] Even in her own home, she was not
entirely her own mistress.

Husbands could pose greater problems than mothers for
female ascetic devotees who wished to remain at home:[71]
take the case of Melania the Younger. Married in her
early teens, Melania for years attempted to convince her
husband Pinian to adopt the ascetic life she so much desired (he was willing to do so only if she would first
bear him two children to inherit their enormous property).[72] So desperate did Melania become that she attempted to flee the marriage.[73] Recognizing that her husband
was still in his prime[74] (as Augustine wrote of Pinian,
he had "a strong natural capacity for enjoying this
world"),[75] Melania shrewdly wooed him to the ascetic
cause by stages.[76] Eventually he consented to her request, and she surged valiantly ahead with her ascetic
resolution.

These stories illustrate the difficulties of practicing "house asceticism" when you were not your own
master. Once husbands or parents relinquished their
power, the way was opened for women to live in the ascetic style they pleased.[77] Given such problems, Ambrose's
words to a hypothetical Christian maiden ring true: "If

you conquer your home, you can conquer the world."[78]
Male ascetics, by contrast, encountered fewer impedi-
ments: once they were of age, the only relatives who
might block their ascetic determination were their wives,
and the wives of the males we have considered either died
before their husbands made their renunciations,[79] or
accompanied their spouses into ascetic retreat.[80]

If the women's style of "home monasticism" resembled
the men's, so did their pattern of activity, although our
sources emphasize more prominently the menial chores the
women undertook, from scrubbing vegetables to nursing
the sick,[81] than they do for the men. Although spinning
and weaving are recommended to female ascetics,[82] it is
clear that such work did not support the ascetic aristocrats: the funds for their own or their community's
upkeep came from inherited wealth. Augustine and Ambrose
inform us that they knew of nuns who supported themselves
by their own labor,[83] but the aristocrats we are investi-
gating did not so toil. Both in the monastery and in
"home asceticism," servants were the norm for the women,
as for the men.[84]

The daily activity of the women revolved around worship. The nuns in Melania the Younger's convent in
Jerusalem spent much of their time in reciting the daily
and nightly offices.[85] In Paula's monastery, the women
participated in worship six times a day, learned Scripture, and made garments.[86] Some, like Melania the
Younger, studied religious literature, and made copies
of Scripture.[87] Her grandmother, Melania the Elder,
also engaged in higher theological study: we are told
she devoured the writings of the Eastern fathers, and was
interested in ascetic literature as well.[88] The actual
labor demanded of these ascetic women, however, seems
little more than what they would have performed as

worldly matrons. The menial tasks they undertook were
designed as exercises in humility and were not prompted
by any necessity to earn a livelihood.[89] In this respect, too, their lives followed the pattern of their male
counterparts. It is not too much to say that they led
"manly" lives, despite the special problems they as women
encountered in achieving their ascetic goals.

The fact that these women lived in a fashion similar
to that of male monastics gave them freedom to pursue
activities that would not have been considered entirely
proper for Christian matrons in the world, activities
that were for the ascetic women not only permitted, but
sanctioned, by churchmen. Take the issue of traveling:
proper Christian wives did not wander about the world
unaccompanied by husbands or fathers, yet such "wandering" was acceptable for these ascetics when it was blessed with the name of pilgrimage[90] or when undertaken as
religious duty. Both Paula and Melania the Elder
traveled extensively throughout the East on the routes
that soon would be well-worn by Christian tourists.[91]
They were greeted along the way by the most notable monks
and bishops of their day,[92] who heaped honors on their
heads and presented them with tokens of esteem: several
sources report that Melania the Elder was the happy
recipient of Macarius the Alexandrian's sheepskin that a
hyena had brought to him in gratitude for his miraculous
cure of her blind cub.[93] As for Melania the Younger,
she journeyed throughout Italy, North Africa, Egypt, and
Palestine; after the deaths of her mother and husband,
she traveled to Constantinople, where she pressured her
still-pagan uncle Volusian into a deathbed conversion.[94]
Thus permission to travel, granted under the rubric of
pilgrimage and missionary effort, was one privilege that
these "manly" women received.

A second indication that they enjoyed greater freedom than their married Christian sisters lies in the
praise their instructional and intellectual efforts were
awarded. Palladius describes Melania the Elder as "most
erudite"; he claims she read the Greek church fathers'
writings seven or eight times over.[95] Her studiousness
bore fruit in her role as Christian counselor and
teacher. She is credited with rescuing that monastic
superstar, Evagrius Ponticus, from a relapse into worldly
life by her counsel and prayers.[96] In addition, she is
said to have convinced heretics who denied the Holy
Spirit of orthodox truth, and to have converted a man
named Apronianus to an ascetic form of Christianity.[97]

Melania the Younger followed her grandmother's steps.
We are told that she attempted to convert "Samaritans,
pagans, and heretics."[98] While in Constantinople, she
entered the debate on Nestorianism: the Latin text of
her *Life* says that she instructed illustrious women on
correct Christological doctrine;[99] the Greek version includes cultivated men in the ranks of those she enlightened.[100] While in the eastern capital, she is also said
to have "edified" the emperor Theodosius.[101]

As for Marcella in Rome, Jerome tells us that she
took a stand against Origenism and publicly refuted its
partisans, including priests and monks.[102] Marcella assumed the role of Scripture expert in Rome after Jerome
left for the East, solving many dilemmas for the male
clerics who sought her out--although Jerome remarks that
she made it seem as if her answers came from himself or
some other male, so that she did not violate the Biblical
injunction against women teaching.[103] Once again, activities our writers would not have countenanced, had these
women been Christians in secular life, are not only tolerated, but are praised when performed for the advancement

of the Christian religion. Thus the women's ascetic professions allowed them new freedoms, freedoms Christian
authors customarily granted only to men.

But their freedom stemmed not solely from their
asceticism: the money and status they brought with them
from their old lives gave them a certain power as well.
Supposedly they had divested themselves of property and
riches, yet even after their "divestments" they do not
lack funds to build monasteries and give financial assistance to fellow ascetics.[104] When their own supplies of
money dwindle, they know where to find further resources
among their worldly acquaintances and relations.[105] Nor
were the women averse to having their generosity recognized, despite the Biblical injunction that we should not
let our left hand know what our right is doing.[106] A
revealing story about Melania the Elder illustrates this
point: when Melania contributed three hundred pounds of
gold to Pambo, one of the desert fathers, he took no
notice of the amount, but simply instructed his steward
to distribute it to the poorer brothers. Melania, however, hungered for praise: didn't Pambo want to know how
much money was in the basket? His answer was calculated
to deflate her pride: since you offered it to God, not
to me, keep quiet![107]

Nor were these women loathe to remind others of their
aristocratic connections when the situation called for
drastic action. Again, we are instructed by a story
about Melania the Elder. When the consul of Palestine,
unaware of her background, was about to jail her for aiding some Egyptian holy men in exile at Diocaesarea, she
acquainted him with her impressive pedigree, letting him
know whose daughter she was, whose wife she had been.
She continued, "I have told you this plainly so that you
may avoid falling under legal charges unknowingly." The

judge, recognizing the *gaffe* that had been committed,
offered an appropriately obsequious apology and gave her
permission to mingle with the exiles as much as she
pleased. Palladius, who tells the story, thought her behavior appropriate: when you are dealing with insensi-
tive people, he writes, it is sometimes necessary to
pull rank.[108]

The correspondence of Augustine also provides us with
evidence that these aristocratic women were not uncon-
scious of their importance to the church, an importance
related directly to their wealth. Augustine's letters
125 and 126 tell of an imbroglio that he fell into with
the mother of Melania the Younger, Albina, who had joined
her daughter in ascetic renunciation. (The author of the
Life of Melania the Younger passes over the incident in
silence, perhaps for the obvious reason that it was discrediting to Melania's mother.) Albina, so highly
praised in the *Vita* as a saintly woman,[109] claimed that
the citizens of Hippo had clamored for her son-in-law
Pinian to be ordained as their priest just so they could
lay claim to his fortune--and she apparently did more
than hint that she suspected Augustine's motivation as
well.[110] Given the rudeness of the charge, Augustine's
reply is remarkably restrained: he will not rebuke her
or give way to invective; he simply wants to clear up
what he views as a misunderstanding.[111] Albina is mistaken about the motivation of the good people of Hippo
who had demanded Pinian's ordination: they loved Pinian
for his many virtues, not for his money.[112] Although
others might think Pinian had perjured himself in taking
an oath to regard Hippo as his home, Augustine is ready
to consider the vow fulfilled at least spiritually.[113]

Female behavior of the sort just described in the
cases of Melania and Albina accords poorly with the

"lowliness" to which these Christian women had voluntarily stooped. On the contrary, they appear to have
enjoyed the best of both worlds: their ascetic professions gave them certain freedoms similar to those granted
men, while their money and aristocratic connections permitted an assertiveness surprising to note among the meek
who will inherit the earth.[114] The earth was theirs before their ascetic renunciations, and they appear to have
sacrificed less of it than we might have expected in
their adoption of asceticism.

When we look at various features of these ascetics'
lives--that they practiced house asceticism, often in
cities; that they lived under no set rules; that they
had money at their disposal and decided, by themselves,
how to distribute it--we are struck with the similarities
between their monastic style and that of the monks Jerome
calls "Remnuoth," and Cassian and Benedict, the
"Sarabaites."[115] To Jerome, the Remnuoth are "very inferior" monks; they follow neither the anchorite nor the
cenobite pattern. They tend to live in cities. They
will not subordinate themselves to anyone, nor do they
follow a rule, "but do precisely what they choose," unlike the cenobites whose life is based on obedience.[116]
Both Jerome and Cassian concede with regret that this
type of monk is dominant in some districts.[117] For Cassian, the most despicable feature of the Sarabaites is
that they are under no rule; they do not submit themselves to the elders, but prefer to manage their own
affairs. Living in their own homes, pursuing the professions they had practiced before their ascetic decisions,
they remain free. Not under an abbot or elders, they
come and go as they please, wander where they will. Cassian admits that they do contribute some of their money
to the poor--but claims they sin even in their charity,

because they are filled with pride.[118] Benedict's version, probably adopted from Cassian's, adds that the
Sarabaites, dwelling in two's and three's, are "without
a shepherd and in their own sheepfolds."[119]

The lives of the aristocratic ascetics we are con-
sidering seem remarkably similar to those of the
Sarabaites.[120] Although the former did not work to earn
a living, as did the Sarabaites, they too were not cloistered and they determined their own ascetic styles. For
however much our ascetics fasted, however chaste they
remained, however generously they gave to the poor, they,
like the Sarabaites, were independent and beholden to no
authority, not to an ascetic master, a rule, or an abbot.
Given their harsh judgment on the Sarabaites, it is surprising that the churchmen who describe the pattern of
the nobility's ascetic renunciation find no fault with
it; especially surprising is their failure to criticize
the free mode of life practiced by the aristocratic
females in retreat. Could it be that the Sarabaites had
not provided such generous assistance to ascetic causes
as had Paula, Marcella, and the Melanias, and thus did
not enjoy the protection from attack that the women received?

Would a cenobitic regime tame these women? The evidence is mixed for the three who organized cenobia about
which we have information. Paula, we gather, remained
peacefully in her Bethlehem convent for the rest of her
day's, under Jerome's close scrutiny. His authoritative
presence may have been a decisive influence: Palladius
bluntly claims that Jerome stifled her development and
bent her to his own purposes.[121] She was, nonetheless,
the head of the convent she had had erected, and she
gathered prospective nuns to it:[122] she was her own
mistress in ascetic seclusion.

The two Melanias follow patterns different from
Paula's. Melania the Elder, although abbess of a convent
on the Mount of Olives whose construction she had
financed,[123] did not spend her latter days there in iso-
lation. When she was sixty, she returned to Italy to
direct the fortunes of her family: she feared for the
worldliness of her son, Valerius Publicola, and for the
possible failure of ascetic fervency in his daughter,
Melania the Younger.[124] She did not return to Palestine
for ten years, so long did it take her to be assured of
the younger Melania's dedication and to visit ascetic
friends, such as Paulinus of Nola and the monks of Egypt.
She died shortly after her return to the Holy Land in
410.[125]

Melania the Younger also established a convent in
Jerusalem, but unlike her grandmother and Paula, she refused to accept its headship, a fact that her biographer
attributes to her great humility. We learn, however,
that she undercut the abbess' authority by bringing
extra provisions to the nuns without the mother superior's knowledge.[126] Her "humility," in other words, did
not prevent her from subverting the discipline of the
abbess she had herself chosen. Having accepted her
worldly uncle's invitation to Constantinople, she mingled
there with royalty and nobles.[127] "Stability" was not
yet part of these women's ascetic commitment, as it was
soon to be for cloistered nuns.[128]

The prestigious backgrounds with which these women
entered life were never entirely blotted from consciousness, even in their ascetic renunciations. They paid for
the convents they established, they directed them, they
left them at will, they picked their successors.[129]
Whether in their homes or in the convents they had
founded, they were never entirely tamed. They had left

domesticity, not to be domesticated again. The ascetic
style they cultivated provided them with opportunities
that later nuns, under vows of strict renunciation of
property, obedience to authority, and stability, never
experienced; their money and class furnished them with a
strong sense of their own value.

In several respects, these women furnish us with instructive models. Although the monks and churchmen whose
writings constitute our evidence were eager to paint them
as paragons of docility, we from a perspective of fifteen
hundred years cherish more the courage, intelligence, and
ardor of these social iconoclasts. The fact that they
were exceptional should not preclude our understanding
them as harbingers of the future: in the process of
social liberation, one century's exception becomes the
commonplace of the next. Thus while the church fathers
thought the female ascetics "virile," we might rather
label their behavior "androgynous."

The church offered to these aristocratic women the
only possible career outside the domestic. In eagerly
grasping the opportunity proffered, they forged a daringly
novel style of life for themselves, yet retained a traditional function characteristic of the wealthy, the benefiting of society through their largesse. The asceticism
of these women, then, can be understood as resulting in
social utility as well as personal liberation. Indeed,
without their generous charity, they might not have been
accorded their lasting fame. As it was, they had left
the palaces of their earthly fathers to discover that the
mansions of their Heavenly One[130] offered no less freedom
and even greater acclaim.

NOTES

[1]Mark 10:31= Matthew 19:30= Luke 13:30 ("some").

[2]For examples of celibacy as the "angelic" life, see Peter Nagel, *Die Motivierung der Askese in der alte Kirche und der Ursprung des Mönchtums*, Texte und Untersuchungen zur Geschichte der altchristlichen Literatur 95 (Berlin: Akademie Verlag, 1966), chap. 3.

[3]Jerome, *Ep*. 108, 14 (CSEL 55, 324); *Vitae Melaniae* 36; 39; 51 (*Vie de Sainte Mélanie. Texte grec, introduction, traduction et notes*, ed. Denys Gorce, Sources Chrétiennes 90 [Paris: Les Editions du Cerf, 1962], pp. 194; 200, 202; 224, 226).

[4]Melania the Younger's welcome by Serena: *Vita Melaniae* 11; 12 (Gorce, *Vie*, pp. 146, 148).

[5]Paulinus, *Ep*. 29, 12 (CSEL 29, 259), (*Letters of Paulinus of Nola, II*, trans. P.G. Walsh, Ancient Christian Writers 36 [Westminster, Md.: Newman Press, 1967], p. 115).

[6]Jerome, *Ep*. 130, 6 (CSEL 56, 181-182), written in 414, after the sack of Rome.

[7]Jerome, *Ep*. 127, 5 (CSEL 56, 194). For an overview of the complaints, see L. Gougaud, "Les Critiques formulées contre les premiers moines d'occident," *Revue Mabillon* 24 (1934): 145-163.

[8]Ambrose, *Ep*. 27 (Maur. 58), 3 (CSEL 82, 181).

[9]Eunapius, *Vitae Sophistarum* 472; Libanius, *Oratio* 30, 8.

[10]Rutilius Claudius Namatianus, *De Reditu Suo* 1, 430; 519-526: monastic teaching has a worse effect on young men than Circe's magic, for the latter only transformed their bodies, while the former transforms their souls. For a discussion, see Pierre de Labriolle, "Rutilius

Claudius Namatianus et les moines," *Revue des Etudes Latines* 6 (1928): 30-41, and Gougaud, "Les Critiques," pp. 155-159.

[11] Salvian, *De Gubernatione Dei* 4, 7, 32-33 (CSEL 8, 74-75).

[12] Even churchmen complained: see Sulpicius Severus, *Vita S. Martini* 9 (CSEL 1, 119).

[13] Paulinus, *Ep.* 22, 2 (CSEL 29, 155).

[14] Palladius, *Historia Lausiaca* 66, 1 (*The Lausiac History of Palladius*, II, ed. Cuthbert Butler [Cambridge: Cambridge University Press, 1904], p. 162); Ambrose, *De Virginibus* I, 11, 65 (PL 16, 218); *Vita Melaniae* 12 (Gorce, *Vie*, pp. 150, 152). On the "economics" of ascetic renunciation of the wealthy, especially females, see Evelyne Patlagean, *Pauvreté économique et pauvreté sociale à Byzance 4ᵉ-7ᵉ siècles*, Civilisations et Sociétés 48 (Mouton: Ecole des Hautes Etudes en Science Sociales, 1977): 129-131.

[15] *Codex Theodosianus* VI, 2, 8; XVI, 2, 20; XVI, 2, 27, Jerome, *Ep.* 52, 6 (CSEL 54, 425) comments on such a law. Yet the *Vita Melaniae* 12 (Gorce, *Vie*, p. 152) claims that Honorius helped Melania and Pinian sell their possessions in various provinces. If it were Serena who arranged for his aid, the decree stood in danger of annulment when she was condemned by the senate. See note 24 below.

[16] Jerome, *Epp.* 53, 11 (CSEL 54, 464-465); 66, 8 (CSEL 54, 656-657). Jerome himself apparently did not renounce everything at once, for in 397 he writes of sending his brother to the West to sell some of their real estate (*Ep.* 66, 14 [CSEL 54, 665]). On Melania the Elder's lack of total renunciation, see Francis X. Murphy "Melania the Elder: A Biographical Note," *Traditio* 5 (1947): 65-66. A popular story of the time concerned a senator who upon making his declaration for asceticism kept back some of his money, not wanting to be supported by the labor of his hands. Supposedly Basil of Caesarea said to him, "You have spoiled the senator and not made a monk" (taking *syncletium* not as a proper name, but as *synklētikos*= senator); John Cassian, *De Institutis Coenobiorum* VII, 19 (CSEL 17, 143-144) and the *Verba Seniorum* 6, 10 (PL 73, 890). See Owen Chadwick, *John Cassian*, 2nd ed. (Cambridge: Cambridge University Press, 1968), p. 45.

[17]Jerome, *Ep.* 66, 8 (CSEL 54, 656); Acts 5:1-12.

[18]Luke 18:22.

[19]Jerome, *Ep.* 118, 6 (CSEL 55, 443).

[20]Mark 3:33= Matthew 12:48.

[21]A good example of this highly regarded virtue is provided in *Vita Melania* 44 (Gorce, *Vie*, p. 212). The concept was toned down in the West; see Derwas J. Chitty, *The Desert A City: An Introduction to the Study of Egyptian and Palestinian Monasticism under the Christian Empire* (Oxford: Basil Blackwell, 1966), p. 52. That Evagrius Ponticus, a leading champion of *apatheia*, was a close friend of Melania the Elder is useful to recall in this context (Palladius, *Historia Lausiaca* 38, 8-9 [Butler, *Lausiac History*, pp. 119-120]).

[22]Sulpicius Severus, *Dialogus* I, 22 (CSEL 1, 174); Palladius, *Historia Lausiaca* 6, 2 (Butler, *Lausiac History*, p. 22); 35, 8 (Butler, p. 103); Athanasius, *Vita S. Antonii* 5 (PG 26, 845-846); Paulinus, *Ep.* 29, 10 (CSEL 29, 257). On property problems: Palladius, *Historia Lausiaca* 6, 2 (Butler, *Lausiac History*, p. 22); Jerome, *Epp.* 118, 4 and 6 (CSEL 55, 439 and 443); 79, 4 (CSEL 55, 91); 66, 3 (CSEL 54, 649-650); 108, 5 (CSEL 55, 310); Paulinus, *Ep.* 29, 9-10 (CSEL 29, 255-257); 39, 2 (CSEL 29, 335-336); Basil of Caesarea, *Regulae Fusius Tractatae* 9 (PG 31, 941-944); *Sayings of the Fathers* V, 162 (tr. from Syriac by E.A. Wallis Budge, *The Book of Paradise Being the Histories and Sayings of the Monks and Ascetics of the Egyptian Desert by Palladius, Hieronymus and Others*, Lady Meux Manuscript 6 [London: n.p., 1904], I, p. 637). Philip Rousseau has suggested, regarding Eastern ascetics, that the issue was one of authority; see "Blood-Relationships among Early Eastern Ascetics," *Journal of Theological Studies*, n.s. 23 (1972): 144. The thesis seems equally appropriate for the Western ascetics.

[23]Basil of Caesarea, *Regulae Fusius Tractatae* 32, 2 (PG 31, 995); Numbers 14:4.

[24]Despite *Vita Melania* 7 (Gorce, *Vie*, p. 138), Pinian was not yet old enough to dispose of his own property; a special dispensation would have been required: *Codex Theodosianus* II, 17, 1; *Codex Justinianus* II, 45, 1-2.

See Gorce, *Vie*, pp. 138 n. 1 and 152 n. 4; Paul Allard, "Une Grande Fortune romaine au cinquième siècle," *Revue des Questions Historiques* 81 (1907): 21; Georges Goyau, *Sainte Mélanie (383-439)* (Paris: J. Gabala, 1909), p. 70; R.W. Lee, *The Elements of Roman Law*, 3rd ed. (London: Sweet & Maxwell, 1952), pp. 89-90.

[25] Jerome, *Ep.* 107, 5 (CSEL 55, 296).

[26] Ambrose, *De Virginibus* I, 11, 65-66 (PL 16, 218).

[27] For example, Paula was Pammachius' mother-in-law; Marcella and Pammachius were cousins; Paulinus and Melania the Younger were related, although the exact relationship is debated (see Paulinus, *Ep.* 29, 5 [CSEL 29, 251]); the younger Paula and Melania the Younger were second cousins. See A.H.M. Jones, J.R. Martindale, and J. Morris, *The Prosopography of the Later Roman Empire, Vol. I: A.D. 260-395* (Cambridge: Cambridge University Press, 1971), *stemmata* 13, 20, and 23. For a discussion of some of the links, see chap. 5 ("The Aristocratic Cousinhood") of M.T.W. Arnheim's *The Senatorial Aristocracy in the Later Roman Empire* (Oxford: Clarendon Press, 1972).

[28] Jerome, *Epp.* 66, 4, 6, 11 (CSEL 54, 651, 654, 661); 118, 5 (CSEL 5, 441).

[29] Jerome, *Ep.* 127, 1 (CSEL 56, 146). For the date of Marcella's conversion to asceticism as it relates to the origins of Roman monasticism, see Rudolf Lorenz, "Die Anfänge des abendländischen Mönchtums im 4. Jahrhundert," *Zeitschrift für Kirchengeschichte* 77 (1966): 3-8; G.D. Gordini, "Origine e sviluppo del monaschesimo a Roma," *Gregorianum* 37 (1956): 220-260; Ernest Spreitzenhofer, *Die Entwicklung des Alten Mönchtums in Italien von seinen ersten Anfängen bis zum Auftreten des heil. Benedict* (Vienna: Heinrich Kirsch, 1894), pp. 5-9, 29ff. For a discussion of the dating of the community of Roman ascetic women dedicated to St. Agnes, see Philbert Schmitz, "La Première Communauté de vierges a Rome," *Revue Bénédictine* 38 (1926): 189-195.

[30] Jerome, *Epp.* 108, 1 (CSEL 55, 306); 130, 6 (CSEL 56, 181).

[31] Paulinus, *Ep.* 29, 6 (CSEL 29, 252).

198   *Ascetic Piety and Women's Faith*

^{32}Jerome, *Epp.* 52, 5, 6, 9 (CSEL 54,422, 425, 430); 60,
11 (CSEL 54, 563); 69, 5 (CSEL 54, 687); 125, 16 (CSEL 56,
136); Basil of Caesarea, *Regulae Brevius Tractatae* 94 (PG
31, 148); *Regulae Fusius Tractatae* 11 (PG 31, 948);
Apophthegmata Patrum, Arsenius 36 (PL 65, 101); Augustine,
De Opere Monachorum 21 (25) (CSEL 41, 570); 25 (32) (CSEL
41, 577-579). Also see Karl Suso Frank, *Grundzüge der
Geschichte des Christlichen Mönchtums* (Darmstadt: Wis-
senschaftliche Buchgesellschaft, 1975), p. 39; and Philip
Rousseau, *Ascetics, Authority, and the Church in the Age
of Jerome and Cassian* (Oxford: Oxford University Press,
1978), p. 207.

^{33}Friedrich Prinz, *Frühes Mönchtum im Frankenreich.
Kultur und Gesellschaft in Gallien, den Rheinlanden und
Bayern am Beispiel der monastischen Entwicklung (4. bis
8. Jahrhundert)* (Munich/Vienna: R. Oldenbourg Verlag,
1965), pp. 47-57: Lorenz, "Die Anfänge," p. 12; Chadwick,
Cassian, p. 9; and Frank, *Grundzüge*, pp. 39, 43.

^{34}Some examples: for Isidore, see Palladius, *Historia
Lausiaca* 1, 4 (Butler, *Lausiac History*, p. 16); for Amoun,
see *Historia Monachorum in Aegypto* 22, 1 (A.-J. Festugière, ed., Studia Hagiographa 53 [Brussels: Société
des Bollandistes, 1971], p. 128); for Arsenius, see
Apophthegmata Patrum, Arsenius 42 (PL 65, 42).

^{35}Some examples: Paul the Simple, a herdsman, see
Palladius, *Historia Lausiaca* 22, 1 (Butler, *Lausiac History*, p. 69); John of Lycopolis, a builder, see Palladius,
Historia Lausiaca 35, 1 (Butler, p. 100); Sisinnius, a
slave, see Palladius, *Historia Lausiaca* 49, 1 (Butler,
p. 143); Amoun of Nitria, a balsam grower, see Palladius,
Historia Lausiaca 8, 3, (Butler, p. 27); Moses the Ethiopian, a houseman and a robber, see Palladius, *Historia
Lausiaca* 19, 1 (Butler, pp. 58-59).

^{36}Some examples: Theon, *Historia Monachorum* 6, 3
(Festugière, *Historia*, pp. 44-45); Or, *Historia Monachorum*
2, 5 (Festugière, pp. 36-37); Paphnutius, see Palladius,
Historia Lausiaca 47, 3 (Butler, *Lausiac History*, p. 137);
Cassian needed an interpreter since some of the desert
fathers spoke only Coptic (Cassian, *Conlationes* II, 16,
1 [CSEL 13, 439]). On Greek culture in the Syriac monastic tradition, see Pierre Canivet, *Le Monachisme syrien
selon Théodoret de Cyr*, Théologie Historique 42 (Paris:
Editions Beauchesne, 1977), pp. 248-253.

[37]On the church's traditional ideals regarding married women, see, for example, Clement of Alexandria, *The Instructor* 3, 11; Ambrose, *Concerning Virgins* 1, 6; Jerome, *Against Jovinian* 1, 47; John Chrysostom, *Homily 20 on Ephesians* and *Homily 10 on Colossians*.

[38]Both Melanias are called "manly": Paulinus, *Ep.* 29, 6 (CSEL 29, 251); Palladius, *Historia Lausiaca* 9 (Butler, *Lausiac History*, p. 29); *Vita Melaniae* 39 (Gorce, *Vie*, p. 200). For other examples and discussion, see Elizabeth A. Clark, *Jerome, Chrysostom, and Friends: Essays and Translations* (New York: Edwin Mellen Press, 1979), pp. 15, 19, 55-56.

[39]On the "house monasticism" of these aristocrats, see Frank, *Grundzüge*, pp. 15, 17, 36-37, 47; Lorenz, "Die Anfänge," pp. 6-7; Gordini, "Origine," pp. 238-240, 244-245, 256-257; Joseph T. Lienhard, *Paulinus of Nola and Early Western Monasticism* (Cologne/Bonn: Peter Haustein Verlag, 1977), p. 110; Karl Suso Frank, *Frühes Mönchtum im Abendland, I* (Zürich/Munich: Artemis Verlag, 1975), pp. 14-15.

[40]Augustine, *De Moribus Ecclesiae Catholicae* I, 33, 70 (PL 32, 1339-1340); Possidius, *Vita S. Aurelii Augustini* 3 (PL 32, 36): Augustine returned "propriam domum agrosque." See Georges Folliet, "Aux Origines de l'ascetisme et du cénobitisme africaine," *Saint Martin et son temps*, Studia Anselmiana 46 (Rome: Herder, 1961), pp. 39, 43.

[41]Palladius, *Historia Lausiaca* 37, 12 (Butler, *Lausiac History*, p. 113).

[42]On Paulinus' arrangements, see Paulinus, *Ep.* 5, 4 (CSEL 29, 27); *Carmina* 11, 11 (CSEL 30, 39); 21, 386-560, for numerous references to his buildings and property (CSEL 30, 171-176).

[43]Paulinus, *Ep.* 24, 3 (CSEL 29, 204): "domus tuae hospes es, ut sis hospitium domus."

[44]Jerome, *Epp.* 125, 6 (CSEL 56, 123); 66, 6 (CSEL 54, 654). Palladius, in *Historia Lausiaca* 62 (Butler, *Lausiac History*, p. 157), says that Pammachius gave away some of his wealth, but part of it remained to be given to the poor after his death. On the property qualification for

the senate, see Goyau, *Sainte Mélanie*, p. 68; Theodor
Mommsen, *Römisches Staatsrecht* (1887; reprint of 3rd ed.,
Basel: Benno Schwabe & Co., 1952), I, 498-9, n. 2.

[45]These are Paulinus' consoling words to Sulpicius
Severus, *Ep.* 24, 2 (CSEL 29, 203); see also Paulinus, *Ep.*
16, 9 (CSEL 29, 122-123).

[46]On wandering ascetics, see Nagel, *Die Motivierung*,
chap. 9; Hans von Campenhausen, *Die Asketische
Heimatlosigkeit im Altkirchlichen und Frümittelalterlichen
Mönchtum*, Sammlung Gemeinverständlicher Vorträge und
Schriften aus dem Gebiet der Theologie und Religionsge-
schichte 149 (Tübingen: J.C.B. Mohr [Paul Siebeck], 1930),
pp. 10-15; Gordini, "Origine," p. 237. For the mockery,
see Jerome, *Ep.* 22, 28 (CSEL 54, 185).

[47]For example, those of Paulinus and Sulpicius
Severus. For a discussion of the social dimensions of
letter writing in late antiquity, see J.H.W.G.
Liebeschuetz, *Antioch: City and Imperial Administration
in the Later Roman Empire* (Oxford: Clarendon Press,
1972), pp. 18-21, and J.F. Matthews, "The Letters of
Symmachus," *Latin Literature of the Fourth Century*, ed.
J.W. Binns (London: Routledge & Kegan Paul, 1974).

[48]Paulinus, *Ep.* 23, 6 (CSEL 29, 162-163).

[49]For example, Paulinus' *Natalica* in honor of St.
Felix. For their audience, see P.G. Walsh, "Paulinus of
Nola and the Conflict of Ideologies in the Fourth Cen-
tury," *Kyriakon: Festschrift Johannes Quasten*, 2, ed.
P. Granfield and J.A. Jungmann (Münster Westf.: Verlag
Aschendorff, 1970), p. 568; and P.G. Walsh, "Introduc-
tion," *The Poems of Paulinus of Nola*, Ancient Christian
Writers 40 (New York: Newman Press, 1975), pp. 1-29.

[50]Paulinus, *Ep.* 5, 22 (CSEL 29, 39).

[51]Jerome, *Ep.* 125, 11 (CSEL 56, 130); Paulinus, *Ep.*
5, 15-16 (CSEL 29, 34-35), on the joys of working in
Felix's garden.

[52]Palladius, *Historia Lausiaca* 61, 7 (Butler, *Lausiac
History*, p. 157).

[53]John Cassian, *De Institutis Coenobiorum* X, 22-23 (CSEL
17, 192). For examples of the desert fathers' work, see
Palladius, *Historia Lausiaca* 7, 4-5 (Butler, *Lausiac History*, pp. 25-26); 32, 9 (Butler, pp. 95-96); 22, 5
(Butler, p. 71); 2, 2 (Butler, p. 17); *Historia Monachorum*
13, 1 (Festugière, *Historia*, p. 98); *Vita Pachomii, Les
Vies coptes de Saint Pachôme et de ses premiers successeurs*, trans. L.-Th. LeFort, Bibliothèque du Muséon 16
(Louvain: Bureaux du Muséon, 1943), pp. 4, 94-95; *S.
Pachomii Regula*, praefatio 2; 6 (*Pachomiana Latina*, ed.
Amand Boon, Bibliothèque de la Revue d'Histoire Ecclésias-
tique 7 [Louvain: Bureaux de la Revue, 1932], pp. 5-7).
Also see Arthur T. Geoghegan, *The Attitude towards Labor
in Early Christianity and Ancient Culture* (Washington,
D.C.: Catholic University Press, 1945), pt. 2, chap. 5.
For attitudes toward labor in Syriac monasticism, see
Canivet, *Le Monachisme syrien*, pp. 221-226.

[54]Sulpicius Severus, *Vita S. Martini* 10 (CSEL 1, 120).

[55]Augustine, *De Opere Monachorum* 25, 33 (CSEL 41,
579-580). Also see Augustine, *Ep.* 211, 9 (CSEL 57, 361-
362) for special relaxations of rules for upper-class
nuns; and Geoghegan, *The Attitude*, pp. 203-205. See
Lorenz, "Die Anfänge," pp. 57-61.

[56]Augustine, *De Opere Monachorum* 25, 33 (CSEL 41,
580).

[57]Jerome, *Epp.* 23, 2 (CSEL 54, 212); 47, 3 (CSEL 54,
346); 108, 5-6 (CSEL 55, 310-311); 127, 8 (CSEL 56, 151);
Commentarius in Epistolam ad Ephesios, praefatio, liber
2 (PL 26, 507); *Vita Melaniae* 7; 36; 41 (Gorce, *Vie*, pp.
140; 194; 204); Palladius, *Historia Lausiaca* 61, 6 (Butler, *Lausiac History*, p. 157).

[58]Paulinus of Milan, *Vita S. Ambrosii* 4 (PL 14, 28).

[59]Sulpicius Severus, *Dialogus* II, 12 (CSEL 1, 194-
195). For arrangements in Gaul, see René Metz, "Les
Vierges chrétiennes en Gaule au IVe siècle," *Saint Martin
et son temps*, pp. 109-132.

[60]The decree was confirmed by the council of Carthage
in 397. See J.D. Mansi, ed., *Sacrorum Conciliorum Nova
et Amplissima Collectio* (Florence: 1759), III, p. 923,
canon 31; see also Folliet, "Aux Origines," p. 32. That

"home asceticism" was considered the correct way for
virgins to live is also shown in Eusebius of Emesa's
homily *De virginibus* (Homily VII, 22 and 24).

[61]Jerome, *Ep*. 22, 38 (CSEL 54, 203). Jerome's connection of a woman's "having her own property" and "being
honored by all" is instructive.

[62]Jerome, *Ep*. 46, 2, 10, 12, 13 (CSEL 54, 330, 339,
341-344). Also see Chadwick, *Cassian*, p. 115, and
Francine Cardman, "The Rhetoric of the Holy Places:
Palestine in the Fourth Century," paper given at the
Eighth International Conference on Patristic Studies,
Oxford, England, Sept. 7, 1979. On Jerome's change of
mind about visitors to Palestine, see Rousseau, *Ascetics*,
pp. 115-123.

[63]Jerome, *Ep*. 117, 3 (CSEL 55, 425).

[64]Some examples of pregnant nuns: Palladius, *His-
toria Lausiaca* 69, 1 (Butler, *Lausiac History*, p. 164);
Niceta of Remesiana, *De Lapsu Susannae* (ed. Klaus Gamber
[Regensburg: Friedrich Pustet, 1969]); also see Jerome,
Ep. 147, 6 (CSEL 56, 321-322).

[65]For a fuller discussion of the practice in ancient
Christianity and references, see Elizabeth A. Clark,
"John Chrysostom and the *Subintroductae*," *Church History*
46 (1977): 171-185.

[66]John Chrysostom's treatises on the *subintroductae*
provide us with the fullest information; they are edited
by Jean Dumortier, *Saint Jean Chrysostome: Les Cohabita-
tiones suspectes; Comment observer la virginité* (Paris:
Société d'Edition "Les Belles Lettres," 1955); English
translation in Clark, *Jerome, Chrysostom, and Friends*,
pp. 158-248. For specific arguments here mentioned, see
Adversus Eos Qui apud Se Habent Subintroductas Virgines
6; 7 (Dumortier, pp. 63-67) and *Quod Regulares Feminae
Viris Cohabitare Non Debeant* 4; 5; 7 (Dumortier, pp. 109-
111, 117-118).

[67]John Chrysostom, *Quod Regulares* 11 (Dumortier, pp.
134-135).

[68]Jerome, *Ep*. 117, 8 (CSEL 55, 431).

[69]Jerome, *Ep.* 123, 13 (CSEL 56, 88); for further examples of marriage as "slavery," and discussion, see Clark, *Jerome*, pp. 17-19, 53, 244.

[70]Jerome, *Epp.* 32, 2 (CSEL 54, 252-253); 127, 2, 4 (CSEL 56, 146, 148-149).

[71]For examples, *Questions and Answers on the Ascetic Life* XV, 4 (trans. Budge, *The Book of Paradise*, pp. 806-807); Jerome, *Ep.* 122, 1, 4 (CSEL 56, 56-57, 69-71).

[72]*Vita Melaniae* 1 (Gorce, *Vie*, p. 132). Couples separating sexually after producing two children is a regular feature of hagiographic literature: see Evelyne Patlagean, "Sur la limitation de la fécondité dans la haute époque byzantine," *Annales Economies, Sociétés, Civilisations* 24 (1969), 1358. On the property, see Mariano Rampolla del Tindaro, *Santa Melania Giuniore, senatrice romana: documenti contemporanei e note* (Roma: Tipografia Vaticana, 1905), pp. 166-183; Allard, "Une Grande Fortune," pp. 9-18, 27; Goyau, *Sainte Mélanie*, pp. 4-9.

[73]*Vita Melaniae* 4 (Gorce, *Vie*, p. 132).

[74]*Vita Melaniae* 8 (Gorce, *Vie*, p. 142).

[75]Augustine, *Ep.* 126, 7 (CSEL 44, 13): "quanto flagrantius in nostro Piniano amare potuerunt tantam mundi istius cupiditatem..."; *The Confessions and Letters of St. Augustin*, trans. J.G. Cunningham, A Select Library of the Nicene and Post-Nicene Fathers of the Christian Church, ser. 1, vol. 1 (New York: Charles Scribner's Sons, 1886), p. 457.

[76]*Vita Melaniae* 8; 9 (Gorce, *Vie*, pp. 140; 142, 144).

[77]Paula and Melania the Elder were widows; Melania the Younger was given ascetic freedom by her husband; Marcella's mother died by 387, mentioned by Jerome, *Commentarius in S. Pauli ad Galatas*, praefatio (PL 26, 331). After Jerome's departure from Rome and probably after Albina's death, Marcella took in a young virgin, Principia, who remained with her until the time of Marcella's death (*Ep.* 127, 8, 13, 14 [CSEL 56, 151, 155-156]).

[78]Ambrose, *De Virginibus* I, 11, 63 (PL 16, 217): "Si vincis domum, vincis saeculum."

[79]As in the cases of Pammachius (see Paulinus, *Ep.*,
13 [CSEL 29, 84-107], Jerome, *Ep.* 66 [CSEL 54, 649-665])
and Sulpicius Severus, who remained on good terms with
his mother-in-law after his wife's death; see Sulpicius
Severus, *Ep.* 3 (CSEL 1, 146-151).

[80]As in the case of Paulinus, who took his wife
Therasia into ascetic retreat with him; he refers to her
in his letters by such phrases as "mea conserva" (e.g.,
Ep. 5, 19 [CSEL 29, 38]).

[81]Jerome, *Epp.* 66, 13 (CSEL 54, 664); 77, 6 (CSEL 55,
43); 108, 20 (CSEL 55, 336).

[82]Jerome, *Epp.* 108, 20 (CSEL 55, 335); 130, 15 (CSEL
56, 195).

[83]Augustine, *De Moribus Ecclesiae Catholicae* I, 31,
68 (PL 32, 1339); 33, 70 (PL 32, 1340); Ambrose, *De
Virginibus* I, 10, 60 (PL 16, 216).

[84]On servants: Jerome, *Epp.* 130, 13 (CSEL 56, 192);
108, 2 (CSEL 55, 308); 79, 8 (CSEL 55, 97); 123, 14
(CSEL 56, 89-90).

[85]*Vita Melaniae* 42; 46; 47 (Gorce, *Vie*, pp. 208; 214;
216).

[86]Jerome, *Ep.* 108, 20 (CSEL 55, 335).

[87]*Vita Melaniae* 23; 26 (Gorce, *Vie*, pp. 174; 178).
On the survival of Melania's transcriptions, see Rampolla,
Santa Melania, p. lxii and Gorce, *Vie*, p. 178 n. 2.

[88]On Melania the Elder's reading, see Palladius,
Historia Lausiaca 55, 3 (Butler, *Lausiac History*, p. 149;
taking the chapter to be about Melania; see C.H. Turner's
note in *Journal of Theological Studies* 6 [1905]: 352-
354, and Butler's acknowledgment, *Journal of Theological
Studies* 7 [1906]: 309); also see Paulinus, *Ep.* 29, 14
(CSEL 29, 261).

[89]Jerome, *Epp.* 66, 13 (CSEL 54, 663-4); 77, 6 (CSEL
55, 43).

[90]On the transformation of ascetic wandering into
peregrinatio, see Campenhausen, *Die Asketische Heimatlosigkeit*, pp. 1-15.

[91] Jerome, *Ep.* 108, 7-14 (CSEL 55, 312-325); Palladius, *Historia Lausiaca* 46, 2-3 (Butler, *Lausiac History*, pp. 134-135). On another famous female pilgrim, see John Wilkinson, *Egeria's Travels* (London: SPCK, 1973).

[92] Jerome, *Ep.* 108, 14 (CSEL 55, 324); Palladius, *Historia Lausiaca* 46, 2 (Butler, *Lausiac History*, p. 134).

[93] Palladius, *Historia Lausiaca* 18, 27-28 (Butler, *Lausiac History*, p. 57), but according to the *Historia Monachorum* 21, 16 (Festugière, *Historia*, p. 119), the skin remained with the brothers. Could this be the *tunica* Paulinus sent on to Sulpicius Severus, telling him he received it from Melania? See Paulinus, *Ep.* 29, 5 (CSEL 29, 251).

[94] *Vita Melaniae* 19; 20; 34; 50; 55 (Gorce, *Vie*, pp. 166; 168; 190; 224; 236); she was also in Nola with Paulinus in 406 (*Carmen* 21, 272ff. [CSEL 30, 167ff.]).

[95] Palladius, *Historia Lausiaca* 55, 3 (Butler, *Lausiac History*, p. 149); see note 88 above.

[96] Palladius, *Historia Lausiaca* 38, 8-9 (Butler, *Lausiac History*, pp. 119-120).

[97] Palladius, *Historia Lausiaca* 46, 6; 54, 4 (Butler, *Lausiac History*, pp. 136; 146-147).

[98] *Vita Melaniae* 29 (Gorce, *Vie*, p. 184).

[99] *Vita Melaniae* 54 (Latin version, Rampolla, *Santa Melania*, p. 30). It is helpful to recall that the probable author of the *Vita* was a Monophysite; see Rampolla, *Santa Melania*, pp. lxx-lxxvi; Chitty, *The Desert*, p. 102; Goyau, *Sainte Mélanie*, p. viii.

[100] *Vita Melaniae* 54 (Greek version, Gorce, *Vie*, p. 232).

[101] *Vita Melaniae* 56 (Gorce, *Vie*, p. 238).

[102] Jerome, *Ep.* 127, 9 (CSEL 56, 152).

[103] Jerome, *Ep.* 127, 7 (CSEL 56, 151); I Timothy 2:12; I Corinthians 14:34.

104Jerome, *Ep.* 108, 20 (CSEL 55, 334-335); Palladius, *Historia Lausiaca* 46, 6 (Butler, *Lausiac History*, p. 136). Melania the Younger, according to her *Vita*, wanted to be enrolled with the poor on the lists of the Jerusalem church (*Vita* 35, [Gorce, *Vie*, p. 194]); but she does not seem to have lacked funds for her projects, even so.

105Palladius, *Historia Lausiaca* 54, 2 (Butler, *Lausiac History*, p. 146).

106Matthew 6:3.

107Palladius, *Historia Lausiaca* 10, 2-4 (Butler, *Lausiac History*, p. 30).

108Palladius, *Historia Lausiaca* 46, 3-4 (Butler, *Lausiac History*, pp. 134-135): it is unclear from the text whether Melania or Palladius made this remark; Robert T. Meyer assigns it to Palladius (*Palladius, The Lausiac History*, Ancient Christian Writers 34 [Westminster, Md.: The Newman Press, 1965], pp. 124, 206 n. 416).

109*Vita Melaniae* 33; 40 (Gorce, *Vie*, pp. 188, 190; 202).

110Augustine, *Epp.* 125, 2 (CSEL 44, 3-4); 126, 7 (CSEL 44, 12-13). Augustine claims in *Ep.* 125, 2 that they did not give any money to *people* in Thagaste, so the citizens of Hippo should have known not to expect anything from them; yet *Ep.* 126, 7 makes clear that they gave funds to the *church* at Thagaste; *Vita Melaniae* 21 (Gorce, *Vie*, p. 172) confirms this version, reporting that the church at Thagaste became rich through their generosity.

111Augustine, *Epp.* 125, 2 (CSEL 44, 3); 126, 1, 7, 8 (CSEL 44, 7-8, 12-14).

112Augustine, *Ep.* 126, 7 (CSEL 44, 13).

113Augustine, *Epp.* 126, 3-4, 12-13 (CSEL 44, 9-11, 17-18); 125, 4 (CSEL 44, 6-7).

114Matthew 5:5.

[115]Jerome, *Ep.* 22, 34 (CSEL 54, 196-197); John Cassian, *Conlationes* III, 18, 7 (CSEL 13, 513-516); *Benedicti Regula* 1, 6-9 (CSEL 75, 18). See Rousseau, *Ascetics*, p. 209, and Chadwick, *Cassian*, pp. 51-53, 65.

[116]Jerome, *Ep.* 22, 34, 35 (CSEL 54, 197). He may be attacking the Remnuoth in *Ep.* 125, 16 (CSEL 56, 135) when he criticizes monks who carry on the same work they practiced in secular life. Jerome thinks the cenobitic life is better than the eremitic, especially for women, whose minds tend to degenerate if they are left alone (*Ep.* 130, 17 [CSEL 56, 198]). Also see *Ep.* 125, 9, 15 (CSEL 56, 127-128, 133-134).

[117]Jerome, *Ep.* 22, 34 (CSEL 54, 197); John Cassian, *Conlationes* III, 18, 7 (CSEL 13, 516).

[118]John Cassian, *Conlationes* III, 18, 7 (CSEL 13, 514-515); also see Rousseau, *Ascetics*, p. 209.

[119]*Benedicti Regula* 1, 8 (CSEL 75, 18); see Chadwick, *Cassian*, p. 154.

[120]See Rousseau, *Ascetics*, p. 219.

[121]Palladius, *Historia Lausiaca* 41, 2 (Butler, *Lausiac History*, p. 128). Palladius, as a warm supporter of the circle of Melania the Elder, cannot be expected to have kind words for Jerome.

[122]Jerome, *Ep.* 108, 20 (CSEL 55, 335).

[123]Palladius, *Historia Lausiaca* 46, 5 (Butler, *Lausiac History*, p. 135). See Francis X. Murphy, *Rufinus of Aquileia (345-411): His Life and Works* (Washington, D.C.: Catholic University Press, 1945), p. 53, for a discussion of Rufinus and Melania as the first Latins to start ascetic foundations in Palestine. Also see G.D. Gordini, "Il monachesimo romano in Palestina nel IV secolo," *Saint Martin et son temps*, pp. 85-107, who stresses the influence of Egyptian monastic practices on the Roman foundations in Palestine; nonetheless, he must concede that social distinctions were retained in Paula's convent and that there was not much attention to manual labor (pp. 102-104).

[124]Paulinus, *Ep.* 45, 2 (CSEL 29, 381); Palladius, *Historia Lausiaca* 54, 3 (Butler, *Lausiac History*, p. 146).

[125]Paulinus, *Ep.* 29, 12-14 (CSEL 29, 258-262); Palladius, *Historia Lausiaca* 54, 3-6 (Butler, *Lausiac History*, pp. 146-147). On the dating, see Murphy, "Melania," pp. 73-77.

[126]*Vita Melaniae* 41 (Gorce, *Vie*, p. 206): this despite her lecturing the nuns on obedience (*Vita Melaniae* 44 [Gorce, pp. 210, 212]).

[127]*Vita Melaniae* 53; 54; 56 (Gorce, *Vie*, pp. 230; 232; 238).

[128]Stability was already evidenced in the oldest nuns' rule known to us, that of Caesarius of Arles, *Regula ad Virgines* 2 and 50 (*Sancti Caesarii Arlatensis Opera Varia*, ed. G. Morin [Maretioli: 1942] II, 102, 115-116). The first version was composed in 512, the final version given in 534. See Mary Caritas McCarthy, *The Rule for Nuns of St. Caesarius of Arles* (Washington, D.C.: Catholic University Press, 1960), pp. 63-66; 164; also see the older work, Carl Franklin Arnold's *Caesarius von Arlate und die Gallische Kirche Seiner Zeit* (Leipzig: J.C. Hinrich'sche Buchhandlung, 1894), 406-419.

[129]*Vita Melaniae* 41; 68 (Gorce, *Vie*, pp. 204, 206; 266); Jerome, *Ep.* 108, 14, 20, 30 (CSEL 55, 325, 335, 348); Palladius, *Historia Lausiaca* 46, 5 (Butler, *Lausiac History*, p. 135); 54, 6 (Butler, p. 148).

[130]John 14:2.

AUTHORITY AND HUMILITY: A CONFLICT OF VALUES IN FOURTH-CENTURY FEMALE MONASTICISM

Byzantinische Forschungen

9 (1985), 17-33

That humility was of central importance to the Christian life is made abundantly clear in the New Testament.[1]
Yet the first generations of Christians, if not the
impoverished outcasts imagined by earlier scholars,[2]
nonetheless included few if any aristocrats for whom
humility might be an unfamiliar virtue.[3] By about
A.D. 200, however, Clement of Alexandria knew Christians
sufficiently wealthy to be troubled by Jesus' counsel to
sell our goods for the sake of the poor,[4] and in the
fourth century the conversion of the monied aristocrats
began in earnest.[5] Not least among the patrician con-
verts to ascetic Christianity were women who renounced
their societal roles in order to found and direct monasteries for females. That both their noble backgrounds
and their authoritative leadership of monasteries might
militate against the humility they as female Christian
ascetics should espouse is obvious.[6] The evidence provided about the women by the Church Fathers does indeed
suggest that the potential conflict of humility and
authority called for a skillful resolution, in literature
as well as in life.

Is not the Fathers' extravagant praise for the
humility of their female subjects, when coupled with

their deafening silence regarding the women's authoritative leadership, paradoxical? Why should the women's
humility be accorded such honor when their leadership in
founding and directing monasteries receives practically
no mention? It is evident that humility must in fact be
cultivated if aristocratic nuns were to live together
amicably with those from the lowest social classes in
monastic seclusion: that theme punctuates two early
monastic Rules composed especially for women, Augustine's
Epistle 211 and Caesarius of Arles' *Rules for Nuns*.[7] We
may also take for granted that the Fathers wished to
represent their admired female friends as conforming to
such Biblical injunctions as I Timothy 2:11-15 that enjoined women to be silent and submissive. Yet something
more appears to be at issue in the exaltation of the
women's humility and the neglect of their authority that
prompts a re-examination of the sources pertaining to
their monastic leadership.

The three fourth-century women serving as subjects
for the investigation founded monasteries for females in
the East: Olympias, confidante of John Chrysostom;
Melania the Elder, monastic companion of Rufinus of
Aquileia; and Paula, the friend of Jerome.[8] Their life
patterns are remarkably similar. Each was a wealthy
aristocrat who, when prematurely widowed, devoted her
energies as well as her fortune to the founding and
directing of a monastery. Although contemporary documents
tell less about the women's supervision of monasteries
than about their Christian virtues, the evidence nonetheless enables us to locate the type of authority they
wielded and to hypothesize why that authority was not
openly lauded in the sources.

Olympias' grandfather, Ablabius, although reputedly
of undistinguished background,[9] was praetorian prefect of

Constantinople and served as consul in A.D. 331.[10] Her
father ranked among the *comites* and her husband of brief
duration, Nebridius, served as prefect of Constantinople
in A.D. 386.[11] When she was widowed at twenty, Olympias
was so prized as a potential mate that Theodosius I
attempted to force her into marriage with one of his
relatives.[12] Resisting both his threats and his entice-
ments, Olympias vowed herself to Christian celibacy and
was ordained a deaconess in the early 390s.[13] Her financial contributions to the church of Constantinople were
stunning: "Ten thousand pounds of gold, twenty thousand
of silver, all her real estate in Thrace, Galatia, Cappadocia Prima, and Bithynia," in addition to several
houses in the Eastern capital and its suburbs.[14] Both
Palladius and the anonymous author of her *Vita*[15] report
that she "maintained" John Chrysostom as bishop of
Constantinople, as she had done his predecessor, Nec-
tarius.[16] Even after Chrysostom's exile, Olympias
supplied him with money to provide for the needs of his
retinue, to redeem captives, to assist the poor.[17]
Visiting clergy also benefited from Olympias' largesse:
she opened a house for their use in Constantinople and
furnished them with funds.[18]

Most important, Olympias erected a monastery for
females near the Constantinople cathedral and enrolled
about 250 women in it, of whom fifty were her own servants
and four her own relatives (the latter were required to
make over their possessions to the convent before they
were granted admission).[19] Since in Raymond Janin's
judgment the first orthodox monastery for men in the city
cannot be dated before A.D. 382 and the first women's
monastery was most likely founded near the end of the
fourth century,[20] it is safe to assume that Olympias'
community was among the earliest such institutions for

women in the Eastern capital. The sources reveal little,
however, about Olympias' direction of her convent. Instead, much is reported about her Christian virtues:
that she had no vanity or conceit,[21] that she revered
members of the clergy,[22] that she spent her life in tears
of repentance.[23] Chrysostom in his seventeen extant
letters to Olympias from exile stresses how remarkable
her ascetic practices were, given her luxuriously soft
upbringing.[24] Her patience in suffering, he writes, is
"the queen of goods, the most beautiful of crowns."[25] To
enumerate her good deeds would be as futile as to count
the waves of the sea.[26] Chrysostom's adulation of
Olympias often strains the limits of the modern reader's
trust, fashioned as it is in accordance with the extrava-
gances of late ancient rhetoric. Yet Chrysostom relates
not a single word about Olympias as founder and director
of the Constantinople monastery. Indeed, his picture of
the modest, retiring Olympias does not entirely square
with the notices in other sources that she was courageous
enough to defy the wills of an emperor and a city prefect.[27]

　　The case of Melania the Elder is likewise puzzling.
Daughter and granddaughter of Roman consuls, a member of
the distinguished gens Antonia, Melania was widowed at an
early age.[28] Leaving Rome in the 370s, she journeyed to
the East and founded monasteries for men and women on the
Mount of Olives in A.D. 378 or 380, paid for from her own
considerable fortune.[29] Her companion Rufinus of
Aquileia took charge of the men's monastery and Melania,
the one for females. Yet neither Rufinus nor her friends
Palladius and Paulinus of Nola (who was also her cousin)[30]
describe the monasteries she organized; Palladius merely
remarks in passing that the community for women housed
fifty virgins.[31] Although Melania's charitable[32] and

courageous[33] deeds, self-imposed poverty,[34] and extreme
ascetic practices[35] are frequently mentioned, Palladius
and Paulinus disclose nothing about her role as monastic
leader, even though she provided the funds for her monastery and left money to endow it when she died.[36]

Melania was not the only fourth-century member of the
Roman nobility to found a monastery for women in the Holy
Land: Jerome's friend Paula did the same in Bethlehem.
In his encomium of Paula, *Epistle* 108, Jerome dwells upon
her aristocratic background: she was descended from the
Scipios, the Gracchi, and Agamemnon, while her husband
Julius Toxotius had the blood of Aeneas in his veins.[37]
When Toxotius died, Paula remained in Rome for five
years, practicing home asceticism in her own palace.[38]
In A.D. 385, she left Rome for the East, accompanied by
her daughter Eustochium and her female servants.[39] After
an extended tour of Egypt and the Holy Land, she settled
in Bethlehem where she built monasteries for both sexes,
superintending the women's community herself.[40] So
numerous were the women who flocked to her convent that
Paula divided them into three companies. Jerome's description implies that the division may have been made on
the basis of social class: he says of the women that
there were "tam nobiles quam medii et infimi generis."[41]
Although Jerome praises the women's work in making garments for themselves and others,[42] it does not appear
that their labor supplied the funds by which the monastery was maintained. One of the several testimonies to
this fact lies in Jerome's comment, after Paula's death,
to her daughter and successor Eustochium that now she
would have "crowds of brothers and sisters" to support;
however heavy the burden, it would be "inpius" to cast
off the monks and nuns dependent upon her.[43] His words
indicate that the money for the monasteries' operation
had indeed been supplied by Paula.

Just as with Olympias and Melania, so with Paula are
humility and self-sacrifice more praised than leadership.
Jerome reports that she cultivated lowliness, shunned
glory.[44] During her visit to Egypt, she protested that
the desert fathers received her with too much honor.[45]
"Humility is the first virtue of Christians," Jerome
writes of Paula, "and so great was the humility by which
she cast herself down that those who had seen her, and
those who wanted to see her because of her celebrated
reputation, would not have believed that it was she, but
the lowliest of her servant women."[46] Her lowliness, not
her competent direction of a monastery, is clearly
Jerome's chief concern.

One possible explanation for why the Fathers did not
dwell on the women as monastic leaders was that the
authority they exercised was based neither on the offices
they held nor on the functions they performed, but on
their personal status. Max Weber's typology of authority
is here useful to the discussion. These three monastic
directors wielded, in Weber's terminology, a traditional
type of authority, indeed a patriarchally traditional
one.[47] Their authority cannot be characterized either as
Weber's rational/legal type in which generalized, impersonal rules prevail and a clear-cut separation exists
between the official and the private spheres,[48] or as the
charismatic type Weber most frequently ascribes to
founders of religious movements.[49] To be sure, as
"ascetic virtuosi,"[50] Olympias, Melania the Elder, and
Paula possessed a certain charisma derived from their
awesome renunciations, but their source of authority as
monastic leaders did not rest primarily on their followers' perception of them as possessors of special
divinely-granted powers.[51] Even though the women's
breaking of societal norms in their decision for

asceticism can scarcely be labeled traditional,[52] the
type of authority they possessed can: it was derived
from their own monied and aristocratic backgrounds.

Several characteristics of traditional authority as
outlined by Weber seem especially relevant to the analysis. First, traditional authority does not clearly
distinguish between the private and the public roles of
the leader: his or her status is "total."[53] Traditional
authority here sharply contrasts with rational/legal
authority in which a manifest separation of the public
and private spheres exists.[54] Also unlike rational/legal
authority is a second, correlative characteristic of
traditional authority, especially the patriarchally traditional type: it makes little or no distinction between
the leader's own property and the property of the group.[55]
The leader, for example, equips his retainers,[56] shares
his house, food, and drink with them.[57] Third, in traditional authority the leader's assistants and close
followers are usually persons whose loyalty is based on
their status as relatives, slaves, or other dependents.[58]
The obedience the leader commands thus corresponds closely to a form of filial piety, posits Weber.[59] Fourth,
patriarchally traditional authority tends to provide for
succession of leadership by inheritance within the kinship group,[60] rather than by election or appointment on
grounds of merit. Fifth, traditional authority is not
likely to operate through a set of impersonal, written
rules, as does rational/legal authority, even though
such rules may exist.[61]

These five characteristics are prominent in descriptions of the women and monasteries here considered. All
three monasteries were not only founded but also funded
by the women who became their superiors. The monasteries' property was in essence *their* property: they had

purchased it, erected the monastic buildings. Indeed, it
can be posited that the women's ownership and control of
the monastic property was the decisive determinant of
their authority. This economic factor clearly distinguishes the women's patriarchally traditionalist authority from authority held by charismatic endowment. Weber
is unequivocal in his insistence that charismatic authority "recognizes no appropriation of positions of power by
virtue of the possession of property, either on the part
of a chief or of socially privileged groups."[62]
Olympias, Melania the Elder, and Paula, by contrast, fail
to exemplify the "anti-economic" tendency Weber asso-
ciates with early charismatic monasticism,[63] whose practitioners lived either from gifts or by begging.[64]
Despite the fact that the communities of these women were
among the earliest we know outside of Egypt and hence
theoretically could be expected to conform more closely
to Weber's ideal type than later monasteries, such an
expectation is not confirmed by the sources: the monasteries were supported by the women's inherited wealth.
In this as in other ways, the Latin aristocratic ascetics
deviate from what is commonly assumed to be the norm of
early Christian asceticism.[65]

    As for the composition of the original group of nuns
in the women's monasteries, the relatives and servants of
Paula and Olympias who followed them into ascetic retreat
formed the nucleus of the monastic establishment.[66]
Loyalty would hence continue to be granted on a personal
basis to the former mistress or relative, not to an impersonal order. Concerning the succession of leadership
in the convents, it is also clear that Paula's and
Olympias' kin inherited the founder's authority over the
monasteries. Jerome reports that Paula's daughter
Eustochium succeeded her as director,[67] and the *Vita*

Melaniae Junioris provides evidence that Paula's granddaughter and namesake continued in the third generation
as the head of the Bethlehem convent.[68] As for Olympias'
monastery, the *Vita Olympiadis* plainly states that its
next two mother superiors, Marina and Elisanthia, were
the founder's own relatives.[69] The traditional pattern
of succession by inheritance[70] apparently obtained in
these two convents as long as the ascetic lifestyle permitted.

The fifth characteristic, that traditional authority,
unlike rational/legal authority,[71] does not tend to
operate through written rules, deserves a more extended
consideration. Weber posits that although such rules
may exist in situations of traditional authority, it is
the personal status of the leader that is determinative.[72]
This is precisely the case for the three monasteries
under consideration: regulations of some sort were in
effect, possibly written ones, but they are not appealed
to in the sources as empowering the monastic directors.
Some regulatory principles must have sustained the monasteries, as they do all institutions, especially as women
joined who were not the foundresses' relatives and former
servants, and who hence could not necessarily be expected
to accord their superior the filial obedience characteristic of traditional authority. The original principle
of authority must somehow be modified to allow for the
changing situation: in Weber's phrase, "routinization"
must take place. Although Weber uses the word "routinization" to describe the process by which *charismatic*
leadership becomes stabilized,[73] it is an apt term with
which to describe the process by which leadership is per-
petuated when the original situation of traditional
authority no longer obtains. In the case of monasticism,
one important manifestation of "routinization" would be

the adoption of and adherence to a Rule, a standard
authority apart from the person of the monastic founder.
Hence the evidence pertaining to the use of monastic
Rules in the sources under discussion is germane to the
analysis of women's monastic leadership. The evidence
suggests that Rules were indeed present early in the
monasteries' histories, but that they were not seen as
determining the authority of the original foundresses.

The *Vita Olympiadis*, for example, reports that
Marina, the next director of the convent after Olympias,
"performed and fulfilled" that which had been entrusted
to her by Olympias, "preserving safe and governing the
whole caravan of her flock."[74] The fourteenth-century
Byzantine historiographer Nicephorus Callistus adds the
more precise note that Marina was entrusted to observe
τὸν τοῦ μοναστηρίου κανόνα.[75] And Elisanthia, the second
mother superior after Olympias, "preserved unchanged the
entire Rule she had received from that pious and blessed
soul," according to the *Vita Olympiadis*.[76] The Rule is
again mentioned in an account relating to the transfer of
Olympias' bones, composed by Sergia, director of Olympias' convent in the 630s. Sergia states that "Olympias'
Rule" had remained in effect until the convent burned
during the Nika rebellion of A.D. 532.[77] When the convent was rebuilt, the Rule was presumably adopted again,
for Sergia concludes her *Narratio* with the pious wish
that the Rule transmitted down to her time will be
observed in the future.[78] What this Rule was, we do not
know. There is no mention of its content in any known
source pertaining to Olympias. Although it may well have
been in effect during her lifetime, it was not the factor
determining her authority.

From the sources we have considered pertaining to
Paula and Melania the Elder, even less can be gleaned

about possible Rules existing in their monasteries. Yet
supplementary documents suggest that the monasteries may
indeed have had Rules. Neither Rufinus, nor Palladius,
nor Paulinus--the three men who wrote the most about
Melania--mentions that Melania governed her nuns through
a Rule. Yet it was Rufinus who translated Basil of
Caesarea's Rules into Latin, conflating the two Rules
into one.[79] Although the translation was not made until
Rufinus returned West in A.D. 397,[80] it is likely that he
knew them at an earlier date. Indeed, the Rufinus
scholar Francis X. Murphy earlier posited that Basil's
Rules were in fact used in Rufinus' and Melania's monasteries.[81]

Melania may have received advice on running a monastery from another source as well: Evagrius Ponticus, the
famous Origenist theoretician of asceticism whom Melania
had rescued for the ascetic life,[82] wrote a work often
called, in translation, "The Mirror for Nuns."[83] That
title, however, is inexact in more than one respect: the
Greek title, Παραίνεσις πρὸς παρθένον, indicates that it
is *one* nun who is addressed. Is it not likely, as Joseph
Muyldermans has argued, that the παρθένος to whom the
work was directed was Evagrius' old friend, Melania the
Elder?[84] Muyldermans' suggestion is strengthened by the
additional information that it was none other than
Rufinus himself who translated the work into Latin.[85]
Nevertheless, it is clear that even if Melania did have a
monastic Rule for her community, the men who wrote about
her did not deem her leadership to be grounded in such a
Rule, for they mention it not once.

The evidence pertaining to Paula's monastery is
similar. Jerome in *Epistle* 108 briefly describes the
operation of Paula's Bethlehem community and from his
words we infer that regulations of some sort were in

effect there. He reports, for example, that disobedient nuns were excluded from the common refectory, that meat was allowed only to the sick, that the nuns all dressed alike.[86] But *what* Rule may have undergirt such regulations is never revealed. We do know, however, that it was Jerome who translated Pachomius' Rule from its Greek version into Latin, and he testifies that he did so explicitly for Eustochium's use in governing the sisters of the Bethlehem convent.[87] It is not inconceivable that some provisions of the Egyptian Rule were upheld in Paula's community even during her lifetime. Indeed, when Jerome implies that the ascetic life practiced by Rufinus and Melania the Elder in Jerusalem was not as rigorous as that practiced at Bethlehem (Jerome calls Rufinus a Croesus, a Crassus, a Sardanapalus),[88] we might conclude that the Bethlehem contingent favored the more severe Egyptian practices over the milder ones of Basil's Rule[89]--although the venom Jerome spews forth at Rufinus probably discredits his testimony about him.

The authority wielded by these female monastic founders, then, does not appear to have been dependent upon their offices or upon Rules, as is characteristic of rational/legal authority. Their leadership derived ultimately from their family wealth and status. Perhaps this is one reason why the Fathers did not think to mention the offices the women held, how they carried out their duties as superiors of convents, or from what Rules they derived their authority--questions that we who live in a world regulated largely by rational/legal authority would like answered. Those are questions of interest to our time, but apparently not to fourth- and fifth-century monastic writers. Rather, by their emphasis on the women's humility and abject lowliness, the Fathers were in effect highlighting, by way of contrast, the true source of authority the women possessed: status, family background, wealth. Blueness of blood implied a power that Rules, however painstakingly penned, would find difficult to match.

NOTES

[1]For example, Matthew 5:3; 18:1-5; 20:26-28; 23:11-12; Mark 9:33-37; 10:15, 43-45; Luke 1:38, 52; 14:7-14; 18:9-14; 22:27; Acts 20:19; Romans 12:16; Ephesians 4:2; Colossians 3:12; James 1:9-10; 4:6; I Peter 5:5-6.

[2]See discussions and reassessments in E.A. Judge, *The Social Pattern of the Christian Groups in the First Century* (London, 1960), chap. 5; Martin Hengel, *Property and Riches in the Early Church*, trans. J. Bowden (London, 1974), 27-37; Gerd Theissen, "Soziale Schichtung in der korinthischen Gemeinde," *ZNW*, 65 (1974), 232-272; Gerd Theissen, "Die Starken und Schwachen in Korinth," *Evth*, 35 (1975), 155-172; Abraham Malherbe, *Social Aspects of Early Christianity* (Baton Rouge, London, 1977), 8-9, 29-41; L. William Countryman, *The Rich Christian in the Church of the Early Empire: Contradictions and Accommodations* (New York, Toronto, 1980), 1-18.

[3]The editor of Acts is especially concerned to represent Christianity as appealing to the powerful or at least not outrightly condemned by them. See, for example, Acts 13:7-12; 18:12-17; 24-26, and comments by Ernst Haenchen, *The Acts of the Apostles: A Commentary*, trans. B. Noble et al. (Philadelphia, 1971), 403, 658-659, 663, 670, 674, 679, 691-692.

[4]Clement of Alexandria, *Quis Dives Salvetur?*, ed. O. Stählin, GCS 17 (Leipzig, 1909), 157-191; the treatise is a commentary on the story of the rich young man in Mark 10:17-32= Matthew 19:16-30= Luke 18:18-30.

[5]André Chastagnol, "Le Sénateur Volusien et la conversion d'une famille de l'aristocratie romaine au Bas-Empire," *REA*, 58 (1956), 241-253; Peter Brown, "Aspects of the Christianization of the Roman Aristocracy," *JRS*, 51 (1961), 1-11 (= *Religion and Society in the Age of Saint Augustine* [New York, 1971], 161-182); A.H.M. Jones, "The Social Background of the Struggle between Paganism and Christianity," in A. Momigliano, *Paganism and Christianity in the Fourth Century* (Oxford,

1963), 17-37; Charles Pietri, "Esquisse de conclusion:
l'aristocratie chrétienne entre Jean de Constantinople
et Augustin d'Hippone," *Jean Chrysostome et Augustin*,
actes du colloque de Chantilly, 22-24 septembre 1974, ed.
C. Kannengiesser (Paris, 1975), 283-305; Anne Yarbrough,
"Christianization in the Fourth Century: The Example of
Roman Women," *ChH*, 45 (1976), 149-165.

[6]For an analysis of the status elevation the Fathers
accorded these aristocratic ascetics, see Elizabeth
Clark, "Ascetic Renunciation and Feminine Advancement,"
AthR, 63 (1981), 240-257.

[7]Augustine, *Ep.* 211, 5-6, ed. A. Goldbacher, CSEL 57
(Vienna, Leipzig, 1911), 359-361; Caesarius of Arles,
Regula Sanctarum Virginum 21, ed. G. Morin (Bonn, 1933),
9.

[8]Macrina, sister of Basil of Caesarea and Gregory of
Nyssa, and the fifth-century Melania the Younger are
other monastic founders whose careers bear study.

[9]Libanius, *Oratio* 42, 33, ed. R. Foerster (Leipzig,
1906), III, 318; Eunapius, *Vitae Sophistarum* 463, ed.
W.C. Wright (London, New York, 1922), 384.

[10]*Vita Olympiadis* 2, ed. A.-M. Malingrey, SC 13 bis
(Paris, 1968), 408; Palladius, *Historia Lausiaca* 56, ed.
C. Butler (Cambridge, 1904), II, 150; A.H.M. Jones, J.R.
Martindale, J. Morris, *The Prosopography of the Later
Roman Empire, Vol. I: A.D. 260-395* (Cambridge, 1971),
3-4.

[11]*Vita Olympiadis* 2, ed. Malingrey, 408, 410; Jones
et al., *Prosopography*, I, 818-819, 620; Palladius, *Historia Lausiaca* 56, ed. Butler, II, 150; Palladius,
Dialogus de Vita S. Joannis Chrysostomi 56, ed. P.R.
Coleman-Norton (Cambridge, 1928), 98.

[12]*Vita Olympiadis* 3, ed. Malingrey, 410, 412; Palladius, *Dialogus* 60, ed. Coleman-Norton, 106-108.

[13]*Vita Olympiadis* 3-6, ed. Malingrey, 412, 414, 416,
418, 420; Palladius, *Dialogus* 56; 60, ed. Coleman-Norton,
98, 108-109; Sozomen, *Historia Ecclesiastica* VIII, 9, 1,
ed. J. Bidez and G.C. Hansen, GSC 50 (Berlin, 1960), 361.

[14]*Vita Olympiadis* 5, ed. Malingrey, 416.

[15]Perhaps Heraclides, bishop of Nyssa around A.D. 440:

so Ernst Honigmann, *Patristic Studies*, ST 173 (Vatican City, 1953), 106, 113-116.

[16]Palladius, *Dialogus* 61, ed. Coleman-Norton, 109-110; *Vita Olympiadis* 7; 8; 14, ed. Malingrey, 420, 422, 436.

[17]*Vita Olympiadis* 8; 14, ed. Malingrey, 422, 436; Sozomen, *Historia Ecclesiastica* VIII, 27, 8, ed. Bidez and Hansen, 388.

[18]*Vita Olympiadis* 14, ed. Malingrey, 436, 438; Palladius, *Dialogus* 56-57; 61, ed. Coleman-Norton, 99-102, 110; John Chrysostom, *Epistulae ad Olympiadem* 8 (= Migne 2), 10a, ed. A.-M. Malingrey, SC 13 bis (Paris, 1968), 198.

[19]*Vita Olympiadis* 6, ed. Malingrey, 418; see also Raymond Janin, *La Géographie ecclésiastique de l'empire byzantin. I, 3: Les Eglises et les monastères* (Paris, 1953), 395-396.

[20]Janin, *Eglises*, 3-4.

[21]*Vita Olympiadis* 13, ed. Malingrey, 434; John Chrysostom, *Epistulae ad Olympiadem* 15, 15, 1a; 8 (= Migne 2), 5c-d; 9c, ed. Malingrey, 356, 178, 196.

[22]*Vita Olympiadis* 14; 15, ed. Malingrey, 436, 438, 440; Palladius, *Historia Lausiaca* 56, ed. Butler, II, 150.

[23]*Vita Olympiadis* 15, ed. Malingrey, 440.

[24]John Chrysostom, *Epistulae ad Olympiadem* 8 (= Migne 2), 5c, ed. Malingrey, 176, 178.

[25]John Chrysostom, *Epistulae ad Olympiadem* 17 (= Migne 4), 2a, ed. Malingrey, 372.

[26]John Chrysostom, *Epistulae ad Olympiadem* 8 (= Migne 2), 5d, ed. Malingrey, 178.

[27]*Vita Olympiadis* 3-4, ed. Malingrey, 410, 412, 414; Sozomen, *Historia Ecclesiastica* VIII, 24, 4-7, ed. Bidez and Hansen, 382.

[28]Palladius, *Historia Lausiaca* 46, ed. Butler, II, 134; Paulinus of Nola, *Ep.* 29, 8, ed. W. von Hartel, CSEL 29 (Prague, Vienna, Leipzig, 1894), 253-254; Jones, et al., *Prosopography*, I, 592-593.

[29]Palladius, *Historia Lausiaca* 46; 54, ed. Butler, II, 135-136, 147-148; Paulinus of Nola, *Ep.* 29, 10, ed. Hartel, 257.

[30]Paulinus of Nola, *Ep.* 29, 5, ed. Hartel, 251.

[31]Palladius, *Historia Lausiaca* 46, ed. Butler, II, 135.

[32]Palladius, *Historia Lausiaca* 10; 46; 54, ed. Butler, II, 30, 136, 146, 147-148; Paulinus of Nola, *Ep.* 29, 11, ed. Hartel, 257-258.

[33]Melania provides refuge for fugitives from Arian persecution and intimidates a Palestinian judge who attempts to convict her: Paulinus of Nola, *Ep.* 29, 11, ed. Hartel, 257-258; Palladius, *Historia Lausiaca* 46, ed. Butler, II, 134-135.

[34]Palladius, *Historia Lausiaca* 54, ed. Butler, II, 146; Paulinus of Nola, *Ep.* 29, 12, ed. Hartel, 259-260.

[35]Melania did not wash: see Palladius, *Historia Lausiaca* 55, ed. Butler, II, 148-149 (a passage now thought to concern Melania). Her couch was the ground, according to Paulinus of Nola, *Ep.* 29, 13, ed. Hartel, 260.

[36]Palladius, *Historia Lausiaca* 54, ed. Butler, II, 148.

[37]Jerome, *Ep.* 108, 1; 3; 4, ed. I. Hilberg, CSEL 55 (Vienna, Leipzig, 1912), 306, 308, 309.

[38]Jerome, *Ep.* 108, 5; 34, ed. Hilberg 310, 351.

[39]Jerome, *Ep.* 108, 6; 11; 14, ed. Hilberg, 310-312, 320, 325.

[40]Jerome, *Ep.* 108, 7-14; 20, ed. Hilberg, 312-325, 334-335.

[41]Jerome, *Ep.* 108, 20, ed. Hilberg, 334-335.

[42]Jerome, *Ep.* 108, 20, ed. Hilberg, 335.

[43]Jerome, *Ep.* 108, 30, ed. Hilberg, 348.

[44]Jerome, *Ep.* 108, 3, ed. Hilberg, 308-309.

[45]Jerome, *Ep.* 108, 14, ed. Hilberg, 324.

[46]Jerome, *Ep.* 108, 15, ed. Hilberg, 325.

[47]Max Weber, *Economy and Society: An Outline of Interpretive Sociology*, ed. G. Roth and C. Wittich, trans. E. Fischoff et al. (New York, 1968), I, 231; III, 1006-1008.

[48]Weber, *Economy*, I, 215, 217; explicated by Talcott Parsons in Max Weber, *The Theory of Social and Economic Organization*, trans. A.M. Henderson and T. Parsons (New York, London, 1947), 57-67.

[49]Weber, *Economy*, I, 241-245; III, 1111-1120. For a summary of recent criticism of Weber's notion of charismatic authority, see Bengt Holmberg, *Paul and Power; The Structure of Authority in the Primitive Church as Reflected in the Pauline Epistles* (Lund, 1978), chap. 5.

[50]Weber, *Economy*, I, 245; III, 1170.

[51]Charisma is attributed, not "individual psychological equipment": Holmberg, *Paul*, 176.

[52]Their revolutionary break from societal expectations would be more characteristic of Weber's charismatic authority; see Weber, *Economy*, I, 244-245.

[53]Implicit in Weber, *Economy*, I, 226-241; contrasted with rational/legal authority, I, 219; explicitly developed by Parsons, in Weber, *Theory*, 58, 61.

[54]Weber, *Economy*, I, 218-223.

[55]Weber, *Economy*, I, 219.

[56]Weber, *Economy*, I, 230.

[57]Weber, *Economy*, III, 1008.

[58]Weber, *Economy*, I, 227-228, 230; III, 1006; a characteristic similar to charismatic authority, III, 1122.

[59]Weber, *Economy*, III, 1007.

[60]Weber, *Economy*, I, 231.

[61]Weber, *Economy*, I, 219, 227, 231; III, 1006; explicated by Parsons, in Weber, *Theory*, 60-61.

[62]Weber, *Economy*, I, 244.

[63]Weber, *Economy*, III, 1168.

[64]Weber, *Economy*, I, 244-245.

[65]For other deviations, see Clark, "Ascetic Renunciation," *passim*.

[66]*Vita Olympiadis* 6; 15, ed. Malingrey, 418, 440;
Jerome, *Ep*. 108, 11; 14, ed. Hilberg, 320, 325.

[67]Jerome, *Ep*. 108, 15; 30, ed. Hilberg, 327, 348-349.

[68]*Vita Melaniae Junioris* 68, ed. Gorce, SC 90 (Paris,
1962), 264: Paula arrives at Melania the Younger's
deathbed "with all her household." In *Vita Melaniae
Junioris* 63, ed. Gorce, 254, Melania and Paula celebrate
the Nativity in Bethlehem. The younger Paula was the
daughter of the elder Paula's son Toxotius and his wife
Laeta.

[69]*Vita Olympiadis* 6-7; 10; 12, ed. Malingrey, 418,
420, 426, 432, 434.

[70]Weber, *Economy*, I, 231; explicated by Parsons in
Weber, *Theory*, 61-62.

[71]Weber, *Economy*, I, 219; explicated by Parsons in
Weber, *Theory*, 57-58.

[72]Weber, *Economy*, I, 227; explicated by Parsons in
Weber, *Theory*, 60-61.

[73]Weber, *Economy*, I, 246-254; III, 1121-1123.

[74]*Vita Olympiadis* 12, ed. Malingrey, 432.

[75]Nicephorus Callistus, *Ecclesiasticae Historiae* XII,
24, PG 146, 1013.

[76]*Vita Olympiadis* 12, ed. Malingrey, 432, 434.

[77]Sergia, *Narratio de translatione S. Olympiadis* 2,
ed. Delehaye, *AnalBoll*, 16 (1897), 44.

[78]Sergia, *Narratio* 14, ed. Delehaye, 51.

[79]Latin translation in PL 103, 485-554. See also
Francis X. Murphy, *Rufinus of Aquileia (345-411): His
Life and Works* (Washington, D.C., 1945), 50 n. 86, 63,
89-91; Ferdinand Laun, "Die beiden Regeln des Basilius,
ihre Echtheit und Entstehung," *ZKircheng*, 44 (1925), 10-
29.

[80]Rufinus, *Praefatio ad Regulam S. Basilii*, PL 103,
485-486; for Rufinus' return to the West in A.D. 397, see
Murphy, *Rufinus*, 50 n. 86; C.P. Hammond, "The Last Ten
Years of Rufinus' Life and the Date of His Move South
from Aquileia," *JThS*, n.s., 28 (1977), 384; Nicole Moine,
"Melaniana," *RAug*, 15 (1980), 31.

[81]Murphy, *Rufinus*, 70.

[82]Palladius, *Historia Lausiaca* 38, ed. Butler, II,
119-120.

[83]Greek text edited by Hugo Gressmann in *TU* 39, 4
(Leipzig, 1913), 146-151.

[84]Joseph Muyldermans, ed. and trans., *Evagriana
Syriaca. Textes inédits du British Museum et de la
Vaticane* (Louvain, 1952), 30.

[85]For clues that Rufinus translated Evagrius' *Rule
for Nuns*, see Jerome, *Ep.* 133, 3, ed. I. Hilberg, CSEL 56
(Vienna, Leipzig, 1918), 246-247; Gennadius, *De viris
illustribus* 17, PG 58, 1070; D.A. Wilmart, "Les Versions
latines des Sentences d'Evagre pour les vierges," *RBén*,
28 (1911), 143-144, 148-151.

[86]Jerome, *Ep.* 108, 20, ed. Hilberg, 335-336.

[87]Jerome, *Praefatio, S. Pachomii Regula*, 1, ed. A.
Boon (Louvain, 1932), 3-5.

[88]Jerome, *Apologia contra Rufinum* I, 17, PL 23, 430;
III, 4, PL 23, 480-481; *In Nahum* III, PL 25, 1261.

[89]Murphy, *Rufinus*, 61-62.

INTRODUCTION TO JOHN CHRYSOSTOM,
ON VIRGINITY; AGAINST REMARRIAGE

The Edwin Mellen Press (1983)

John Chrysostom--so called for his "golden-mouthed" oratory[1]--composed more treatises on asceticism and marriage than any other Greek-writing church father. Because of his enormous literary production and his eventful life, we are better acquainted with Chrysostom than we are with many other ancient figures. Although the sources leave some basic questions unanswered, and the highly rhetorical style in which Chrysostom wrote, heady with exaggeration, numbs the modern reader, our knowledge of his life and ascetic concerns is nonetheless pertinent to understanding his treatises *On Virginity* and *Against Remarriage*, here published in English translation for the first time.

Chrysostom's contemporaries or near-contemporaries Palladius, Socrates, Sozomen, and Theodoret commented on his life, yet their notices leave modern scholars uncertain as to the date of his birth: estimates have ranged from A.D. 344 to 354.[2] Although the traditional reading of these ancient histories took Chrysostom's father, Secundus, to be *magister militum* of Syria,[3] A.H.M. Jones has more recently argued that Secundus should be demoted to a "high grade civil servant."[4] If Jones' interpretation is correct, the reports of Socrates and Sozomen that Chrysostom came from a noble family may need reassess-

ment.[5] In any event, Secundus died a few years
after his marriage, leaving his twenty-year-old widow,
Anthusa, with two small children.[6] The patristic sources
add that Chrysostom trained for the bar[7] or (in an alternate interpretation) for work in the office of an
imperial clerk.[8] Some also state that he studied with
the famous rhetorician of Antioch, Libanius,[9] and with
the philosopher Andragathius.[10]

Antioch, the city of Chrysostom's birth and upbringing, was a thriving Syriac metropolis of perhaps 200,000
persons. Until Constantinople's rise in the fourth century, it had been the third city of the Empire, ranking
behind only Rome and Alexandria.[11] Christians, Jews, and
pagans all flourished there.[12] By decree of the Council
of Nicaea in A.D. 325, it had been made a patriarchate
whose territory was co-extensive with the civil diocese
of the Orient.[13] Chrysostom's baptism when he was about
eighteen years old[14] and his subsequent training by
Christian teachers, including the noted Biblical scholar,
Diodore of Tarsus,[15] took place in Antioch.

From his youth, Chrysostom showed a keen personal
interest in asceticism.[16] Palladius notes that John
spent four of his formative years under the tutelage of
an ascetic named Syrus in monastic retreat on the
mountains outside Antioch. For another two years,
Chrysostom lived a solitary's life in a cave.[17] Only
ill-health, brought on by his rigorous regimen, convinced
him to abandon eremiticism and return to Antioch.[18]
Probably already a lector in the church at Antioch before
his retreat to the wilderness,[19] Chrysostom upon his return was ordained deacon in A.D. 381 and, five years
later, priest.[20] It was in his Antiochene period, most
likely when he served as deacon, that Chrysostom composed
his first treatises advocating asceticism, including the
two contained in this volume.[21]

The better-known and more eventful portion of
Chrysostom's life falls after his call to the bishopric
of Constantinople in A.D. 397. His struggles there with
other clergy, royalty, and the unregenerate rich, the
attack upon him by Theophilus of Alexandria, and his two
sentences of exile (the last of which also saw his death
in A.D. 407) are more fully covered by the ancient historians than his earlier years.[22] It is nonetheless
clear that he manifested a strong ascetic bent from the
time of his baptism to that of his downfall--indeed,
according to Palladius, his downfall was in part occasioned by the ascetic reforms he pressed upon his
reluctant clergy and the "society Christians" of
Constantinople.[23] Commentators agree that during his
years as cleric at Antioch, Chrysostom was exceptionally
keen for the ascetic life.[24] Later, as priest and
bishop, he toned down his advocacy of rigorous asceticism[25] and adopted a view that has been described as less
"eschatological" and more "incarnational."[26]

In addition to the treatises that comprise this
volume, Chrysostom wrote other works during his years at
Antioch that manifest similar ascetic themes. In the
*Comparison of the Power, Riches, and Excellence of a King
and a Monk*, for example, Chrysostom, adapting motifs from
Stoic diatribe, argues that a monk who practices the
"philosophic" virtues of Christianity, defined in accordance with asceticism, is truly more regal than the
monarch engaged in the cares of the world.[27] Whereas the
king fights mere barbarians, the monk casts down
demons;[28] the king's possessions are buried with this
life, while the monk's spiritual wealth lasts eter-
nally,[29] and so forth. In *Against the Opponents of the
Monastic Life*, Chrysostom wars against those who succumb
to the love of riches and to sexual desire[30] (pederasty

receives special condemnation).[31] Similarly, he advocated in his *Letter to a Young Widow*, composed in A.D.
380 or 381, that widows not remarry.[32] Two early letters
Chrysostom wrote to a "fallen" friend, Theodore, also
counsel sexual denial: Theodore, having lapsed from his
ascetic commitment through his passion for a certain
Hermione, is urged by Chrysostom to abandon her and return to the ascetic life.[33] In addition, at least one of
Chrysostom's two treatises against "spiritual marriage"
(the practice of ascetic men and women living together)
may have been composed during the 380s in Antioch.[34]
Later in Chrysostom's career, his numerous commentaries
and homilies on Genesis and the New Testament books, as
well as his homilies praising female saints and martyrs,
all resound with ascetic themes. Thus *On Virginity*
(dated to the 380s or the early 390s)[35] and *Against Remarriage* (dated A.D. 383-386)[36] are in the company of
many other writings by Chrysostom that celebrate the
ascetic life. To be sure, his championing of virginity
was far from novel in his time. In fact, scholars think
his treatise *On Virginity* borrowed themes from similar
works composed a few years earlier by Basil of Ancyra,[37]
Eusebius of Emesa,[38] and Gregory of Nyssa.[39]
Chrysostom's treatises translated below, then, are just
one manifestation of the ascetic fervor of late ancient
Christianity.

　　Enough manuscripts remain of the two treatises here
translated (some of which date to the tenth century)[40]
to ensure reasonable confidence in the Greek text. The
Greek texts used by Sally Shore for her translation are
those established by Herbert Musurillo for *On Virginity*
and by Gerard Ettlinger for *Against Remarriage* and published in volumes 125 and 138, respectively, of Sources
Chrétiennes.[41]

II

Although it has been posited that Chrysostom's
treatise *On Virginity* can be read as an extended commentary on I Corinthians 7,[42] it is immediately apparent to
the contemporary reader that it constitutes no simple
explication of the Pauline text, no more than *Against
Remarriage* does. Despite Chrysostom's constant appeal to
Paul, so changed was the intellectual and social setting
of late fourth-century Christianity that his interpretation of I Corinthians would no doubt have startled its
author in several ways. It is not simply the passage of
time that separates Chrysostom from Paul. Chrysostom's
fine training in Greek literature and philosophy[43] was
far superior to whatever rudimentary classical education
we may imagine Paul received. In addition, his position
as deacon and priest in the church of Antioch involved
him in an ecclesiastical organization much larger and
more elaborately structured than that of Corinth in the
mid-first century. Yet these and other factors mean
little in themselves unless we appreciate what such
changes signaled for Chrysostom's understanding of Paul.

In I Corinthians 7, Paul made clear that despite the
usefulness of marriage as a check for sexual desire,
celibacy was preferable.[44] He hoped that Christians
would choose his path of celibacy as the one most expedi-
tious for the period before the eschaton's arrival.[45] By
the late fourth century, celibacy was considered the most
exalted way of life for Christians. Virginity and widowhood were no longer, as Paul saw them, simply conditions
in which persons might best preserve their energies for
the service of the Lord; they were now "professions" for
which a solemn pledge was taken. Chrysostom thus has
something more definite in mind when he speaks of widows
and virgins than Paul apparently did. For example, when

commenting on Paul's opinion that a virgin did not sin if
she married,[46] Chrysostom feels constrained to remark
that Paul most certainly could not have been speaking of
a girl who had formally renounced marriage for virginity,
for if such a girl were to wed, she would be committing
an unforgivable sin. Rather, on Chrysostom's reading of
the passage, Paul intended to characterize a young woman
who had not yet decided whether to marry or to profess
virginity.[47] Likewise for widows: Paul could not mean
(according to Chrysostom) that a woman who had vowed herself to perpetual widowhood in the Christian church was
still free to remarry.[48] To pledge oneself in widowhood
while contemplating a second marriage would be to break
a promise.[49] It is evident that to be a virgin or a
widow in Chrysostom's time implied a more fixed status
than it had in Paul's.

Although when Chrysostom wrote the treatises under
consideration there were only a few monasteries for
women in Asia Minor,[50] many women committed to a celibate
life had banded together in groups or had simply continued to live in their families' homes.[51] We know less
than we wish about early monasticism for women in the
area. Yet churches supported massive numbers of such
female celibates, as is revealed by Chrysostom's chance
comment that 3000 widows and virgins were assisted by the
church at Antioch.[52] The ascetic fervor that attended
the cessation of the persecutions and the sudden acceptance of the Christian faith is a familiar theme to
historians of late antiquity; whatever reasons may be
posited for the phenomenon, it is clearly attested in the
sources. Whether or not *On Virginity* was written for the
explicit purpose of recruiting virgins,[53] it nonetheless
depicts the rewards of celibacy and the difficulties of
marriage in ways that must have been attractive to many
Christians of Chrysostom's age.

Although Chrysostom agreed with Paul that celibacy
was preferable to marriage, their reasons differed:
Paul's view that virginity should be favored because of
the imminence of the eschaton was re-interpreted by
Chrysostom to fit a late fourth-century context. Paul
believed, as he set forth in I Thessalonians 4:15, that
Jesus would return to usher in the Kingdom of God during
the lifetimes of many in his audience. Thus it is not
surprising to find him in I Corinthians 7 arguing that
because of the "impending distress" the single state was
to be advocated. Since the time had "grown short," as
Paul put it, it would be better not to entangle oneself
in marriage, for the unmarried person was freer to serve
the Lord in the brief interim before the Kingdom's
arrival.[54]

Chrysostom's treatment of Paul's words reminds us
how rapidly the eschatological hope of early Christianity
faded, how speedily the enthusiasts for the Kingdom's
arrival were viewed as unpopular eccentrics, if not
worse.[55] So removed from Paul's eschatological expectation is Chrysostom that he cannot comprehend the plain
meaning of the text. Since he, like his contemporaries,
no longer expected an immediate cessation of this world,
all Paul's comments about the eschaton must be understood
as pertaining to the individual's afterlife in heaven.
Indeed, Chrysostom addresses the (to him) puzzling
problem of why Paul only seemed to speak of celibacy's
advantages for the present life, rather than of those for
the next.[56] Chrysostom's answer is that Paul's approach
was conditioned by pedagogical considerations: since
people tend to be more concerned with the here-and-now
than with the heavenly afterlife, Paul, skillful teacher
that he was, leads them from their present lowly concerns
to a higher "philosophy" (Chrysostom's customary term for

Christian truth) by addressing their immediate anxieties
first.[57] Chrysostom is quick to admit that virginity has
its present advantages, as Paul had suggested,[58] but the
future rewards in heaven capture his imagination at least
equally.[59] The account we must give of ourselves in the
heavenly court, before the divine Judge, he thinks,
should always weigh on our minds--and that judgment will
take place upon an individual's death, not at the
eschaton's arrival.[60]

This change in eschatological expectation forms the
background to two prominent themes reiterated throughout
Chrysostom's works: that while we live on this earth, we
are to lead the life of the angels as much as possible if
we wish to join them in their heavenly home later,[61] and
that celibate women can expect to greet Jesus as their
Bridegroom when they enter the heavenly mansions after
death.[62] The motivation for celibacy, in other words,
has been significantly altered since the time of Paul.
No longer seen primarily as a practical measure to expe-
dite Christian living while we await God's Kingdom,
celibacy has now acquired an "ontological" status that
raises humans to a semi-divine existence in the midst of
the present era and prepares them for incorporation into
the ranks of those angelic powers who Jesus allegedly
declared neither married nor gave in marriage.[63]

If virginity or celibacy was viewed as an "angelic"
way of life, it is easy to understand why Chrysostom
thought it more elevated than marriage. Yet in a neat
inversion of his own argument, he posits that virginity
is the true *human* condition, not just the angelic one.
Virginity was the condition in which Adam and Eve were
created and in which God had intended that they remain.[64]
By adopting virginity, we not only become more godly, we
are also recalled to our true human nature. Chrysostom

elaborates this point at some length. Sexual desire, he
says, was not "naturally" implanted in humans at their
creation as part of their biological constitution.[65] It,
along with marriage and sexual reproduction, resulted
from the Fall in the Garden of Eden[66]--a view that Paul
would no doubt have found astounding. Although Paul had
suggested in Romans 5 that death entered the world
through the sin of Adam, he nowhere hinted at Chrysostom's conclusion, that marriage was introduced only as a
consequence of the Fall. Yet Chrysostom, using Hesiod's
image of Decency and Reverence abandoning the earth at
the end of the Golden Age,[67] described the Fall as the
time when the beauty of virginity abandoned the first
couple, leaving them to become "earth and ashes"--and to
discover the solace of marriage.[68] As Chrysostom bluntly
put it, "For where death is, there is marriage."[69] To
the obvious question of how the human race could have
multiplied without sexual intercourse, Chrysostom
answered that God could have created other humans without
recourse to sexual means, just as he created the angels
and archangels (who suffer no population deficiency),
and, for that matter, as he created Adam and Eve.[70]
Furthermore, Christians should understand that children
are never simply begotten by "natural" means in marriage;
their creation is always by God's will and word, as is
made clear by such Old Testament examples as Abraham and
Sarah's belated conception of Isaac.[71] In any case, the
Bible teaches us that it is not the lack of sexual intercourse that brings about the demise of the human race,
but rather sin, as we can see in the case of Noah's
flood.[72]

 Since the Fall, the two functions that marriage
serves are procreation and the taming of sexual desire.[73]
For Chrysostom, both are dubious justifications for the

marital state. He notes that for Christians who look to
a heavenly afterlife, the desire for children is an
inappropriate motivation for marriage.[74] Chrysostom
notes that Paul himself never mentioned the production
of children as a justification for marriage: the only
rationale the apostle gave for marriage was the contain-
ment of sexual desire[75]--or, as Chrysostom more crudely
puts it, for "the suppression of licentiousness and
debauchery."[76] Marriage, a concession to our weakness,[77]
a rescue from impurity,[78] is for those who are still
"caught up in their passions, who desire to live the life
of swine and be ruined in brothels."[79]

Yet Chrysostom's view of marriage is not wholly negative. Marriage was useful in its time, he concedes. In
the "childhood" of our race, we needed such infant fare.
But, like fledglings, we must learn to fly and leave the
maternal nest.[80] Chrysostom here bases his argument on
Paul's: that Christians must become adults and put away
"childish things,"[81] yet they must be given "milk" before
they are ready for "solid food."[82] Marriage, then, for
Chrysostom, was one of the indulgences allowed by the Old
Law, i.e., the Old Testament.[83] It does not detract from
the relative goodness of marriage that now a more perfect
standard is recommended to us, one consonant with the
greater overflow of the Spirit's power since the advent
of Christ.[84]

Chrysostom's eagerness to defend marriage as a relative good despite its disadvantages stems in large part
from the battle the orthodox church had waged in earlier
years against the Gnostics' depreciation of the created
world; in Chrysostom's time, the struggle persisted
against the Manichean ascetics.[85] Although Paul in I
Corinthians may have addressed an ascetic contingent who
disapproved of marriage,[86] it is unlikely that he was

confronting a full-blown Gnostic attack on marriage.
Later New Testament writings hint that the attack on
marriage may have become more acute after Paul's time.[87]
Certainly the church fathers from the late second century
on had to take care that their negative remarks about
marriage not be interpreted as supporting the views
attributed to some Gnostics that human sexual functioning, reproduction, and marriage were traps set by the
evil powers to ensnare humans.[88]   In *On Virginity*, Chrysostom singles out Marcion, Valentinus, and Mani as the
three heretical leaders who, he says, led their followers
to eternal perdition through their teachings about the
created order, virginity, and marriage.[89]   The burden of
Chrysostom's complaint is that the ascetic heretics are
wrongly motivated in their espousal of virginity:[90]   they
insult God[91] and slander his creation by treating
marriage with such contempt.[92]   The heretics, he argues,
are almost compelled to lives of virginity because of
their desire to abstain from the evil of marriage,[93]
whereas true virtue must be more than simple abstention
from evil.[94]   In fact, the heretics inadvertently reduce
the glory of virginity by their deprecation of marriage,
for if virginity is understood merely as better than
something inferior, i.e., marriage, it cannot be viewed
as a very laudable end.[95]   Chrysostom's argument that
praising marriage also serves to glorify virginity[96]
should be understood in the context of his anti-Gnostic
polemic. Indeed, it was imperative for Chrysostom to
uphold the goodness of marriage, amid his many criticisms
of it, if he himself wished to avoid charges of Manicheanism.[97]   Thus the conflict of orthodox Christianity
with Gnostic and Manichean groups after the time of Paul
added a dimension to the debate on marriage that was
absent from the apostle's arguments.

Still another way in which Chrysostom's discussion
of marriage and celibacy differs from Paul's lies in
Chrysostom's attitudes toward women. Paul's views on the
female sex have been much debated in recent years,[98] but
even taking Paul at his most conservative, we find
nothing in the genuinely Pauline epistles to rival the
deprecating comments Chrysostom makes about Eve and her
descendants. For example, Paul in Romans writes of
Adam's sin and its consequences for the human race, but
does not mention Eve in this passage.[99] Chrysostom, however, attributing the derogatory comments about women in
the Pastoral Epistles to Paul,[100] blames Eve for her
treachery in the sin.[101] It was she who subjected man to
death.[102] It was women who were the cause of the Great
Flood and who destroyed, or attempted to destroy, the Old
Testament heroes.[103] Woman at creation was intended to
be a helper to man,[104] but she did not adhere to this
high purpose.[105] She now "helps" man by bearing his
children and allaying his sexual desire, but Chrysostom
scoffs at the worth of such assistance to Christians.[106]
Women who still make "the demands of wives" rather than
embracing chaste frugality are in fact dangers to their
husbands, not aids.[107] To be sure, Chrysostom's words
about women are not entirely condemnatory; he can even
sympathize with the oppression and outright cruelty to
which they are often subjected in marriage.[108] Nonetheless, his views on Eve and other women are far more
biting than anything in Paul's letters.

Lastly, Chrysostom's views on marriage and virginity
are influenced by some features of late ancient ethical
discussion that had made little if any impact on Paul's
thinking. To begin, we should note that Chrysostom
thinks of Christian teaching not so much as divine revelation as "philosophy,"[109] indeed, as the highest

imaginable wisdom. As such, Christianity had both its
theoria and its *praxis*: it taught the loftiest contemplation, yet offered sage advice for daily living. To
cast the discussion of virginity and marriage in the
framework of "philosophy" gives it a decidedly abstract
flavor that was foreign to Paul's advice, geared to
address a pressing practical problem. Chrysostom's discussion throughout shows that he borrows from the
traditions of Greek philosophy. For example, he adapts
Plato's image in *Phaedrus* 246A-248E of reason as the
charioteer reining in the unruly horses of the passions
to describe the virgin who as charioteer keeps the
"horses" of her tongue, her ears, her feet, and so forth,
under control.[110] An appeal to revelation has here been
supplanted by an appeal to Greek ethical writings. Likewise, Chrysostom's treatment of riches is in strict
accord with the classical praises of simple living (whose
benefits include good health, hearty appetite, sound
sleep)[111] that are more reminiscent of Stoic and Cynic
diatribe[112] than of the New Testament.

   Nowhere is the influence of the Greek ethical tradition more prominent in Chrysostom's writings than in his
discussion of the relationship between virtue and free
choice. Behind Chrysostom's insistence that virtue is
not genuine if it is not freely chosen, the result of
reasoned decision, lies the entire Greek ethical tradition from Socrates onward.[113] Only when we make a
decision can we be credited with acting well, Chrysostom
argues.[114] So strong was Chrysostom's desire to emphasize the role of choice[115] that modern commentators have
sometimes felt obliged to defend him from charges of
Semi-Pelagianism.[116] Indeed, when we note how sharply
Chrysostom must bend Paul's words to make the apostle's
celibacy a matter of his own choice and effort, not (as

Paul himself said) a gift from God, we can see the point
of the charge. Chrysostom thus argues that when Paul
attributed his virginity to God's gift, he was simply
exhibiting humility. What Paul calls "gifts" are really
virtuous deeds. Paul's continence resulted from his own
effort. Chrysostom remarks that he stresses this point
so that no one will imagine that he or she need not
strive in order to uphold celibacy.[117] Paul thus functions as a model for others who struggle to live without
sexual relation.[118]

   Chrysostom's emphasis on personal effort is important
for his advocacy of virginity and widowhood: they are
states of life that are (in the Stoic phrase he borrowed)
"up to us."[119] If we do not exercise sexual self-
control, we have only ourselves to blame and must concede
that we simply did not make the effort,[120] an effort that
must not be postponed if we are to receive the appropriate heavenly crown.[121] The decision for celibacy must be
a completely free one.[122] No one should imagine, for
example, that a widow could be "compelled" to remarry.[123]
There is no "compulsion" involved in her choice. And if
she makes the decision for celibacy, there can be no
going back on it without her breaking a solemn promise to
God.[124] Chrysostom compares the choice of celibacy to an
athlete's decision to enter a contest: the athlete
freely decides whether or not to participate, but once he
enters the stadium, there is no more choice; the "law of
the contest" then prevails.[125]

   Chrysostom's insistence that celibacy must involve
free decision accords well with his understanding of virginity and widowhood as governed by the "counsels of
perfection."[126] In the patristic era, the notion became
common that not all of the ethical injunctions given in
the New Testament need be taken in their strictest sense

by every Christian. There was a minimum standard of
morality incumbent upon all Christians, to be sure: no
Christian should murder, steal, deny the faith, and so
forth. But it was understood that only some Christians
would be strong enough to renounce property and the
sexual life. For those willing to accept and act upon
those "counsels of perfection," a more glorious reward in
heaven was envisaged. This double-tiered concept of
merit was particularly prominent in the church fathers'
discussions of marriage and virginity. For Chrysostom,
Christians are of course permitted to marry, although
marriage should never be viewed as an opportunity for
sexual excess or soft living.[127] But those who opt for
the more perfect way can expect a more brilliant reception in heaven.[128] And if graded rewards are available
to Christians, it is important that celibacy with its
highest reward be a freely-chosen state. As Chrysostom
phrased it, Christ quite intentionally did not compel
people to virginity by making it a law for all of his
followers, since then no "honor" would have been attached
to the state: virginity would simply have been a duty
required of all Christians.[129]

In *On Virginity*, Chrysostom uses the argument linking
celibacy and free choice to good effect in his opening
attack against the heretical virgins: they are not
really virgins since they have not chosen their virginal
condition.[130] Because they view marrriage as an evil,
they have not made a genuine decision for virginity. Yet
by their avoidance of the perceived evil of marriage,
they have deprived themselves of the reward they expected
to receive since they did not freely choose the virginal
life.[131] Such heretics want to make virginity an obliga-
tion, not a matter of virtuous choice, and herein lies
the error of their position.[132] Chrysostom points out

that Paul, unlike the heretics, never spoke of marital
intercourse as defiling; according to Chrysostom, Paul
rather believed that sex was simply a waste of one's
time.[133] If marriage is not a genuinely good option for
Christians, Chrysostom continues, it makes no sense to
praise virgins, no more than we laud eunuchs for their
sexual chastity. Indeed, heretical virgins share
mutilation with eunuchs, for although the latter have
suffered bodily castration, the heretical virgins have
had their "upright thoughts" cut off by the devil![134]

The moral framework within which Chrysostom constructs his argument about virtue's link with choice is
thus significantly different from that of Paul, whose
ethical position rested on a belief that God gave various
spiritual gifts (*charismata*) to different Christians for
the upbuilding of the community.[135] To some, like Paul,
the Spirit had granted a gift of celibacy, but not all
would receive that gift and hence not all could be expected to follow his course.[136] Although Chrysostom in
his voluminous writings speaks much of grace, on the
issue of celibacy he emphasizes human effort almost
exclusively. He stresses the "up-to-us"-ness of human
action as much as the Stoic philosophers did, for he,
like they, believed that praise and blame could not be
assigned unless virtuous action were freely chosen or
rejected.[137]

A third aspect of Chrysostom's writings on celibacy
that is directly borrowed from the world of classical
literature--an aspect that does not appear in Paul's
letters--are the *topoi* on marriage, the common-place
examples and arguments that highlighted the problems
occasioned by marriage and wives. Although Paul, for his
part, thinks of marriage as a bond between the
partners,[138] and mentions the worldly anxieties that

marriage may bring,[139] he does not belabor the
disadvantages--indeed, the horrors--of the married estate
as Chrysostom, following many classical writers, does.
Especially in describing the woes of marriage Chrysostom
makes free use of the commonplaces to be found in classical literature.[140] In doing so, Chrysostom goes far
beyond Paul's modestly expressed view that marriage was a
"bond." Thus according to Chrysostom, marriage is even
worse than slavery: slaves have the hope that they can
buy their freedom, but for the married there is no such
escape, since divorce is not permitted to Christians.[141]
In an outburst of rhetorical extravagance, Chrysostom
compares married couples to fugitive slaves whose legs
have been shackled together; if they wish to move at
all, they are forced to limp in concert.[142] Moreover,
since a Christian man is sexually subject to his wife,[143]
he is in effect trapped into sexual chastity.[144] No
doubt this seemed like a shocking form of bondage to many
among Chrysostom's readers, accustomed to a more relaxed
sexual standard for men.[145] Although the husband is the
master of the household, Chrysostom admits, what advantage is this if he himself is enslaved?[146]

Developing Paul's notion of marriage as a "bond,"
Chrysostom fully exploits the pagan *topoi* on marriage.
As the latter brought home, marriage means that each
partner must put up with the other's faults. The husband
must endure his wife even if she is "wicked, carping, a
chatterbox, extravagant."[147] Unlike the pagan authors,
however, Chrysostom in these treatises stresses mostly
the woes of marriage that beset women, rather than those
that beset men--an approach no doubt conditioned by his
subject and his audience. He thus brings the trials of
marriage home to his female readers. If the wife dis-
covers that her husband has "morally depraved" desires,

she must nonetheless follow him.[148] Men may strike their
wives, cover them with abuse, subject them to the
contempt of the servants: how many ways men have found
to punish their wives, Chrysostom exclaims![149] The
jealous husband--a stock character in Chrysostom's
analysis--encourages the servants to spy upon his wife's
every deed, word, yes, upon her every sigh. But if she
tries to accuse him of wrongdoing, he will teach her to
keep silent fast enough. He can even have her executed,
if he wishes, Chrysostom notes.[150] Inequality of
economic status presents further problems in the relationship,[151] but even if the two are on a par as far as
property is concerned, the potential equality is ruined
by "the rule of subordination" in marriage, by which the
wife is subject to her husband.[152]

Next Chrysostom asks his readers to consider the
fears that attend the girl even before her husband is
picked. Will he suit her? What are his habits? Will
she please him? She is subject to the decision of her
father or guardian,[153] and becomes, in effect, the
embarrassed subject of a financial transaction between
two men.[154] Next she must worry about childlessness, or
conversely, about bearing too many children.[155] Even if
a child is safely born, after the pains and dangers of
labor, its fate is a source of worry for years to
come.[156] A matron's entire life is spent in constant
anxiety about the death of loved ones--and her antici-
pated fear is as difficult to bear as the grief resulting
from an actual death.[157] The problems occasioned by
lazy, gossiping, and vindictive servants illustrate still
another disadvantage of marriage.[158]

The woes of second marriage are even more graphically
depicted by Chrysostom. To all the problems of first
marriage are now added the hostilities and jealousies

incumbent upon the new relationship. Step-children pose
special difficulties. Irrational jealousies toward the
spouse's dead partner prevail.[159] In particular does
Chrysostom dwell upon the suspicions that lurk in the
mind of the new husband as well as those of outsiders:
how can the woman be considered trustworthy, if she
desecrated the memory of her dead husband by marrying
again?[160] What does the second husband feel when he
joins his bride on the marriage bed she shared with her
first?[161] The new husband always lives with the suspicion that he himself is being scorned since the very fact
that his wife remarried shows her "faithlessness" to the
man of her youth.[162] And, when it comes to plain talk,
Chrysostom reminds us that a man can never love a widow
in the frenzied passion with which he embraces a virgin
bride, for he always has in mind that she has known
another man.[163] Every husband, Chrysostom insists, wants
to think that he is his wife's "first and only master
(*kyrios*)."[164]

On the point of second marriage, Chrysostom, like
other Christian writers, follows the classical ideal of
the *univira*, the once-married woman. Despite changes in
legislation and mores during the Empire that granted more
freedom to women, especially freedom to divorce, the
traditional ideal of the monogamous woman was enshrined
in literature as well as life.[165] From that pagan,
especially Roman, ideal, Christian critics of second
marriage such as Tertullian and Jerome,[166] as well as
Chrysostom, borrowed much. Their denunciations of second
marriage stand in contrast to Paul's timid suggestion
that widows might, in his opinion, be happier if they
remained single.[167] Yet even Paul's hesitant recommenda-
tion was not accepted by all New Testament writers. The
author of I Timothy, for example, believed that younger

widows should remarry, and that no woman should be
counted on the rolls of the church's widows until she
reached sixty years of age.[168]

Chrysostom's denunciation of second marriage is, in
comparison, sharp. One might think, he argues, that
widows would have learned from hard experience the
problems of marriage and would not need guidance from him
to encourage them to celibacy.[169] Widows who ponder remarriage must suffer from amnesia regarding the conditions of marriage--unless, of course, they are motivated
by desire for worldly possessions, or worse yet, by
"incontinence."[170] Only total inexperience with marriage
could explain why any female would seek it out,[171] and
such inexperience a widow cannot claim. A monogamous
woman has at least exhibited a dignified self-control,
but a woman who remarries reveals that she has a "weak
and carnal soul."[172] In such ways does Chrysostom alter
the values of the earlier Christian tradition.

In so depicting the woes of marriage, Chrysostom
undoubtedly meant to encourage his audience toward celibacy. He reminds them that virgins avoid all the afore-
mentioned problems: not only do they receive a higher
heavenly reward than the married, they also win the
advantages of an unharried earthly life.[173] The virgin,
unlike the matron, has no worry except to present her
beautiful soul to her heavenly Bridegroom.[174] (The
Bridegroom Jesus, according to Chrysostom, accepts celibate widows to himself as well.)[175] We might imagine,
given Chrysostom's emphasis on moral effort, that he
would concede to married people extra heavenly "credit"
for the trials they have endured in wedlock. Not so. In
the case of marriage, effort does not count, only the
triumph over evil, and celibates have a much keener edge
on achieving it, in Chrysostom's opinion.[176]

Indeed, when the virgin contemplates the high reward she will receive, her abstinence will be easy to bear,[177] whatever her struggle may have been.[178] Of course, Chrysostom asserts, she must have a pure soul as well as a pure body:[179] decorum, devotion, and perfect conduct are all essential to true virginity.[180] Those who are merely bodily virgins but who have not exemplified other Christian virtues--such as the foolish virgins of Matthew 25 and probably the heretical ones as well--will end up in hell.[181] Chrysostom is eager to insist that mere externals, such as shabby clothing, cannot make a true virgin.[182] Genuine Christian virgins must be completely unconcerned with worldly matters,[183] totally detached from material affairs.[184] In this condition, the virgin will be prepared to marry God and to receive the wedding gifts of heaven.[185] The benefits of celibacy thus provide a pleasing contrast to the woes of marriage.

In so describing the trials of marriage and the glories of virginity, Chrysostom has gone far beyond his Pauline source. The two treatises of Chrysostom that follow are therefore no straightforward retelling of I Corinthians 7. Christianity's entrance to the world of "high" classical culture, its abandonment of an immediate eschatological expectation, its struggle against Gnosticizing heretics, its reflection on the origin and consequences of the Fall, its acceptance of gradation in moral standards for Christians proportioned to their varying degrees of religious commitment, all contributed to make Chrysostom's commentary upon the Pauline chapter as much an *eisegesis* as an *exegesis*.

NOTES

[1]The first recorded use of "Chrysostomos" for Bishop
John was in A.D. 553 by Pope Vigilius, *Constitutum
Vigilii Papae de tribus capitulis* (PL 69, 101):
"...Joannis Constantinopolitani episcopi, quem Chrysos-
tomum vocant...." Of Chrysostom, the *Suda* reports,
"...his tongue was more fluent than the cataracts of the
Nile" (*Suidae Lexicon*, ed. Ada Adler [Leipzig: B.G.
Teubner, 1931], II, 463 [p. 647, 31-32]).

[2]Aimé Puech, *Saint John Chrysostom, 344-407*, 2nd ed.,
tr. M. Partridge (London: R. and T. Washborne, Ltd.,
1917), p. 3 (between A.D. 344 and 347); Anatole Moulard,
Saint Jean Chrysostome. Sa vie, son oeuvre (Paris:
Procure Générale du Clergé, 1941), p. 12 (A.D. 349);
Chrysostomus Baur, *John Chrysostom and His Time*, tr. M.
Gonzaga (Westminster, Md.: Newman Press, 1959), I, 3
(A.D. 354); Jean Dumortier, "La Valeur historique du
Dialogue de Palladius et la chronologie de Saint Jean
Chrysostome," *Mélanges de Science Religieuse* 7 (1951),
56 n.3. Dates in Chrysostom's early life as given by
Robert E. Carter, "The Chronology of Saint John Chrysos-
tom's Early Life," *Traditio* 18 (1962), 357-364 are:
Chrysostom was born in A.D. 349, baptized in A.D. 368;
spent A.D. 372-378 in ascetic retreat.

[3]Based on Palladius, *Dialogus de Vita S. Joannis
Chrysostomi*, ed. P.R. Coleman-Norton (Cambridge: Cambridge University Press, 1928), V, 18 (p. 28).

[4]A.H.M. Jones, "St. John Chrysostom's Parentage and
Education," *Harvard Theological Review* 46 (1953), 171.

[5]Socrates, *Historia ecclesiastica* VI, 3 (PG 67, 665);
Sozomen, *Historia ecclesiastica* VIII, 2 (PG 67, 1513);
Palladius reports that John Chrysostom's parents were
eugenōs (*Dialogus* V, 18 [Coleman-Norton, p. 28]).

[6]John Chrysostom, *De sacerdotio* (PG 48, 624-625); *Ad
viduam juniorem* 2 (PG 48, 601).

[7]Socrates, *Historia ecclesiastica* VI, 3 (PG 67, 665); Palladius, *Dialogus* V, 18 (Coleman-Norton, p. 28).

[8]Jones, "Chrysostom," p. 151.

[9]Socrates, *Historia ecclesiastica* VI, 3 (PG 67, 665); Sozomen, *Historia ecclesiastica* VIII, 2 (PG 67, 1513). Doubts on the relationship have been raised by Paul Petit, *Les Etudiants de Libanius* (Paris: Nouvelles Editions Latines, 1957), p. 41, and by A.J. Festugière, *Antioche païenne et chrétienne: Libanius, Chrysostome et les moines de Syrie* (Paris: Editions E. de Boccard, 1959), pp. 409-410.

[10]Socrates, *Historia ecclesiastica* VI, 3 (PG 67, 665); Sozomen, *Historia ecclesiastica* VIII, 2 (PG 67, 1513).

[11]Paul Petit, *Libanius et la vie municipale à Antioche au IVe siècle après J.-C.* (Paris: Librairie Orientaliste Paul Geuthner, 1955), pp. 165-190; J.H.W.G. Liebeschuetz, *Antioch: City and Imperial Administration in the Later Roman Empire* (Oxford: Clarendon Press, 1972), pp. 92-96; Glanville Downey, *Ancient Antioch* (Princeton: Princeton University Press, 1963, chaps. 7-9. The statistic of 200,000 residents is based on John Chrysostom, *In S. Ignatium Martyrem* (PG 50, 591). See Ausonius, *Ordo urbium nobilium* XI, 4 for Antioch as equal to Alexandria.

[12]Petit, *Libanius*, pp. 191-216; Festugière, *Antioche*, passim; Liebeschuetz, *Antioch*, pp. 220, 227; Glanville Downey, *A History of Antioch in Syria from Seleucus to the Arab Conquest* (Princeton: Princeton University Press, 1961), pp. 447-450; Alain Natali, "Christianisme et cité à Antioche à la fin du IVe siècle d'après Jean Chrysostome," in *Jean Chrysostome et Augustin: Actes du colloque de Chantilly, 22-24 septembre 1974*, ed. Charles Kannengiesser (Paris: Editions Beauchesne, 1975), pp. 41-59; Wayne A. Meeks and Robert L. Wilken, *Jews and Christians in Antioch in the First Four Centuries of the Common Era* (Missoula, Mont.: Scholars Press, 1978); C.H. Kraeling, "The Jewish Community at Antioch," *Journal of Biblical Literature* 51 (1932), 130-160. According to Chrysostom, Christians at Antioch in his time numbered 100,000 persons (*Hom. 85 Matt.* 4) (PG 58, 762).

[13]Downey, *A History of Antioch*, p. 351; E.S. Bouchier, *A Short History of Antioch, 300 B.C.-A.D. 1268* (Oxford: Basil Blackwell, 1921), pp. 146-147.

[14]Moulard, *Saint Jean Chrysostome. Sa vie*, p. 13; Baur, *John Chrysostom* I, 85.

[15]Socrates, *Historia ecclesiastica* VI, 3 (PG 67, 665, 668); Sozomen, *Historia ecclesiastica* VIII, 2 (PG 67, 1516); John Chrysostom, *In Diodorum Tarsensem* (PG 52, 761-766). Festugière, *Antioche*, p. 183, writes that Diodore of Tarsus taught at Antioch from about 372-375.

[16]Socrates, *Historia ecclesiastica* VI, 3 (PG 67, 668); Sozomen, *Historia ecclesiastica* VIII, 2 (PG 67, 1516).

[17]Palladius, *Dialogus* V, 18 (Coleman-Norton, p. 28). On the development of monasticism in Syria, see Arthur Vööbus, *History of Asceticism in the Syrian Orient*. II: *Early Monasticism in Mesopotamia and Syria* (Louvain: CSCO, 1960); Pierre Canivet, *Le Monachisme syrien selon Théodoret de Cyr* (Paris: Editions Beauchesne, 1977), esp. chaps. 8-10; Jean Gribomont, "Le Monachisme au IVe s. en Asie Mineure: de Gangres au Messalianisme," *Studia Patristica* II (=*Texte und Untersuchungen* 64) (Berlin: Akademie-Verlag, 1957), 400-415; S. Jargy, "Les Premiers Instituts monastiques et les principaux répresentats du monachisme syrien au IVe siècle," *Proche Orient Chrétien* 4 (1954), 109-117. On Chrysostom and monasticism, see Jean-Marie Leroux, "Monachisme et communauté chrétienne d'après Saint Jean Chrysostome," *Théologie de la vie monastique*, vol. 49 (Paris: Aubier, 1961), 143-191, and "Saint Jean Chrysostome et le monachisme," in *Jean Chrysostome et Augustin*, ed. Kannengiesser, pp. 125-144; Ivo Auf der Maur, *Mönchtum und Glaubensverkündigung in den Schriften des hl. Johannes Chrysostomus* (Freiburg: Universitätsverlag, 1959).

[18]Palladius, *Dialogus* V, 18 (Coleman-Norton, p. 29).

[19]Palladius, *Dialogus* V, 18 (Coleman-Norton, p. 28); Baur, *John Chrysostom*, I, 85; Moulard, *Saint Jean Chrysostome. Sa vie*, p. 21.

[20]Palladius, *Dialogus* V, 19 (Coleman-Norton, p. 29); Socrates, *Historia ecclesiastica* VI, 3 (PG 67, 668). For a chronological summary, see Festugière, *Antioche*, pp. 413-414; Baur, *John Chrysostom*, I, 143; Moulard, *Saint Jean Chrysostome. Sa vie*, pp. 21, 30; Peuch, *Saint John Chrysostom*, p. 16.

[21]According to Socrates, the following of Chrysostom's treatises were composed in Antioch (*Historia*

ecclesiastica VI, 3 [PG 67, 669]): *Against the Jews; On the Priesthood; Against Stagirius; On the Incomprehensibility of the Divine Nature; On the Women who Lived with Ecclesiastics.* For a discussion of Chrysostom's early ascetic treatises, including the modern dating of the two in this volume, see below, pp. ix-x.

[22]Socrates, Sozomen, Palladius devote most of their discussions of Chrysostom to his Constantinople period; the section of Theodoret's *Church History* on Chrysostom is entirely about his life in Constantinople.

[23]Palladius, *Dialogus* V, 19-20 (Coleman-Norton, pp. 31-33); XVIII, 62 (Coleman-Norton, pp. 112-113).

[24]Bernard Grillet, "Introduction générale," *John Chrysostome. La Virginité* (Paris: Les Editions du Cerf, 1966), p. 23; Moulard, *Saint Jean Chrysostome. Sa vie,* pp. 47-50; Baur, *John Chrysostom* I, 164-170.

[25]E.g., Bernard Grillet, "Introduction générale," *Jean Chrysostome. La Virginité*, pp. 67, 72; Bruno Vandenberghe, "St. Jean Chrysostome: pasteur des jeunes époux," *La Vie Spirituelle* 89 (1953), 39; Herbert Musurillo, "The Problem of Ascetical Fasting in the Greek Patristic Fathers," *Traditio* 12 (1956), 7-8.

[26]Carter, "Chronology," p. 371.

[27]The treatise is in PG 47, 387-392. See the discussion in Robert E. Carter, "Saint John Chrysostom's Rhetorical Use of the Socratic Distinction Between Kingship and Tyranny," *Traditio* 14 (1958), 368-369.

[28]*Comparatio potentiae, divitarum et excellentiae regis, cum monacho* 2 (PG 47, 389).

[29]*Comparatio* 4 (PG 47, 390-392).

[30]*Adversus oppognatores eorum qui vitam monasticam inducunt* II, 3; 9; 10 (PG 47, 335, 345, 346-347).

[31]*Adversus oppognatores* III, 8 (PG 47, 360-363); see Festugière, *Antioche*, pp. 195-208.

[32]*Ad viduam juniorem* (PG 48, 599-610).

[33]*Ad Theodorum lapsum* (PG 47, 277-316).

[34]According to Socrates, *Historia ecclesiastica* VI,
3 (PG 67, 669), one of the treatises was written in
Antioch. Palladius, on the other hand, says the problem
arose during Chrysostom's time in Constantinople
(*Dialogus* V, 19 [Coleman-Norton, p. 31]). It has been
suggested by Jean Dumortier, "La Date des deux traités de
Sainte Jean Chrysostome aux moines et aux vierges,"
Mélanges de Science Religieuse 6 (1949), 251-252, that
the two treatises were originally written in Antioch and
re-issued in Constantinople. The two treatises are
Adversus eos qui apud se habent virgines subintroductas
(PG 47, 495-514) and *Quod regulares feminae viris cohabi-
tare non debeant* (PG 47, 513-532); English translation
by Elizabeth A. Clark in *Jerome, Chrysostom, and Friends:
Essays and Translations* (New York and Toronto: Edwin
Mellen Press, 1979), pp. 158-248.

[35]Bernard Grillet's dating for the *De Virginitate* is
around 382 A.D. ("Introduction générale," *Jean Chrysostome. La Virginité*, p. 25), against Herbert Musurillo's
dating of the treatise to A.D. 392 ("Some Textual
Problems in the Editing of the Greek Fathers," *Studia
Patristica* III =Texte und Untersuchungen 78 [Berlin:
Academie-Verlag, 1961], p. 92).

[36]Bernard Grillet, "Introduction générale," *Jean
Chrysostome. A une jeune veuve. Sur le mariage unique*
(Paris: Les Editions du Cerf, 1968), p. 14, dates
Against Remarriage to between A.D. 383 and 386.

[37]Basil of Ancyra (=Pseudo-Athanasius), *De vera
virginitate* (PG 28, 251-282); see also Michel Aubineau,
"Les Ecrits de Saint Athanase sur le virginité," *Revue
d'Ascétique et de Mystique* 31 (1955), 144-151.

[38]See David Amand de Mendieta, "La Virginité chez
Eusèbe d'Emèse et l'ascéticisme familial dans la première
moitié de IVe siècle," *Revue d'Histoire Ecclésiastique*
50 (1955), 790ff.

[39]See text in Michel Aubineau, ed., *Grégoire de
Nysse. Traité de la virginité* (Paris: Les Editions du
Cerf, 1966). Aubineau dates the treatise to A.D. 371
(p. 31).

[40]See Herbert Musurillo, "Introduction au texte
grec," *Jean Chrysostome. La Virginité*, pp. 77-83, and
Gerard H. Ettlinger, "Introduction au texte grec," *Jean
Chrysostome. A une jeune veuve. Sur le mariage unique*,
pp. 97-98.

[41]See notes 24 and 36 for bibliographical information.

[42]Grillet, "Introduction générale," *Jean Chrysostome. La Virginité*, p. 8.

[43]For discussion, see P.R. Coleman-Norton, "St. Chrysostom and the Greek Philosophers," *Classical Philology* 25 (1930), 305-317; Harry Hubbell, Chrysostom and Rhetoric," *Classical Philology* 19 (1924), 261-276; Jean Dumortier, "La Culture profane de S. Jean Chrysostome," *Mélanges de Science Religieuse* 10 (1953), 53-62; Anton Naegele, "Johannes Chrysostomos und sein Verhältnis zum Hellenismus," *Byzantinische Zeitschrift* 13 (1904), 73-113.

[44]I Corinthians 7:1-9, 25-40.

[45]I Corinthians 7:25-35.

[46]I Corinthians 7:28.

[47]*On Virginity* XXXIX, 1 (Musurillo, p. 228). English title and Roman numeration will be used hereafter, in accordance with Shore's translation.

[48]*On Virginity* XXXIX, 2 (Musurillo, pp. 228, 230).

[49]*Against Remarriage* 3 (Ettlinger, p. 174). English title will be used hereafter, in accordance with Shore's translation.

[50]See note 17 above for bibliography on early monasticism in Syria. The information about women's monasticism in fourth-century Syria is disappointingly thin: see Vööbus, *History of Asceticism*, II, 372.

[51]See note 38 above; for "home asceticism" in the West, see Elizabeth A. Clark, "Ascetic Renunciation and Feminine Advancement: A Paradox of Late Ancient Christianity," *Anglican Theological Review* 63 (1981), 240-257, and references therein.

[52]*Hom. 66 Matt.*, 3 (PG 58, 630).

[53]Grillet, "Introduction générale," *Jean Chrysostome, La Virginité*, p. 45: the treatise is addressed to those already converted to the virginal life.

[54]I Corinthians 7:25-29.

[55]The condemnation of the Montanist movement by second and third-century writers is a case in point.

[56]*On Virginity* XLIX, 1-2 (Musurillo, pp. 274, 276).

[57]*On Virginity* XLIX, 5-6 (Musurillo, p. 280).

[58]*On Virginity* XLIX, 8 (Musurillo, p. 282).

[59]*Ibid.*

[60]*On Virginity* LXXIII, 3-4 (Musurillo, pp. 352, 354).

[61]*On Virginity* XI, 1 (Musurillo, p. 126): virginity makes angels out of us.

[62]*On Virginity* LIX (Musurillo, pp. 318, 320); *Against Remarriage* 6 (Ettlinger, p. 198). The virgin yearns for death because then she will see her Bridegroom face to face; the heretical virgins will not, because they are not betrothed to Christ (*On Virginity* I, 1 [Musurillo, p. 92]).

[63]Mark 12:25 = Matthew 22:30 = Luke 20:35-36.

[64]*On Virginity* XIV, 3; 5; 6 (Musurillo, pp. 140, 142).

[65]*On Virginity* XIV, 3 (Musurillo, p. 140).

[66]*On Virginity* XIV, 5; 6; XV, 2 (Musurillo, pp. 142, 146).

[67]Hesiod, *Works and Days* 197-200.

[68]*On Virginity* XIV, 5 (Musurillo, p. 142).

[69]*On Virginity* XIV, 6 (Musurillo, p. 142). Chrysostom's views on this topic echo those of Gregory of Nyssa. The view that marriage was not part of God's created order but the result of the Fall was strongly combatted by the Latin-writing theologian Augustine in a variety of treatises.

[70]*On Virginity* XIV, 6 (Musurillo, pp. 142, 144).

[71]*On Virginity* XV, 1 (Musurillo, p. 144).

[72]*On Virginity* XVIII (Musurillo, p. 156).

[73] *On Virginity* XIX, 1 (Musurillo, p. 156).

[74] John Chrysostom, *In propter fornicationes* 3 (PG 51, 213); *Hom. 20 Gen.* 1 (PG 53, 167); *Hom. 18 Gen.* 4 (PG 53, 154).

[75] *On Virginity* XIX, 1 (Musurillo, p. 156); I Corinthians 7:2, 8-9, 36.

[76] *On Virginity* XIX, 1 (Musurillo, p. 158).

[77] *On Virginity* XV, 2 (Musurillo, p. 146).

[78] *On Virginity* XIX, 2 (Musurillo, p. 158); IX, 1 (Musurillo, p. 120); marriage is compared with a dam that contains the flood of sexual desire.

[79] *On Virginity* XIX, 2 (Musurillo, p. 158).

[80] *On Virginity* XVI, 1; 2 (Musurillo, pp. 146, 148); XVII, 1-2; 5 (Musurillo, pp. 150, 154).

[81] I Corinthians 13:11.

[82] I Corinthians 3:1-2; also see Hebrews 5:12-13.

[83] *On Virginity* XLIV, 1 (Musurillo, pp. 250, 252).

[84] *On Virginity* LXXXIV, 1 (Musurillo, p. 390); LXXXIII, 1-2 (Musurillo, pp. 386, 388). For some positive themes in Chrysostom's evaluation of marriage, see T. Špidlík, "Il matrimonio, sacramento di unità, nel pensiero di Crisostomo," *Augustinianum* 17 (1977), 221-226; and Anatole Moulard, *Saint Jean Chrysostome. Le Défenseur du mariage et l'apotre de la virginité* (Paris: Librairie Victor Lecoffre, 1923), esp. pt. I, chaps. 2-5.

[85] For example, Clement of Alexandria, *Stromateis* III; Jerome, *Epp.* 22, 13; 48, 2; 133, 9; *Adversus Jovinianus* I, 3.

[86] Unless one takes the Corinthian enthusiasts as outright Gnostics and attributes to them the sentiment of I Cor. 7:1: "It is better for a man not to touch a woman." See C.K. Barrett, *A Commentary on the First Epistle to the Corinthians* (London: Adam and Charles Black, 1968), pp. 154-155; John C. Hurd, Jr., *The Origin of I Corinthians* (New York: Seabury Press, 1965), pp. 154-163. On the Gnostic question, see Walter Schmithals,

Gnosticism in Corinth, tr. J.E. Steely (Nashville:
Abingdon Press, 1971), and *Paul and the Gnostics*, tr.
J.E. Steely (Nashville: Abingdon Press, 1972).

[87]I Timothy 4:3; Matt. 19:10-12 and Col. 2:23 suggest
an ascetic movement as well.

[88]See note 85 above and Hans Jonas, *Gnosis und
Spätantiker Geist* (Göttingen: Vandenhoeck & Ruprecht,
1964), I, 233-238; J.P. Broudéhoux, *Mariage et famille
chez Clément d'Alexandrie* (Paris: Beauchesne, 1970), pp.
27-61.

[89]*On Virginity* III (Musurillo, pp. 100, 102); II, 1
(Musurillo, p. 98).

[90]*On Virginity* II, 2 (Musurillo, p. 100); IV, 2
(Musurillo, p. 104).

[91]*On Virginity* V, 1 (Musurillo, p. 106).

[92]*On Virginity* VIII, 1 (Musurillo, p. 114).

[93]*On Virginity* I, 2 (Musurillo, pp. 92, 94); II, 2
(Musurillo, p. 100); VIII, 3 (Musurillo, p. 116).

[94]*On Virginity* I, 3 (Musurillo, p. 94).

[95]*On Virginity* X, 1 (Musurillo, p. 122).

[96]*Ibid.*

[97]Moulard, *Saint Jean Chrysostome. Le Défenseur*,
pt. I, chap. 3.

[98]See especially Robin Scroggs, "Paul and the Escha-
tological Woman," *Journal of the American Academy of
Religion* 40 (1972), 283-303; Elaine H. Pagels, "Paul and
Women: A Response to Recent Discussion," *Journal of the
American Academy of Religion* 42 (1974), 538-549; more
recently see Raoul Mortley, *Womanhood. The Feminine in
Ancient Hellenism, Gnosticism, Christianity, and Islam*
(Sydney: Delacroix Press, 1981), pp. 45-54.

[99]Romans 5:12-14, 18-19. But see II Corinthians
11:3.

[100]E.g., I Timothy 2:14; *On Virginity* XLVI, 1
(Musurillo, p. 258).

[101] *On Virginity* XLVI, 1 (Musurillo, pp. 256, 258).

[102] *On Virginity* XLVI, 2 (Musurillo, p. 258).

[103] *Ibid.*

[104] Genesis 2:18; *On Virginity* XLVI, 1 (Musurillo, p. 256).

[105] *On Virginity* XLVI, 5 (Musurillo, pp. 260, 262).

[106] *On Virginity* XLVI, 5 (Musurillo, p. 262).

[107] *On Virginity* XLVII, 2 (Musurillo, p. 266).

[108] *On Virginity* LII, 2-7 (Musurillo, pp. 288, 290, 292, 295, 296, 298); LVI, 1 (Musurillo, p. 304); LVII, 1-7 (Musurillo, pp. 308, 310, 312, 314); LXVII (Musurillo, pp. 336, 338); and especially XL, 3 (Musurillo, p. 234). There is never equality in marriage, whatever the woman's economic situation: *On Virginity* LV (Musurillo, p. 302).

[109] See, for example, *Hom. 8 Rom.* 1 (PG 60, 455); *Hom. 10 Rom.* 3 (PG 60, 473); *Hom. 10 Rom.* 5 (PG 60, 480); *Hom. 3 Phil.* 1 (PG 52, 197).

[110] *On Virginity* LXIII, 3 (Musurillo, p. 328).

[111] *On Virginity* LXX, 1-2 (Musurillo, p. 346); LXXI (Musurillo, pp. 346, 348). Also see Chrysostom's *Comparatio* for similar arguments concerning the superiority of a monk's life to a king's.

[112] See A. Uleyn, "La Doctrine morale de S. Jean Chrysostome dans le Commentaire sur S. Matthieu et ses affinités avec la diatribe," *Revue de l'Université d'Ottawa* 27 (1957), 103-105, 120-136.

[113] See especially Louis Meyer, "Liberté et moralisme chretién dans la doctrine spirituelle de Saint Jean Chrysostome," *Recherches de Science Religieuse* 23 (1933), 283-305.

[114] *On Virginity* LXXVII, 6 (Musurillo, p. 374).

[115] *On Virginity* VIII, 3 (Musurillo, p. 116).

[116] E.g., V.J. Stiglmayr, "Zur Aszese des heiligen Chrysostomus," *Zeitschrift für Aszese und Mystik* 4 (1929), 38-39; Meyer, "Liberté," p. 295.

[117]*On Virginity* XXXVI, 1-3 (Musurillo, pp. 212, 214, 216).

[118]*On Virginity* XXXV, 2 (Musurillo, p. 210).

[119]A phrase from Stoic ethics often used by Chrysostom. See Anne-Marie Malingrey, "Introduction," *Jean Chrysostome. Lettres à Olympias. Vie anonyme d'Olympias*, 2nd ed. (Paris: Les Editions du Cerf, 1968), p. 54.

[120]*On Virginity* XXXIX, 3 (Musurillo, p. 230).

[121]*On Virginity* LXXXIV, 3-4 (Musurillo, pp. 392, 394).

[122]*On Virginity* LXXVI, 1 (Musurillo, p. 364).

[123]*Against Remarriage* 6 (Ettlinger, p. 194).

[124]*On Virginity* XXXIX, 1-2 (Musurillo, pp. 228, 230).

[125]*On Virginity* XXXVIII, 1-2 (Musurillo, p. 226).

[126]So called from the wording of Matthew 19:21, "If you would be perfect...." See C. Baur, "Der Weg der Vollkommenheit nach dem heiligen Joh. Chrysostomus," *Theologie und Glaube* 20 (1928), 27, 37; Louis Meyer, "Perfection chrétienne et vie solitaire dans la pensée des St. Jean Chrysostome." *Revue d'Ascetique et de Mystique* 14 (1933), 234. For an argument against Chrysostom having a two-tiered morality, see C. Baur, "Das Ideal der christlichen Vollkommenheit nach dem hl. Johannes Chrysostomus," *Theologie und Glaube* 6 (1914), 573-574; Stiglmayr, "Zur Aszese," pp. 40-41, 46.

[127]See, for example, *On Virginity* L, 1-2 (Musurillo, pp. 284, 286); LXXXII, 4 (Musurillo, p. 386).

[128]Jerome's interpretation of the parable of the sower provides a particularly apt illustration of this point. The "100-fold harvest" he takes to mean the reward awaiting virgins, the "60-fold harvest" is that the widows will receive, while married people can expect only the "30-fold harvest": *Against Jovinian* I, 3; *Ep.* 48, 2.

[129]*On Virginity* II, 2 (Musurillo, p. 100).

[130]*On Virginity* I, 1 (Musurillo, p. 92).

[131]*On Virginity* I, 2-3 (Musurillo, pp. 94, 96).

[132]*On Virginity* VIII, 3 (Musurillo, p. 116).

[133]*On Virginity* XXX, 2 (Musurillo, p. 192).

[134]*On Virginity* VIII, 5 (Musurillo, p. 118).

[135]I Corinthians 12:4-31. For Chrysostom's understanding of the *charismata*, see Adolf Martin Ritter, *Charisma im Verständnis des Johannes Chrysostomos und seiner Zeit* (Göttingen: Vandenhoeck & Ruprecht, 1972), pp. 53-98.

[136]I Corinthians 7:7.

[137]See Malingrey, "Introduction," p. 54. On *prohairesis*, see Edward Nowak, *Le Chrétien devant la souffrance. Etude sur la pensée de Jean Chrysostome* (Paris: Beauchesne, 1972), pp. 57-63.

[138]I Corinthians 7:3-4.

[139]I Corinthians 7:32-34.

[140]For Chrysostom's use of the *topoi* on marriage, see Moulard, *Saint Jean Chrysostome. Le Défenseur*, pp. 202-217; Grillet, "Introduction générale," *A une jeune veuve. Sur le mariage unique*, pp. 76-77; and Leroux, "Monachisme," pp. 155, 165; for Gregory of Nyssa's use of similar *topoi* and references, see Aubineau, *Grégoire de Nysse. Traité de la Virginité*, pp. 87-96.

[141]*On Virginity* XXVIII, 3 (Musurillo, p. 184), XL, 1 (Musurillo, p. 232).

[142]*On Virginity* XLI, 2 (Musurillo, pp. 236, 238).

[143]*On Virginity* XLI, 2 (Musurillo, p. 236); XXVIII, 1 (p. 182).

[144]*On Virginity* XXVIII, 1 (Musurillo, p. 182); XXXII, 3 (Musurillo, p. 196).

[145]See Derrick Sherwin Bailey, *Sexual Relation in Christian Thought* (New York: Harper & Row, 1959), p. 11.

[146]*On Virginity* XLI, 2 (Musurillo, p. 236).

[147]*On Virginity* XL, 1 (Musurillo, p. 232).

[148] *On Virginity* XLVII, 5 (Musurillo, p. 270).

[149] *On Virginity* XL, 2-3 (Musurillo, p. 234).

[150] *On Virginity* LII, 1-7 (Musurillo, pp. 228, 290, 292, 294, 296). Certainly the right of a husband to murder his complaining wife with impunity did not exist in Chrysostom's time. Supposedly before the issuance of *lex Julia de Adulteriis*, between 18 and 16 B.C., a husband who caught his wife in an act of adultery could execute her on the spot, without benefit of trial (so Aulus Gellius, *Noctes Atticae* 10, 23, 5). But even by the first century B.C., *manus* marriage was passing away in favor of freer forms that gave the husband less absolute power over his wife. Chrysostom, here as elsewhere, appeals to older customs. See Percy E. Corbett, *The Roman Law of Marriage* (Oxford: Clarendon Press, 1930), pp. 127-135.

[151] *On Virginity* LIII-LV (Musurillo, pp. 298, 300, 302).

[152] *On Virginity* LV (Musurillo, p. 302).

[153] *On Virginity* LVII, 1-2 (Musurillo, pp. 308, 310).

[154] *On Virginity* LVII, 3 (Musurillo, p. 310).

[155] *On Virginity* LVII, 4 (Musurillo, p. 310).

[156] *On Virginity* LVII, 5 (Musurillo, pp. 312, 314).

[157] *On Virginity* LVI, 1-2 (Musurillo, pp. 304, 306).

[158] *On Virginity* LXVII (Musurillo, pp. 336, 338).

[159] *On Virginity* XXXVII, 3 (Musurillo, pp. 220, 222); *Against Remarriage* 2 (Ettlinger, p. 170); 6 (Ettlinger, p. 192).

[160] *On Virginity* XXXVII, 1 (Musurillo, p. 218).

[161] *Against Remarriage* 2 (Ettlinger, p. 170).

[162] *Against Remarriage* 6 (Ettlinger, p. 192).

[163] *Against Remarriage* 5 (Ettlinger, pp. 188, 190).

[164] *Against Remarriage* 5 (Ettlinger, p. 190).

[165]See, for example, discussions and examples in Gordon Williams, "Some Aspects of Roman Marriage Cere-monies and Ideals," *Journal of Roman Studies* 48 (1958), 16-29; Marjorie Lightman and William Zeisel, "Univira: An Example of Continuity and Change in Roman Society," *Church History* 46 (1977), 19-32.

[166]For their attacks on remarriage, see especially Tertullian, *De exhortatione castitatis* and *De monogamia*; Jerome, *Epp.* 54; 79; 123.

[167]I Corinthians 7:39-40.

[168]I Timothy 5:9-14.

[169]*Against Remarriage* 5 (Ettlinger, p. 188).

[170]*Against Remarriage* 1 (Ettlinger, p. 162).

[171]*Against Remarriage* 1 (Ettlinger, p. 160); 5 (Ettlinger, p. 188).

[172]*Against Remarriage* 2 (Ettlinger, p. 168).

[173]*On Virginity* XLIX, 8 (Musurillo, p. 282); LII, 8 (Musurillo, p. 284); LXV (Musurillo, p. 332).

[174]*On Virginity* LIX (Musurillo, pp. 318, 320); LX, 1 (Musurillo, p. 320).

[175]*Against Remarriage* 6 (Ettlinger, pp. 196, 198).

[176]*On Virginity* XLV, 1 (Musurillo, pp. 254, 256). Thus the heretical virgins will find that their effort has not counted; their virginity resulted from the wrong motivation (*On Virginity* IV, 3 [Musurillo, pp. 104, 106)].

[177]*On Virginity* LXIV (Musurillo, p. 330).

[178]*On Virginity* XXXIV, 1 (Musurillo, pp. 198, 200); 4 (Musurillo, p. 202).

[179]*On Virginity* V, 2 (Musurillo, p. 108); VI, 1 (Musurillo, p. 108).

[180]*On Virginity* LXXX, 2 (Musurillo, p. 380).

[181]*On Virginity* LXXXII, 3 (Musurillo, p. 384); cf. Chrysostom's comments on the "foolish virgins" of Matthew 25 in *Vidua eligatur* 15 (PG 51, 336); *Hom. 78 Matt.* (PG 58, 711-718).

[182]*On Virginity* VII, 1-2 (Musurillo, p. 112).

[183]*On Virginity* LXXVII (Musurillo, p. 366).

[184]*On Virginity* LXVIII (Musurillo, pp. 338, 340, 342).

[185]*On Virginity* LIX (Musurillo, pp. 318, 320).

JOHN CHRYSOSTOM AND THE SUBINTRODUCTAE

Church History 46 (1977), 171-185

When physical affections are destroyed and
tyrannical desire extinguished, then no
hindrance will any longer stand in the way of
men and women being together, because all evil
suspicion will be cleared away and all who
have entered the kingdom of heaven can maintain
the way of life of the angels and spiritual
powers, through the grace and love of our Lord
Jesus Christ, to whom with the Father and the
Holy Spirit be glory, honor, and dominion from
age to age. Amen.[1]

I

With these words, John Chrysostom concludes his first
treatise on the *subintroductae*, one of the most fascinating groups of women encountered anywhere in the annals
of church history. As defined by Hans Achelis, whose
Virgines Subintroductae[2] remains the classical exposition
of the subject, the *subintroductae* were "female Christian
ascetics who lived together with men, although both
parties had taken the vow of continency, and were ani-
mated with the earnest desire to keep it."[3] Such virginal couples were united in a "permanent, intimate
relation,"[4] spiritual marriage, which Derrick Sherwin
Bailey has vividly described as "the cohabitation of the
sexes under the condition of strict continence, a couple

sharing the same house, often the same room, and sometimes the same bed, yet conducting themselves as brother
and sister."[5] The man--who may or may not have been a
cleric--usually took the woman into his house, although
occasionally the female might invite the man to share her
residence, especially if she were a widow with private
means. The relationship shocked Chrysostom and his contemporaries; nonetheless, Achelis has argued (we think
correctly) that it was motivated by spiritual concerns:
"brotherly love was supposed to take the place of the
love of marriage."[6] The man and woman, he claimed, became "Platonic lovers."[7]

There are numerous references to the practice in
Christian literature from the late second century on-
wards. Our earliest evidence is found in the *Similitudes
of Hermas*. In this work, Hermas' female companions, to
whom he has been entrusted, assure him, "You will sleep
with us as a brother, not as a spouse. You are our
brother, we intend to live with you, for we love you
dearly."[8] Also from the second century we have the
testimony of Irenaeus, who informs us that the Valen-
tinians occasioned scandal by allowing "brothers" and
"sisters" to live together--but it became evident that
chastity had been violated when some of the "sisters" became mothers.[9] There also survive two letters of pseudo-
Clement on virginity, dating from the late second or
early third century, in which the author warns the
brethren against dwelling with maidens;[10] Jesus' words
to Mary Magdalene after his resurrection, "Touch me not"
(John 20:17), are used as grounds for condemnation of
those who live with women and "sleep where they sleep."[11]
Spiritual marriage was likewise known to the Latin-
writing fathers Tertullian[12] and Cyprian.[13] Another
pre-Nicene record of the practice is found in

pseudo-Cyprian's *De singularitate clericorum.*[14]   Later
in the fourth century we have the evidence of Eusebius
of Emesa, who advises young women wishing to adopt the
virginal life to remain at home under the watchful eye
of the *pater familias*, rather than to move in with
strange men.[15]   (It has been postulated that Chrysostom
was familiar with Eusebius' treatise dealing with this
theme.[16])   All three Cappadocian fathers speak of the
subintroductae,[17] and Jerome's sarcastic reference to
the "beloved women" (*agapetae*) as "one-man whores"
(*meretrices univirae*) is famous.[18]   Last, the pseudo-
Titus epistles, stemming in all probability from Pris-
cillianist circles of the fifth century, present still
later testimony concerning spiritual marriage.[19]   Thus
both orthodox and heterodox authors were familiar with
the practice; the evidence for it, while not boundless,
is substantial.[20]

     Moreover, we have records of numerous church councils
which condemned spiritual marriage. In Eusebius of
Caesarea's *Church History*, we learn that one of the
accusations made against Paul of Samosata was that he had
scandalized the church by living with young girls, a
practice which apparently contributed to his condemnation
by the Synod of Antioch in 267-268.[21]   The oriental
bishops who had penned the condemning epistle concerning
Paul reported that the Antiocheans had even coined a
special name for these female companions: *gynaikes
syneisaktoi.*[22]   Hence the word "syneisaktism" has been
used to refer to the custom.

     At least six church councils of the fourth century,
including the famous Council of Nicaea in 325, banned the
practice, which must nonetheless have continued to
flourish, for decrees were pronounced against it into the
early middle ages.[23]   Nor was syneisaktism a phenomenon

peculiar to one locality; it can be found in Ireland,[24] Syria,[25] North Africa,[26] and many other centers of Christianity.[27] As Roland Seboldt asserted, following Achelis, "Of one thing we can be sure: there was hardly a church province in ancient Christianity in which spiritual marriages were unknown."[28]

What is more problematic, and has in fact been the subject of furious debate, is the origin of Christian syneisaktism. Achelis, adopting the thesis of Eduard Grafe,[29] argued that I Corinthians 7:36-38 is a reference to the custom, which he thought was condoned by Paul himself.[30] A brief examination of the passage and its possible interpretations may be helpful before we discuss Chrysostom's views on the matter.[31]

Part of the debate over I Corinthians 7:36-38 has been stimulated by perplexing difficulties of translation.[32] What, for example, does *hyperakmos* mean? Does it refer to the man, who is "full of vitality"? Or to the young woman? If the latter, is she "past her prime" or "in the flower of her youth"?[33] And to whom does *gameitōsan* ("let *them* marry") refer? (Paul has not presented us with a potential bridegroom for the woman.) Shoud *gamizō* be translated as "marry" or "give in marriage"?[34] The variations in translation have of course reflected differences of opinion regarding the situation presupposed in the text. Traditionally the passage has been interpreted to refer to a father who had asked Paul for advice concerning his virgin daughter: should he have her marry or keep her as a virgin? A variant on this interpretation hypothesizes that the young woman was already engaged, and the couple (or the father) was wondering whether, given the impending end of the world and the urgency of Christian commitment, she should consummate her pledge.[35]

Achelis, in contrast, popularized the view that
I Corinthians 7:36-38 is the first reference in Christian
history to syneisaktism.[36] According to his reading of
the text, Paul is replying to the query of a male celibate who was, alas, plagued by sexual feelings for his
subintroducta.[37] Paul advised that it would be preferable in this situation for her to leave him and marry
someone else, but that in other circumstances, if the
man could control his lustful desires, he would do well
to "keep his virgin." Paul did not condemn spiritual
marriage, Achelis insisted; to the contrary, he recognized the real advantages it might offer celibate men
and women of his era.[38] Among the modern supporters of
Achelis' thesis are D.S. Bailey,[39] John C. Hurd, Jr.,[40]
and Jean Héring, who goes so far as to assert that
Achelis' interpretation is "the only plausible explanation of our passage."[41] Those who disagree with Achelis
do so not only on the grounds of the textual difficulties; they also posit that Paul in his apostolic wisdom
could never have given his imprimatur to a situation
which must have encouraged sexual temptation, if not
overt sexual activity.[42]

Why, then, did none of the church fathers with the
exception of Ephraem the Syrian interpret I Corinthians
7:36-38 this way?[43] One answer is that the fathers could
not imagine their hero Paul sanctioning a practice which,
by their time, had brought trouble and disrepute to the
church. Chrysostom sided with the majority of his contemporaries in taking the Pauline passage to refer to a
father and a daughter.[44] However, in his *Homily 19 on
I Corinthians*, we can sense his bewilderment at the
wording of the text. He comments on Paul's choice of
language, "Here he seems to be talking about marriage,
but all that he says relates to virginity."[45] Chrysostom

did not pause to inquire whether Paul might have been
describing "virginal marriage"; since he was to write two
treatises condemning the *subintroductae*, he was not
likely to admit that Paul had permitted men and women to
live together in chastity.

II

Chrysostom's two treatises on syneisaktism (scholars
debate whether they were composed during his diaconate
in Antioch in the 380s or early 390s, or after he
ascended the episcopal chair of Constantinople in 397)[46]
are among the most interesting and clever of his writings. In these short works, he employs all of his
rhetorical skills to exhort the virgins and the monks
living with them to abandon their housekeeping arrangements.[47] As a spiritual physician, he wished to heal the
sick rather than condemn them. (How much he hoped the
"diseased" would cooperate, rather than behaving like
some who, when stricken with fever, eat and drink the
forbidden fare which only serves to aggravate their
condition!)[48] Both his psychological analysis and his
Biblical arguments in these treatises are to the point,
which cannot be said for all of Chrysostom's writings.
Unlike Jerome, who denounced the *subintroductae* as
harlots and gleefully noted the frequency with which the
supposed virgins were betrayed by their "swelling
wombs,"[49] Chrysostom did not charge all such couples with
this misdeed. He generously admitted that many of them,
innocent of sexual relations, had retained their bodily
purity,[50] although he leads us to understand that some
few of the women had indeed needed the services of a mid-
wife.[51] Rather, Chrysostom cited other reasons for his
condemnation of spiritual marriage. Among these (which
will be discussed in the following pages) we may note:
the arousal of lust; the offense to "weaker brothers;"

the opportunity for enemies of the Church to criticize
her; the "adultery" of the brides of Christ; the necessity of suffering and denial in the Christian life; the
dubious practical benefits secured by the relationship;
the sacrifice of the freedom virginity was intended to
bring; and the overturning of the sexual roles and functions which "nature" as well as God had ordained.

For Chrysostom, living together without indulging in
sexual intercourse could only serve to fan the flames of
lust. The married man, to whom sexual opportunity was
ever present, often became satiated and lost the passion
he earlier felt for his bride. As for the woman, the
cares of the household and the bodily strain of childbearing and childrearing took a heavy toll upon her
physical beauty--and her diminished attractiveness no
doubt served to dampen further her husband's already
wilting ardor. But with the *subintroductae* and their
monks, desire was intensified with the passage of time
because it was never satisfied.[52] The constant association of the two--eating, talking, laughing together--
promoted a state of perpetual sexual arousal.[53] Chrysostom compared a monk who consented to live in this fashion
to someone who had a table of delicacies set before him,
but was instructed not to eat, or to one ravaged by
thirst, who was led to a stream but not permitted to
drink.[54] The combination of simultaneous temptation and
deprivation is a well-known form of torture; the ancients
described it in the myth of Tantalus, to which Chrysostom
alludes, and God employed it to punish the first couple
after he expelled them from Eden (they were kept near
the lovely garden which they no longer could enter).[55]

Moreover, Scripture affirms that men who lust after
women with their eyes have already committed adultery
with them in their hearts (Matt. 5:27-28); by that

standard of judgment, Chrysostom reckoned, these monks
must be guilty of a thousand adulteries daily![56] True
chastity means that we wage war constantly against our
passions, not that we exacerbate them. Both the monks
and the virgins are guilty in this regard, but Chrysostom assigned the greater blame to the women; they, like
prostitutes or adulteresses, were responsible for the
man's madness.[57] Some of the virgins, he ruefully noted,
spent as much time on their personal appearance and
wardrobes as actresses![58] Wearing perfume and enticing
men with their eyes or their walk were activities more
appropriate to harlots than to brides of Christ.[59]

Chrysostom was convinced that, in any case, it was
sexual desire which bound a man to a woman. In one of
his more misogynistic moods he puzzled, "Why else would
a man put up with the faults of a woman? He would find
her despicable (*eukataphronētos*)."[60] If the monks
enjoyed their female companions, it must be for the same
reason that other men find women attractive: the simple
pull of lust. When those heroes of the faith who don
sackcloth, cover their bodies with chains, fast and
deprive themselves of sleep "can hardly restrain the
frenzy of sexual desire," how can those of more earth-
bound constitution expect to escape it?[61] It was not
spiritual love which drew the couples together, Chrysostom assumed, but concupiscence in disguise.

Moreover, the couples living in this fashion irri-
tated Chrysostom with their claims that they could withstand the temptations constantly present to them due to
their tougher moral fiber. In his response to their
boast, he borrowed Paul's words regarding the eating of
meat offered to idols as support for his case. Paul had
claimed that, although he was entitled to eat meat, he
would never do so if he thereby caused another to "fall,"

If need be, he would become a "vegetable-eater" to win
the weak (Romans 14; I Corinthians 8). This argument
was readily adaptable to Chrysostom's purposes: the men
and the *subintroductae* living together were not taking
into account the offense they gave to those of less
rugged character (or of wilder imagination?) who assumed
that the couples indulged in sexual intercourse and were
scandalized. A true Christian, Chrysostom asserted,
would be willing to renounce his position of "strength"
in order to encourage brothers in the faith; that would
be manifesting genuine Christian *agapē*. If the good
resulting from syneisaktism outweighed the damage it
wreaked, he would be willing to sanction the practice,
even if some minor offense were caused thereby.[62] But
since there is no advantage whatsoever to the practice
(as he will show), and great harm comes to the Church
through the gossiping of non-Christians and the
blaspheming of God's name--not to speak of the damage to
the parties themselves[63]--the custom should be abandoned
at once.

Informing Chrysostom's argument is a view of the
faith which requires a Christian to deny himself and be
prepared for suffering. Christianity is not truly practiced by those who indulge themselves in comforts, who
attempt to secure a soft and easy life. Rather, the
faith entails staunch self-denial and asceticism. Christ
told us to take up our crosses and follow him (Matt. 16:
24), but the monks who live with virgins have abandoned
their "crosses" like cowardly soldiers who, instead of
marching steadfastly into battle, toss away their shields
and retreat to the women's quarters.[64] Paul's testimony
that he crucified himself to the world and the world to
himself (Gal. 6:14) is one which these couples would do
well to take to heart; his willingness to suffer for God

should provide a paradigm for our behavior.[65] Although
Chrysostom regretfully admitted that martyrdom, the
ultimate in self-denial, was no longer possible for
Christians, he hinted that those who from their love of
God struggle to overcome carnal lust can expect the
martyrs' reward.[66]

Another religiously-grounded argument employed by
Chrysostom was that female virgins have pledged their
troth to Jesus; by taking up with other men, they violate
their promises and become "adulteresses." Here Chrysostom, as did many other church fathers, relied heavily on
the imagery of the Song of Songs, Matthew 28, and
Ephesians 5. According to him, Christ as the heavenly
Bridegroom is awaiting his virgins, who should keep themselves worthy of him and the bridal chamber into which
they will eventually be initiated.[67] Jesus will demand
of them not only purity of body, but unspotted souls as
well--and the *subintroductae*, Chrysostom thought, would
have a harder time meeting the latter requirement than
the former.[68] True virginity, he did not tire of reiter-
ating in his treatise devoted to that subject, embraces
both body and soul; the virgin must take care lest her
intact body harbor a rotten soul.[69] Her spiritual
beauty, rather than her physical charms, will be the
quality rendering her attractive to her future spouse.[70]
And she should not regret her renunciation of associations with men here on earth, for her heavenly husband
will prove to be a more passionate "lover" than any mere
human![71] The "brides of Christ" who behave like prostitutes, even if they do not actually pronounce the words
of Proverbs 7:17-18, are unworthy of this high calling.[72]

In addition to such arguments, Chrysostom also
appealed to the couples on practical grounds. All the
reasons they adduced for the usefulness of the custom

are challenged by him. The men claimed that they were
protecting the women, helping them to manage their
finances (if they were rich) or providing for their
physical needs (if they were poor). Replied Chrysostom,
why should men dedicated to God immerse themselves in
business affairs at all? Supposedly they have embraced
the ideal of poverty, yet they complicate their lives
with the anxieties about money, property, servants. God
wishes us to despise riches and renounce our attachments
to worldly things. The story in Acts 6 contains a moral
for us: the apostles turned the management of the
widows' food dole over to others when that function began
to interfere with their spiritual duties.[73]

Moreover, even if the monks asserted that they were
helping poor women, what possible good could it do to
provide material aid if in the process they were destroy-
ing the women's spirits and barring the gates of heaven
to them?[74] If the men argue that aiding indigent virgins
is a way of demonstrating Christian charity, Chrysostom
points out to them that there are plenty of old, blind,
sick, and impoverished people of *both* sexes who would be
fitting recipients of their generosity--not just comely
young maidens.[75] If they plead that they need a woman to
manage the household, make the beds, cook, and so forth,
Chrysostom laughs them to shame: a man could perform
these tasks just as well for another man[76]--and besides,
then each pair would need only one bed, one set of
covers, and one pillow.[77] When the women in turn complained that due to their weakness they needed a man's
help, Chrysostom cleverly reminded them that the men had
already pleaded *that* argument: that *they* needed a
woman's aid in order to manage. Chrysostom suggested
that if the women were such invaluable servants to the
men, could they not help each other out, employing their

domestic skills for their own benefit? Men are not able
to provide women with any service which they could not
perform for themselves (except, of course, with that
which the virgins have supposedly renounced). If the
women need someone to run errands on their behalf in
public places, a servant or an older woman would be
well-suited for such tasks.[78] Chrysostom's argument, we
can see, was two-pronged: on the one hand, we ought to
be able for the most part to attend to our own needs,[79]
and, on the other, if we do require aid, a person of the
same sex can more easily provide it, for men understand
men's needs best, and women, women's.[80]

In addition, by their absorption with housekeeping
details, these men and women bind themselves in servitude
to "the world," the very thing from which the state of
virginity was supposed to free them.[81] Instead of re-
joicing in the liberty which Christ had given them, they
have submitted to a new kind of slavery, the anxieties
of married life,[82] even though they were not married.
Unlike the widows who with good sense rejected a second
marriage as a "yoke of servitude," the *subintroductae*
willingly rushed into such slavery.[83] Chrysostom reminded his female audience of Paul's argument in I Corinthians 7:34: the unmarried woman was to be free to care
for the things of the Lord,[84] but the *agapetae* did not
enjoy that liberty, what with the cooking, making of
beds (Chrysostom generously granted that there was more
than one),[85] and other domestic duties they must perform,[86] not to speak of the business affairs in which
they often engaged.[87] It irked Chrysostom that these
couples tried, in effect, to have the best of both the
virginal and the married states. If they were going to
live together, one senses him saying, they ought to
endure *all* the woes of marriage, including the screaming

children, which by spiritual marriage they had avoided.[88]
Probably he also thought it unfair that the *subintroduc-*
tae, relieved of the childrearing cares of married women,
kept their youthful bloom until they were forty and
rivalled the beauty of teen-age brides![89] Perhaps Chrysostom secretly wished that the monks and the virgins
would find their living arrangements less pleasant and
agreeable than apparently they did.

Last, it plagued Chrysostom that in syneisaktism,
the distinctive male and female characteristics and roles
were overturned. The monk acquired "womanish" traits by
his constant association with the female sex. By sitting
with women while they spun and weaved, he absorbed
women's words and habits,[90] and became affected by the
talkativeness and "servile mentality" of that sex.[91]
Instead of pursuing activities fit for a male, he spent
his days running errands for his female companion, calling at shops to see if madame's mirror was ready yet, if
her bowl had been repaired.[92] Chrysostom sternly reminded the monks that Christ had armed them to be soldiers
in a noble fight, to cast down demons and wage spiritual
warfare, not to devote their days to waiting on girls
who were worth "only three obols."[93] Perhaps the latter
complaint touches the heart of Chrysostom's objections:
the man in such a relationship usually served the woman
more than she did him.[94] Paul told us in I Corinthians
7:23, "Do not become servants of men"--and how much more
we should not make ourselves servants of women![95] These
domesticated monks were as tame as lions whose manes had
been clipped and whose teeth and claws broken off; the
men, like their feline counterparts, had become "softer
than wax."[96] How unfitting it was for a monk who pro-
fessed Christian freedom to submit himself to such ser-
vility; the peace he might have found in the celibate
life had been exchanged for slavery.[97]

The female virgins, for their part, also acquired
undesirable and "unnatural" characteristics. They
adopted lordly ways and thought it laudable that they
ruled over men. In their wish to assume the dominant
role, they had forgotten that women who bring men under
their authority are not respected.[98]   (Women honor those
who rule over them, not those who submit to them, Chrysostom claimed,[99] neatly expressing the traditional view
of female psychology.) It was an outrage for the virgin
to try to be the "head" rather than the "body" and rele-
gate the male to her lowly status. If such a reversal
of roles was objectionable in marriage, it was even worse
in the case of the virgins and the monks. These women
should remember God's word subjecting them to the male;
"And your desire shall be for your husband, and he shall
rule over you" (Gen. 3:16) and "the head of the woman is
the man" (I Cor. 11:3).[100] That peculiarly female vice,
vanity, had led these unfortunates into a mode of life
for which Chrysostom had no good word.[101] All in all,
syneisaktism was a practice which, to Chrysostom's eyes,
dishonored the individuals, the Church, and God, while
providing no compensating benefits.

                                  III
     What, from a later point of view, can we make of the
phenomenon of syneisaktism? Was it simply the practical
advantages of communal living which recommended the custom and ensured its popularity? There is no doubt some
point to this argument. In an age when convents for
women were rare and in some areas unknown, spiritual
marriage might be one solution to the virgin's quest for
suitable domestic arrangements.[102] Some wealthy widows,
such as Jerome's friends Paula and Marcella, might be
able to maintain from their own resources a household and
servants, but not every young woman was so fortunately

endowed. Chrysostom indicated the enormity of the
problem when he reported that the Antiochene church
alone in his period had over three thousand widows and
virgins enrolled on its lists.[103] Would not living with
a man dedicated to chastity who could help with financial
and domestic matters be of great benefit to an unprotected
girl? And in return the man would receive the advantages
of her housekeeping services.

   We doubt, however, that the popularity of syneisaktism resulted from practical considerations alone, even
though these may have played an important role. Two
other reasons present themselves for consideration.
First, although Achelis professes his uncertainty about
the motives of the couples,[104] he hints at an answer
which has much to commend it: the attractiveness of
"Platonic love" to those who recognize in a member of the
opposite sex their own visions and ideals.[105] Syneisaktism, we think, offered to men and women a unique opportunity for friendships which involved a high degree of
emotional and spiritual intimacy. It is of interest in
this regard that both Chrysostom and Jerome, outspoken
critics of spiritual marriage, had longstanding relationships with women. In Chrysostom's case, it is dubious
that they ever (with the exception of his love for
Olympias) achieved a closeness which could be called
"emotional intimacy." (His rather wooden notes to women,
complaining about the weather, his indigestion, and the
lack of mail do not suggest that he was "intimate" with
many of his correspondents.)[106] To the contrary,
Chrysostom expressed shock that men and women would spend
as much time together as did the *subintroductae* and their
male companions. From his point of view, such a way of
life was inappropriate not only to virgins, but to
married women as well. As he makes clear in his many

treatises, wives are to be sober, quiet, and unobtrusive.
They are to obey their husbands' commands and frequently
recall, with humility and repentance, their implication
in Eve's sin, which required them henceforth to be submissive to men.[107]

For the virgins and their companions, all such rules
had been dashed to the ground. Their intimate association to Chrysostom could only imply that the proper male
and female roles had been discarded. God, he thought,
had ordained women to one role and men to another, and
never should the sexes doubt what these were.[108] Females
through martyrdom (in the past) or ascetic devotion (in
his own day) might be fortunate enough to appropriate
some of the nobler masculine qualities (courage, for
example),[109] but nowhere did Chrysostom indicate that
women should be praised for assertiveness or the adoption
of the types of behavior permitted to men. The laws of
God and "nature" would be put in jeopardy if the partners
in spiritual marriage veered too far in the direction
of "unisexuality," or even became more like one another.
The androgynous ideal was one which Chrysostom could have
espoused only very tentatively, if at all.

These couples, we think, were tending toward the
recognition of the possibility of friendship between the
sexes, something considered improbable in the ancient
world. To the classical mind, friendship in its truest
sense meant a kind of parity between two people,[110] and
women, by virtue of their inferior nature and status,
could thus rarely qualify as suitable candidates for
friendship with men. Chrysostom was very conscious that
the monks and virgins were friends; he used the word
philia to describe their relationship on at least four
occasions.[111] The fact that he thought men and women
capable of such a relationship at all indicates that he

was breaking with traditional attitudes. (Love between
the sexes, even as the basis for marriage, was rather
rare in Christian circles of the fourth century, Jean
Dumortier has pointed out.)[112] Chrysostom, although
conscious of the possibility of such friendships, was
very wary of their consequences. He resolved his
ambivalence by proclaiming that *philia* between a man and
woman--theoretically an option--must be renounced if it
makes love for Jesus impossible, as he plainly thought
syneisaktism did. We want to be able to say to Christ
at our future meeting, "For you and your honor we have
despised intimacy and triumphed over pleasure, have
troubled our souls, and set aside all *philia* and personal
preference; we have chosen you and our love for you above
all things."[113] To those virgins who were enmeshed in
the bonds of spiritual marriage, Chrysostom penned his
warning words, "You must be ready to bear and suffer all
things rather than desert the *philia* of Christ."[114]

Today, when men and women are re-examining their
sexual roles and relationships, it is tempting to depict
these early Christian couples as trying in the face of
criticism and condemnation to create new forms of relationship, to discard the older stereotypical ideas of
appropriate sexual behavior. Alas, most of our information about them and their lives comes from the accounts
of their accusers. We will probably never know how they
would have described their own relationships.

But is it out of place to imagine that they would
have stressed the spiritual component of their association? Would they have pictured themselves as attempting
to live the life of the Kingdom here and now? Would they
have argued that God had promised to the followers of his
Son superhuman power to withstand temptations to which
ordinary mortals might succumb?[115] Would they have

claimed, with Paul, that in Jesus there is "no male and
female" (Gal. 3:28)? Wayne Meeks wrote, in discussing
Paul's encounters with the early Christian communities,
"it is at least a plausible conjecture that the symbolic
identification of male and female among them was a
significant part of their 'realized eschatology.'"[116]
We think that such an understanding might also be applicable to the phenomenon of spiritual marriage. Although
Chrysostom urged his audience to live like the intellectual and incorporeal powers above,[117] he clearly wished
to exempt the mingling of the sexes from that foretaste
of heavenly life. The monks and the virgins, on the
other hand, perhaps thought that God had already given
them the impassibility of the angels. We know at least
that they argued they had been granted superior strength
to resist sexual sin,[118] although Chrysostom believed
that people who talked in this fashion fancied they were
living among stones, not among flesh-and-blood humans.[119]
His response to their position is found in the quotation
with which we began the paper: it is only later on, in
the heavenly realms, after death, that men and women will
be able to enjoy free associations with impunity. From
his point of view, the *subintroductae* and the monks had
prematurely assumed that they had shed their bodily
desires. Chrysostom, less given to illusions of heavenly
incorporation, felt obliged to remind them they were
still of the earth, earthy.

NOTES

[1]John Chrysostom, *Adversus eos qui apud se habent subintroductas virgines* 13 (J.P. Migne, *Patrologiae Cursus Completus: Series Graeca* [Hereafter, PG] 47, 514). Hereafter abbreviated as *Adv. eos.* The numberings of the sections given in Migne do not always correspond with those of other editions.

[2]Hans Achelis, *Virgines Subintroductae: Ein Beitrag zum VII Kapitel des I. Korintherbriefs* (Leipzig, 1902).

[3]Hans Achelis, "Agapetae," *Encyclopedia of Religion and Ethics,* ed. James Hasting (New York, 1926), 1:177.

[4]Achelis, *Virgines,* p. 27.

[5]Derrick Sherwin Bailey, *Sexual Relation in Christian Thought* (New York, 1959), p. 33.

[6]Achelis, "Agapetae," p. 178.

[7]Achelis, *Virgines,* p. 73.

[8]*Similitudes* 9, 10f; also see 10, 3. Pierre de Labriolle, "Le 'Mariage spirituel' dans l'antiquité chrétienne," *Revue Historique* 137 (1921): 210, denies that the *Similitudes* can be used as an apology for spiritual marriage.

[9]Irenaeus, *Adversus haereses* 1, 6, 3.

[10]Pseudo-Clement, *Epistola* 1, 10; *Ep.* 2, 1 and 10.

[11]Pseudo-Clement, *Ep.* 2, 15.

[12]Tertullian, *De exhortatione castitatis* 12; *De monogamia* 16.

[13]Cyprian, *Ep.* 62 and *Ep.* 6, 5 (PL numberings; Oxford *Ep.* 4 and *Ep.* 13).

[14]Text in S. Thasci Caecili Cypriani, *Opera Omnia*, ed. W. Hartel (*Corpus Scriptorum Ecclesiasticorum Latinorum* 3, 3) (Vienna, 1871), pp. 173-220. The treatise is discussed by Achelis, *Virgines*, pp. 36-42.

[15]Eusebius of Emesa, *Homilia* 7, 20 and 22. The subject is discussed in David Amand de Mendieta, "La Virginité chez Eusèbe d'Emèse et l'ascétisme familial dans la première moitié du IVᵉ siècle," *Revue d'Histoire Ecclésiastique* 50 (1955): 777-820.

[16]Bernard Grillet, "Introduction," *Jean Chrysostome: La Virginité* (Paris, 1966), p. 37, n. 1, asserts that Chrysostom may have been familiar with Eusebius' writings.

[17]Gregory of Nyssa, *De virginitate* 23; Basil of Caesarea, *Ep.* 55; Gregory of Nazianzus, *Epigrammata* 10-20.

[18]Jerome, *Ep.* 22, 14. 𝒐𝓃𝑒-𝓂𝒶𝓃 𝓌𝒽𝑜𝓇𝑒𝓈

[19]English translation in *New Testament Apocrypha*, ed. W. Schneemelcher-E. Hennecke (Philadelphia, 1963-1966), 2: 141-164.

[20]See Achelis, *Virgines*, pp. vii-viii; and Roland H. A. Seboldt, "Spiritual Marriage in the Early Church: A Suggested Interpretation of I Cor. 7:36-38," *Concordia Theological Monthly* 30 (1959): 176-184 for further references.

[21]Eusebius of Caesarea, *Historia ecclesiastica* 7, 29.

[22]Eusebius of Caesarea, *His. eccles.* 7, 30. Felix Quadt, "Subintroductae Mulier," *Zeitschrift für Katholische Theologie* 34 (1910): 228-231, disagrees with Achelis' view that *syneisaktoi* was translated as *subintroductae* for the first time in the sixth century; he presents evidence from an early fifth-century translation of the canons of the Sixth Synod of Carthage (419) for his opinion.

[23]See Labriolle, "Le 'Mariage spirituel,'" p. 222 for a list of councils condemning the practice. Achelis (*Virgines*, p. 35) thinks that the medieval decrees are protesting against outright concubinage, not spiritual marriage.

[24]Roger Reynolds, "Virgines Subintroductae in Celtic Christianity," *Harvard Theological Review* 61 (1968): 547-566.

[25]Arthur Vööbus, *History of Asceticism in the Syrian Orient* (Louvain, 1958), 1:78-83.

[26]Achelis (*Virgines*, p. 13) discusses the evidence for Montanist adoption of the practice in North Africa. Tertullian and Cyprian witness to the practice in this area.

[27]Achelis, *Virgines*, p. 60, for a list.

[28]Roland Seboldt, "Spiritual Marriage," p. 184, and Achelis, *Virgines*, p. 59.

[29]Eduard Grafe, "Geistliche Verlöbnisse bei Paulus," *Theologische Arbeiten aus dem rheinischen wissenschaftlichen Prediger-Verein*, N. F. 3 (1899): 57-69.

[30]Achelis, *Virgines*, pp. 21-29.

[31]Numerous commentaries have been written on these verses. See Seboldt, "Spiritual Marriage"; John J. O'Rourke, "Hypotheses Regarding I Corinthians 7:36-38," *The Catholic Biblical Quarterly* 20 (1958): 292-298; and Werner Georg Kümmel, "Verlobung und Heirat bei Paulus (I Cor. 7:36-38)," *Neutestamentliche Studien für Rudolf Bultmann* (Berlin, 1954), pp. 276-277, n. 1, for references. Also see the commentaries mentioned below.

[32]See John C. Hurd, Jr., *The Origin of I Corinthians* (New York, 1965), pp. 172-175.

[33]See Hurd, *Origin*, p. 173; E.B. Allo, *Saint Paul, première epître aux Corinthians*, 2nd ed. (Paris, 1956), p. 192; and Achelis, *Virgines*, p. 22.

[34]See Kümmel, "Verlobung," pp. 287-288; Allo, *Saint Paul*, pp. 192-193; O'Rourke, "Hypotheses," p. 294; Seboldt, "Spiritual Marriage," pp. 107-108, as well as the standard commentaries on I Corinthians by C.K. Barrett and Hans Conzelmann for discussions of this translation problem.

[35]Advocated by Kümmel, "Verlobung," pp. 275-295, and followed by Henry Chadwick, "'All Things to All Men' (I Cor. 9:22)," *New Testament Studies* 1 (1954): 267, and by C.K. Barrett, *A Commentary on the First Epistle to the Corinthians* (London, 1968), p. 184.

[36]Achelis thinks there are pre-Christian precedents for the practice in Philo's description of the Therapeutae. See Achelis, *Virgines*, pp. 29-31. A. Oepke, "*gynē*," *Theological Dictionary of the New Testament*, ed. G. Kittel, trans. and ed. G.W. Bromiley (Grand Rapids, 1964), 1:779 thinks there were also pagan precedents, and refers us to R. Reitzenstein's *Hellenistische Wundererzählungen* (Stuttgart, 1963), pp. 146f.

[37]Achelis, *Virgines*, pp. 21-23.

[38]Achelis, *Virgines*, p. 28.

[39]Bailey, *Sexual Relation*, p. 33.

[40]Hurd, *Origin*, pp. 179-180.

[41]Jean Héring, *The First Epistle of Saint Paul to the Corinthians*, trans. from the 2nd French ed. by A.W. Heathcote and P.J. Allcock (London, 1962), p. 64.

[42]See O'Rourke, "Hypotheses," p. 294.

[43]So Henry Chadwick, "'All Things,'" p. 267. For Ephraem's view on this matter, see Arthur Vööbus, *Celibacy, A Requirement For Admission to Baptism in the Early Syrian Church* (Stockholm, 1951), pp. 23-25.

[44]John Chrysostom, *De virg.* 78.

[45]John Chrysostom, *Homilia 19 I Cor.*, 6.

[46]Socrates (*Hist. eccles.* VI, 3) gives the earlier date; Palladius (*Dialogus* 5), the later. Jean Dumortier, "La Date des deux traités de Saint Jean Chrysostome aux moines et aux vierges," *Mélanges de Science Religieuse* 6 (1949), thinks that they were originally written in 381-383 (Jerome, he postulates, used the second treatise in writing *Ad Eustochium*), but this does not preclude Chrysostom's having published them again in Constantinople when confronted with the same problem (pp. 251-252).

[47]Achelis, *Virgines*, p. 52 thinks the men were monks only, not clerics, or Chrysostom could have used the canons of Nicaea against them. He also suggests that the situation in Constantinople, in which rich women took men into their homes, was an unusual arrangement (pp. 52-53, 56).

[48]*Adv. eos* 1 (PG 47, 496) and 2 (PG 47, 497).

[49]Jerome, *Ep.* 22, 13 and 14.

[50]*Quod regulares feminae viris cohabitare non debeant* 5 (PG 47, 523). (Hereafter abbreviated as *Quod reg.*) Also *Adv. eos* 2 (PG 47, 497).

[51]*Quod reg.* 2 (PG 47, 516).

[52]*Adv. eos* 1 (PG 47, 496).

[53]*Adv. eos* 3 (PG 47, 498).

[54]*Adv. eos* 1 (PG 47, 496-497).

[55]*Adv. eos* 2 (PG 47, 497).

[56]*Hom. 17 Matt.*, 2.

[57]*Quod reg.* 1 (PG 47, 515) and 3 (PG 47, 519-520).

[58]*Quod reg.* 7 (PG 47, 528). Chrysostom reminds them that Adam and Eve were content with garments of skins! (*Quod reg.* 7, [PG 47, 527-528]).

[59]*Quod reg.* 1 (PG 47, 515) and 3 (PG 47, 501).

[60]*Adv. eos* 5 (PG 47, 502).

[61]*Adv. eos* 5 (PG 47, 501).

[62]*Adv. eos* 3 (PG 47, 499) and 3 (PG 47, 498); *Quod reg.* 5 (PG 47, 522). John Hurd, *Origin*, p. 181, stresses the similarity between Paul's approach to marriage problems and his approach to the difficulties arising from the meat offered to idols.

[63]*Adv. eos* 4 (PG 47, 499); *Quod reg.* 6 (PG 47, 527).

[64] *Adv. eos* 6 (PG 47, 502-503).

[65] *Adv. eos* 5 (PG 47, 501).

[66] *Adv. eos* 13 (PG 47, 514).

[67] *Quod reg.* 2 (PG 47, 516).

[68] *Quod reg.* 6 (PG 47, 526).

[69] *De virg.* 6.

[70] *Quod reg.* 7 (PG 47, 528).

[71] *Quod reg.* 9 (PG 47, 532).

[72] *Quod reg.* 1 (PG 47, 515).

[73] *Adv. eos* 6 (PG 47, 503).

[74] *Adv. eos* 6 (PG 47, 504).

[75] *Adv. eos* 7 (PG 47, 504-505).

[76] *Adv. eos* 9 (PG 47, 507). One wonders if Chrysostom's contemporaries believed this argument.

[77] *Adv. eos* 9 (PG 47, 508).

[78] *Quod reg.* 4 (PG 47, 520).

[79] *Quod reg.* 4 (PG 47, 521).

[80] *Adv. eos* 9 (PG 47, 508) and *Quod reg.* 4 (PG 47, 520).

[81] *Hom. 19 I Cor.*, 6.

[82] *Quod reg.* 8 (PG 47, 530).

[83] *Quod reg.* 9 (PG 47, 530).

[84] *Adv. eos* 6 (PG 47, 504).

[85] *Adv. eos* 9 (PG 47, 508).

[86] *Adv. eos* 9 (PG 47, 507).

[87]*Adv. eos* 6 (PG 47, 503-504).

[88]*Adv. eos* 1 (PG 47, 496).

[89]Ibid.

[90]*Adv. eos* 10 (PG 47, 509).

[91]*Adv. eos* 11 (PG 47, 510).

[92]*Adv. eos* 9 (PG 47, 508).

[93]*Adv. eos* 10 (PG 47, 509).

[94]*Adv. eos* 9 (PG 47, 507).

[95]*Adv. eos* 10 (PG 47, 509).

[96]*Adv. eos* 10 (PG 47, 510).

[97]*Adv. eos* 11 (PG 47, 511).

[98]*Quod reg.* 6 (PG 47, 524).

[99]*Adv. eos* 11 (PG 47, 511).

[100]*Quod reg.* 6 (PG 47, 524). Chrysostom appears to have forgotten that the profession of virginity removed the curse of Genesis 3:16 from women, a point he made in this very treatise and elsewhere. See *Quod reg.* 8 (PG 47, 530) and *De virg.* 65.

[101]*Quod reg.* 5 (PG 47, 523).

[102]Jean Dumortier, "Le Mariage dans les milieux chrétiens d'Antioche et de Byzance d'après Saint Jean Chrysostome," *Lettres d'Humanité* 6 (1947): 149. Achelis, *Virgines*, p. 28, notes that many of these women were not content to take a subordinate place in a married couple's home, assuming servant duties.

[103]*Homilia 66 Matt.*, 3.

[104]Achelis, *Virgines*, p. 4.

[105]Ibid., pp. 72-75.

[106]Olympias was without doubt his true soul-mate. But his other letters are not nearly so personal. Chrysostom's letters are found in PG 52.

[107]For example, see *Serm. 5 Gen.*, 1 and 3; *Hom. 26 I Cor.*, 2. See Elizabeth A. Clark, "Sexual Politics in the Writings of John Chrysostom," *The Anglican Theological Review* 59 (1977): 3-20.

[108]*Hom. 5 Tit.*, 4.

[109]*Ep.* 94; *De virg.* 7; *De S. Droside* 3.

[110]See Aristotle, *Eth. Nic.* VIII, 6-8 (1158b1-1159b20).

[111]*Adv. eos* 10 (PG 47, 510) and 13 (PG 47, 514); *Quod reg.* 6 (PG 47, 524) and 8 (PG 47, 529).

[112]Dumortier, "Mariage," p. 107.

[113]*Adv. eos* 13 (PG 47, 514).

[114]*Quod reg.* 6 (PG 47, 525).

[115]Achelis, *Virgines*, p. 74.

[116]Wayne A. Meeks, "The Image of the Androgyne: Some Uses of a Symbol in Earliest Christianity," *History of Religions* 13 (1973-1974): 202.

[117]*Adv. eos* 13 (PG 47, 513).

[118]*Adv. eos* 4 (PG 47, 500).

[119]*Adv. eos* 5 (PG 47, 501).

VITIATED SEEDS AND HOLY VESSELS:
AUGUSTINE'S MANICHEAN PAST

Conference on "Images of the Feminine in Gnosticism"
Claremont, California (1985)

I

The chasm between Augustine's youthful yearning for
scientific certainty[1] and his later admissions of ignorance[2] is but one indication of his progressively
"darkening" vision.[3] Although this ignorance prompted
his praise of God's mysterious omnipotence,[4] the older
Augustine, far from grasping the design of the universe,[5]
could fathom neither how fetuses were formed nor how they
received their souls.[6] Yet worse than scientific ignorance was heresy, and at the end of his life, Augustine
found that his theology of reproduction brought charges
of "Manicheanism" against him.[7] Pelagian critics such as
Julian of Eclanum alleged that Augustine's theory of
original sin, transmitted through the sex act and corrupting the offspring conceived, was a throwback to the
Manichean notion of "natural evil" that Augustine had
accepted in his youth.[8] According to Julian, both
Augustine's "Manichean" (i.e., overly-ascetic) view of
marriage and his "Manichean" (i.e., Docetic and Apollinarian) Christology stemmed in part from his deficient
understanding of human biology. In the course of the
controversy--which we know only from Augustine's
rejoinders to Julian--Julian moved from a more general

accusation of "Manicheanism" to pinpoint the source of
Augustine's error: his view of "vitiated seeds."

Julian's charge cannot be immediately dismissed, for
despite Augustine's belief that human seed was the car-
rier of Adam's sin, he could not explain the mechanism
by which this happened. Although Augustine appealed to
Virgin Birth theory, Catholic teaching on marriage and
asceticism, Scripture, pagan learning, common experience,
and horticulture to bolster his supposition of the *tradux
peccati*, he managed only to offer his opponent unwitting
support. To the end, Augustine foundered on the "scientific" points raised by Julian. Although the mixing of
seeds with evil is given a very different--indeed,
contrasting--evaluation in Augustine's myth of Eden than
in the Manichean foundation myth (and thus arguably is
"anti-Manichean"), the very fact that the mixing of
seeds with evil is the key to *both* myths suggests that
Julian had ferreted out in Augustine's theology of reproduction a carry-over from Manicheanism. To unravel
the charge will lead us through the development of
Julian's argument and back to Augustine's Manichean past.

II

Although the early Pelagian controversy centered on
the explanation of God's goodness and justice in relation
to human sin, the issues pertaining to sexuality, marriage, and the transmission of original sin that became
central in Julian's attack were present in Augustine's
first anti-Pelagian treatise, *De peccatorum meritis et
remissione*, dated to 412 A.D. Here Augustine formulates
his view that original sin is revealed in the "disobedient
excitation of the members"[9] that causes all children to
be born with concupiscence;[10] the "injury" is transferred
to infants through the "sinful flesh" of those who

produce them.[11] Psalm 51:5 is enlisted in support of the
theory: "I was brought forth in iniquity, and in sin did
my mother conceive me."[12] Augustine also appeals to his
earlier ascetic writings to demonstrate the sinfulness
revealed in our "disobedient members."[13] From Virgin
Birth theory he borrows the theme that Jesus' sinlessness
stems from his not having been conceived "through concupiscence and a husband's embrace."[14] Augustine further
notes the Christological correlate of his views: Jesus
did not have our "sinful flesh," but only the "likeness
of sinful flesh" (Romans 8:3),[15] nor as an infant did he
suffer "weakness of mind."[16] Moreover, the treatise reveals that by 412 the Pelagians had posed the questions
with which Augustine would struggle until his death in
430: why do regenerated Christians not beget regenerated
children?[17] Why if we have remission of sins through
Christ do we still suffer death, on Augustine's theory a
penalty for sin?[18] Is the soul propagated or not?[19]

Augustine's anti-Pelagian works of the next five
years add nothing new to the "biology" underlying the
debate.[20] Then, between 417 and 419, Augustine began to
explore the *process* by which original sin was transmitted.
He now details how the sin in Eden affected human sexual
functioning and speculates on what the first couple's
relationship would have been if they had remained sinless. The best-known elaboration of these views is found
in Book XIV of *The City of God*: if Adam and Eve had not
sinned, there would have been no unruliness of lust to
disturb peace of mind and blot out mental functioning.[21]
Although Adam and Eve would have engaged in sexual intercourse in order to reproduce,[22] their sexual organs would
have moved at the command of their wills, tranquility
would have prevailed, defloration and labor pains would
have been unknown.[23] No quarrel would have existed

between lust and the will; rather, the genital organs
would have moved at the will's command, as do our other
bodily parts.[24] That the sin in Eden affected all later
humans is proved to Augustine by both our unruly sexual
members and our sense of shame at sexual intercourse.[25]
Significantly, Augustine borrows a phrase from Virgil's
Georgics to describe how the first man would have begotten
children calmly had the sin not intervened: Adam would
have resembled the farmer who prepares his mares for the
seed to be sown "on the field of generation."[26]

   Horticultural analogies are used in Augustine's other
writings from this period as well. In *Epistle* 184A,
dated to 417 A.D., Augustine expresses the same theory of
ideal sexual relations in Paradise that he did in *The
City of God*.[27] Here for the first time he finds an
example that will provide his controlling metaphor to
illustrate the transmission of sin: from the cultivated
olive tree are produced only wild olive trees, not cultivated ones. God providentially provided this dendrologi-
cal example to teach us that regenerated parents pass on
to their offspring only their old "carnal" natures, not
their state of spiritual rebirth.[28] Augustine uses the
example of the olive trees again in a letter to Pope
Sixtus and in *On the Grace of Christ and Original Sin*,[29]
both dated to 418 A.D. "Seeds" are now manifestly on his
mind. He explains to Albina, Melania the Younger, and
Pinianus, recipients of the *De gratia Christi*,[30] that God
constitutes and blesses the seeds of his creatures,
despite the transmission of the original sin through
them.[31] He also draws implications for Virgin Birth
theory from his evaluation of human seed: Christ's birth
is different from ours because he was not *seminatus* or
conceptus in carnal concupiscence; and Ambrose's words
that the Holy Spirit's "immaculate seed" (rather than a

husband's spoiled seed) caused Mary's impregnation are
cited.[32] Thus we can safely assert that Augustine's
interest in the "biology" of original sin had already
been piqued by the year in which Julian most likely wrote
his first attack upon Augustine, 419.

The course of the controversy between Julian and
Augustine developed as follows: after the condemnation
of Julian and other Pelagian bishops in 418, those condemned wrote to friends in Rome and to Count Valerius at
the imperial court in Ravenna defending their cause and
alleging that the opinions of Augustine (and others) on
marriage were "Manichean."[33] In 419, Augustine wrote
Book I of the *De nuptiis et concupiscentia*, championing
his theories against the "new heretics" who said he condemned marriage,[34] and sent it to Count Valerius who
(according to Augustine) had observed "marital
chastity."[35]

Apparently Augustine did not know the full details of
the Pelagian charges when he wrote Book I of *De nuptiis*,
for in the book he merely repeats arguments that he had
already elaborated before Julian's attack. Thus he upholds the goodness of creation in general and human
nature in particular.[36] He repeats his interpretation of
Eden *wie es gewesen ist* and how it should have been.[37]
He discusses shame's entrance to the world.[38] He
describes his sexual and marital ethic[39] and links it to
his understanding of the Virgin Birth and the marriage of
Joseph and Mary.[40] Borrowing points from his anti-
Manichean writings, he explains and defends the polygamy
of the patriarchs.[41] Last, he again calls up his example
of the seed of the olive tree that produces only wild
olives to explain how regenerated parents produce unre-
generated children.[42] (God's "pruning" is necessary to
remove the corruption from the carnal seed, and this is

accomplished through baptism.[43]) Augustine in Book I of
De nuptiis seems unaware that Julian had more detailed
and trenchant criticism of his theory of the *tradux
peccati*.

When Julian read Book I of the *De nuptiis*, he launched
a more probing attack upon Augustine's theology of reproduction. Extracts of his now-lost work, addressed to a
certain Turbantius, were given to Count Valerius, who in
turn despatched them to Augustine. Augustine responded
with Book II of the *De nuptiis*.[44] About the same time,
he wrote *Contra duas epistolas Pelagianorum*, again
defending his views against Julian.[45] Meanwhile, Augustine received all four volumes of Julian's treatise
addressed to Turbantius, of which he had earlier seen
only extracts, and responded more fully with the *Contra
Julianum*.[46] Without seeing (as far as we know) this response of Augustine, Julian wrote an even longer, eight-
book treatise against his Catholic opponent, to which
Augustine replied in the last, exhaustive work of his
life, the *Contra secundam Juliani responsionem opus
imperfectum*.[47]

Judging from Book II of the *De nuptiis* onward, we can
see that Julian was arguing from different grounds than
Augustine: for Julian, Augustine's theology of original
sin was the superstructure resting on a very dubious
biological substructure, and he resolved to force Augustine to explicate the biological underpinnings of his
theory. Although in the face of Julian's assault, Augustine grudgingly and belatedly allowed that there *might*
have been sexual desire in a sinless Eden (albeit very
different from the raging lust we now feel),[48] his attempt
to explain his theory of vitiated seeds succeeded only in
leaving him more liable to charges of "Manicheanism."
Julian's insinuations about the "Manichean" remnants in

Augustine's theology are indeed more precise than some
modern critics have acknowledged.[49]

To be sure, Julian's charge of "Manicheanism" that
prompted Book II of the *De nuptiis* rested also on some
broader issues of the Pelagian-Augustinian debate:
whether sin was a matter of nature or will,[50] how creation could be said to be good if children were born
evil,[51] how God's justice could be squared with the
condemnation of infants for what they personally did not
choose.[52] Augustine probably would have preferred to
keep the argument on grounds such as these, for here he
could wax eloquent on God's justice and mercy, on human
sinfulness and regneration, and could appeal to Scripture and his revered ecclesiastical predecessors,
especially Ambrose, to bolster his argument. Although
Julian also could argue theologically, citing Biblical
verses and writings of earlier church fathers,[53] he
wanted Augustine to make explicit the biology of the
tradux peccati, for here he could show that Augustine's
views were unscientific, ridiculous--and deeply "Manichean." Augustine could no longer rest his case, as he
had so often done in his anti-Manichean writings, on an
argument from the unity of God's goodness and justice, or
on his understanding that evil was no substance but a
lack. He would have to answer Julian's questions, and
his counter-attack would have to be on Julian's own
ground.

III

Book II of the *De nuptiis* shows how Julian proceeded
in his attempt to discredit Augustine. Just what *is* it
about marriage, he asks, that the Devil can claim its
offspring as his own? It can't be the difference between
the sexes, for God made us in two sexes. It can't be the

union of male and female, for God blessed this in
Genesis 1:28 and 2:24. It can't be human fecundity,
for reproduction was the reason why marriage was insti-
tuted.[54] Augustine's response--"none of the above, but
carnal concupiscence"[55]--leads Julian to his next task,
to show that Augustine's understanding of "concupiscence"
was not properly scientific.

Here Augustine gave him easy assistance, for in
several places, Augustine had already affirmed that
"concupiscence" was not necessarily a sexual term, since
we can have "lust" for vengeance, money, victory, and
domination, among other things.[56] Moreover, for Augustine there were good kinds of "concupiscence": the lust
of the spirit against the flesh (Galatians 5:17), for
instance, or the lust for wisdom (Wisdom 6:21).[57] But
usually for Augustine, concupiscence had a specifically
sexual reference--and a negative connotation.[58] As
Augustine cites him in *De nuptiis* II, Julian wished to
substitute phrases such as "the natural appetite"[59] or
"the vigor of the members"[60] for concupiscence. Augustine was quick to note (and to complain) that Julian's
terminology removed the issue from the realm of religious
or moral discourse.[61] Yet Julian does not in his treatise to Turbantius argue at length about the implications
of "nature," as he will later; he is content to affirm
that God is the creator of sexual desire and of the seeds
formed by it.

The ways in which Julian shifted the discussion away
from theology *per se* and toward a "bio-theology" of reproduction are revealed in his handling of several
Scriptural passages. When, for example, Genesis 4:25
states that Seth was the seed God raised up from Adam,
Julian interprets the verse to mean that God stirred up
sexual desire in Adam, through which the seed was

"raised" in order to be "poured" into Eve's womb.[62] God,
he asserts, is the ultimate cause of the seminal elements
present in our bodies[63] (this is the meaning of I Corinthians 15:38, "God gives to every seed its own body"),[64]
as well as of the "ardor" and the pleasure--but the seed
is formed through sexual desire.[65] Using another agricultural metaphor, Julian reminds Augustine that wheat
from stolen seeds produces no worse a crop--that is, that
seed itself is not affected by an adulterous relationship.[66] Seed is a biological phenomenon, whatever the
morality of human agents.

Julian also turned to Romans 1:27 (Paul's condemnation of homosexuality) to champion the "naturalness" and
hence the goodness of sexual desire. If Paul condemns
the "unnatural use," he must intend to praise the
"natural use," i.e., heterosexual relations. To Julian's
mind the misuse that "Sodomites" make of their sexual
organs provides no basis for adopting a "Manichean"
stance against heterosexual relations.[67]

We also learn from *De nuptiis* that Julian interpreted
the story in Genesis 20:18 (God's closing of the wombs of
the women in Abimelech's household as a punishment) to
mean that God removed the women's sexual desire. Augustine replies, So what? Lust isn't essential to women's
sexual and reproductive role, as it is to men's. If God
were going to take away lust as a hindrance to begetting,
he should have taken it from the men rather than the
women.[68] Julian later will argue that through such expressions, Augustine seems to make males more responsible
for the transmission of sin than females.[69]

Julian has thus pressed Augustine into a discussion
of more specifically sexual issues in *De nuptiis* II. To
be sure, by using the example of the seed of the olive
tree three times in *De nuptiis* I,[70] Augustine set the

stage for the discussion of seeds on which Julian would
needle him in subsequent books. In *De nuptiis* II, however, the argument is not pressed very far, and Augustine
reverts to his vision of Adam the Edenic farmer, sowing
his sperm with the calm and rational purpose with which
he would sow seeds of corn.[71]

Gathering from Augustine's discussion in the *Contra
Julianum*, we can posit that Julian became more interested
in the issue of "seeds" between the time of his first
attack upon Augustine and his book to Turbantius that
prompted the *Contra Julianum*. From Book III of the
Contra Julianum on, seeds come in for extensive discussion. Augustine's position is this: he agrees with
Julian that God makes all men from seed, but (unlike
Julian) he believes that it is seed already condemned
and vitiated.[72] Against Julian, Augustine holds that the
seed is created by God directly and does not receive its
formation from "lust."[73] Thus the child that results is
a divine work, not a human one.[74] If God were to with-
draw his good action in producing seeds, caring for them,
and quickening the fetus, there would be no begetting,
and what was already begotten would lapse into nothing-
ness.[75]

Augustine argues that although the seed was in essence
good, the Devil "sowed the fault" in it--a phrase that
alludes to Genesis 3 as well as the parable of the
tares.[76] In support of his view, he cites Romans 5:12.[77]
and his own *De nuptiis*: "the semination of the children
in the body of that life would have been without that
disease without which it cannot now exist in the body of
this death."[78] It is a tribute to God's mercy that he
does not withhold his creative power even from the seed
"vitiated by the paternal prevarication."[79] Augustine
suggests that perhaps a regenerated man has two kinds of

seeds: the immortal ones from which he derives life, and
the mortal ones through which "he generates the dead,"[80]
i.e., doomed children.

As cited in the *Contra Julianum*, Julian devised new
arguments after he read *De nuptiis* I that he here employs
in addition to his earlier charges.[81]   Some of his new
arguments rest on Aristotelian analysis, a point noticed
by Augustine[82] as well as by modern commentators.[83]
First, Julian undertakes what Augustine calls a "medical
dissection" of concupiscence using Aristotelian categories.   Thus Julian writes that the "genus" of concupiscence lies in "the vital fire" (a term borrowed from
Stoic analysis),[84] its "species" in the genital activity,
its "mode" in the conjugal act, and its "excess" in the
intemperance of fornication.[85]   Augustine, who considers
concupiscence a moral category,[86] is annoyed that Julian
censures only the excess of concupiscence, not the thing
itself; he must imagine that concupiscence constitutes
an original endowment of humankind, present even in
Paradise.[87]   Julian indeed *does* believe this: according
to him, concupiscence was one of the original senses
humans received,[88] a point he will further develop.

A second argument mounted by Julian involves
Aristotle's discussion of accidents inhering in subjects:
"that which inheres in a subject cannot exist without
the thing which is the subject of its inherence." Julian
concludes, "...therefore, the evil which inheres in a
subject cannot transmit its guilt to something else to
which it does not extend, that is to say, to the offspring."[89]   Aristotle was right: accidental properties
cannot "wander off" from their proper subject to
another.[90]   Julian faults two points in Augustine's view.
First, he writes, "natural things cannot be transformed
by an accident," hence human nature cannot be changed

forever by one act of a man's will.[91] Second, if parents
don't have something (namely, sin), they can't transmit
it; if on the other hand they do transmit it, as Augustine holds, they never lost it (in regenerating baptism).[92] Augustine's image of the olive tree is ridiculous; illustrations cannot help us to defend points that
by their very nature are indefensible.[93] If Augustine
wants to indulge in horticultural examples, why doesn't
he turn to Matthew 7:17-18, the good tree that bears
good fruit, which illustrates the goodness of human
nature and what is produced from it?[94]

Julian also appeals to religious arguments: God's
power and goodness are called into question if we believe
that "in the womb of a baptized woman, whose body is the
temple of God," is formed a child under the power of the
Devil.[95] And last, Julian faults Augustine's notion of
sin: "How could a matter of will be mixed with the creation of seeds?"[96] From Julian's standpoint, Augustine
has confused a matter of morals (the will's determination
of sin) with a biological issue (the creation of sperm).

Augustine found Julian's arguments dangerous. Armed
with Julian's exaltation of concupiscence, married
people might be encouraged to indulge in sexual relations
whenever they wanted. Did Julian so behave in his own
marriage, Augustine nastily inquires?[97] Any sexual act,
so long as it was heterosexual, would have to be praised
on the basis of Julian's analysis of Romans 1:27.[98] We
could not categorically state that consent to concupiscence was an evil (as Augustine thinks it is), since the
thing itself would be a good.[99]

In response to Julian's point about qualities inhering in a subject, Augustine agrees with Julian (and
Aristotle) that they do so inhere and that they do not
"wander." But he holds that qualities can pass by

"affecting" other things. Thus Ethiopians beget black
children (the blackness "affects" the children's bodies);
the color of Jacob's rods "affected" the color of the
lambs produced.[100] A medical writer (later identified
as Soranus) testifies that an ugly king had his wife
gaze at a portrait of a handsome man while they had
sexual relations so that the child would be "affected."[101]
Moreover, parents *can* transmit accidental qualities: a
man who lost the sight of one eye produced a son with
sight in one eye, so that what had been an "accident" for
the father became "natural" for the son. And parents can
also transmit what they *don't* themselves have, as is
proved by the same father's producing a fully-sighted
son[102] and by circumcised fathers begetting sons with
foreskins![103] Thus with so much "scientific" evidence,
why can't we believe that original sin "affects" an offspring?[104] In addition to his genetics of "affection,"
Augustine also speaks of the transfer of properties by
"contagion,"[105] in which "another quality of the same
kind is produced," as when diseased parents transmit
their affliction to their offspring.[106]

As for Julian's objection that the omnipotent God
could not let the fetus of a baptized woman fall under
the power of the Devil, Augustine misconstrues his point
(namely, that God is simultaneously powerful, just, *and*
merciful). Augustine thus rebukes Julian for thinking
that enclosure in a narrow womb could limit or defile
God,[107] an argument used by both pagan and Manichean
opponents of the Incarnation.[108] Augustine responds that
God is everywhere and is defiled by nothing. Besides,
infants in the womb are not really part of their mothers'
bodies, as is evidenced by the fact that they have to be
baptized separately, for a fetus, who is "not a temple
of God," is created in a woman who is.[109]

As for Julian's argument that sin is a matter of will
and has nothing to do with the biological phenomenon of
the creation of seeds, Augustine rejects it because he
rejects Julian's restriction of sin to the act of a
single rational being. He writes, if the will could *not*
be mixed with seeds, there would be no way to hold that
infants are "dead."[110] That is, of course, Julian's very
point: infants *cannot* be held responsible for sin.
Augustine's zeal to damn upbaptized infants seemed cruel
and unjust to Julian;[111] Augustine's counter-argument
(that Julian himself is "cruel" in not opening Christ's
saving grace to infants)[112] is beside the point, given
Julian's understanding of sin and human development.

In the work that prompted the *Contra Julianum*, Julian
also must have pressed Augustine on the consequences of
his theory of original sin for his understanding of
marriage and the Virgin Birth. Many years earlier,
Augustine had elaborated his notion of the threefold
goods of marriage (offspring, fidelity, the sacramental
bond)[113] and had affirmed Mary's virginal vow and her
perpetual virginity.[114] In *De nuptiis* I, he had re-
affirmed the threefold goods,[115] and had used his interpretation of them to argue that Joseph and Mary had a
genuine marriage. Joseph and Mary shared "affection of
soul" and hence deserve to be called "parents" (Luke
2:41), just as Mary is called a "wife" (Matt. 1:20).[116]
Reflecting on the "bond" between Joseph and Mary, Augustine avers the permanence of marriage even when there are
no offspring, or when one partner commits adultery or
insists on divorce.[117] A sexless marriage is sanctioned
for those with sufficient fortitude.[118]

As early as *De nuptiis* II, Julian reveals his discomfort with Augustine's praise of sexless marriage and his
view, derived from Ambrose, that Jesus was free from

"sinful fault" because he was not born from sexual union. Does Julian dare to call Ambrose a Manichean (as Jovinian had), counters Augustine?[119] At least Jovinian never denied the necessity of Christ's saving grace to redeem babies from the Devil![120] Julian, although an advocate of the Virgin Birth, disliked Augustine's use of the example of Joseph and Mary to suggest that sexual union was not necessary in marriage. "Show me any bodily marriage without sexual union!" he demands of Augustine.[121] Augustine, for his part, scorned Julian's notion of marriage as overly sexual: does Julian imply that the "shedding of seed" is the ultimate pleasure of the union, rather than the conception and birth of a child?[122] Augustine was gradually abandoning a sexual understanding of marriage and stressing more centrally the bond between partners. To Julian, this movement betokened "Manicheanism."

Such criticisms are amplified by Julian in the treatise to which Augustine responded in the *Contra Julianum*. "Marriage consists of nothing else than the union of bodies," Julian wrote.[123] Since Joseph and Mary never engaged in sexual intercourse, they cannot be considered married.[124] On Augustine's view of their relationship, we might infer that Adam and Eve could have been "married" in Eden without sexual union.[125] When Augustine asserts that Christ was born sinless because he was born "not of the seed of man,"[126] or, alternately, because he was not begotten from "the concupiscence of sexual intercourse,"[127] Julian puts some difficult questions to him.

First, even if Joseph was not involved in Christ's conception, why did not Mary have "concupiscence" from her own birth that she transferred to her son (recall that for Julian, this was a natural quality, akin to the five senses).[128] If she came from the stock of Adam, she

must have given him the same flesh that we have, flesh
(*contra* Augustine) that is not sinful.[129] If Augustine
insists that Jesus did not have one of the senses with
which we are born, Jesus is not a human being and Augustine is guilty of Apollinarianism.[130] Moreover, since
Augustine does not hesitate to assert that Christ's body
was of a "different purity" from the bodies of other
humans because of the lack of concupiscence (and hence
original sin) involved in his conception,[131] Julian
suspects him of harboring a Docetic i.e., "Manichean,"
view of Jesus.

Thus we see that in Julian's first two attacks on
Augustine, he pinpointed some problematic aspects of
Augustine's theology of reproduction that kindle his
suspicions of Augustine's orthodoxy: that ideal marriage
might not involve sexual relations, that sexual intercourse transmits original sin, that Jesus does not share
all our human qualities. These points Julian will pursue
in his last work against Augustine that is excerpted in
Augustine's *Opus imperfectum*.

IV

From Julian's words cited in the *Opus imperfectum*, we
gather that he had reflected further on the implications
of Augustine's theology and was prepared for a still
lengthier attack. Five points either absent from or
undeveloped in the earlier controversy emerge as central
in Julian's last set of charges. First, Julian adds a
new "science" to those from which he had drawn his
earlier arguments: anthropology, understood in the
modern, not the classical theological sense. Anthropological data were useful to Julian in demolishing Augustine's appeal to the shame surrounding nudity and sexual
intercourse as evidence for original sin. Julian earlier

had explained that Adam and Eve at first had gone naked
because they had not yet developed the art of making
clothing, a product of "human inventiveness" that came in
time.[132] Thus for Julian, the use of clothing was not
related to sin's entrance to the world and the desire to
cover the unruly genitals, as it was in Augustine's interpretation.[133]

In his last anti-Augustinian work, Julian drew arguments from the Cynic philosophers, who faulted customary
ideas of shame; from the animals, who exhibit no shame at
their public sexual activities;[134] and from the diverse
customs of human beings. Borrowing Aristotle's notion
that virtuous behavior depends on knowing which people
may perform what activities in which circumstances and
how,[135] Julian observes that we do not shun nudity at the
baths, but clothe ourselves for public assemblies; that
our nightgowns are loose and *seminudus*, but our street
attire covers us more carefully; that we don't blame
artisans, athletes, or sailors (witness Peter in John
21:7) for their state of undress since their activities
require it. Moreover, the Scots and other barbarians go
naked without shame. Augustine's teaching that universal
shame accompanies nudity is "destroyed" by such evidence,
Julian asserts.[136] Augustine's appeal to "universal
facts" turns out to be an appeal to culturally-conditioned
behavior that is not universal. More important, from
Julian's viewpoint, Augustine veers dangerously close to
a condemnation of the human body that can be labeled
"Manichean."

Julian's next piece of anthropological evidence concerns birthing experience. Against Augustine's view
that labor pains are the penalty for original sin, Julian
suggests that such pains are natural to the human (and
animal) condition, and hence are not to be associated

with sin.[137] Surely Augustine must realize that the
intensity of labor pains varies widely among human beings.
Rich women suffer more than poor ones, and barbarian and
nomadic women give birth with great ease, scarcely inter-
rupting their journeys to bear children. How then can
Augustine say that labor pains are universal and the
penalty for sin?[138] He has not taken a properly
scientific approach to the issue.

Julian's second new argument concerns the origin of
the soul, a question on which Augustine had consistently
pronounced his ignorance.[139] Augustine had been content
to affirm the existence of original sin, whether we believe that the soul's corruption came about with the
body's conception, or that the soul was corrupted after
having been placed by God in the body "as in a faulty
vessel."[140] He had earlier advised Julian to adopt the
position of the mother of the seven Maccabean brothers,
who confessed her ignorance about the soul's origin.[141]
Julian now pressed the Creationist view against Augustine's notion of a *tradux peccati*. Since the soul is a
new creation of God and does not come from the bodily
seed, how can it be said to pass sin from parents to offspring?[142] And Julian claims that he knows Augustine's
position, even if Augustine doesn't: since Augustine believes that sin becomes mixed with the seeds and makes
the *conceptus* guilty,[143] he is a Traducian,[144] and Traducians are to be equated with Manicheans.[145] Both
Traducians and Manicheans assert that evil contracted
from some ancient and unfortunate event is passed down by
reproduction through the ages. When Augustine argues
that all men are "in Adam" and thus receive his sin, he
must mean that the soul as well as the body is transmitted, for to be a "man" means to have both.[146] Doesn't
Augustine know that Traducianism was condemned both in

Tertullian's and in Mani's teachings?[147] Although the
Traducians (i.e., Augustine) find themselves "shut up in
the cave of the Manicheans," Julian, by expounding his
own theories, will turn the key so the captives may make
their escape from confinement![148]

Third, we learn from reading the *Opus imperfectum*
that Julian now developed a more explicit argument about
the immutability of "nature." Against Augustine's view
that all human nature was ever after changed by Adam's
sin,[149] Julian argues that "human nature" (including our
senses and concupiscence)[150] does not change since God
bestows our essential human constitution[151] and neither
sin nor grace has the power to change our essential
being.[152] The things Augustine believes were penalties
for the first sin--labor pains, sweat, work, the submis-
sion of women to man--are all part of the original order
of nature and thus are unchangeable.[153] If original sin
had truly become part of our nature, as Augustine holds,
it could not be eradicated.[154]

Julian's reflection on "nature" leads him to a fourth
accusation, that Augustine's views on Jesus' conception
and physical constitution have a Docetic or Apollinarian
(i.e., "Manichean") cast. Although Julian champions the
Virgin Birth,[155] he suspects that Augustine's praise of
the virginal conception stems mainly from his desire to
avoid a "damnable sexual connection," not (as Julian
thinks) to demonstrate God's power through a miracle.[156]
To say, as Augustine does, that Jesus had no *concupiscentia sensuum* is to say that he has different flesh than we
do, and this is "Manichean."[157] Since Jesus ate, slept,
sweated, worked, bled, and grew a beard, he must have had
the same bodily *concupiscentia* as we do. His willingness
to take all our bodily organs ("which Mani's impiety
refuses to give him") reveals the great love the Savior

felt for us.[158] Moreover, Julian draws the conclusion of
Augustine's position for ethics: what kind of model for
us can Jesus be if he did not have a real human nature?
Why praise his chastity if he had no "virility," if his
chastity stemmed only from "sexual weakness?" What
meaning have his forty-day fast and the Cross if he felt
no pain?[159]

Augustine defends his position by differentiating the
senses (which Jesus had) from concupiscence (which he did
not have).[160] He even allows that if Jesus had wanted to
beget children, he could have; after all, he was not a
eunuch, incapable of *seminandi filiorum*.[161] But Augustine rejects Julian's moral theory, because it implies
that virtue is measured by the degree of struggle. On
this theory, Christ would have had greater virtue if he
had had a greater *libido*.[162] We should rather exempt
Christ from that disruptive war between the flesh and the
spirit the rest of us suffer.[163] Christ had a holy body,
free from all offense because his conception did not
involve the *commixtio* of the sexes.[164] It is blasphemous
for Julian to put the divine flesh of Christ on a par
with our own, which suffers the discord between its
desires and the spirit.[165] And Augustine insists that
his own position is *not* Manichean.[166]

Last, and for our purposes most important, Julian
launches a sharper attack upon Augustine's view of seeds
and their connection with sin. Strictly speaking, Julian
probably accepted the same medical theory as Augustine
that deemed male seed largely responsible for the creation of a child.[167] (His claim that children are born *de
vi seminum* is meant to challenge Augustine's view that
sin is transmitted through the reproductive act,[168] not
to stand as a biological statement about the relative
contributions of male and female.) However, in his

treatise that elicited the *Opus imperfectum*, Julian
needles Augustine on a point at which he had hinted
earlier, but develops only here: Augustine, by connect-
ing original sin with the male seed, suggests that sin is
a peculiarly male problem.[169] Julian attacks Augustine's
argument from two directions: from the interpretation of
Romans 5:12 ("through one man sin entered the world")
and from a discussion of Virgin Birth theory.

Fortunately for Julian, Romans 5:12 was one of
Augustine's favorite texts which he had employed throughout the entire Pelagian controversy.[170] Julian argues
that since Paul asserts that sin came into the world
"through one man," he could not possibly mean "through
generation," for everyone knows that reproduction takes
two.[171] Julian intends his readers to conclude, on the
basis of Paul's words, that sin arose through *imitation*
of the first man, not by transmission.[172]

Nonsense! Augustine rejoins. If Paul had wished to
claim that sin arises by imitating bad examples, he would
have mentioned the woman, since she sinned first and gave
the example of sin to the man.[173] Paul is correct in
saying that sin entered through the male because it
enters through the *semen generationis* which is cast off
from the male and through which the woman conceives.[174]
Paul writes as he did because it is "not from the seed
which conceives and bears" (i.e., the woman's contribution to conception) "that generation takes its beginning,
but from the male seed (*a viro seminante*)."[175] Since the
man's *seminatio* precedes the woman's conceiving, Paul
speaks correctly. Everyone knows that women "conceive"
or "bear," but they don't "generate."[176] The Bible confirms the point, Augustine claims, for in it, a woman
doesn't *genuit*, only a man does.[177] There can be no
mistaking Augustine's meaning when he expresses himself

so plainly and so often: the offspring contracted the
original sin from Adam, the male who engendered; the
woman receives the already vitiated seed from him, conceives, and gives birth.[178]

Augustine's notion of the *tradux peccati* also relates
to his discussion of the Virgin Birth. It is because
Christ is not conceived *ex semine* of a man that he is
liber a nexu seminatricis concupiscentiae.[179] It was
because (*propterea*) Christ was not conceived *virili
semine* but by the Holy Spirit that he lacks carnal concupiscence and thus is able to release others from original
sin, not contract it himself by being "generated."[180]

Julian presses this point by asking Augustine to comment on John 14:30, that the Devil found no trace of sin
in Christ. If original sin is "natural," as Julian
thinks Augustine believes, why didn't the Devil find a
trace of it in Christ? Augustine replies (as we would
now expect) that Christ does not have "sinful flesh" because he alone was not born from the "commingling of the
sexes."[181]

Julian argues that if sin is natural to the human
condition, then Christ either was born culpable, or he
was not made a man[182]--and Augustine will be shown to
hold a Docetic (i.e., "Manichean") Christology. Julian,
of course, wishes us to deny the premise (that sin is
natural to the human condition), but his argument has the
effect of pushing Augustine even closer to stating that
the male gives original sin. Julian presses further:
if, as Augustine claims, sin is a condition of the flesh,
Christ should have contracted sin from his mother[183]
(recall here Augustine's theory of "affection"). Augustine admits in reply that Mary, by condition of her own
birth, would have been "submitted to the Devil" (i.e.,
under the sway of original sin) if the grace of

regeneration had not loosed that condition.[184] This is
as close as Augustine comes to espousing the later doctrine of the Immaculate Conception of Mary, a doctrine
necessary if Augustine and others want to avoid the
conclusion that Mary could have transmitted to Christ the
sin present in her from her own birth. Julian here
emerges as an important contributor to the development of
the argument regarding the Immaculate Conception.

Julian finds Augustine's views so anti-sexual, anti-
body, and anti-scientific, that he cannot resist
imagining what Augustine's notion of ideal reproduction
would be. He goes Augustine's image of the "happy
farmer"[185] one better: Augustine would have preferred
for the world to be so constituted that wombs and penises
would have been unnecessary. The woman's entire body
would have been fecund, like the earth; children would
have "sweated forth" from the pores and joints of her
body (like lice, Julian adds). The male would have
assisted her in her reproductive task, but not with his
genitals, which would have been replaced with ploughshares
and hoes. Thus he would plough her and "forest" the
unbridled fecundity of her body.[186] Poor woman, scraped
over by ploughs and hoes! Such sentiments are worthy of
Manicheans, Julian concludes, who blame God's works and
deny that God created our bodily parts to be so perfect
that we cannot imagine any better ones.[187]

Julian has forced Augustine to make plain the anti-
sexual and anti-scientific roots of his theology of sin.
Yet Augustine has conceded only one point: that in a
sinless Eden, there might have been *libido*, although one
controlled by the will, not the unruly and disobedient
libido we know today.[188] For the rest, Augustine repeats
the same arguments in the *Opus imperfectum* that he had
raised earlier in the controversy.[189] Despite the fact

that Augustine won the controversy in terms of the later
course of Catholic theology, it is not so clear that he
won the debate with Julian. Had Julian responded to the
Contra Julianum and the *Opus imperfectum*, we suspect he
would have faulted Augustine for becoming progressively
more "Manichean" as the controversy unfolded. Early on,
the accusation was simply that the theory of original
sin made marriage and the reproductive process seem evil;
as the debate proceeded, the charge became considerably
more precise.

   Julian came to the controversy well-armed with
Augustine's writings, especially with such anti-Pelagian
treatises as *On the Remission of Sins*,[190] *Against the Two
Letters of the Pelagians*,[191] *On the Grace of Christ*,[192]
and *On Nature and Grace*.[193] He also knew Augustine's
Confessions.[194] But what he knew of Augustine's anti-
Manichean writings remains less clear. Julian faults
Augustine for changing his theology between the period
after his conversion and the present,[195] an accusation
which suggests that he had read some of Augustine's early
anti-Manichean writings. Yet actual citations from the
anti-Manichean books are much harder to locate than one
would imagine on the basis of Albert Bruckner's claim
that Julian had studied both the anti-Manichean and the
anti-Pelagian works of Augustine.[196] I have found no
sure references to any anti-Manichean work of Augustine
except *On Two Souls*[197] in the citations from Julian.

   From whatever source, Augustine or the Manicheans
themselves, Julian knew at least the outlines of the
Manichean foundation myth.[198] He was familiar with some
of their ritual practices, such as the Elect's eating of
fruit to release the particles of God trapped therein.[199]
He tells us that years before on a visit to Carthage, he
had met Augustine's friend Honoratus, "a Manichean like

you," with whom he discussed the origin of the soul.[200]
Most important, Julian knew and cited from Mani's (or the
Manichean) *Epistle to Menoch*, a work unknown to Augustine,[201] and from Mani's *Epistle to Patricius*.[202] The
former in particular he put to good purpose, showing how
Mani's notion of the transmission of souls[203] and his
belief that *concupiscentia* is the strategem by which the
Devil snares humans[204] were similar to Augustine's teaching. He points out that Mani, like Augustine, frequently
cites Paul's words in Roman 7:19, "The good I want I do
not do, and I do the evil I do not want."[205] Both Mani
and Augustine subscribe to the view that the human race
degenerated from its original state.[206] Both think
concupiscence is the origin of evil.[207] If Mani's name
did not appear in the title of his *Epistle to Menoch*,
Julian concludes, people would think the work had been
written by Augustine![208]

Yet the one piece of Manichean lore which would have
been most useful to him in his quarrel with Augustine he
seems not to know: the myth of the seduction of the
archons. Although it was *against* this myth--and its
real-life consequences--that Augustine had constructed
his sexual and marital ethics, yet, I posit, it was this
myth that gave Augustine his first explanation of how
seeds became corrupted. Even if Julian did not know this
aspect of the Manichean myth, he knew that Augustine's
version of the *tradux peccati* through seed sounded "Manichean" to his ears. To Augustine's Manichean past we
thus must turn.

V

Augustine, by his own account, had been a Manichean
Auditor for nine years.[209] Struggling to answer questions about the presence of evil in the world, Augustine

turned to the Manichean myth of the ancient battle that
had resulted in God's defeat by Darkness and his entrap-
ment, as pieces of Light, in matter.[210] The human soul
was seen as part of God's nature,[211] the body as the
product of malevolent forces.[212] Two natures, good and
evil, thus warred within humankind.[213]

One consequence of the Manichean view of human nature
was that Christ could not be ascribed a fleshly body or
birth from a woman. Indeed, Augustine's Manichean
opponents consistently denied the reality of Christ's
birth.[214] According to the Manichean Faustus, Jesus
enjoined his disciples to teach others the commandments,
not that he was born.[215] When Jesus asked, "Who are my
mother and my brothers?" and then gestured to the crowd
before him, he meant to indicate that he had no fleshly
human relations.[216] The Manicheans also attacked the
genealogies in Matthew and Luke, pointing out their
discrepancies, as a way to discount Jesus' birth.[217]
According to Augustine, even the Manichean attack upon
the polygamy, sexual profligacy, lying, and other dubious
acts of the patriarchs was motivated by their desire to
discredit the Incarnation by slandering Christ's ances-
tors.[218] Since the Manicheans did not believe that
Christ was born, they of course rejected theories about
the virginity of Mary before, during, and after Jesus'
birth that were gaining acceptance in the late fourth
century.[219]

Specifically, the Manicheans complained that "con-
fining" Christ to a womb limited God's nature[220] and
subjected him to "defilement."[221] Those who wish to
avoid their own future reincarnations, asserted the Manichean Secundinus, should not shut Christ up in a womb![222]
The *Manichean Psalm-Book* provides further examples of
this aspect of Manichean teaching:

...He (Jesus) was not born in a womb corrupted:
not even the mighty were counted worthy of him
    for him to dwell beneath their roof,
that he should be confined in a womb of a woman
    of low degree(?)[223]
Many the marvels of thy begetting, the wonders
    of thy cross....
When I say 'thy begetting,' yet who created
    thee?...
They came to the son of God, they cast him
    into a filthy womb....
(I) hear that thou didst say: "I am the Light
    of the world."...
(Then) who gave light to the world these
    nine months?
When I say "The son was begotten(?)," I
    shall find the Father also at his side.
Shall I lay waste a kingdom that I may fur-
nish a woman's womb?
Thy holy womb is the Luminaries that con-
    ceive thee.
The trees and the fruits--in them is thy
    holy body.[224]

Over against these Manichean views, the young Augustine
confessed his belief in the genuine humanity of Jesus.
Far from the "feigned flesh" that the Manicheans attribute to Christ,[225] Augustine in his anti-Manichean
writings upholds the reality of Jesus' flesh, both pre-
and post-resurrection,[226] and attacks the Apollinarian
denial of a human mind to Christ.[227] Christ was so much
part of the human race, Augustine asserts in these early
writings, that he even took mortality from his mother.[228]
Against the Manichean belief that a human birth would
have "confined" Jesus to the womb, Augustine constantly

affirms that God is everywhere and cannot be subjected to
"confinement."[229] He did not abandon the government of
the earth and the heavens, or leave the presence of his
Father, when he became man.[230]

Nor is Christ "contaminated" by his sojourn in a
woman's womb.[231] Augustine mocks his Manichean opponents:
certainly the womb of the Virgin Mary was purer than the
manured ground that grows the fruit in which Manicheans
think Jesus was trapped![232] Mary's virginity before,
during, and after Jesus' birth are guarantees for Augustine that her vessel remained "undefiled."[233] Her womb
is like a marriage chamber in which the humanity and the
divinity became "one flesh," and from which Christ
emerged, like "a bridegroom leaving his chamber."[234]
Augustine scoffs at Manicheans who disdain to think of
Christ in Mary's womb, yet (according to their myth) subject God to imprisonment in the wombs not just of
ordinary women, but even of beasts.[235] Manicheans would
undoubtedly have preferred Mary to engage in sexual
intercourse without reproduction than in motherhood without sexual intercourse, given their perverted ethical
views.[236]

Augustine in his anti-Manichean writings cites Romans
8:3 ("the likeness of sinful flesh") to argue the *reality*
of Christ's body against the Manicheans,[237] an ironic
note, given Julian's claim that Augustine's constant
appeal to this verse only reveals the Docetic, i.e.,
"Manichean," tendency of his Christology.[238] For Julian,
a Christ without *concupiscentia*, or ignorance as an
infant, or struggle against temptation, is not a genuinely human Christ but a "Manichean" one.[239] Yet Augustine
had earlier staunchly defended the real flesh and real
birth of Jesus against Manichean detractors.

A second consequence of the Manichean myth was the
prohibition against reproduction, which further entrapped
particles of God's substance in fleshly darkness. Sexual
activity was allowed to Manichean Auditors with the
stipulation that they circumvent conception. That Augustine learned Manichean contraceptive techniques (a
primitive form of the "rhythm" method[240] and perhaps
coitus interruptus[241]) is suggested not just by his
explicit testimony,[242] but also by his failure to produce
any children during his long period as a Manichean--a
period in which he engaged in regular sexual activity.[243]

As a Catholic convert, Augustine became sharply
critical of Manichean sexual practice and theory. He
thought the Manichean boast of continence was false.[244]
Reporting on the dubious sexual morality of Manicheans,
he insinuates that they eat human seed, as well as fruits
and vegetables, to free the divine light within.[245]
While they frown on motherhood, they boast that prostitutes "spare God";[246] probably they would have preferred
the prophet Hosea's woman to have remained a prostitute
than to have become an honorable wife and mother![247]

Against Manichean theory, Augustine developed a pro-
reproductive and anti-contraceptive marital ethic that
became the hallmark of Catholic sexual teaching until our
own century.[248] For Augustine the Catholic, *only* the
desire to produce children rescues sexual intercourse for
God's good plan. Thus "offspring" stand in first place
among the threefold goods of marriage in his earlier
writings.[249] He defends the polygamy and sexual activities of the patriarchs from Manichean attacks: our
Hebrew forefathers, he claims, wished only to raise up
children for God, a fitting goal for the period in which
they lived, even if not so glorious now that Christian
virginity is an option.[250] The use of contraceptive

measures is thus tantamount to "adultery" for Augustine, since it strikes against a central purpose of marriage,[251] which Manicheans who use the woman's sterile period for sexual intercourse attempt to thwart.[252] Moreover, it is in Augustine's anti-Manichean polemic that he develops his infamous interpretation of the sin of Onan in Genesis 38: God punished him (and should punish others who imitate him) for practicing *coitus interruptus*.[253]

Most important for our purposes, Augustine understands the function of the Manichean foundation myth to be a justification and court of appeal for Manichean sexual practices. When Manicheans teach that Adam was produced from the abortive princes of darkness and that through the "stirring up" of the evil part of his soul he was led away into sexual intercourse, they merely seek to excuse their own indulgence in sexual acts not motivated by the desire for reproduction.[254]

Moreover, Augustine precisely pinpoints the myth of the archons as the sanction for Manichean sexual perversity. Making fun of the Manichean belief that the sun is a ship which sails through the heavens, Augustine continues:

> This really is tolerable, however it may make us
> laugh or weep. But what is intolerable is your
> wicked notion about beautiful young women and
> men coming forth from the ship, whose great
> beauty of form inflames the rulers of darkness,
> the males for the women and the females for the
> men, so that the members of your god are re-
> leased from this loathsome and nasty shackling
> in their members by means of burning lust and
> eager concupiscence.[255]

The myth to which Augustine here alludes is mentioned at least seven times in his writings--six times in his anti-Manichean works and once in *De haeresibus*.[256] Brief references or allusions to the story are made in other places as well.[257] The fullest version of the myth is found in *De natura boni* 44. Augustine there speaks of the Manichean belief that God's nature has gotten mixed into all bodies and seeds, and is fettered to them.

> For they say that the powers of light are
> transformed into beautiful males and are set
> opposite the females of the race of darkness,
> and that the same powers of light are again
> transformed into beautiful females and are
> set opposite the males of the race of dark-
> ness. And they say that through their beauty
> they might inflame the filthiest *libido* in
> the princes of darkness. In this way, vital
> substance (*vitalis substantia*), i.e., the
> nature of God which they say is bound in their
> bodies, is loosed from their members relaxed
> through concupiscence; it flies away and it
> is freed after it has been taken up and
> purged.

Augustine continues, citing from Book 7 of Mani's *Thesaurus*:

> ...by this handsome sight of theirs, ardor
> and *concupiscentia* increase. Thus the chain
> of their very worst thoughts is loosened and
> the living soul which was held by their mem-
> bers is relaxed by this occasion, escapes,
> and is mixed with its own most pure air.
> When the souls are cleansed through and
> through, they ascend to the shining ships
> which have been readied for their sailing
> and for transporting them to their own
> country. But indeed, that which still

bears the stains of the adverse race descends
bit by bit through heat and fires, and is
mixed with trees and other plants and with
all seeds, and is tinged with diverse colors.
The figures of the beautiful males and females also appear
to the "fiery" and the "cold and moist" heavenly powers,
who likewise release their "life."[258]

When Faustus, Augustine's Manichean opponent, complains about the patriarchs' sexual practices, Augustine
rejoins: could *anything* the patriarchs did be as bad as
the Manichean teaching which affirms that God's substance,
confined in our bodies, is there subjected to the violent
motion of sexual acts and is released in ejaculation--
that very God who gave up his members to the *libido* of
the male and female powers of the race of darkness?[259]

Augustine repeats the story in his *Contra Felicem,*[260]
and the anathema that the defeated Felix signs is concerned almost exclusively with this aspect of the Manichean myth:

I, Felix, used to believe in Mani, but now I
anathematize him, his doctrine, and the
seducing spirit that was in him. He said that
God had mixed a portion of himself with the
race of darkness, and that to free it in so
immoral a way, he transformed his virtues
into women over against the men, and again
into men over against the female demons, so
that afterward he fixed in a globe of darkness the rest of these parts of himself.
All these things and other blasphemies of
Mani, I anathematize.[261]

Augustine gives the following additions to the Manichean myth in the *Contra Faustum*:

...in that battle, when their Primal Man en-
snared the race of darkness by deceitful
substances, princes of both sexes of that
source were captured and from them the world
was constructed. And among those used in the
formation of the heavens were some pregnant
females. When the sky began to revolve, they
were not able to stand the rotation, and
these females cast off aborted fetuses, both
male and female, which fell from the heavens
to the earth. Here they lived, and grew;
they had sexual relations and produced offspring. This they say was the origin of
all flesh which is in the earth, the water,
and the air.[262]

It is striking that Augustine, who mocks the myth
frequently in his anti-Manichean writings, never once
elaborates it in his lengthy books against Julian, despite Julian's constant charge that Augustine is still a
Manichean, and Augustine's just-as-constant denial of the
charge. Both he and Julian frequently mention the Manichean myth of the mixing of God's nature with evil,
Julian complaining that the theory of original sin
"mixed" evil with the nature of the good and hence is
Manichean.[263] Since Julian had pinpointed with some
specificity the biological problem in Augustine's theory--
the vitiated seeds--he could have put the Manichean myth
of the archons' seduction to good use had he known it:
he could have claimed that it provided the precise Manichean background of and correlate to Augustine's theory.
I suggest that Augustine neither could nor wished to
answer Julian's question of how sin came to be mixed with
seeds. Having decisively rejected his Manichean past,
why should he bring to Julian's attention that other

foundation myth to which, forty years earlier, he had
subscribed?[264] It was enough to have built a Catholic
sexual ethic that condemned lust without reproductive
intent, an ethic that countered by inversion the very
meaning of the Manichean myth. His Manichean past haunted
him enough in Julian's charges without adding fuel to
his opponent's fire.

VI

Social historians have recently suggested that
periodization in history would look far different if it
were based on changes that have primarily affected *women*
rather than men. Thus Joan Kelly writes:

What feminist historiography has done is to
unsettle such accepted evaluations of historical periods. It has disabused us of the
notion that the history of women is the same
as the history of men, and that significant
turning points in history have the same impact for one sex as for the other. Indeed,
some historians now go so far as to maintain
that, because of women's particular connection with the function of reproduction,
history could, and should, be rewritten
and periodized from this point of view,
according to major changes affecting child-
birth, sexuality, family structure, and so
forth.[265]

If we accept the challenge here presented (although Kelly
herself expresses reservations on the project this nar-
rowly construed),[266] we could assert that the half-
century from 380 to 430 A.D. was of world-historical
importance not only because of the battle of the Frigidus
or the sack of Rome, but also because in those years were

firmed up the doctrines that for twelve centuries and
more would ensure an ambiguous theological evaluation of
reproduction, the "career" followed by the vast majority
of women. Peter Brown has recently observed that Augustine, in contrast to his predecessors who championed an
"ascetic paradigm,"[267] was more accepting of our bodily
nature--but to Julian, and to many of our contemporaries,
there were remnants in Augustine's work that still
breathed his Manichean past.[268]

NOTES

[1]*Confessiones* III, 10(6); VII, 8-10(6) (CCL 27, 31-32, 97-99); *Contra epistolam Manichaei quam vocant fundamenti* 5; 12; 14; 18 (CSEL 25, 197, 208, 210-212, 215).

[2]Ibid.; also see his confession in *De animae et ejus origine* IV, 6(5) (CSEL 60, 386), that he was ignorant about many topics pertaining to the human body. Augustine suffered profound disappointment that the Manicheans could not deliver the "truth" they constantly promised.

[3]For the fading of Augustine's early optimism, see Peter Brown, *Augustine of Hippo: A Biography* (Berkeley; Los Angeles: University of California Press, 1967) ch. 15.

[4]See especially Augustine's expressions of wonder at miracles in *De civitate Dei* XXII, 8 (CCL 48, 815-827).

[5]Like many of his era, Augustine had early been interested in astrology, and had hoped the Manicheans would furnish answers to his questions. See especially *Confessiones* IV, 4-5(3); V, 3-6(3) (CCL 27, 41-42, 58-60) and Brown, *Augustine*, pp. 56-58 for discussion. Later in the *Confessions*, Augustine chastizes those who praise the wonders of nature but do not look within themselves (X, 15[8] [CCL 27, 162-163]) and the "futile curiosity," masked as scientific interest, which stems from slavery to the senses (X, 54[35] [CCL 27, 184]).

[6]*Confessiones* IX, 73(13); *De animae et ejus origine* I, 25(15); IV, 5(4); 6(5) (CSEL 60, 323-325, 384-385, 386); and *Epp.* 143, 5-11; 164, 7, 19; 166 (a short treatise on the origin of the soul); 180, 2 (CSEL 44, 255-261, 538, 545-585, 698). The soul's origin will become a topic for dispute in the quarrel between Julian and Augustine; see below, pp. 308-309.

[7]Earlier, around 400 A.D., the Donatist leader Petilian had charged Augustine with his Manichean past. Petilian's allegations, however, do not appear to center

on Augustine's theology. See Augustine, *Contra litteras Petiliani* III, 11(10); 19(16); 20(17) (CSEL 52, 172, 177-178). See William Frend, "Manicheanism in the Struggle Between Saint Augustine and Petilian of Constantine," *Augustinus Magister. Congrès International Augustinien, Paris, 21-24 Septembre, 1954* (Paris: Etudes Augustinien-nes, 1954) II, 859-865, esp. 864-865. See also Frend's brief overview of Manicheanism in North Africa: "The Gnostic-Manichean Tradition in Roman North Africa," *Journal of Ecclesiastical History* 4 (1953) 13-26; and the two magisterial volumes by François Decret, *Aspects du Manichéisme dans l'Afrique Romaine. Les controverses de Fortunatus, Faustus et Felix avec Saint Augustin* (Paris: Etudes Augustiniennes, 1970) and *L'Afrique Manichéene (IVᵉ-Vᵉ siècles). Etudes historique et doctrinale* (Paris: Etudes Augustiniennes, 1978).

[8]*Contra duas epistolas Pelagianorum* I, 4(2); 10(5) (CSEL 60, 425, 431); *De nuptiis et concupiscentia* II, 15(5); 34(9); 38(23); 49(29); 50(29) (CSEL 42, 266-268, 288, 291-292, 304, 305); *Contra secundum Juliani respon-sionem opus imperfectum* I, 24; 115 (CSEL 85[1], 21, 132-133); and many other places.

[9]*De peccatorum meritis et remissione* I, 57(29) (CSEL 60, 56).

[10]*De peccatorum meritis* II, 4(4) (CSEL 60, 73).

[11]*De peccatorum meritis* III, 2(2) (CSEL 60, 130).

[12]*De peccatorum meritis* III, 13(7) (CSEL 60, 140).

[13]*De peccatorum meritis* I, 57(29) (CSEL 60, 56).

[14]*De peccatorum meritis* I, 57(29); II, 38(24) (CSEL 60, 57, 110).

[15]*De peccatorum meritis* II, 38(24); 48(29) (CSEL 60, 110, 118), citing Romans 8:3.

[16]*De peccatorum meritis* II, 48(29) (CSEL 60, 119).

[17]*De peccatorum meritis* II, 39(25) (CSEL 60, 111): If Hebrews 7:9-10 testifies that Levi paid tithes in the loins of Abraham, the Pelagians ask why should we not think that regeneration is received by those still in the loins of baptized and regenerated fathers?

[18]*De peccatorum meritis* II, 53(33) (CSEL 60, 123).

[19]*De peccatorum meritis* II, 59(36) (CSEL 60, 127-128).
Augustine responds with the answer to which he will forever adhere: we don't know, since Scripture gives no
"certain and clear proofs." Augustine even rallies
Pelagius' support for his caution: III, 18(10) (CSEL 60,
144). On this point, it is useful to recall that Augustine was well aware of the theological difficulties
positions about the soul might entail: see *Ep.* 73, 6(3)
(CSEL 34, 270-271) for his acknowledgment of reading
Jerome's *Contra Rufinum*, a central document of the
Origenist debate. Also see Augustine's *Epp.* 143, 6-11;
164, 19-20(7); 166; 180, 2 (CSEL 44, 255-261, 538-539,
545-585, 698) for further reflections on the origin of
the soul.

[20]Nothing new, for example, is contained in *De natura
et gratia* (dated to 415); *De perfectione iustitiae
hominis* (dated to 415); *De gestis Pelagii* (dated to
early 417) on the "biology" of original sin.

[21]*De civitate Dei* XIV, 10; 15-16 (CCL 48, 430-431,
437-439).

[22]An advance over his earlier position, when he was
dubious on the point. Now he affirms that "reproduce and
multiply" meant genuinely sexual relations, not an allegory about spiritual qualities "multiplying" (*De civitate
Dei* XIV, 22 [CCL 48, 444]). For the development of
Augustine's position, see Michael Müller, *Die Lehre des
hl. Augustinus von der Paradiesesehe und ihre Auswirkung
in der Sexualethik des 12. und 13. Jahrhunderts bis
Thomas von Aquin* (Regensburg: Verlag Friedrich Pustet,
1954) 19-26.

[23]*De civitate Dei* XIV, 23; 26 (CCL 48, 444-446, 449-450).

[24]*De civitate Dei* XIV, 23; 24 (CCL 48, 444-448).

[25]*De civitate Dei* XIV, 18-20 (CCL 48, 440-443).
Augustine in ch. 20 (unlike elsewhere) denies that
Diogenes the Cynic could have had sexual intercourse in
public: the act would not have been pleasurable.

[26]*De civitate Dei* XIV, 23 (CCL 48, 446), citing
Georgics III, 136--although Virgil's horses are far
lustier than Augustine's ideal first couple.

[27]*Ep.* 184A, 3(1) (CSEL 44, 733-734).

[28]*Ep.* 184A, 3(1) (CSEL 44, 734).

[29]*Ep.* 194, 44(10) (CSEL 57, 211); *De gratia Christi et de peccato originali* II, 45(40) (CSEL 42, 202).

[30]*De gratia Christi* I, 1(1) (CSEL 42, 125). The association of the family with Pelagianism has been explored by Peter Brown, "The Patrons of Pelagius: The Roman Aristocracy Between East and West," *Journal of Theological Studies*, n.s. 21 (1970) 56-72 (=*Religion and Society in the Age of Saint Augustine* [New York: Harper & Row, 1972] 208-226), and by Elizabeth A. Clark, *The Life of Melania the Younger: Introduction, Translation and Commentary* (Studies in Women and Religion 14; New York; Toronto: Edwin Mellen Press, 1984), 143-144.

[31]*De gratia Christi* II, 46(40) (CSEL 42, 204): but only humans, not animals, suffer the "fatal flaw" transmitted through those seeds, for animals do not possess reason and thus cannot partake of either the misery or the blessedness appropriate to humans.

[32]*De gratia Christi* II, 47(41) (CSEL 42, 205-206), citing Ambrose's *Expositio evangelii secundam Lucam* II, 56; *Ep.* 184A, 3(1) (CSEL 44, 733).

[33]*Contra duas epistolas Pelagianorum* I, 3(1); 4(2) (CSEL 60, 424-425). On the history of the quarrel between Julian and Augustine, see Albert Bruckner, *Julian von Eclanum. Sein Leben und Seine Lehre. Ein Beitrag zur Geschichte des Pelagianismus* (TU 15, 3; Leipzig: J.C. Hinrichs, 1897); Yves de Montcheuil, "La Polémique de Saint Augustin contre Julien d'Eclane d'après l'*Opus Imperfectum*," *Recherches de Science Religieuse* 44 (1956) 193-218; François Refoulé, "Julien d'Eclane, Théologien et Philosophe," *Recherches de Science Religieuse* 52 (1964) 42-84, 233-247; shorter summaries in Michel Meslin, "Sainteté et mariage au cours de la seconde querelle pélagienne," *Mystique et Continence. Travaux scientifiques du VIIe Congrès International d'Avon* (Les Etudes Carmélitaines; Paris: Desclée de Brouwer, 1952) 294-295; Brown, *Augustine*, ch. 32; Emile Schmitt, *Le Mariage chrétien dans l'oeuvre de Saint Augustin. Une théologie baptismale de la vie conjugale* (Paris: Etudes Augustiniennes, 1983) 56-61.

[34]*De nuptiis et concupiscentia* I, 1(1) (CSEL 42, 211).

[35]*De nuptiis* I, 2(2) (CSEL 42, 212-213).

[36]*De nuptiis* I, 23(21) (CSEL 42, 236).

[37]*De nuptiis* I, 6(5); 7(6) (CSEL 42, 216-219).

[38]*De nuptiis* I, 24(22); 6(5); 8(7) (CSEL 42, 237, 216-217, 219-220).

[39]*De nuptiis* I, 5(4); 9(8); 11(10); 13(11); 17(15); 19(17); 23(21) (CSEL 42, 215-216, 220-221, 222-223, 225, 229-230, 231-232, 236).

[40]*De nuptiis* I, 12(11); 13(11); 1(1) (CSEL 42, 224-225, 211).

[41]*De nuptiis* I, 9(8); 10(9) (CSEL 42, 221-222).

[42]*De nuptiis* I, 21(19); 37(32); 38(33) (CSEL 42, 234, 248-249).

[43]*De nuptiis* I, 38(33) (CSEL 42, 249).

[44]*De nuptiis* II, 1(1); 2(2) (CSEL 42, 253, 254); *Opus imperfectum*, praefatio (CSEL 85[1], 3); *Retractiones* II, 53, 1 (CCL 57, 131). Also see Albert Bruckner, *Die Vier Bücher Julians von Aeclanum an Turbantius. Ein Beitrag zur Charakteristik Julians und Augustins* (Neue Studien zur Geschichte der Theologie unde der Kirche 8; Berlin: Trowitzsch & Sohn, 1910), for a discussion of the treatise that prompted *De nuptiis* II, with a reconstruction of the fragments contained in Augustine's work.

[45]*Contra duas epistolas Pelagianorum* I, 3(1); 4(2); 9(5)-10(5); II, 1(1) (CSEL 60, 424-425, 429-431, 460-461).

[46]*Contra Julianum* I, 1(1)-3(1) (PL 44, 641-643); *Retractiones* II, 62, 1 (CCL 57, 139).

[47]*Opus imperfectum*, praefatio (CSEL 85[1], 3-4).

[48]*Contra duas epistolas Pelagianorum* I, 10(5); 31(15); 34(17); 35(17) (CSEL 60, 431, 448, 450-451, 451-452); *Opus imperfectum* II, 122 (CSEL 85[1], 253); also the new *Ep.* 6*, 5; 7 to Atticus (CSEL 88, 34-35, 35-36) on the difference between *concupiscentia nuptiarum*, which *would* have been present in Paradise even if Adam and Eve had not sinned, and *concupiscentia carnis*, which would not.

[49]See, for example, the rather loose accusations of Augustine's "Manicheanism" in Alfred Adam, "Der manichäische Ursprung der Lehre von den zwei Reichen bei Augustin," *Theologische Literaturzeitung* 77 (1952);

385-390, and idem., "Das Fortwirken des Manichäismus bei Augustin," *Zeitschrift für Kirchengeschichte* 69 (1958) 1-25. He is rightly criticized by W. Geerlings, "Zur Frage des Nachwirkens des Manichäismus in der Theologie Augustins," *Zeitschrift für Katholische Theologie* 93 (1971) 45-60.

[50]*De nuptiis* II, 15(5) (CSEL 42, 266-267).

[51]*De nuptiis* II, 50(29); 31(16); 36(21) (CSEL 42, 305, 284-285, 290-291).

[52]The case of babies is raised in *De nuptiis* II, 4(2); 24(11); 49(29); 56(33); 60(35) (CSEL 42, 256, 276, 304-305, 313-314, 318-319); more explicitly argued in *Contra Julianum* III, 11(5); V, 43(10) (PL 44, 708, 808-809); *Opus imperfectum* II, 28; 236, 2 (CSEL 85[1], 181-183, 349).

[53]See Julian's appeal to Ambrose in *Opus imperfectum* IV, 121 (PL 45, 1415-1416), since Augustine had effectively co-opted Ambrose for his side of the debate. Julian got bored with Augustine's constant citations of Ambrose: *Opus imperfectum* IV, 109 (PL 45, 1404).

[54]*De nuptiis* II, 13(4) (CSEL 42, 264-265).

[55]*De nuptiis* II, 14(5) (CSEL 42, 265).

[56]*De civitate Dei* XIV, 15 (CCL 48, 438). For discussion of the meaning of "concupiscence" for Augustine, and differences between his view and that of Julian, see Meslin, "Sainteté," 298-299, 300-301, 303; Refoulé, "Julien," 70-71; Schmitt, *Le Mariage*, 95-105; G.I. Bonner, "*Libido* and *Concupiscentia* in St. Augustine" (Studia Patristica 6 [TU 81]; Berlin: Akademie-Verlag, 1962), 303-314; François-Joseph Thonnard, "La Notion de concupiscence en philosophie augustinienne," *Recherches Augustiniennes* 3 (1965) 59-105, esp. 80-95; Athanase Sage, "Le Péché originel dans la pensée de saint Augustin, de 412 à 430," *Revue des Etudes Augustiniennes* 15 (1969) 75-112, esp. 91-97; Emanuele Samek Lodovici, "Sessualità, matrimonio e concupiscenza in sant' Agostino," in *Etica sessuale e matrimonio nel cristianesimo delle origini*, ed. Raniero Cantalamessa (Studia Patristica Mediolanensia 5; Milan: Università Cattolica del Sacro Cuore, 1976), esp. 251-262.

[57]*De nuptiis* II, 23(10) (CSEL 42, 275).

[58]Made clear already in *De civitate Dei* XIV, 16 (CCL 48, 438-439).

[59]*De nuptiis* II, 17(7) (CSEL 42, 269).

[60]*De nuptiis* II, 59(35) (CSEL 42, 317).

[61]*De nuptiis* II, 17(7) (CSEL 42, 269-270).

[62]*De nuptiis* II, 19(8) (CSEL 42, 271). Augustine's response: the author means only that God gave him a son.

[63]*De nuptiis* II, 26(13); 41(26) (CSEL 42, 279, 294).

[64]*De nuptiis* II, 27(13) (CSEL 42, 279). Augustine rejoins, Paul is talking of seeds of corn, not human seeds.

[65]*De nuptiis* II, 25(12) (CSEL 42, 277).

[66]*De nuptiis* II, 40(25) (CSEL 42, 293-294).

[67]*De nuptiis* II, 35(20) (CSEL 42, 289). Augustine rejoins, Paul means only to contrast the "natural use" with the "unnatural," not to give special praise to sexual relations. Later Augustine adds that on Julian's premises, he would have no way to criticize the emission of seed for other than reproductive purposes: II, 59(35) (CSEL 42, 317-318).

[68]*De nuptiis* II, 30(15) (CSEL 42, 283-284).

[69]See below, p. 311.

[70]*De nuptiis* I, 21(19); 37(32); 38(33) (CSEL 42, 234, 248-249).

[71]*De nuptiis* II, 29(14) (CSEL 42, 283).

[72]*Contra Julianum* III, 33(17) (PL 44, 719).

[73]*Contra Julianum* IV, 12(2) (PL 44, 742).

[74]*Contra Julianum* V, 34(8) (PL 44, 804).

[75]*Contra Julianum* VI, 59(19) (PL 44, 858).

[76]*Contra Julianum* III, 51(22) (PL 44, 728); cf. Matt. 13:24-30.

[77]*Contra Julianum* III, 51(22) (PL 44, 728).

[78]*Contra Julianum* III, 59(26) (PL 44, 732), citing *De nuptiis* I, 1(1).

[79]*Contra Julianum* VI, 5(2); cf. 26(9) (PL 44, 823-824, 837-838).

[80]*Contra Julianum* VI, 14(5) (PL 44, 831).

[81]E.g., God's closing the wombs of the women of Abimelech's house is interpreted as the removal of lust from the women (*Contra Julianum* III, 37[19] [PL 44, 721-722]) (Augustine here takes the story as an illustration of how "contagion" can pass); that the "power of the seeds" produces children from adultery as well as from marriage (*Contra Julianum* III, 53[23] [PL 44, 729-730]); that "reproductive heat" is good in its own way (*Contra Julianum* IV, 7[2] [PL 44, 739]); that "natural concupiscence" is a good (*Contra Julianum* IV, 52[8] [PL 44, 764]).

[82]*Contra Julianum* V, 51(14); VI, 55(18)-56(18) (PL 44, 812, 855-856).

[83]See Bruckner, *Julian*, 90-99; Refoulé, "Julien," 233-247; François-Joseph Thonnard, "L'Aristotélisme de Julien d'Eclane et saint Augustin," *Revue des Etudes Augustiniennes* 11 (1965) 295-304.

[84]On the "heat" of the soul in Stoic philosophy, see Eduard Zeller, *Die Philosophie der Griechen in Ihrer Geschichtlichen Entwicklung*, 3rd ed. (Leipzig: Fues's Verlag, 1880), III[1], 194-197, with references to the primary sources.

[85]*Contra Julianum* III, 26(13) (PL 44, 715).

[86]Ibid.

[87]*Contra Julianum* III, 27(13); V, 27(7) (PL 44, 716, 801).

[88]*Contra Julianum* IV, 65(14) (PL 44, 769-770).

[89]*Contra Julianum* V, 51(14) (PL 44, 812).

[90]*Contra Julianum* V, 51(14) (PL 44, 813). Besides, says Julian, even if infants contract evil, a merciful God would cleanse them of it (V, 53[15] [PL 44, 813]). Cf. Aristotle, *Categories* 2, 1a 23-29. I thank Michael Ferejohn for assistance with this reference.

[91]*Contra Julianum* VI, 16(6) (PL 44, 831-832).

[92]*Contra Julianum* VI, 18(7) (PL 44, 833).

[93]*Contra Julianum* VI, 15(6) (PL 44, 831).

[94]*Contra Julianum* I, 38(8) (PL 44, 667).

[95]*Contra Julianum* VI, 43(14) (PL 44, 846).

[96]*Contra Julianum* VI, 24(9) (PL 44, 837): "Qui fieri potest ut res arbitrii conditioni seminum misceatur?"

[97]*Contra Julianum* III, 28(14) (PL 44, 716). Cf. Paulinus of Nola's epithalamium on the occasion of Julian's marriage: the chastity of the couple is praised; Paulinus even hopes they will not consummate their marriage (*Carmen* 25, 233-234 [CSEL 30, 245]).

[98]*Contra Julianum* III, 40(20) (PL 44, 722).

[99]*Contra Julianum* IV, 12(2) (PL 44, 742).

[100]*Contra Julianum* V, 51(14) (PL 44, 812).

[101]Ibid. In *Retractiones* II, 62, 2 (CSEL 57, 139) Augustine reports that he mistakenly wrote that Soranus had given the king's name (Dionysius); he hadn't, and Augustine must have gotten the name from elsewhere. Augustine's reference is important because it shows he knew something of Soranus' works, which were in Latin translation by the later fourth century. See note 167 below.

[102]*Contra Julianum* VI, 16(6) (PL 44, 832).

[103]*Contra Julianum* VI, 18(7); 20(7) (PL 44, 833, 834).

[104]Julian, of course, believes in sin "by imitation." See his interpretation of Romans 5:12, given below, p. 311.

[105]*Contra Julianum* V, 51(14) (PL 44, 813).

[106]*Contra Julianum* VI, 55(18) (PL 44, 855).

[107]*Contra Julianum* VI, 43(14) (PL 44, 846-847).

[108]See below, pp. 316-318, for discussion of this point.

[109]*Contra Julianum* VI, 43(14) (PL 44, 847).

[110] *Contra Julianum* VI, 24(9)   (PL 44, 837).

[111] *Contra Julianum* V, 43(10)   (PL 44, 808-809).

[112] *Contra Julianum* VI, 9, 24   (PL 44, 836-837); also see *Contra duas epistolas Pelagianorum* I, 11(6); IV, 5(4); 9(5) (CSEL 60, 431-432, 525, 530); *Opus imperfectum* I, 32; II, 236, 2 (CSEL 85^1, 24-25, 349).

[113] *De bono conjugali* 3(3); 4(4); (CSEL 41, 190-193).

[114] *De sancta virginitate* 2(2); 3(3); 4(4); 27(27) (CSEL 41, 236-238, 264).

[115] *De nuptiis* I, 11(10); 23(21) (CSEL 42, 222-223, 236).

[116] *De nuptiis* I, 12(11); 13(11-12) (CSEL 42, 224-226).

[117] *De nuptiis* I, 19(17)   (CSEL 42, 231).

[118] *De nuptiis* I, 13(12)   (CSEL 42, 226).

[119] *De nuptiis* II, 15(5)   (CSEL 42, 267).

[120] *De nuptiis* II, 15(5)   (CSEL 42, 268).

[121] *De nuptiis* II, 37(22) (CSEL 42, 291).

[122] *De nuptiis* II, 19(8)   (CSEL 42, 271).

[123] *Contra Julianum* V, 62(16)   (PL 44, 818). Augustine fears that this definition would allow adultery and other sexual relationships to count as marriage.

[124] *Contra Julianum* V, 46(12)   (PL 44, 810). Scripture calls Joseph Mary's husband because it follows the common view (V, 47[12]   [PL 44, 810-811]).

[125] *Contra Julianum* V, 48(12)   (PL 44, 811). Augustine denies the charge.

[126] *Contra Julianum* II, 8(4)   (PL 44, 678-679); Ambrose is cited as being in agreement (II, 10[5] and 15[6] [PL 44, 681, 684]).

[127] *Contra Julianum* V, 54(15)   (PL 44, 814).

[128] See above, p. 301.

^{129}*Contra Julianum* V, 52(15)   (PL 44, 813):   Paul in Romans 8:3 does not mean to imply that bodies are sinful.

^{130}*Contra Julianum* V, 55(15)   (PL 44, 814).

^{131}*Contra Julianum* V, 52(15)   (PL 44, 814-815).

^{132}*Contra Julianum* IV, 81(16)   (PL 44, 780). Augustine responds, was it sin that made us so clever? Julian also apparently argued that the parts Adam and Eve covered were their "sides," not their genital organs. Augustine faults both Julian's Greek and his shamelessness: is he raising the *perizoma* up to their shoulders and leaving the turbulent members in full view? *Contra Julianum* V, 7 (2) (PL 44, 785-786).

^{133}See especially *De civitate Dei* XIV, 17 (CCL 48, 439-440).

^{134}*Opus imperfectum* IV, 43   (PL 45, 1362). Augustine replies (1362-1363) that animals don't suffer concupiscence as humans do and hence have no shame about their sexual acts.

^{135}Aristotle, *Nicomachean Ethics* II, 2, 4; 6, 11; 6, 18; 9, 2; 9, 7.

^{136}*Opus imperfectum* IV, 44   (PL 44, 1363-1364). Augustine responds (1364-1365) that we should look to the "parents of all nations," Adam and Eve, not just to a particular group like the Scots. The first couple were not originally corrupted with evil doctrine, as were the Cynics, nor did they have to work (as Peter did; his nudity is excused).

^{137}*Opus imperfectum* VI, 26   (PL 45, 1562). Augustine responds (1563) we do not know what animals feel when they give birth. Do their sounds portend joyous song or grief? Perhaps they feel pleasure, not pain? Cf. *De Genesi contra Manichaeos* II, 29(19)   (PL 34, 210).

^{138}*Opus imperfectum* VI, 29   (PL 45, 1577). Augustine responds (1578), so what if the pain varies; *all* women still suffer; hence all are affected by original sin.

^{139}See note 6 above.

^{140}*Contra Julianum* V, 17(4)   (PL 44, 794).

^{141}*Contra Julianum* V, 53(15)   (PL 44, 814), citing II Maccabees 7:22. Neither is Augustine ashamed of his ignorance: *Opus imperfectum* II, 178, 3   (CSEL 85[1], 299).

[142]*Opus imperfectum* II, 24, 1 (CSEL 85[1], 178).

[143]*Opus imperfectum* II, 8   (CSEL 85[1], 168).

[144]*Opus imperfectum* I, 6; II, 14   (CSEL 85[1], 9, 172).

[145]*Opus imperfectum* I, 27; 66; II, 27, 2; 202; III, 10 (CSEL 85[1], 23, 64, 181, 314, 355).

[146]*Opus imperfectum* II, 178, 2   (CSEL 85[1], 298). Augustine does not know *how* all men were "in Adam," but asserts *that* they were.

[147]*Opus imperfectum* II, 178, 1   (CSEL 85[1], 297). Actually, the Church had not officially pronounced on whether Traducianism or Creationism was correct.

[148]*Opus imperfectum* II, 27, 2   (CSEL 85[1], 181).

[149]*Opus imperfectum* VI, 37   (PL 45, 1596).

[150]*Opus imperfectum* III, 142   (CSEL 85[1], 447-448). In I, 71, 2   (CSEL 85[1], 81), concupiscence is called a "natural and innocent *affectio.*"

[151]*Opus imperfectum* III, 109, 2-3; 142, 2; IV, 120; V, 46   (CSEL 85[1], 429, 447; PL 45, 1414, 1482).

[152]*Opus imperfectum* I, 96; II, 94   (CSEL 85[1], 111, 227).

[153]*Opus imperfectum* VI, 26; 27; 29   (PL 45, 1561-1562, 1566-1568, 1577).

[154]*Opus imperfectum* I, 61   (CSEL 85[1], 58).

[155]*Opus imperfectum* I, 141, 1   (CSEL 85[1], 158):   those who refuse to believe the doctrine are called "vessels of earth" by Julian (cf. Isaiah 45:9).

[156]*Opus imperfectum* I, 66   (CSEL 85[1], 64).

[157]*Opus imperfectum* IV, 47; VI, 41   (PL 45, 1365, 1604).

[158]*Opus imperfectum* IV, 53 (PL 45, 1369-1370); cf. IV, 50 (PL 45, 1368).

[159]*Opus imperfectum* IV, 50   (PL 45, 1368).

[160]*Opus imperfectum* IV, 48; 69; 29 (PL 45, 1366, 1379, 1353).

[161]*Opus imperfectum* IV, 49; 52 (PL 45, 1367, 1369).

[162]*Opus imperfectum* IV, 49; 52; 53 (PL 45, 1367-1368, 1369, 1370).

[163]*Opus imperfectum* IV, 49 (PL 45, 1367).

[164]*Opus imperfectum* IV, 134 (PL 45, 1429).

[165]*Opus imperfectum* IV, 122 (PL 45, 1418).

[166]*Opus imperfectum* VI, 33 (PL 45, 1586-1587).

[167]See Galen, *Peri physikōn dynameōn* II, 3:   the semen works like an artist (e.g., Phidias) on the woman's blood; it is the active principle, the blood provides the "matter." According to Soranus (*Gynecology* I, 3, 12), the "female seed" seems not to be used in generation, since it is excreted. Soranus' *Gynecology* was influential in the West by the late fourth century (Owsei Temkin, *Soranus' Gynecology* [Baltimore: Johns Hopkins Press, 1956] xxix). For Augustine, children are "poured off" (*transfunduntur*) from the man to the woman: *Opus imperfectum* II, 178, 2 (CSEL 85[1], 299).

[168]E.g., *Opus imperfectum* II, 40; 41; 112 (CSEL 85[1], 191-192, 243).   Julian reports on various medical opinions about the creation of the seed in *Opus imperfectum* V, 11 (PL 45, 1440).

[169]See above, p. 299.   Readers may rightly argue that already in *De civitate Dei* XIV, 16, Augustine's description of original sin manifesting itself was depicted in typically male examples (erection and impotence).

[170]See Augustine's use of Romans 5:12 in *De perfectione iustitiae hominis* 39(18); 44(21); *De gratia Christi* I, 55(5); II, 34(29); *De nuptiis* I, 1(1); II, 3(2); 8(3); 15(5); 20(8); 24(11); 37(22); 42(26); 45(27); 47(27); *De peccatorum meritis* I, 8(8); 9(9); 10(9); 11(10); III, 8(4); 14(7); 19(11); *De spiritu et littera* 47(27); *De natura et gratia* 9(8); 46(39); 48(41); *De anima et ejus origine* I, 28(17); II, 20(14); *Contra duas epistolas Pelagianorum* IV, 7(4); 8(4); 21(8).

[171]*Opus imperfectum* II, 56, 1; 75 (CSEL 85[1], 203, 218).

[172]*Opus imperfectum* II, 56, 1; 61; 194 (CSEL 85[1], 203, 207-208, 309).

[173]*Opus imperfectum* III, 85, 1 (CSEL 85[1], 411-412). Julian's explanation for why the man is named although the woman sinned first is that fathers have more *auctoritas* than women; possessing the *potestas* of the male sex, a man's example (Adam's) would carry more weight than a woman's (Eve's): *Opus imperfectum* II, 190 (CSEL 85[1], 307).

[174]*Opus imperfectum* II, 56 (CSEL 85[1], 204-205). In II, 173, 1 (CSEL 85[1], 293), Augustine asserts that we have a choice of just two views: the one here espoused or that Eve is included with Adam in the phrase "one man." Augustine does not pursue the latter alternative.

[175]*Opus imperfectum* II, 83 (CSEL 85[1], 221).

[176]*Opus imperfectum* III, 85, 4 (CSEL 85[1], 413).

[177]*Opus imperfectum* III, 88, 3-4 (CSEL 85[1], 415-416).

[178]*Opus imperfectum* II, 179 (CSEL 85[1], 299-300).

[179]*Opus imperfectum* IV, 104 (PL 45, 1401). Cf. other expressions of this idea in Augustine's sermons, such as that Jesus was "conceived in a womb no seed had entered" (*Sermo* 192 [Ben.], 1 [PL 38, 1012]); and that he was "born of his Father without time, of his mother without seed" (*Sermo* 194 [Ben.], 1 [PL 38, 1015]). Augustine's Christmas sermons in particular often mention the "seedless" conception of Jesus, but since the sermons are difficult to date, they are not useful in an historical argument as are treatises or letters that can be dated with some precision.

[180]*Opus imperfectum* VI, 22 (PL 45, 1553).

[181]*Opus imperfectum* IV, 79 (PL 45, 1384).

[182]*Opus imperfectum* IV, 80 (PL 45, 1384-1385).

[183]*Opus imperfectum* IV, 51 (PL 45, 1369).

[184]*Opus imperfectum* IV, 122 (PL 45, 1418). On Augustine's Mariological theory, see Joseph Huhn, "Ein Vergleich der Mariologie des Hl. Augustinus mit der Hl. Ambrosius in ihrer Abhängigkeit, Ahnlichkeit, in ihrem Unterschied," in *Augustinus Magister. Congrès International Augustinien, Paris, 21-24 Septembre, 1954* (Paris:

Etudes Augustiniennes, 1954), I, 221-239; Henri Frévin,
*Le Mariage de Saint Joseph et de la sainte Vierge. Etude
de théologie positive de Saint Irénée à Saint Thomas*
(Cahiers de Joséphologie 15, 2; Montréal: Centre de
Recherche et de Documentation Oratoire Saint-Joseph,
1967), 239-267. For background, see Hugo Koch, *Virgo
Eva-Virgo Maria. Neue Untersuchungen über die Lehre von
der Jungfrauschaft und der Ehe Mariens in der ältesten
Kirche* (Arbeiten zur Kirchengeschichte 25; Berlin; Leip-
zig: Verlag Walter de Gruyter & Co., 1937).

[185]*De civitate Dei* XIV, 23 (CCL 48, 446); *Opus imperfectum* V, 14 (PL 45, 1444-1445).

[186]Does Julian here hint that he approves of
"bridling" women's fecundity through contraceptive
measures?

[187]*Opus imperfectum* V, 15 (PL 45, 1445).

[188]*Opus imperfectum* I, 68, 5 (CSEL 88[1], 75): originally libido was never contrary to the movement of the
will. In II, 122 (CSEL 85[1], 253) Augustine gives three
choices: either there was no *libido* in Eden before sin;
or, there was *libido*, but it didn't go before the will or
mind; or at least it didn't exceed them. Also see *Contra
duas epistolas Pelagianorum* I, 10(5); 31(15); 35(17)
(CSEL 60, 431, 448, 451-452) for the possibility of
libido and "motion of the members" in Eden. In the new
Ep. 6* to Atticus (5, 1; 7, 2 [CSEL 88, 34, 35-36]),
Augustine distinguishes the *concupiscentia nuptiarum*
which would have been present, from the *concupiscentia
carnis*, which would not.

[189]Scripture affirms original sin (Ecclesiasticus
40:1 is a favorite proof text; see *Opus imperfectum* I,
27; 49; VI, 3; 23 [CSEL 85[1], 23, 41-42; PL 45, 1507,
1556]); the church fathers affirm original sin (Ambrose's
Commentary on Luke is cited over three dozen times, by my
count); Julian would push all the woes of this life into
Paradise (*Opus imperfectum* I, 67, 7; III, 154; 187, 2-3;
IV, 114; V, 23; VI, 16; 21 [CSEL 85[1], 72, 459-460, 488-
489; PL 45, 1408, 1458, 1537-1538, 1549-1550]); that
Julian is cruel not to allow Christ's grace to be effective for babies (*Opus imperfectum* I, 32; 54; II, 2; 117;
236, 3; III, 48; 126; 146 [CSEL 85, 24-25, 49-50, 165,
249, 350, 388, 441, 452-453]); that he does not hold a
Manichean "mixing of natures" (*Opus imperfectum* I, 85;
120; VI, 20; 25; 36; 41 [CSEL 85[1], 98, 136; PL 45, 1547,
1559, 1592, 1608]); Julian's praise of concupiscence and

the sexual relation puts illicit and licit sexual relations on the same footing (*Opus imperfectum* III, 209
[CSEL 85[1], 502-503]).

[190]Shown in *Opus imperfectum* II, 178, 1; IV, 104
(CSEL 85[1], 297; PL 45, 1399).

[191]Shown in *Opus imperfectum* II, 178, 2 (CSEL 85[1],
298).

[192]Shown in *Contra Julianum* IV, 47(8) (PL 44, 762).

[193]Shown in *Contra Julianum* V, 10(3) (PL 44, 788).

[194]Shown in *Opus imperfectum* I, 25 (CSEL 85[1], 22).

[195]*Contra Julianum* VI, 39(12) (PL 44, 843).

[196]Bruckner, *Julian*, p. 85.

[197]Shown in *Opus imperfectum* I, 44; V, 40 (CSEL 85[1],
31; PL 45, 1476).

[198]See *Contra Julianum* VI, 68(22); (PL 44, 864); *Opus
imperfectum* I, 49, 1; 2 (CSEL 85[1], 41, 115); perhaps also
V, 15 (PL 45, 1445).

[199]*Opus imperfectum* VI, 23 (PL 45, 1555).

[200]*Opus imperfectum* V, 26 (PL 45, 1464).

[201]*Opus imperfectum* III, 166; cited from 172 on (CSEL
85[1], 469, 473ff.). Augustine doesn't know the letter
(III, 172, 3 [CSEL 85[1], 473]). Mani's authorship has
been doubted (though not the Manichean origin of the
work) by G.J.D. Aalders, "L'Epître à Menoch, attribuée
à Mani," *Vigiliae Christianae* 14 (1960) 245-249.

[202]*Opus imperfectum* III, 186, 2 (CSEL 85[1], 484).
Augustine in *Contra epistolam fundamenti* 12 (CSEL 25,
207-208) cites Mani's words responding to Patticius. The
name is now known from the *Cologne Mani Codex* (#89:
"Pattikios"); see discussion in Decret, *L'Afrique Mani-
chéenne*, 117-122.

[203]*Opus imperfectum* III, 173; 174 (CSEL 85[1], 474,
475).

[204]*Opus imperfectum* III, 174 (CSEL 85[1], 475). Manichean documents consistently condemn lust and reject

"defiling intercourse."   See, for example, Psalm 270, 1.
29; Psalm 268 11. 31-32 (*A Manichean Psalm-Book, Part II*,
ed. C.R.C. Allberry [Manichean Manuscripts in the Chester
Beatty Collection II; Stuttgart: W. Kohlhammer, 1938],
88, 86); *Kephalaia* 78, 11. 19-20; 94, 11. 20-21 (*Manichäische Handschriften der Staatlichen Museen Berlin* I,
ed. Hugo Ibscher [Stuttgart: W. Kohlhammer Verlag, 1940],
190, 239).

[205] *Opus imperfectum* III, 185 (CSEL 85[1], 483).

[206] *Opus imperfectum* III, 186, 2 (CSEL 85[1], 484); cf.
Contra epistolam fundamenti 12 (CSEL 25[1], 208).

[207] *Opus imperfectum* III, 187, 1-5 (CSEL 85[1], 485-487).

[208] *Opus imperfectum* III, 187, 7 (CSEL 85[1], 488).

[209] *Confessiones* III, 11, 20; IV, 1, 1 (CCL 27, 38,
40); *Contra epistolam fundamenti* 10 (CSEL 25, 206); *De
moribus Manichaeorum* 68(19) (PL 32, 1374); *De moribus
ecclesiae catholicae* 18, 34 (PL 32, 1326).   Pierre
Courcelle (*Recherches sur les Confessions de Saint Augustin* [2nd ed.; Paris: Editions E. de Boccard, 1968], 78)
has argued for a Manichean period of at least ten years.

[210] For overviews of Manicheanism and the Manichean
myth, see Hans Jonas, *The Gnostic Religion. The Message
of the Alien God and the Beginnings of Christianity* (2nd
ed., revised; Boston: Beacon Press, 1963), ch. 9; Henri-
Charles Puech, *Le Manichéisme. Son fondateur-sa doctrine*
(Musée Guimet, Bibliothèque de Diffusion 56; Paris:
Civilisations du Sud, 1949); Geo Widengren, *Mani and
Manichaeism* (New York; Chicago; San Francisco: Holt,
Rinehart and Winston, 1963), esp. chs. 3 & 4; L.J.R. Ort,
*Mani. A Religio-Historical Description of His Per-
sonality* (Supplementa ad Numen, Altera Series 1; Leiden:
E.J. Brill, 1967); H.J. Polotsky, "Manichäismus," *PW*
Suppl. Bd. VI (1935), 240-271; C. Colpe, "Manichäismus,"
RGG[3] (1960), IV, 714-722.

[211] *De anima et ejus origine* I, 24(15); II, 4(2); 6(3)
(CSEL 60, 323); *De Genesi contra Manichaeos* II, 11(8);
38(25) (PL 34, 202, 216); *De moribus Manichaeorum* 11, 21
(PL 32, 1354); *Contra Faustum* XX, 98 (CSEL 25,[1], 705)
among many references.

[212] *De Genesi contra Manichaeos* II, 38(26) (PL 34,
217); *Contra Faustum* XX, 22 (CSEL 25[1], 565-566).

[213]*De duabus animabus* I, 1 (CSEL 25^1, 51); *Opus imperfectum* VI, 6 (PL 45, 1510-1511).

[214]*Contra Faustum* II, 1; XVI, 4; XXVI, 6; XXVIII, 2; XXXII, 7 (CSEL 25^1, 253, 442-443, 734-735, 744-745, 766); *Contra epistolam fundamenti* 9 (CSEL 25^1, 202).

[215]*Contra Faustum* V, 3 (CSEL 25^1, 273). On Faustus (and with a restoration of his *Capitula*), see Paul Monceaux, *Le Manichéen Faustus de Milev: Restitution de ses Capitula* (Extrait des Mémoires de l'Academie des Inscriptions et Belles-Lettres 43; Paris: Imprimerie, 1924).

[216]*Contra Faustum* VII, 1 (CSEL 25^1, 303); Denis *Sermo* 25, 5 (*Miscellanea Agostiniana. Vol I: Sancti Augustini Sermones* [Rome: Tipografia Poliglotta Vaticana, 1930], 160).

[217]*Contra Faustum* II, 1; III, 1; VII, 1 (CSEL 25^1, 253-254, 261-262, 302-303); also see *Sermo* 51, 11(7)-16(10); 27(17) (PL 38, 339-342, 348-349); *De consensu Evangelistarum* II, 2(1)-16(5) (PL 34, 1071-1079); *Retractiones* II, 16; 55, 3 (CCL 57, 103, 134).

[218]*Contra Faustum* XXII, 64 (CSEL 25^1, 660). Much of *Contra Faustum* XXII is dedicated to this issue, as is a surprisingly large portion of *De bono conjugali*.

[219]*Contra Faustum* XXIX, 1; 4 (CSEL 25^1, 743, 747). According to Faustus, Jesus became Son of God at his baptism, not at his birth: *Contra Faustum* XXIII, 2 (CSEL 25^1, 707-709).

[220]A point also worried about by pagan critics of Christianity; see Augustine's correspondence with Volusian: *Epp.* 135, 2; 137, 1, 2; 2, 4 (CSEL 44, 91, 98, 100-101).

[221]*Confessiones* III, 7, 12 (CCL 27, 33); *Contra Secundinum* 23 (CSEL 25^2, 940); *Contra Faustum* XX, 11; XXIII, 10 (CSEL 25^1, 549-550, 716-717).

[222]*Epistola Secundini* (CSEL 25^2, 899).

[223]Psalm 245, ll. 23-26 (cf. Luke 7:2-6), Allberry, *Manichean Psalm-Book, Part II*, 52. I thank my colleague Orval Wintermute for assistance with the text. For a discussion of Manichean views of Christ, see Eugen Rose, *Die Manichäische Christologie* (Studies in Oriental

Religions 5; Wiesbaden: Otto Harrassowitz, 1979), esp.
121-123.   Augustine asks of the Manicheans, if you discount Jesus' birth, why do you allow Mani to be born?:
Contra epistolam fundamenti 8 (CSEL 25[1], 201-202).   On
Manichean views of Jesus in Eastern Manichean texts, see
O.G. von Wesendonk, "Jesus und der Manichäismus,"
Orientalische Literaturzeitung 30 (1927) 221-227; and
Ernst Waldschmidt and Wolfgang Lentz, "Die Stellung Jesu
im Manichäismus," *Abhandlungen der Preussischen Akademie
der Wissenschaften, philosophisch-historische Klasse,*
1926-1927, no. 4, 1-131.

[224]A Psalm to Jesus, 11. 19-32, *passim* (Allberry, *A
Manichean Psalm-Book, Part II,* 120-121).   The "begetting"
of Christ, for the Manicheans, always means the heavenly
begetting from the Father.   That Jesus' body was present
in the fruit of trees was the background of the notion
of *Jesus patibilis* (see, e.g., *Contra Faustum* XX, 11
[CSEL 25[1], 549-550]).   The Psalm to Jesus also (1. 31)
mocks the Magi, another feature of the Christian birth
story that probably was repulsive to those whose leader
had suffered the ill will of the Magi.

[225]*De continentia* 23(9); 24(10) (CSEL 41, 170);
Contra duas epistolas Pelagianorum IV, 5(4) (CSEL 60,
525).

[226]*Confessiones* VII, 19, 25 (CCL 27, 108-109); *De
bono conjugali* 26(21) (CSEL 27, 220-221); Mai *Sermo* 95,
3 (*Miscellanea Agostiniana* I, 342); Guelferbytana Append.
VII, 1 (*Miscellanea Agostiniana* I, 581-582); Morin *Sermo*
17, 1-2 (*Miscellanea Agostiniana* I, 659); and numerous
other places in Augustine's doctrinal, moral works, letters and sermons.   For a review of Augustine's
Christology, see Tarsicius J. van Bavel, *Recherches sur
la Christologie de Saint Augustin.   L'humain et le divine
dans le Christ d'après Saint Augustin* (Paradosis X; Fribourg: Editions Universitaires, 1954).

[227]*Confessiones* VII, 19, 25 (CCL 27, 109); *De anima
et ejus origine* I, 31(18) (CSEL 60, 332); Denis *Sermo* 5,
7 (*Miscellanea Agostiniana* I, 28); and numerous other
places.   See van Bavel, *Recherches,* 122-128.

[228]*Contra Adimantum* 21 (CSEL 25[1], 180); *Contra
Felicem* II, 11 (CSEL 25[2], 840).

[229]*Contra Faustum* XXIII, 10 (CSEL 25[1], 716); *Contra
epistolam fundamenti* 20 (CSEL 25[1], 216); *Confessiones* V,
2, 2 (CCL 27, 57).

[230]*Contra Faustum* XXIII, 10 (CSEL 25[1], 716).

[231]*Contra epistolam fundamenti* 8 (CSEL 25[1], 202); *Contra Faustum* XX, 11 (CSEL 25[1], 549-550); *Confessiones* V, 10, 20 (CCL 27, 69); *De bono viduitatis* 13(10) (CSEL 41, 319); *Sermo* 12, 12(12); 51, 3(2); 215, 3 (PL 38, 106, 334, 1073).

[232]*Contra Faustum* XX, 11 (CSEL 25[1], 549).

[233]A particularly strong theme in Augustine's sermons. See, for example, *Sermones* 51, 18; 184, 1; 186, 1; 188, 4; 189, 2; 190, 2-3; 191, 2-4; 192, 1; 193, 1; 195, 1; 170, 3, 3; 291, 6; 231, 2, 2; 215, 2; and numerous others.

[234]Citing Psalm 19:5: found in such works as *Sermones* 191, 2(1); 192, 3(3); 195, 3; 126, 6(5); 291, 6 (PL 38, 1010, 1013, 1018, 701, 1319); *Tractatus in Johannis Evangelium* 8, 4 (CCL 36, 84); *Ennarationes in Psalmos* 148, 8 (CCL 40, 2171).

[235]*Contra Secundinum* 23 (CSEL 25[2], 940); *Contra Faustum* III, 6 (CSEL 25[1], 267-268).

[236]*Contra Faustum* XXX, 6 (CSEL 25[1], 755).

[237]*Contra Adimantum* 21 (CSEL 25[1], 180).

[238]*De nuptiis* I, 13(12) (CSEL 42, 226); *Contra Julianum* V, 55(15) (PL 44, 815); *Opus imperfectum* IV, 60; 79; VI, 34 (PL 45, 1375, 1384, 1588). Interestingly, a Manichean Psalm (probably) cites the verse as part of its Docetic Christology (Allberry, *Manichean Psalm-Book II*, 194 [1. 1]).

[239]See above, pp. 309-310.

[240]*De moribus Manichaeorum* 18, 65 (PL 32, 1373). See John Noonan, *Contraception. A History of its Treatment by the Catholic Theologians and Canonists* (New York; Toronto: New American Library, 151-154). According to Soranus' *Gynecology* I, 10, 36 (pp. 34, 36 Temkin), the woman's fertile period came at the end of menstruation; if some argue for other times, don't pay attention to such "unscientific" arguments.

[241]So Noonan deduces from *Contra Faustum* XXII, 30 (CSEL 25[1], 624): in intercourse, the Manicheans "pour out their God by a shameful slip" (Noonan, *Contraception*, 153-154). Recall Augustine's interpretation of the sin of Onan as *coitus interruptus*; see below, p. 320.

[242]*De moribus Manichaeorum* 18, 65, (PL 32, 1373):   the Manicheans advised Augustine to refrain from sexual relations during the woman's fertile period. Cf. *Confessiones* IV, 2, 2 (CCL 27, 41):   on how we begrudge the birth of children, though love them after they arrive; and *Contra Faustum* XX, 23 (CSEL 25[1], 567), on married Manichean Auditors who have children, "albeit they beget them against their wills."

[243]On Augustine's early sex life, see *Confessiones* II, 2, 2; 4; III, 1, 1; VI, 11, 20-15, 25; VIII, 17 (CCL 27, 18, 19, 27, 87-90, 124). On a (probable) later reflection concerning his relationship with his mistress, see *De bono conjugali* 5(5) (CSEL 41, 193-194). Peter Brown has wisely warned us not to view Augustine's relationship with his mistress in terms of "animal passions"; the "late Roman caste system" provides a better explanation of his behavior (*Augustine and Sexuality* [Berkeley: The Center for Hermeneutical Studies in Hellenistic and Modern Culture, Colloquy, 45, 1983], pp. 1-2).

[244]*Confessiones* VI, 7, 12 (CCL 27, 82); *De continentia* 26(12) (CSEL 41, 175); *Contra duas epistolas Pelagianorum* III, 14(5) (CSEL 60, 503); *De moribus ecclesiae Catholicae* 2(1) (PL 32, 1311); *Retractiones* I, 7, 1 (CCL 57, 18).

[245]*De moribus Manichaeorum* 68; 70-72(19) (PL 32, 1374, 1374-1375); *De continentia* 27(12) (CSEL 41, 177); *De natura boni* 45-47 (CSEL 25[2], 884-888); *De haeresibus* 46, 5; 9; 10; 11 (CCL 46, 313, 314-315, 316); *Contra Fortunatum* 3 (CSEL 25[1], 85); for suspicions about their practices, see also Cyril of Jerusalem, *Catecheses* VI, 33 (PG 33, 597); Possidius, *Vita Augustini* 16 (PL 32, 46-47); cf. Epiphanius on the Barbeliotes, *Adversus haereses* I, 2, 26, 4 (PG 41, 338-339).

[246]*Contra Secundinum* 21 (CSEL 25[2], 938).

[247]*Contra Faustum* XXII, 80 (CSEL 25[1], 682-683).

[248]Augustine's "three goods of marriage" is still the structuring device of Pius XI's encyclical *Casti Connubii* of 1930.

[249]*De moribus ecclesiae Catholicae* 63(30) (PL 32, 1336); *De sancta virginitate* 12(12) (CSEL 41, 244-245); *De bono conjugali* 32(24) (CSEL 41, 226-227).

[250]*Contra Faustum* XXII, 31-32; 43; 45; 47-50; 81 (CSEL 25, 624-627, 635-636, 637, 639-644, 683); *De sancta*

virginitate 1(1) (CSEL 41, 235-236); *De bono viduitatis*
10(7) (CSEL 41, 314-315); and throughout *De bono conjugali*, esp. sections 26-35 (CSEL 41, 221-230). Augustine
rejects the Manichean tendency to pit the asceticism of
some New Testament passages over against the pro-
reproductive view of the Old Testament: *Contra Adimantum*
3; 23 (CSEL 25^1, 118-122, 182); *Contra Secundinum* 21; 23
(CSEL 25^2, 938-939, 941); *Contra Faustum* XIV, 1 (CSEL
25^1, 401-404).

[251] *Contra Faustum* XV, 7 (CSEL 25^1, 429-430).

[252] *De moribus Manichaeorum* 65(18) (PL 32, 1373).

[253] *Contra Faustum* XXII, 84 (CSEL 25^1, 687); also
later in *De adulterinis conjugiis* II, 12, 12 (CSEL 41,
396).

[254] *De moribus Manichaeorum* 73(19) (PL 32, 1375-1376).

[255] *Contra Faustum* XX, 6 (CSEL 25^1, 540).

[256] *Contra Felicem* II, 7; 22 (CSEL 25^2, 834-835, 852);
Contra Faustum VI, 8; XX, 6; XXII, 98 (CSEL 25^1, 296-297,
540, 704); *De natura boni* 44 (CSEL 25^2, 881-884); *De
haeresibus* 46, 7-8, 14 (CCL 46, 314-317). The myth of
the seduction of the archons, its variations and precedents have been well explicated by Franz Cumont,
*Recherches sur le Manichéisme. I: La Cosmogonie mani-
chéene d'après Théodore bar Khôni* (Brussels: H. Lamber-
tin, 1908), "Appendice I: La Seduction des archontes,"
54-68. Cumont shows that several variations developed
from the central myth as explicated in Mani's *Thesaurus*,
which had either semen or rain fall from the heavens.
Mani was vague as to the substance, but Christian
writers filled in the details. Probably the Manichean
myth was derived from the older Persian myth of the
primordial battle between the Primal Man and the bull.
For background to the myth in Persian religion, see
R.C. Zaehner, *Zurvan: A Zoroastrian Dilemma* (Oxford:
Clarendon Press, 1955), 183-192. Among Christian authors
who cite the myth are Augustine's friend Evodius, *De fide
contra Manichaeos* 14-16 (CSEL 25, 956-957); Hegemonius,
Acta Archelai 9 (GCS 16, 13, 15) where the substance is
identified as rain and compared with the sweat a man
sheds when he works; Epiphanius, who says he derives his
version from "Archelaus" (*Adversus haereses* II, 2, 66, 32
[PG 42, 80-81]); a remnant in Theodoret, *Compendium
haereticorum fabularum* V, 10 (PG 83, 487), where the substance is again identified as rain; and fully in Theodore
bar Konai, *Liber scholiarum* XI (ed. Addai Scher, CSCO,

Script. Syri 26; Louvain: Secrétariat du CorpusSCO, 1960
[Réimpression anastatique] 316-318; German translation
in Alfred Adam, *Texte zum Manichäismus* [Kleine Texte für
Vorlesung und Ubungen 175, 2nd ed.; Berlin: Walter de
Gruyter, 1969], pp. 20-21). One wonders if recalling the
myth motivated Augustine to note that in the Bible angels
always manifest themselves *clothed* (*Opus imperfectum* IV,
63 [PL 45, 1376]).

[257] E.g., in *De moribus Manichaeorum* 61(19); 73(19);
49-50(16) (PL 32, 1371, 1375-1376, 1365).

[258] *De natura boni* 44 (CSEL 25^2, 881-884).

[259] *Contra Faustum* XXII, 98 (CSEL 25^1, 704-705).

[260] *Contra Felicem* II, 7 (CSEL 25^2, 834-835).

[261] *Contra Felicem* II, 22 (CSEL 25^2, 852).

[262] *Contra Faustum* VI, 8 (CSEL 25^1, 296).

[263] *Opus imperfectum* I, 49; 120; VI, 25 (CSEL 85^1, 41;
PL 45, 1559), and many other passages; also see *De continentia* 14(5) (CSEL 41, 157-158) and *Contra Faustum* II,
6 (CSEL 25, 261).

[264] I remained unconvinced by the intriguing argument
of Pier Franco Beatrice, *Tradux peccati: alle fonti della
dottrina agostiniana del peccato originale* (Studia
Mediolanensia 8; Milan: Vita e Pensiero Università
Cattolica del Sacro Cuore, 1978), 222-259, that Augustine's theory of original sin stemmed from the Encratites,
especially from Julius Cassianus (cited in Clement of
Alexandria, *Stromateis* III), perhaps by way of fourth-
century Messalian teaching. Although there are indeed
similarities between Encratite and Augustinian theory,
Beatrice provides no convincing historical road map of
how Augustine would have known these earlier views.
Beatrice cites in support of his theory a pseudo-Cyprianic
sermon, "De centesima, sexagesima, tricesima" (PL Supplement 1, 53-67) which asserts that baptism cleanses us
from the "delictum primae nativitatis" (col. 54, ll. 5-
7; wrongly cited as col. 64 in Beatrice), but such
generalized views of the matter were also common in
Ambrose, a sure influence on Augustine. Moreover, the
phrase does not pinpoint the problem to the seeds, as
Augustine does. Second, it remains unclear how Augustine, with his limited ability in Greek, would have known
much about the Messalians, an Eastern movement originating

in the mid-fourth century. (The only early Latin source
mentioning the Messalians, the prologue to Jerome's
Dialogue against the Pelagians, which was written in
Palestine, is almost contemporary with the treatises in
which Augustine begins to discuss vitiated seeds, but
post-dates by about two decades Augustine's interest in
Adam's sin, as described in Romans 5.) The sources on
the Messalians are collected in *Patrologia Syriaca* I, 3
(Paris, 1926), clxx-ccxcii. In sum, although Augustine's
general theory of human sinfulness since birth is found
in "orthodox" as well as sectarian and heretical authors,
the motif of seeds becoming mixed with evil can most
likely be linked to his Manichean past.

[265]Joan Kelly, *Women, History and Theory: The Essays
of Joan Kelly* (Chicago; London: University of Chicago
Press, 1984), 3-4.

[266]Kelly, *Women*, 4.

[267]Brown, *Augustine and Sexuality*, 6-11; also see
Margaret R. Miles, *Augustine on the Body* (AAR Dissertation Series 31; Missoula, Mont.: Scholars Press, 1979).

[268]My emphasis thus differs somewhat from Kari E.
Børresen's in *Subordination and Equivalence: The Nature
and Rôle of Woman in Augustine and Thomas Aquinas* (tr.
C.H. Talbot; Washington, D.C.: University Press of
America, 1981), who states that the biological arguments
in the debate between Julian and Augustine are only
"illustrative"; the essential argument is theological
(p. 64). I agree that the essential argument *is* theological, but suggest that the "biological" substructure of
the debate is more important than Børresen indicates. Of
course, part of Julian's tactics was to "caricature"
Augustine so that he looked Manichean (Brown, *Augustine*,
p. 393), but by raising the "biological" argument to a
more important position in the debate as I have done,
Julian's accusation, even if not ultimately convincing,
gains a force it is too often denied. It is not for
nothing that Augustine calls Julian *religiosus physicus*
(*Opus imperfectum* IV, 134 [PL 45, 1429]) and Julian returns the jibe to Augustine: *physicus iste novus* (*Opus
imperfectum* V, 11 [PL 45, 1440]).

PART III

ASCETICISM AND EXEGESIS

HERESY, ASCETICISM, ADAM, AND EVE: INTERPRETATIONS OF GENESIS 1-3 IN THE LATER LATIN FATHERS

The Society of Biblical Literature (1983)

To refute Manichean claims that the Hebrew Scriptures in general and the book of Genesis in particular were crude documents unworthy of acceptance by the erudite, Ambrose and his pupil in exegesis, Augustine, adopted a spiritual reading that relied heavily on allegorical and moral interpretation. Appropriating an exegetical style derived from Philo and Origen, which thanks to the Cappadocian Fathers had emerged in the 370s and 380s as the "thinking man's" approach to Genesis, Ambrose and Augustine labored to demonstrate how the events depicted in the first book of Scripture betokened higher truths that Christian intellectuals need not blush to espouse.[1]

By the first decade of the fifth century, however, the utility of a spiritualized exegesis of Genesis had diminished, for it carried in its wake ascetic implications now attacked as "Manichean." Interpreters who posited a poetic creation prior to a material one, or who turned the physical entities of Genesis 1-3 into allegories of incorporeal truths, could be viewed as denigrating God's good creation, including the human body. To meet such accusations, leveled especially by Jovinian, Augustine developed an earthier, more literal reading of Genesis 1-3. The continuation of this exegetical trend in Augustine's later writings is doubtless due to the

fact that his Pelagian opponents revived Jovinian's
criticism that an ascetically spiritualized interpretation of Genesis debased marriage and sexuality--in other
words, that Augustine's views were "Manichean."[2] The
switch from Augustine's earlier offensive against the
Manichean mockery of Genesis to his self-defense against
charges of "Manicheanism" signals a changed interpretation of Genesis 1-3 that influenced all later Western
theology.

Thus the prevalent opinion that the Pelagian controversy was the decisive factor prompting Augustine to
develop a more "fleshly" reading of Adam and Eve is to be
questioned. To the contrary, this reading was firmly in
place by A.D. 410, before Augustine even knew any Pelagians.[3] Rather, it appears that Augustine revised his
interpretation of Genesis 1-3 to conform his exegesis to
the views on marriage and virginity he had developed as
a resolution to the debate between Jovinian and Jerome.

As Augustine indicates in the *Confessions*, it was
Ambrose who convinced him that a more spiritual exegesis
of the Old Testament both gave meaning to what Augustine
had earlier deemed "the most unlikely doctrines,"[4] and
provided an effective way to refute Manichean slanders on
the books of the Old Law.[5] Yet although Ambrose wrote
several treatises on Genesis in which he ardently strove
to outwit Manichean opponents, he never clearly compre-
hended *which* verses must be defended in their literal
sense in order to avoid the accusation that he denigrated
the goodness of creation, namely, "Reproduce and multiply
and fill the earth," and "They shall be one flesh."[6] So
eager was Ambrose to give an intellectually acceptable
rendition of Genesis that he failed to protect himself
adequately from the charges of "Manicheanism" that
plagued his later years. Ambrose's critics complained

that his ascetic enthusiasm, especially his championing
of Mary's perpetual virginity, compromised the goodness
of reproduction and signalled irreverence toward the
Creator.

Ambrose's earliest foray into the interpretation of
Genesis 1-3 is his *De Paradiso*, dated to A.D. 377. His
exegesis here is partially allegorized and in all likelihood is dependent upon Philo.[7] Thus the trees and rivers
of Paradise symbolize the classical virtues,[8] the birds
and animals brought to Adam for naming represent the
irrational senses,[9] the serpent of Genesis 3 stands for
enjoyment, the woman represents sensation (*aisthēsis*),
and the man is a symbol of reason (*nous*). The story of
the Fall is thus transformed into a morality play in
which the senses, lured by pleasure, bring about the
downfall of reason.[10] But the sexual (or non-sexual)
dimensions of the narrative receive scant attention.[11]

In a letter written ten or twelve years later
(Epistle 45), Ambrose expressed dissatisfaction with the
De Paradiso[12]--but not with his allegorical exegesis. If
anything, his new interpretation is more heavily allegorized, for Paradise is now said to be situated *inside* the
human heart. It is further identified with the "garden
enclosed" of Song of Songs 4:12, which Ambrose takes to
mean either the virgin soul or the Church. Genesis 3
still conveys the warning that reason should not let itself be bested by passion: God's "breathing onto Adam's
face" (Genesis 2:7) was intended to fortify the first man
against lust.[13] The moral of the tale is that Christians
should not allow their understanding to be weakened by
passion, as Adam was dragged down by Eve.[14]

Shortly before he composed the letter in which he
criticized his earlier *De Paradiso*, Ambrose had completed
a treatise on the six days of creation, the *Hexameron*, a

treatise heavily indebted to Basil of Caesarea's work of
the same name.[15] There can be no doubt that one purpose
of Ambrose's *Hexameron* was to refute Manichean cosmology.
In this treatise Ambrose is quick to emphasize, against
the Manicheans, that God did not create evil;[16] that evil
was not produced by an "alien nature," but is a deviation
from virtue;[17] that our formation by the pre-existent
Christ "in the image of God" refutes the Manichean claim
that humans were not created by the divine power.[18]

Ambrose does not, however, exploit such verses as
"Reproduce and multiply" or "They shall be one flesh" in
his exposition of Genesis, no doubt because the Manicheans viewed reproduction as a nasty trick devised by
the dark powers to disperse the defeated principle of
light. To cite "reproduce and multiply" to Manicheans
would scarce convince *them* of the spiritual value of
Genesis. The little that Ambrose here says on matters
sexual falls far short of the polemic regarding bodies as
God's handiwork that comes to prominence two decades
later. Instead, his exposition tends to the moral: that
Adam and Eve were one, she being taken from his rib,
becomes an injunction against adultery;[19] that they were
created in God's image, having been "painted on" by God,
becomes a warning to women not to erase God's art work by
the use of cosmetics.[20] A deeper analysis of sexual
distinction and functioning is largely absent from
Ambrose's account.[21]

Nor does Ambrose exploit the themes of Genesis 1-3 in
his early ascetic writings. In three works dating to
376-377 (*De Viduis*, *De Virginibus*, and *De Virginitate*),
there is little reference to Genesis.[22] Only in *De
Institutione Virginis*, composed at Eastertime 393, does
Ambrose comment in detail on such verses as "It is not
good for a man to be alone" (Genesis 2:18).[23] In a

surprising move, he argues here that in their commission
of sin, Eve is more easily excused than Adam,[24] and that
even her penalty (pain in childbearing) has the recom-
pense of salvation, as we learn from I Timothy 2:15.[25]

This attention to Eve in the *De Institutione
Virginis*, however, serves a larger purpose than simple
explication of the Genesis text: it forms the backdrop
for Ambrose to champion the perpetual virginity of Mary[26]
against the attacks of an unidentified "certain
bishop."[27] To refute these attacks, Ambrose summons the
same arguments used ten years earlier by Jerome in his
defense of the perpetual virginity of Mary against
Helvidius.[28] Thus we are presented with the suggestive
fact that the only treatise in which Ambrose dwells at
any length on a literal interpretation of Genesis 1-3
occurs in one whose major purpose is to defend the perpetual virginity of Mary. Here is the first, rather
tentative recognition by Ambrose that a discussion of
ascetic ideals might have to address the issue of woman
in Genesis 1-3.

Yet Ambrose's last writings, from 394 to 396, show
that he made no progress in modifying his staunchly
ascetic stance through a more literal reading of Genesis
1-3. In these works, he reminds his readers that Adam did
not "know" his wife until *after* they had been ejected
from Paradise.[29] He writes that "flesh was cast out of
Eden through a man and a woman; it was joined to God
through a virgin."[30] He holds that marriage is for weak
men, who like Paul's vegetable-eaters, cannot aspire to
a higher perfection.[31] Thus Ambrose's exposition of
Adam and Eve's relationship did nothing to modify his
continuing enthusiasm for ascetic renunciation. Not surprisingly, some Christians might judge Ambrose's views to
be closer to the Manicheans' than was prudent.

By the early 390s, even before Ambrose composed his
final works, a serious attack upon ascetic ideals had
already been launched and had received ample publicity:
I refer to the affair of Jovinian. Jovinian's polemic
focused on a denial of higher heavenly rewards or extra
merit for ascetics. Rather, he claimed that there was
only one tier of heavenly reward for Christians, that
there would be no otherworldly differentiation on the
grounds of ascetic practice.[32] According to Jovinian,
all who had passed through the Christian baptismal laver
were of equal merit, assuming that virgins, widows, and
the married possessed equal virtue in other respects.[33]
Like most early Christian thinkers, Jovinian argued his
case from the Bible, citing numerous examples of blessed
couples mentioned therein.[34] He also cited the standard
New Testament passages that appeared to laud marriage,
such as I Timothy 5:14 and Hebrews 13:4.[35] And the Song
of Songs, which had been co-opted by fourth-century
ascetics as favoring *their* cause, Jovinian interpreted,
more prosaically, as a paean to marital love.[36]
Ambrose[37] and Augustine[38] report that Jovinian also
denied the perpetual virginity of Mary.

The Roman Church condemned Jovinian; informing Christians at Milan about the condemnation, Pope Siricius
argued that Christianity's preference for virginity
should not be taken to imply its despising of marriage.[39]
The Milanese church also excommunicated Jovinian.[40] Ambrose, reporting his church's action to Siricius, seconds
the view that although marriage is a holy state,
virginity is holier.[41] And after issuing an impassioned
defense of Mary's perpetual virginity,[42] Ambrose concludes by hurling the charge of "Manichean" at
Jovinian,[43] a charge incomprehensible if based on the
content of Jovinian's teaching: Jovinian's views on the

goodness of marriage and of eating food our Creator had
provided can in no way be understood to smack of "Manicheanism." The accusation is understandable, however,
when we consider that it was Jovinian who had called the
ascetic party "Manichean,"[44] i.e., that the ascetic views
upheld by Ambrose and his circle came dangerously close
to denying the goodness of the human body, God's creation. (Augustine's *On Marriage and Concupiscence* reveals
that Jovinian had labeled Ambrose a "Manichean" for his
championing of Mary's perpetual virginity.)[45] Thus it
appears that Ambrose decided the best defense was an
offense: simply throw the charge of "Manichean" back on
Jovinian, no matter how poorly it fitted.

In 393, Jerome took up the cudgels against Jovinian.
He ridicules Jovinian's learning and writing style,[46] and
implies that Jovinian enjoys a plush manner of life too
thoroughly to be counted a true monk.[47] This testimony
to Jovinian's celibate status is important, for it reveals that Jovinian himself was a participant in the
ascetic movement. Jovinian, in other words, can be
understood as protesting Jerome's *excessive* ascetic
ardor, not ascetic ideals themselves. It is clear that
Jerome's argument in the *Adversus Jovinianum* that
Jovinian both had called the ascetic party "Manichean"
and had supported his own pro-marriage position by an
appeal to the opening chapters of Genesis. Jerome thus
begins by defending himself against charges of Manicheanism, Marcionitism, and Encratism: he knows as well
as anybody else that God's first command to humans was
"reproduce, multiply, and fill the earth" (Gen. 1:28).[48]
He quotes a sentence from Jovinian's now-lost treatise
that accused the Ambrose-Jerome contingent of Manicheanism
for their alleged "forbidding" of marriage as well as of
certain foods that God had created for man's good use.[49]

Jerome continues by quoting Jovinian's citations from
Genesis 1:28 and Genesis 9:1 (the repetition of God's
blessing on reproduction after the Great Flood)[50] and he
cites Jovinian's appeal to I Timothy 2:13-15 on the creation and Fall of the first couple, with its suggestion
that women would be saved by childbearing.[51]

Jerome's defense against Jovinian's appeal to the
Biblical text is ingenious. He scores his first point by
noting that Adam and Eve were virgins in Paradise and
ceased to be so only after their expulsion.[52] From this
fact, he concludes that marriage occurred only after the
Fall.[53] Second, he claims that God's injunction to
"reproduce and multiply" was necessary so that "the wood"
might grow before God gave the counsel to "cut it down"
by the practice of virginity.[54] To the followers of
Jesus, a different injunction is given: "The time is
short; let those who have wives live as though they had
none."[55] That virginity was a counsel, not a command,
meant that no condemnation of marriage was intended.[56]
As for Jovinian's use of I Timothy 2:15, that women will
be saved in childbearing if they raise their children in
sōphrosynē, Jerome insists that the correct Latin translation is *castitas*, not *sobrietas*, and consequently he
extracts from the passage the interpretation that women
who raise children *for virginity* are saved, the children
thus making up for their mothers' lack of excellence.[57]

Most interesting, Jerome toys with a speculation
about Adam and Eve's relationship in Eden, a speculation
to which Augustine will return and eventually adopt.
Jerome's wording suggests that he is responding to a
position held by Jovinian:[58]

> If you object [*Quod si objeceris...*] that
> before they sinned, male and female were
> sexually differentiated and that they could

have had union without sin, it is not certain
what might have happened. For we are not able
to know God's judgments, nor can we by our
own choice prejudge his sentence. What did
happen is a perfectly clear fact: they who
had remained virgins in Paradise had sexual
intercourse when they were ejected from
Paradise.
Although Jerome does not here call Jovinian by name, it
is likely that he has him in mind, for he frequently
addresses his opponents in the second person in the
Adversus Jovinianum[59] and elsewhere.[60] This passage,
which to the best of my knowledge has received no scholarly elucidation, is of crucial importance for later
developments: it clues us that Jovinian probably was the
first of the later Latin writers to argue the case that
Adam and Eve could, theoretically,· have had sinless
intercourse in Eden.

  Jerome, as always, could not leave well enough alone.
He raves on: all sexual intercourse is unclean in view
of the purity of the body of Christ.[61] Are we to think
that repentant whores, whose memories are stained by the
recollection of "the inevitable and filthy embraces of a
man" are equal to Christian virgins?[62] Since believers
cannot pray and engage in sexual intercourse at the same
time, and since priests must always be praying, priests
cannot engage in marital intercourse.[63] It is the
unclean animals who entered Noah's ark two by two, that
is, as sexual mates.[64] And Jerome's long citation from
a pagan work *On Marriage*, with which he rounds out his
first book against Jovinian, is one of the most virulent-
ly anti-marital pieces in the patristic corpus.[65]

  Jerome's friends at Rome did their best to suppress
the *Adversus Jovinianum*, much to the author's

annoyance.[66] From his defensive letters to Roman supporters, it is obvious that some Christians were accusing
him of Manicheanism, despite his disclaimers at the
beginning of the treatise.[67] Jerome bristles at the
accusation: *he* is no novice in Scripture; *he* knows that
God's first command was "reproduce and multiply and fill
the earth."[68] He testifies in these letters that he has
repeatedly denounced Manichean and Encratitic views of
marriage.[69] He writes that only heretics would condemn
marriage and "tread under foot the ordinance of God,"[70]
and confirms the sentiment of Ambrose, that marriage is
not criminal but burdensome.[71] With such words, Jerome
managed to convince himself--if nobody else--that he had
spoken "in great moderation" on these matters.[72]

One result of the exchange between Jerome and
Jovinian is justly famous: eight years later, Augustine
felt called to answer the challenging question of whether
Christian virginity could be praised without a simultaneous denunciation of marriage.[73] He hints that some
champions of Christian virginity (namely Jerome) had so
denigrated marriage that Jovinian's party seemed to be
defending Christian truth.[74] Augustine answered the
challenge in two works conceived as companion pieces,
composed in 401: *On the Good of Marriage* and *On Holy
Virginity*. What he did not register clearly in these
treatises, but what he perceived soon thereafter, was
that the charges of "Manicheanism" hurled by Jovinian at
the ascetic party had to be addressed through a new
reading of Genesis 1-3. This different, more literal
reading of the Adam-Eve story surfaced before Augustine
knew about Pelagius' views, and some years would elapse
before he tested his wits--and his interpretation of
Genesis--against those of his clever Pelagian opponent,
Julian of Eclanum.

In 388-389, early in his writing career, Augustine
had composed *On Genesis Against the Manichees*. He tells
us in the *Retractions* that the purpose of the work was to
defend the Old Law against the insults of the Manicheans,[75] who mocked Genesis.[76] Commenting on Genesis
1:26 (humans' creation in the "image of God"), the Manicheans scoffingly inquired if God had nostrils, teeth, a
beard, internal organs? And if pious Christians rejected
such anthropomorphisms, the Manicheans countered that
humans were not then in God's "image."[77] Over against
such calumnies, Augustine announced in *On Genesis Against
the Manichees* that he would go beyond a literal exposition of the text to a "figurative and enigmatic"
interpretation.[78] In the process of spiritualizing
Genesis 1-3, however, Augustine very nearly lost a flesh-
and-blood man and woman.

In addition to the other allegorical interpretations
he propounds in this treatise,[79] Augustine explains that
"reproduce and multiply" (Gen. 1:28) referred only to a
spiritual union, not to a carnal one: carnal fecundity
came into existence only after the Fall.[80] Augustine
does not even allow the birds and fishes to reproduce
physically: the reference in Genesis 1:22 to their
fruitfulness is taken to mean that the Jews "multiplied"
greatly after their dispersion among the Gentiles.[81] In
fact, Augustine writes in *On Genesis Against the Manichees* that Genesis 1 does not pertain to bodily creation
at all, which rather occurred only in Genesis 2, but to
the creation of the "causal reasons."[82] The reference
to the woman's bringing forth is understood spiritually
to mean that the couple will bring forth good works.[83]
And Genesis 3 is taken to contain the now-familiar moral
that "manly reason" should not succumb to *cupiditas*.[84]
Moreover, the Old Latin translation of Luke 20:34 ("the

children of *this* world procreate and are procreated"--
suggesting that there was some other world where they did
not) is interpreted to be a reference to Fallen
humanity.[85] Thus the young Augustine understands Genesis
to teach that, had righteousness prevailed, no sexual
union would have taken place in Eden.

Although, as his later works testify, Augustine did
not abandon allegorical exegesis,[86] some aspects of his
interpretation in *On Genesis Against the Manichees* later
caused him grave discomfort. In the *Retractions*, dated
to A.D. 427, Augustine expressly criticizes his earlier
understanding of "reproduce and multiply" as meaning
spiritual fertility. Having weathered the Pelagian
controversy, he now denies that the first humans would
not have had offspring had they not sinned. He dismisses
his early exegesis with the reminder that "an allegorical
interpretation is not the only one warranted by the words
of Genesis."[87]

Indeed, from the vantage point of 427, Augustine cor-
rects the overly spiritualized interpretations of the
works he wrote during the 390s. "Reproduce and multiply"
is now interpreted as meaning *physical* reproduction: he
admits that he should have clarified this point in *On
True Religion* and the *Commentary on the Lord's Sermon on
the Mount*.[88] Commenting on his treatise of 393, *On Faith
and the Creed*, Augustine now emphasizes his belief in a
genuine bodily resurrection;[89] the same point is scored
in relation to *On the Christian Struggle*, dated to 396.[90]
Contrary to what readers might have gathered from his
Commentary on the Lord's Sermon on the Mount, Augustine
affirms that Adam and Eve ate real food even before their
expulsion from Eden.[91] And referring to a passage in his
Contra Faustum, dated to 397-398, he retreats from the
implication that genital organs are disgraceful.[92] There

can be no doubt from this mass of evidence that Augustine
believed both that his earlier interpretations of Genesis
were too spiritual and that they had made him subject to
criticism.

Augustine began to retreat from his earlier exegesis
of Genesis 1-3 only in 401 and the years following. The
process of retrenchment continued until his last work,
left unfinished at his death, the long second treatise
against Julian of Eclanum.[93] Two events in the early
stages of this process are notable: first, Augustine's
questioning of his earlier spiritualized interpretation
appears initially in the treatise *On the Good of Marriage*
in which he attempts to answer Jovinian without falling
into accusations of "Manicheanism" that Jerome had
encountered; and second, immediately after finishing *On
the Good of Marriage* and its companion piece, *On Holy
Virginity*, Augustine began the *De Genesi ad Litteram*, the
treatise in which his despiritualized interpretation
of Eden first occurs. It is not unreasonable--indeed, it
is highly plausible--to think that there may have been
some connection between these two events.

At the beginning of *De Bono Conjugali*, Augustine
claims that there is now (i.e., in the present treatise)
no need to answer the question of how the command to
"reproduce and multiply" would have been carried out in
Eden had Adam and Eve not sinned. He acknowledges that
many differing opinions exist on the subject, but to
ascertain which of them best fits the Scriptural text
would require an extensive discussion which is not part
of Augustine's immediate concern. He does, however, cite
three possible options: (1) that children would have
been created without sexual intercourse (here he adduced
the examples of Mary's virginal conception and of the
chaste reproductive habits of bees who, according to

Augustine, bring forth progeny without intercourse);[94]
(2) that Genesis 1:28 refers to the "fruitfulness" of
mind and virtue; no carnal reproduction would have
occurred without the sin, which brought death in its
train and hence the need for human replacement (Psalm
137:3 [Vg.: "Thou shalt multiply me in my soul unto
virtue"] is cited in support of this spiritualized interpretation); (3) that the bodies of the first humans were
mortal at creation, but would have been granted
immorality if the couple had not sinned (Adam and Eve
would have reproduced by sexual means, and when the earth
was suitably filled, humans would have been clothed with
immortality; as evidence that God could have preserved
humans from death, Augustine cites the case of the
preservation of the Israelites' clothing during their
forty years of wandering).[95] Whether any of these
opinions is correct, or whether yet another is
preferable, Augustine will not explore at this time: it
would be "tedious," he claims[96]--a point about which he
soon changed his mind.

    Even without Augustine's identifying statement in the
Retractions that *On the Good of Marriage* was directed
against Jovinian and was an attempt to praise virginity
without denigrating marriage,[97] the book's content
closely indicates its concern to seek a better resolution
to the Jovinian-Jerome debate. The questions that Augustine addresses in *On the Good of Marriage* are Jovinian's,
as we know them from Jerome's *Adversus Jovinianum*.
First, Jovinian had asked, "What would happen to the
human race if everyone ceased to propagate?" Augustine
responds much like Jerome before him: the City of God,
the end of time, would come more quickly, for which
Christians might well rejoice.[98]

Second, Jovinian had pointedly inquired that if
virginity were the divinely appointed way of life, how
was the patriarchs' abundant procreation to be explained?
Augustine replies that if the patriarchs had been given
a choice, as later Christians were, they also would have
chosen virginity. But lacking that option, they
obediently and dispassionately followed God's command to
reproduce.[99] By their procreation, they fathered a line
that led to the human Jesus.[100] It is the Manicheans,
writes Augustine, not the orthodox Christians, who
criticize the patriarchs as "lovers of women."[101] (Here
we can recall Faustus the Manichean's witty declination
of the invitation offered in Matthew 8:11 to dine with
Abraham: he had no desire to sit at table with men who
slept with their daughters, "led the life of a goat"
among their many wives, and fathered children by
prostitutes.)[102] According to Augustine, we should refrain from deeming ourselves better than those Hebrew
forefathers who were piously carrying out God's will, not
indulging the flesh.[103] By such comments, Augustine
thinks he has silenced the Manichean critics of the
patriarchs.[104] Moreover, he believes that he has also
silenced Jovinian, by explaining here as well as in *On
Holy Virginity* that the virginal state is nonetheless
superior even to chaste and divinely ordained marriage.[105]
Marriage is good, but virginity is better, and *contra*
Jovinian, the rewards in heaven will not be the same for
virgins and for the married.[106] Like Jerome, Augustine
objects to Jovinian's use of the parable of the Laborers
in the Vineyard (Matthew 20:1-16) to buttress the view
that all faithful Christians shall receive the same
heavenly reward, and he too appeals to John 14:22 ("My
Father's house has many mansions") to indicate the
diversity of heavenly rewards awaiting Christian ascetics
and non-ascetics.[107]

It is clear that Augustine now saw the terms of the
debate as set by the two extremes: Jovinian's view that
marriage was equal to virginity on the one hand, and the
Manichean abhorrence of reproduction on the other.
Augustine seeks the middle position.[108] That Augustine
thought Jerome's view tilted a bit precariously toward
the Manichean side is clear from his subtle corrections
of Jerome in these two treatises. Thus he rejects
Jerome's view that marital intercourse impedes prayer,[109]
and he discards Jerome's interpretation of the parable of
the Sower (that the "onehundredfold harvest" meant
virginity, while the "sixtyfold" stood for widowhood, and
the "thirtyfold," for marriage)[110] with the comment that
the gifts of God's grace are too abundant to be com-
pressed into three categories;[111] Jesus mentioned only
three classifications and left the rest for the reflective to determine.[112]

Yet for all his concern to defend the Catholic sexual
ethic against Jovinian's charge of Manicheanism, Augustine in the two treatises of 401 does not exploit the one
verse in Genesis that would be the most helpful in his
defense--"reproduce and multiply"--although this is
surely the passage he had in mind in his lengthy discussion of the patriarchs' obedience to God's command for
reproduction. Only in his *Literal Commentary on Genesis*,
begun directly after *On Holy Virginity*, does Augustine
finally comprehend the full implication of that decisive
verse for Christian teaching about the goodness of creation. It was this recognition, I submit, that prompted
Augustine to modify, if not abandon, his earlier
spiritualizing interpretation of Genesis in favor of a
more literal, earthier reading of Genesis 1:28.

In the *Retractions*, Augustine reports that in 392 or
393 he had already attempted a literal exegesis of Genesis

but had abandoned his project when he reached Genesis
1:26.[113] Only much later did he return to the work, make
some emendations, and issue it as *De Genesi ad Litteram,
Liber Unus Imperfectus*. Since Augustine never reached
Genesis 1:28 in this first attempt to write a "literal"
commentary on Genesis, we shall never know what his
exegesis of "reproduce and multiply" would have been.

Augustine tried again eight years later. By the time
he had reached the third book of *De Genesi ad Litteram*,
he was raising questions about whether the first human
had had a mortal body, whether he needed to eat, and
what the point of reproduction would have been if death
had not entered the world.[114] One answer he considers
is derived from Philo's speculation on such matters:
Genesis 1 speaks only of the inner, spiritual man; bodies
were not created until the Genesis 2 account. Yet in
the same paragraph Augustine returns to the notion that
perhaps bodies as well as spirits *were* created in
Genesis 1.[115] Moreover, Augustine notes, the mere fact
that "reproduce and multiply and fill the earth" is
commanded in Genesis 1 does not necessarily mean that
Adam and Eve had bodies which were mortal, for "someone"
might postulate that their manner of sexual union was not
motivated by lust and hence they would not have been
subject to death. If this had been the case, reproduction would have ceased after the holy society had reached
its full complement. Augustine does not yet claim this
view for himself. It clearly puzzles him, as his remark
indicates: "Although the idea can be postulated, how to
explain it is another question."[116] Augustine is still
contemplating the matter of human bodies in Book VI of
the *De Genesi ad Litteram*: does Genesis 1 refer only to
the creation of man *in potentia*, with bodies created
later (as might be inferred from Genesis 2),[117] or were
both bodies and souls created in Genesis 1?[118]

By Book IX of the *De Genesi ad Litteram*, however, he
has his revised view on bodies in place and addresses
the question already raised for consideration, but not
resolved, in Book III: the possibility of reproduction
in Eden if Adam and Eve had not sinned. It would be
helpful for our argument if we could date Book IX precisely. Scholarly opinion holds that Books X and XI
reflect issues of the Pelagian controversy and thus must
be dated to after 412, but that Books I-IX were written
earlier.[119] Moreover, in Epistle 143, written in 412,
Augustine mentions that he is still writing his literal
commentary on Genesis.[120] But the question of the dating
of Book IX, which contains the material essential for
our purposes, must be re-examined.

Important clues in Book IX support a dating prior to
the Pelagian controversy. First, as indicated above,
Augustine has already in Book III hinted at the position
he adopts in Book IX. Second, in Book IX he repeats
almost verbatim the position on marriage he had developed
in *On the Good of Marriage*, written in 401. Third, he
states in Book IX that he has recently (*nuper*) published
De Bono Conjugali.[121] The question is, just how long a
time span is *nuper* supposed to cover? One clue can be
found in the first sentence of *On Holy Virginity*, also
written in 401: Augustine reports that he has recently
(*nuper*) composed his treatise *On the Good of Marriage*.[122]
His use of *nuper* in this case to mean the immediate past
months suggests that Book IX of the *De Genesi ad Litteram*
could not date from very many years after 401.

Augustine's more literal interpretation of the Eden
story emerges clearly in Book IX of *De Genesi*. He
reminds his readers that he intends to deal with real
events (*rerum gestarum*), interpreted not allegorically
but according to their proper sense (*propriam*

significationem).[123]   In his new exegesis of Adam and
Eve's relationship in Eden, he accomplished his goal.   In
fact the detailed position that Augustine sets forth in
this book is the very one he expounds several years
later, in the heat of the Pelagian controversy.   Augustine writes in *De Genesi* IX that Adam and Eve would have
reproduced in Eden even if they had remained sinless.[124]
Although they had animal bodies,[125] they did not feel
the appetite of carnal pleasure.[126]   They could have commanded their organs of reproduction in the same way that they commanded other bodily parts, such as their feet. They would have conceived offspring without experiencing bodily passion, and
Eve would have given birth without pain.[127]

Thus even before he became embroiled in the Pelagian
controversy, Augustine had developed an interpretation
of Genesis 1-3 that allowed for possible sexual intercourse and physical reproduction in the sinless Eden.   He
carried this view to his later works against the
Pelagians, such as *On Marriage and Concupiscence*[128] and
his first treatise against Julian,[129] and expounded it in
the *City of God*.[130]   In these writings, Augustine will
argue that despite the transfer of original sin to a
child at its conception, marital intercourse is good.   To
support his view, Augustine will posit that had Adam and
Eve remained righteous in Eden, they would have produced
children through the sexual act, albeit without the dis-
rupting pangs of lust.   This supposition, adopted by
medieval and Reformation theologians as part of the
Augustinian inheritance,[131] was Augustine's strongest
rebuttal to those who claimed that his attitude toward
sexual functioning called into question the goodness of
God's handiwork.

Most significant for our purposes, the arguments with
which Augustine supports his exegesis of Genesis 1-3 on

man and woman in the *De Genesi ad Litteram* are those
that he had developed in reply to Jovinian in *De Bono
Conjugali* and *De Sancta Virginitate* of 401: that
although virginity is presently acclaimed, at the earth's
beginning an abundance of births was needed to ensure
the full number of saints; that the infirmity of the
sexes which now threatens to hurl them into "ruinous
turpitude" is checked by the integrity of marriage; that
any sin surrounding marital intercourse is counted as
venial because of the triple good of marriage, offspring,
fidelity, and the sacramental bond.[132] These points, he
writes, are addressed in his earlier work, *De Bono Conjugali*.[133] Having cited these arguments, Augustine next
criticizes the detractors of procreation, and speculates
on Adam and Eve's reproduction if the Fall had not
occurred, with the conclusions given above.

      In other words, the position Augustine developed in
refuting Jovinian's accusation that Catholic asceticism
was Manichean led within a few years to his earthier
exegesis of sexual matters in Eden. The development of
his argument from *De Bono Conjugali* to Book IX of *De
Genesi ad Litteram* thus demonstrates that Augustine had
formulated a new interpretation of Genesis 1-3 before any
Pelagians criticized the implication of his teaching on
original sin: that intercourse, even within chaste
marriage, was tainted. Augustine's Pelagian opponents
would soon attack with the same Biblical verses--
"reproduce and multiply and fill the earth"[134] and "they
shall be one flesh"[135]--that emerged as central in the
debate between Jovinian and the ascetic party. Ambrose
never saw the potential of those decisive verses in
Genesis, never exploited them as he might have in the
face of accusations of Manicheanism. A decade later,
Augustine, the more consummate theologian, gradually

realized the usefulness of those texts in the service of
Catholic teaching. Sensitive to the needs of Christian
polemic, he clipped the wings of his soaring allegories
on Genesis, and in so doing, provided a more earth-bound
interpretation that was to inform all later Christian
sexual ethics.

NOTES

[1]For Ambrose's indebtedness to Philo and Basil of
Caesarea, see John J. Savage, "Introduction," *Saint
Ambrose, Hexameron, Paradise, and Cain and Abel,* Fathers
of the Church 42 (New York: Fathers of the Church,
1961), pp. vi-viii; and F. Homes Dudden, *The Life and
Times of St. Ambrose* (Oxford: Clarendon Press, 1935),
II: 680-681. On Augustine, see Berthold Altaner,
"Augustinus und Basilius der Grosse: Eine Quellen-
kritische Untersuchung," *Revue Bénédictine* 60 (1950):
17-24 (=*Kleine patristische Schriften,* TU 83 [Berlin:
Akademie-Verlag, 1967], pp. 269-276); "Augustinus und
Origenes," *Historisches Jahrbuch* 70 (1951): 15-41
(=*Kleine patristische Schriften,* pp. 224-252); "Augus-
tinus und Philo von Alexandrien," *Zeitschrift für
katholische Theologie* 65 (1941): 81-90 (=*Kleine
patristische Schriften,* pp. 181-193); "Augustinus,
Gregor von Nazianz und Gregor von Nyssa. Quellenkritische
Untersuchungen," *Revue Bénédictine* 61 (1951): 54-62
(=*Kleine patristische Schriften,* pp. 277-285). Also see
E. Amand deMendieta and S.Y. Rudberg, *Eustathius,
Ancienne version latine des 9 Homélies de l'Hexaméron de
Basile de Césarée,* TU 66 (Berlin: Akademie-Verlag,
1958); Michael Müller, *Die Lehre des Hl. Augustinus von
der Paradiesesehe und ihre Auswirkung in der Sexualethik
des 12. und 13. Jahrhunderts bis Thomas von Aquin*
(Regensburg: Verlag Friedrich Pustet, 1951), pp. 9-32;
Yves M.-J. Conjar, "Le Thème de Dieu-Créateur et les
explications de l'Hexaméron dans la tradition
chrétienne," in *L'Homme devant Dieu: Mélanges offerts au
Pere Henri de Lubac. Exégèse et patristique,* Theologie
56 (Lyon-Fourvière: Aubier, 1963), pp. 185-215. Primary
source texts: Basil, *Hexameron;* Gregory of Nyssa, *De
Hominis Opificio; De Virginitate* 12-14; Origen, *In
Genesim; In Genesim Homiliae* I.

[2]See Augustine, *Contra Julianum* I.1.3; 2.4 (PL 44:
642-643); *De Nuptiis et Concupiscentia* II.5.15; 23.38
(PL 44: 445, 458); *Contra Duas Epistolas Pelagianorum*
I.2.4 (PL 44: 552) for evidence that the Pelagians criticized Augustine's teachings on some of the same grounds

as had Jovinian, and that Augustine recognized the
similarity between the two sets of criticisms. Modern
scholars hold that the unidentified monk of Jerome's
Epistle 50 who in A.D. 394 was publicly attacking the
Adversus Jovinianum in Rome was Pelagius: see Georges de
Plinval, *Pêlage, ses écrits, sa vie, et sa réforme*
(Lausanne: Payot, 1943), p. 53; and especially Robert F.
Evans, *Pelagius, Inquiries and Reappraisals* (New York:
Seabury Press, 1967), pp. 31-37.

[3]For the view that Augustine developed his notion of
possible sexual procreation in a sinless Eden out of the
Pelagian controversy, see, for example, Müller, *Die
Lehre*, p. 19, and Kari Elisabeth Børresen, *Subordination
and Equivalence. The Nature and Role of Woman in Augustine and Thomas Aquinas*, trans. Charles H. Talbot
(Washington, D.C.: University Press of America, 1981;
French original, 1968), p. 38. But as Peter Brown has
convincingly shown, the Pelagian issue was still "very
distant in 410" for Augustine; it was probably the Roman
refugee circles in North Africa who brought wider knowl-
edge of Pelagius' teaching to Augustine's attention.
Only at the end of A.D. 411 did discussion over
Pelagianism arise in Carthage. See *Augustine of Hippo.
A Biography* (Berkeley and Los Angeles: University of
California Press, 1969), pp. 343-345; idem, "Pelagius and
His Supporters: Aims and Environments," *Journal of
Theological Studies*, n.s., 19 (1968): 94, 110 (=*Religion
and Society in the Age of Saint Augustine* [New York:
Harper & Row, 1972], pp. 185, 203); idem, "The Patrons of
Pelagius: The Roman Aristocracy Between East and West,"
Journal of Theological Studies, n.s., 21 (1970): 64
(=*Religion and Society*, p. 217).

[4]*Confessiones* VI.4 (CCL 27: 76-77).

[5]*Confessiones* V.14; VI.4 (CCL 27: 71, 76-77). On
Augustine's exegesis in relation to the Manichees, see
Julien Ries, "La Bible chez Saint Augustin et chez les
manichéens," *Revue des Etudes Augustiniennes* 7 (1961):
231-243; 9 (1963): 201-215; 10 (1964): 309-329; and the
numerous references cited therein; also Arthur Allgeier,
"Der Einfluss der Manichäismus auf die exegetische
Fragestellung bei Augustin," in Martin Grabmann and
Joseph Mausbach, eds., *Aurelius Augustinus. Die Fest-
schrift der Görres-Gesellschaft zum 1500. Todestage des
Heiligen Augustinus* (Köln: J.P. Bachem, 1930), pp. 1-13.

[6]Genesis 1:28; 2:24.

[7]E.g., see *De Paradiso* 2.11 (PL 14: 195-196), cf. Philo, *De Opificio Mundi* 59 and *Legum Allegoriae* I.29; *De Paradiso* 4.25 (PL 14: 301); cf. Philo, *Quaestiones in Genesin* 1.14; *De Paradiso* 15.73 (PL 14: 329); cf. Philo, *De Opificio Mundi* 152.

[8]*De Paradiso* 3.14-18 (PL 14: 296-299).

[9]*De Paradiso* 11.51 (PL 14: 316).

[10]*De Paradiso* 2.11 (PL 14: 295-296); 15.73 (PL 14: 329).

[11]Eve was to be a "helper" in generation (*De Paradiso* 10.48 [PL 14: 315]); the animals are brought to Adam so that he can observe that they are in two sexes and thus contemplate his future lot (*De Paradiso* 11.49 [PL 14: 315-316]).

[12]*Ep.* 45 to Sabinus (PL 16: 1191-1194), written shortly after the *Hexameron* and thus dated to A.D. 387 or 389.

[13]*Ep.* 45.4, 11 (PL 16: 1191, 1192).

[14]*Ep.* 45.17 (PL 16: 1194).

[15]Savage, "Introduction," p. vi; Homes Dudden, *St. Ambrose*, II: 680.

[16]Ambrose, *Hexameron* I.8.30 (PL 14: 150-151).

[17]Ambrose, *Hexameron* I.8.31 (PL 14: 151).

[18]Ambrose, *Hexameron* III.7.32 (PL 14: 181-182).

[19]Ambrose, *Hexameron* V.7.19 (PL 14: 228).

[20]Ambrose, *Hexameron* VI.8.47 (PL 14: 276).

[21]In *De Officiis Ministrorum*, dated to A.D. 386, Ambrose's interest in explaining the Eden tale revolves around social commentary: God's creation of a woman for the man shows the divine intent that humans live in a society (I.28.134-135 [PL 16: 67-68]; I.32.169 [PL 16: 78]).

[22]Brief references to the following points can be found: the fruit trees of Eden mean hospitality (*De Viduis* 1.5 [PL 16: 248-249]); virgins should keep their

doors closed to strangers, as Eve did not (*De Virginitate*
13.81 [PL 16: 300]); the "one flesh" passage is taken as
an injunction against second marriage (*De Viduis* 15.89
[PL 16: 276]). Ambrose rebukes those who condemn
marriage for the wrong reasons (probably the Manicheans),
but he does not put the Genesis account to use in refuting Manichean views of marriage: *De Virginibus* I.7.34
(PL 16: 209). For Ambrose's sources (Cyprian and
Athanasius), see Yves-Marie Duval, "L'Originalité du *De
virginibus* dans le mouvement ascétique occidental.
Ambroise, Cyprien, Athanase," in Duval, *Ambroise de
Milan. XVIᵉ Centenaire de son élection épiscopal* (Paris:
Etudes Augustiniennes, 1974), pp. 21-53.

²³*De Institutione Virginis* 3.22 (PL 16: 325).

²⁴*De Institutione Virginis* 4.25-26 (PL 16: 325-326).

²⁵*De Institutione Virginis* 4.29 (PL 16: 326).

²⁶*De Institutione Virginis*, beginning with 5.33 (PL
16: 328ff.).

²⁷*De Institutione Virginis* 5.35 (misnumbered as 5.36)
(PL 16: 328). The opponent's name, known from other
works, was Bonosus of Naissus. In 391 or 392, a synod of
bishops from upper Italy, over which Ambrose presided,
condemned Bonosus' teaching and remanded him to the
Macedonian hierarchy in his home territory for the
adjudication of his case. The *Epistola de Causa Bonosi*
is variously attributed to Ambrose (PL 16: 1222-1224) or
to Siricius (*Ep.* 9 [PL 13: 1173-1174]). For the attribu-
tion to Siricius, see Wilhelm Haller, *Iovinianus. Die
Fragmente seiner Schriften, die Quellen zu seiner
Geschichte, sein Leben und seine Lehre*, TU 17.2 (Leipzig:
J.C. Hinrichs, 1897), pp. 157-158; for an argument that
the letter should be attributed to Ambrose, and has
resemblances to the *De Institutione Virginis*, see Duval,
"L'Originalité," p. 59 n. 247. On Bonosus, see Homes
Dudden, *Saint Ambrose*, II: 401-403; G. Bardy, "Bonosus,"
Dictionnaire histoire et de géographie ecclésiastiques
(Paris: Librarie Letouzey et Ané, 1937), IX: 1096-1097.
On the council, see *Epistola de Causa Bonosi* 1-2. Dating
of the Council to A.D. 391 in Haller, *Iovinianus*, p. 157;
and to the end of 391 or early 392 in Gerhard Rauschen,
*Jahrbücher der Christlichen Kirche unter dem Kaiser Theo-
dosius dem Grossen. Versuch einer Erneuerung der Annales
Ecclesiastici des Baronius für die Jahre 378-395* (Freiburg im Breisgau: Herder'sche Verlagshandlung, 1897),
pp. 340-341.

[28]*De Institutione Virginis* 5.36-13.81 (PL 16: 329-339); cf. *Adversus Helvidium* (PL 23: 193-216), and see C.W. Neumann, *The Virgin Birth in the Works of Saint Ambrose* (Freiburg im B.: University Press, 1962), pp. 237ff.

[29]Ambrose, *Exhortatio Virginitatis* 6.36 (PL 16: 362), probably dated to A.D. 394.

[30]Ambrose, *Ep.* 63.33 (PL 16: 1249-1250), dated to A.D. 396.

[31]Ambrose, *Ep.* 63.39 (PL 16: 1251); cf. Romans 14:2.

[32]Jerome, *Adversus Jovinianum* I.3 (PL 23: 224). Interestingly, Jerome equates Jovinian's position with that of the ancient Stoic, Zeno (that there are no differentiations within the two categories of virtue, on the one hand, and vice, on the other); *Adversus Jovinianum* II.33, 35 (PL 23: 345, 349).

[33]Jerome, *Adversus Jovinianum* I.3 (PL 23: 224).

[34]*Adversus Jovinianum* I.5 (PL 23: 225-227).

[35]*Adversus Jovinianum* I.5 (PL 23: 227).

[36]*Adversus Jovinianum* I.30-31 (PL 23: 262-266). Also see Jovinian's non-ascetic interpretation of the parable of the Laborers in the Vineyard (all the workers receive one and the same reward) in *Adversus Jovinianum* II.32 (PL 23: 344) and his deviant interpretation of the "many mansions" of John 14:2 to mean "churches scattered throughout the world," rather than as tiers of reward in heaven, as the ascetic party interpreted the verse (*Adversus Jovinianum* II.28 [PL 23: 338-339]).

[37]Ambrose, *Ep.* 42.4 (PL 16: 1172), referring to members of the party of Jovinian who deny degrees of merit and say marriage and virginity have their same reward (*Ep.* 42.2 [PL 16: 1172]).

[38]Augustine, *De Haeresibus* 82 (PL 42: 45-46).

[39]Siricius, *Epistola ad Mediolanensem Ecclesiam* 5 (PL 16: 1171). Siricius sent a similar letter to "diverse bishops": *Ep.* 7 (PL 13: 1168-1172). On these events and those that followed, see John Gavin Nolan, *Jerome and Jovinian*, The Catholic University of America Studies in Sacred Theology, 2d ser., 97 (Washington, D.C.: The

Catholic University of America Press, 1956), pp. 21-23; J. Brochet, *Saint Jérome et ses ennemis* (Paris: Albert Fontemoing, 1905), pp. 70-71 (especially for dating); Ferd. Cavallera, *Saint Jérôme. Sa Vie et son oeuvre*, Spicilegium Sacrum Lovaniense 1 (Louvain: "Spicilegium Sacrum Lovaniense" Bureaux, 1922), I: 150-164; Ilona Opelt, *Hieronymus' Streitschriften* (Heidelberg: Carl Winter's Universitätsverlag, 1973), p. 37; Haller, *Iovinianus*, pp. 126-128; J.N.D. Kelly, *Jerome. His Life, Writings, and Controversies* (New York: Harper & Row, 1975), pp. 179-187; Homes Dudden, *St. Ambrose*, II: 393-397.

[40]Ambrose, *Ep.* 42.13 (PL 16: 1177); the dating of the council has been debated, but probably occurred in A.D. 392 or early 393, see Homes Dudden, *St. Ambrose*, II: 393 n. 1; Rauschen, *Jahrbücher*, pp. 378-379; Jean-Remy Palanque, *Saint Ambroise et l'empire romain. Contribution à l'histoire des rapports de l'église et de l'etat à la fin du quatrième siècle* (Paris: E. de Boccard, 1933), pp. 545-546.

[41]Ambrose, *Ep.* 42.3 (PL 16: 1172-1173).

[42]Ambrose, *Ep.* 42.4-6 (PL 16: 1173-1174).

[43]Ambrose, *Ep.* 42.13 (PL 16: 1176).

[44]Jerome, *Adversus Jovinianum* I.5 (PL 23: 227); Augustine, *De Nuptiis et Concupiscentia* II.23.28 (PL 44: 458).

[45]Augustine, *De Nuptiis et Concupiscentia* II.5.15 (PL 44: 444-445); more generally, Jovinian labeled the Catholic party "Manichean" for upholding the perpetual virginity of Mary: see Augustine, *Contra Julianum* I.2.4 (PL 44: 643).

[46]*Adversus Jovinianum* I.1, 3 (PL 23: 221, 222-223).

[47]*Adversus Jovinianum* I.40 (PL 23: 280). Jerome calls Jovinian an "Epicurus" (I.1; II.36 [PL 23: 221, 349]). He also reports that Jovinian was courted by wealthy Roman nobles (II.37 [PL 23: 351-352]).

[48]Jerome, *Adversus Jovinianum* I.3 (PL 23: 223).

[49]Jerome, *Adversus Jovinianum* I.5 (PL 23: 227).

[50]Jerome, *Adversus Jovinianum* I.5 (PL 23: 225-226).

[51]Jerome, *Adversus Jovinianum* I.27 (PL 23: 259-260).

[52]*Adversus Jovinianum* I.4 (PL 23: 225).

[53]*Adversus Jovinianum* I.16 (PL 23: 246).

[54]*Adversus Jovinianum* I.16 (PL 23: 246).

[55]*Adversus Jovinianum* I.24 (PL 23: 255); I Corinthians 7:29.

[56]*Adversus Jovinianum* I.12 (PL 23: 237); cf. I Corinthians 7:25, 26.

[57]*Adversus Jovinianum* I.27 (PL 23: 260); note a similar interpretation in I.37 (PL 23: 274).

[58]*Adversus Jovinianum* I.29 (PL 23: 263).

[59]*Adversus Jovinianum* I.28 "asserveraveris" (PL 23: 261); II.6 "dixeris" (PL 23: 306); II.24 "tu...proponis" (PL 23: 334); II.25 "audebisne" (PL 23: 336); II.30 "putasne" (PL 23: 341); II.31 "niteris," "negabis" (PL 23: 342); I.36 "dices," "vereris" (PL 23: 271).

[60]Throughout the *Contra Vigilantium* 5-16 (PL 23: 357-368), Jerome addresses his opponent in the second person. In the *Adversus Helvidium*, Jerome sometimes describes his opponent in the third person and sometimes addresses him directly in the second person (PL 23: 193-216).

[61]*Adversus Jovinianum* I.20 (PL 23: 249): "omnis coitus immunda sit."

[62]*Adversus Jovinianum* I.33 (PL 23: 267).

[63]*Adversus Jovinianum* I.34 (PL 23: 269); suggested for lay people as well in I.7 (PL 23: 230).

[64]*Adversus Jovinianum* I.16 (PL 23: 246).

[65]*Adversus Jovinianum* I.47 (PL 23: 288-291). For Jerome's sources, see Pierre Courcelle, *Les Lettres grecques en Occident de Macrobe à Cassiodore* (Paris: E. de Boccard, 1948), pp. 60-62; Opelt, *Hieronymus' Streitschriften*, p. 51 n. 108, and references therein.

[66]Jerome, *Epp.* 48-49 (CSEL 54: 347-387).

[67]Jerome, *Ep.* 49.2 (CSEL 54: 352-355); cf. *Adversus Jovinianum* I.3 (PL 23: 223).

[68]Jerome, *Ep.* 49.2 (CSEL 54: 353).

[69]Jerome, *Ep.* 49.8, 9 (CSEL 54: 361-363, 364).

[70]Jerome, *Ep.* 49.11 (CSEL 54: 366).

[71]Jerome, *Ep.* 49.14 (CSEL 54: 374-375); cf. Ambrose, *De Viduis* 13.81 (PL 16: 273). The fact that Jerome took part of his argument against digamy and for fasting directly from Tertullian perhaps encouraged his sense that he was firmly grounded in the Latin theological tradition; see Fr. Schultzen, "Die Benutzung der Schriften Tertullians *de monogamia* und *de ieiunio* bei Hieronymus *adv. Iovinianum*," *Neue Jahrbucher für Deutsche Theologie* 3 (1894): 387-502, for parallel passages.

[72]Jerome, *Ep.* 49.11 (CSEL 54: 365).

[73]Augustine, *Retractions* II.48.1 (CSEL 36: 157).

[74]Ibid.

[75]Augustine, *Retractions* I.9.1 (CSEL 36: 47). In *De Genesi ad Litteram* VIII.2.5 (PL 34: 373), Augustine writes that in his earlier commentary on Genesis against the Manicheans, he had wanted to show how the New Testament faith is contained in the Old. Since he did not then think all the stories from the Hebrew Scriptures could be taken literally, he interpreted them figuratively; in his present endeavor, however, he says he will take the texts "in their own sense." See also Gilles Pelland, *Cinq Etudes d'Augustin sur le debut de la Genèse* (Tournai: Desclée & Cie; Montréal: Bellarmin, 1972), pp. 17-22.

[76]For Manichean complaints about the book of Genesis and the Old Testament, see, for example, Augustine, *Contra Faustum* IV.1; VI.1; XXII.1, 3, 5 (PL 42: 217, 227, 243, 401, 402, 403). The Manicheans' interest in cosmology probably contributed to Augustine's early and continuing interest in Genesis; see Allgeier, "Der Einfluss," p. 7.

[77]Augustine, *De Genesi contra Manichaeos* I.17.27 (PL 34: 186).

[78]Augustine, *De Genesi contra Manichaeos* II.2.3 (PL 34: 197).

[79]See *De Genesi contra Manichaeos* I.17.28; II.10.13-14; 21.32 (PL 34: 187, 203-204, 212-213).

[80]*De Genesi contra Manichaeos* I.19.30 (PL 34: 187).

[81]*De Genesi contra Manichaeos* I.23.39 (PL 34: 191-192).

[82]*De Genesi contra Manichaeos* II.7.9 (PL 34: 200-201); see Børresen, *Subordination,* p. 16, for discussion.

[83]*De Genesi contra Manichaeos* II.11.15 (PL 34: 204).

[84]*De Genesi contra Manichaeos* II.14.20-21 (PL 34: 206-207).

[85]*De Genesi contra Manichaeos* I.19.30 (PL 34: 187): "Filii enim saeculi hujus generant et generantur...."

[86]See, e.g., *De Civitate Dei* XVIII.44 (CCL 48: 640-641); *De Trinitate* XV.9.15 (CCL 50A: 480-482).

[87]*Retractiones* I.9.4 (CSEL 36: 49).

[88]*Retractiones* I.12.12 (CSEL 36: 63-64), commenting on *De Vera Religione* 46.88; *Retractiones* I.18.8 (CSEL 36: 91), commenting on *De Sermone Domini in Monte* I.15.41.

[89]*Retractiones* I.16.2 (CSEL 36: 84-85), commenting on *De Fide et Symbolo* 10.24.

[90]*Retractiones* II.29.2 (CSEL 36: 134-135), commenting on *De Agone* 32.34.

[91]*Retractiones* I.18.13 (CSEL 36: 95), commenting on *De Sermone Domini in Monte* II.17.56.

[92]*Retractiones* II.33.5 (CSEL 36: 141), commenting on *Contra Faustum* 29.4.

[93]*Opus Imperfectum contra Julianum* IV.19, 39 (PL 45: 1347, 1360); VI.22 (PL 45: 1533); Augustine concedes that maybe there was a sexual impulse in Eden, but asserts that it would have been different from what humans have today. See Yves de Montcheuil, "La Polémique de Saint Augustin contre Julien d'Eclane d'après l'*Opus imperfectum*," *Recherches de Science Religieuse* 44 (1956): 204-206.

[94]A view that Augustine probably derived from Virgil; see *Georgics* IV.197-202.

[95]*De Bono Conjugali* 2.2 (PL 40: 373-375); Deuteronomy 29:5.

[96]*De Bono Conjugali* 3.2 (PL 40: 375): "...quaerero ac disserere longum est."

[97]*Retractiones* II.48.1 (CSEL 36: 156-157). I thus oppose the position of Børresen (*Subordination*, p. 37), who thinks the *De Bono Conjugali* is meant to refute Manichean views. The work indeed does this, but its central aim, by Augustine's own testimony and by the questions that give structure to the book, is to refute Jovinian.

[98]*De Bono Conjugali* 10.10 (PL 40: 381). The same question is asked in *Adversus Jovinianum* I.36; Jerome's reply is that virgins receive the heavenly life on earth (PL 23: 271, 273).

[99]*De Bono Conjugali* 13.15; 16.18; 17.19; 19.22 (PL 40: 384, 386-387, 388-389).

[100]*De Bono Conjugali* 26.34 (PL 40: 395-396).

[101]*De Bono Conjugali* 21.26 (PL 40: 391).

[102]*Contra Faustum* XXII.5; XXIII.1 (PL 42: 403, 509-511).

[103]*De Bono Conjugali* 22.27 (PL 40: 391-392).

[104]*De Bono Conjugali* 25.33 (PL 40: 395).

[105]*De Bono Conjugali* 23.28 (PL 40: 392-393); *De Sancta Virginitate* 9.9 (PL 40: 400).

[106]*De Sancta Virginitate* 19.19; 20.19 (PL 40: 405).

[107]*De Sancta Virginitate* 26.26 (PL 40: 410); cf. *Adversus Jovinianum* II.28, 32 (PL 23: 338-339, 344).

[108]*De Sancta Virginitate* 19.19 (PL 40: 405). Later, when Augustine's opposition shifted, he sought a mean between Manicheanism and Pelagianism. See *Contra Duas Epistolas Pelagianorum* II.2.2; III.9.25; IV.3.3 (PL 44: 572-573, 607-608, 611); *De Nuptiis et Concupiscentia*

II.23.38 (PL 44: 458). Yet in his last work, the *Opus Imperfectum contra Julianum*, Augustine returns to seeking a mean between Mani and Jovinian (I.101 [PL 45: 1116-1117]).

[109]*De Bono Conjugali* 20.23 (PL 40: 389); cf. *Adversus Jovinianum* I.7.34 (PL 23: 230, 269).

[110]*Adversus Jovinianum* I.3 (PL 23: 223); *Epp.* 22.15 (CSEL 54: 163); 49.2 (CSEL 54: 353).

[111]*De Sancta Virginitate* 45.46 (PL 40: 423).

[112]*De Sancta Virginitate* 46.46 (PL 40: 424).

[113]*Retractiones* I.17.1 (CSEL 36: 86-87); for the text of the *De Genesi ad Litteram Opus Imperfectum*, see PL 34: 219-246.

[114]*De Genesi ad Litteram* III.21.33 (PL 34: 293).

[115]*De Genesi ad Litteram* III.22.34 (PL 34: 293-294).

[116]*De Genesi ad Litteram* III.21.33 (PL 34: 293).

[117]*De Genesi ad Litteram* VI.5.7-8; 18.29 (PL 34: 342, 351).

[118]*De Genesi ad Litteram* VI.7.12 (PL 34: 343-344).

[119]P. Agaësse and A. Solignac, "Introduction génerale," *La Genèse au sens literal I-VII*, Oeuvres de Saint Augustin, 7 ser., t. 4, pp. 28-31; J. Mausbach, *Die Ethik des Hl. Augustinus*, 2d ed., (Freiburg im B: Herder, 1929), I: 319--Book IX is dated to A.D. 410.

[120]Augustine, *Ep.* 143.4 (CSEL 44: 254).

[121]*De Genesi ad Litteram* IX.7. 12 (PL 34: 397): "Unde quia satis disseruimus in eo libro quem de Bono Conjugali nuper edidimus...."

[122]*De Sancta Virginitate* 1.1 (PL 40: 397): "Librum de Bono Conjugali nuper edidimus...." A check of Augustine's letters from the years A.D. 400-410 yields no assistance in determining Augustine's usage of "nuper."

[123]*De Genesi ad Litteram* IX.14.24 (PL 34: 402).

[124]*De Genesi ad Litteram* IX.3.6; 9.14 (PL 34: 395, 398).

^{125}*De Genesi ad Litteram* IX.10.17 (PL 34: 399).

^{126}*De Genesi ad Litteram* IX.10.16 (PL 34: 398).

^{127}*De Genesi ad Litteram* IX.10.18 (PL 34: 399).

^{128}*De Nuptiis et Concupiscentia* II.31.53 (PL 44: 467-468).

^{129}*Contra Julianum* III.7.15; 25.27 (PL 44: 709, 731-732).

^{130}*De Civitate Dei* XIV.23, 26 (CCL 48: 444-446, 449-450). See G. Bardy, "Notes complémentaires," *La Cité de Dieu*, Bibliothèque Augustinienne, 5 ser., 35 (Paris: Desclée de Brouwer, 1959), pp. 539-542, for Augustine's views on the mode of procreation in a sinless Eden, according to the *City of God*.

^{131}For example, Thomas Aquinas, *Summa Theologica* Pt. I, Q. 98, arts. 1, 2; Martin Luther, *Lectures on Genesis*, Gen. 2:18.

^{132}*De Genesi ad Litteram* IX.7.12 (PL 34: 397): these points are covered throughout *De Bono Conjugali*, for example, in 3.3; 4.4; 5.5; 6.6; 9.9; 10.11; 11.12; 13.15; 15.17; 17.19 (PL 40: 375, 376, 377, 380, 381-382, 383-384, 385, 386-387).

^{133}*De Genesi ad Litteram* IX.7.12 (PL 34: 397).

^{134}*De Nuptiis et Concupiscentia* I.5.6; 21.23; II.4.12; 9.21; 26.42 (PL 44: 416, 427, 443, 448, 460-461); *Contra Julianum* III.26.60; IV.9.53; 14.69 (PL 44: 732, 764, 772).

^{135}*De Nuptiis et Concupiscentia* II.32.54 (PL 44: 468); *Contra Julianum* III.10.20 (PL 44: 712).

THE USES OF THE SONG OF SONGS:
ORIGEN AND THE LATER LATIN FATHERS

Society of Biblical Literature (1981)

I

Twentieth-century scholars have characterized Origen as mystic, spiritualist, philosopher, as Alexandrian Christian Platonist and "true Gnostic,"[1] yet if we concern ourselves with the history of exegesis, we must apply the historian's tools--as well as the theologian's and the philosopher's--to the subject of our research. Recent scholarly interest has shifted from Origen the mystic to Origen the preacher and exegete, and in doing so has transported us from Alexandria to Caesarea. The Caesarean setting offered Origen fresh challenges that are reflected in his exegetical writings. Scholars' renewed interest in Origen's exegesis and their heightened sensitivity to its *Sitz im Leben* thus form the background to my discussion of his *Commentary* and *Homilies on the Song of Songs*,[2] considered his masterwork by some ancient authorities.[3]

Nonetheless, the motifs in Origen's works on the Song of Songs that illuminate his own historical situation were the very ones most often ignored by later readers with different concerns. For them, the historically "transportable" motif of the soul's relation with Christ was more significant than the more timebound themes pertaining to Jews and Christians (both Catholic and

heretical) in third-century Caesarea. Indeed, the historically interesting features of Origen's exegesis of
the Song of Songs were already irrelevant to the Latin
Fathers of the later fourth century. Although they
probed the Song of Songs for verses pertinent to their
own religious disputes, their appropriation of Origen's
arguments is more selective than we might expect, given
his enormous importance as an exegete and the keen
interest such fourth-century Fathers as Jerome and
Ambrose displayed in his writings.

To be sure, Origen was not the first of the Greek
Fathers to write on the Song of Songs. Hippolytus had
preceded him by a few decades, but of his commentary
there remain only fragments.[4] Origen probably knew the
substance of Hippolytus' commentary,[5] which explicated
the economy of salvation from before creation to the
apostolic mission in the form of a dialogue between
Christ and the Church.[6] Origen develops this dialogue,
but creates another between the individual soul and
Christ.[7]

The Greek text of Origen's writings on the Song of
Songs, like so many of his books,[8] is now lost. Fortunately, parts of his *Commentary* and *Homilies on the Song
of Songs* are extant in Latin translations by Rufinus and
Jerome.[9] Unlike some of their predecessors,[10] modern
researchers agree that although the canons by which
Jerome and Rufinus translated are not ours, their translations preserve at least the substance of Origen's
exegesis.[11] Jerome's translation of the *Homilies*, done
at Rome in about A.D. 383,[12] predates Rufinus' translation of the *Commentary* by about twenty-seven years.[13]
However, the Latin *Homilies* comment only up to Song of
Songs 2:14, and the *Commentary*, preserving less than half
of the ten-book original,[14] covers a scant verse more.

Since only fragments exist of earlier Latin commentaries
on the Song of Songs,[15] Jerome's translation of Origen's
Homilies remains the first surviving Latin work on the
Song of Songs.[16]

Origen's most recent chronologist, Pierre Nautin,
dates the *Homilies on the Song of Songs* to A.D. 239-242
when Origen was in Caesarea. Origen composed the first
books of the *Commentary on the Song of Songs* on a journey
to Athens in 245 and completed the work upon his return
to Caesarea in 246-247.[17] In addition, a few fragments
survive of another treatise on the Song of Songs that
Origen wrote in his youth.[18] The *Homilies* and *Commentary*
were probably addressed to different audiences: whereas
the simple *Homilies* rely heavily on moral and spiritual
exhortation, the longer *Commentary* is more theologically
complex.[19] Jerome recognized the difference between the
two works when he agreed to translate two *Homilies* for
Pope Damasus as a "sample" of Origen's exegesis, but
regretted that attempting the *Commentary* would entail too
much effort and expense[20] (probably a hint that Damasus'
patronage would be welcome). That Origen would write two
works of varying difficulty on the same Biblical book
accords well with his view that Christianity should be
explicated to naive believers as well as to Christian
"gnostics."[21]

According to Origen, "Solomon" had composed the Song
of Songs as an epithalamium couched in the style of a
drama.[22] The Septuagint (at least the Codex Sinaiticus)
and perhaps some manuscripts of the Vetus Latina had
prompted this dramatic interpretation by assigning the
verses to various characters: a bride, a groom, and
choruses of young men and women.[23] Origen appropriates
this scheme for the "literal" exegesis[24] that he offers
at the beginning of each section of the *Commentary*. The

bride's longing for her absent groom, their meetings and
conversations with their companions, comprise the story
line of the alleged drama. Although Origen himself
admitted that the story itself was not very profitable
(it did not even contain a continuous narrative), he
thought that this defect should encourage a deeper probe
for the story's hidden spiritual truth.[25] Beyond the
literal meaning lie allegories pertaining to Christ and
the Church, Christ and the individual soul.[26] What
Origen meant by literal exegesis, however, is not what we
mean. For example, in an allegedly literal interpretation, he identifies the Bridegroom's father as God.[27]

Themes familiar from Origen's other writings, including his earlier Alexandrian works, appear in the *Commentary* and the *Homilies* as well. Thus he claims that as
pagan writers borrowed Hebrew wisdom,[28] so Christians
utilize (but surpass) the precepts of pagan natural and
moral philosophy.[29] He strongly champions personal
responsibility for sinful behavior: we, like Pharaoh,
are to blame for our own "hardening."[30] The theme of
progress in the spiritual life is omnipresent: although
the Church accepts simple believers as well as "the perfect," she encourages the development of the former into
the latter. Thus, in the *Homilies*, Origen asserts that
although the maidens of the chorus (representing the simple
believers[31]) do not yet enjoy the "breasts" of the
Groom[32] that contain treasures of wisdom and knowledge,[33]
he trusts that they will progress from their childish
understanding to a love of the Groom's "breasts."[34] Such
is Origen's confidence in Christianity as *paideia*.[35]

Typical Platonic themes abound in Origen's works on
the Song of Songs, as elsewhere in his writings. The
distinction between archetype and image is played out in
a variety of ways. The "likenesses of gold" (1:11) made

by the Bridegroom's friends for the Bride signify that
the Law and the ritual of the Old Testament were mere
shadows of the truth, the genuine "gold" existing
incorporeally in heaven.[36] In designating humans as "the
image and likeness of God," the Bible also attests the
Platonic notion that earthly things are copies of
heavenly realities.[37] And Origen notes that the Christian belief in the soul's yearning for the intelligible
world above was prefigured by Greek sages who composed
dialogues on the ascent of the soul through love.[38] Thus
Origen's much-noted Platonism is also evident in his
writings on the Song of Songs.

Yet these points are secondary to the distinguishing
motif that grounds Origen's exegesis in a particular time
and place: the union of Jew and Gentile in the Christian
Church. When read with an historian's eye, Origen's
Commentary on the Song of Songs resembles nothing so much
as Romans 9-11, in which Paul's argument for the union of
Jew and Gentile in Christianity reaches its climax.[39]
Later generations, eager to uncover the "mystical"
aspects of Origen's exegesis, abandoned the historical
significance of this point, as shall become clear below.

Origen's treatment of the Pauline theme nonetheless
raises questions for the modern interpreter. Whereas
Romans 9-11 presupposes an identifiable historical moment
(the difficulties occasioned by Gentile recruitment into
an initially Jewish sect), the situation confronting
Origen is more difficult to assess. The historian must
wrestle with two questions: were Origen's comments on
Judaism and his exegesis of the Old Testament prompted by
controversy with actual Jews? Did his stress on the
goodness of the Old Testament and its God counter a
Gnostic or a Marcionite threat?

Scholarly opinion varies on the degree to which
debate with Jews stimulated Origen's work. Pierre
Nautin, for example, has argued that although Origen was
certainly indebted to Jews for points of Scriptural
interpretation, we should not overemphasize the polemical
nature of their relations:[40] Origen's task at Caesarea
was to instruct Christians, not to convert Jews,[41] and
in any case, his relations with rabbis were "sporadic."[42]

Other scholars emphatically stress the positive
significance of Origen's contact with Jews for the
development of his exegesis. Building on ancient testimonies (some from Origen himself) that at Alexandria a
converted Jew served as his Hebrew teacher,[43] that he had
discussions with Jews,[44] and that he cites the opinion
of a contemporary Jew named "Hiullus,"[45] modern commentators have explored Origen's involvement with Jews and
Jewish literature. They posit that Origen must have
employed Jews, or at least Jewish Christians, to copy the
columns of the Hexapla, since his own knowledge of Hebrew
was too limited for him to judge correctly appropriate
divisions in the Hebrew text or to match it with the
parallel columns of Greek.[46] In stimulating articles,
Reuven Kimelman and David Halperin have convincingly
demonstrated the interplay between Origen's exegetical
work and Jewish commentary upon Scripture.[47]

Moreover, N.R.M. deLange has provided strong evidence
for the challenge that the Jewish presence in Caesarea
posed to the Christian community there.[48] DeLange shows
how Origen fought to counter the Jewish syncretism to
which his flock was prone: members of his congregation
attended synagogue on Saturday as well as church on
Sunday, and showed more than an academic interest in
Jewish holidays, fasts, and circumcision.[49] Origen re-
buked Christians who observed Yom Kippur,[50] celebrated

Passover with unleavened bread, adorned themselves for
the Jewish Sabbath.[51] Evidence of these Judaizing
tendencies among Origen's congregation buttresses Lee
Levine's conviction that Judaism was an active force in
Caesarea at this time.[52] The development of Caesarea as
a center of rabbinic studies coincided precisely with
Origen's Caesarean sojourn: Rabbi Hoshaya, whom Levine
calls "the most prominent rabbinic authority of his
generation," began his activities in Caesarea around
A.D. 230.[53]

Did the Jewish presence in Caesarea influence
Origen's works on the Song of Songs? Quite possibly.
Scholars of ancient Judaism agree that Jews before
Origen's time had interpreted the Song of Songs as an
allegory of God's love for Israel,[54] and that some points
in Origen's exegesis may indeed reflect his response to
Jewish interpretations of the book.[55] (The opening lines
of the first *Homily* paraphrase Rabbi Akiba's maxim, "All
the Writings are holy, but the Song of Songs is the Holy
of Holies."[56]) In what follows, I shall argue that
Origen's comments on Jews and Gentiles in his writings on
the Song of Songs are not mere antiquarian excurses on
first-century Christianity, but are relevant to the
Caesarean Church in his own time. In this regard, my
assessment and that of other contemporary scholars re-
vives the insights of Harnack,[57] Bardy,[58] and other
commentators[59] that have sometimes been bypassed by later
interpreters of Origen.

A second question for the historian is whether
Origen's stress on the unity of Jew and Gentile in the
Church and God's "call" to each group--a prominent theme
in his interpretation of the Song of Songs--attempts to
counter a Gnostic threat. Was his exegesis a rebuke to
those contemporaries who severed the New Testament from

the Old, degraded the Creator God, and mocked the history
and the customs of the ancient Israelites?

Although the earlier *On First Principles* surely has
an anti-Gnostic thrust,[60] the question remains whether
Origen there addressed a contemporary Gnostic challenge,
His traditional arguments, amalgamation of Gnostic
opinions, and imprecise allusions to his opponents'
views[61] have been cited as evidence that Origen in *On
First Principles* confronted only an "attenuated image"
of Gnosticism, not a present danger.[62] Yet Eusebius reports that Origen knew Gnostics,[63] and Jerome, that he
debated with the Gnostic Candidus.[64] Moreover, the
evidence from Caesarea and from Origen's exegetical works
composed during his Caesarean period suggests that
Marcionites were active there. Eusebius records that a
Marcionite woman was martyred in Caesarea around 257[65]
and that a Marcionite bishop, probably from Caesarea,
was burned at the stake during Diocletian's persecution.[66]

When the historical data are supplemented by the
exegetical, a strong case can be made that Origen's
Scriptural interpretation was at points prompted not so
much by antiquarian interests as by a present concern to
distinguish Catholic teaching from that of the "heretics." To be sure, in his commentaries and homilies,
Origen often lumps together Marcion, Basilides, and
Valentinus and decries their theology and view of Scripture.[67] Yet numerous points in his exegesis suggest that
he did not simply appropriate a general critique of
Gnosticism from his predecessors, but knew details of
Gnostic or Marcionite interpretation. Whether Origen
himself countered actual Gnostics or Marcionites in
Caesarea, the questions they had posed were still commanding attention. Their objections to the Old Testament

and their refusal to accept one God as the source of both
Testaments still troubled Caesarean Christians.[68]   Just
as Origen aimed to forestall his community's adoption of
Jewish practices, so he tried to expunge Marcionite
Christianity as an option for his flock.

Thus Origen's exegesis makes clear that he knew the
Marcionite Appelles' critique of the tale of Noah's
ark.[69] He knew of heretics who called Moses a murderer
for his killing of the Egyptian in Exodus 2:12.[70] He
knew some denigrators of the Old Testament who claimed
that Numbers 33 (the forty-two stopping places of the
Israelites) was written to "no purpose."[71] He knew of
heretics who attacked Joshua's treatment of the
Gibeonites[72] and of the five kings[73] (Joshua 9-10) as
inhuman. He knew of heretics who cited Jeremiah 13:14
(God's promise of punishment without mercy of the
Judeans) as evidence that the God of the prophets was the
demiurge, not the benevolent deity.[74]

Origen also knew that some New Testament passages had
come under Marcionite and Gnostic attack. He knew, for
example, that Marcionites rejected the accounts of Jesus'
birth since they claimed he was not born of a woman.[75]
He knew that heretics had criticized the parable of the
unforgiving servant (Matthew 18:23-35) on the grounds
that the king's delivering the servant to the tormentors
portrayed God as wrathful.[76] He also knew an interpretation of Matthew 20:21 (the seating arrangements in the
Kingdom of Heaven) that placed Paul on Jesus' right hand
and Marcion on his left.[77] Such evidence suggests that
Marcionite and Gnostic interpretation still confounded
Caesareans in Origen's time.

Origen attempts to refute these Marcionite and Gnostic criticisms by providing alternative explanations for
the alleged (and even admitted) absurdities of

Scripture,[78] the shocking behavior of Old Testament
heroes,[79] and the unworthy depiction of God that his
opponents alleged was everywhere present in the Hebrew
books.[80] He warns Catholic Christians against the
heretical penchant to divide the two Testaments and give
deviant interpretations of their contents.[81] The frequency with which Origen addresses these issues in his
exegetical writings suggests that something more was at
stake than historical reporting of past errors.[82]

Despite their evident differences, one point links
Origen's criticism of Jews and of Gnostics (as well as of
"simple Christians"): to his mind, many of them read the
Bible, especially Hebrew Scripture, too literally.
Origen's rebuttal rests on the acceptance of a spiritual
meaning for the Bible as a whole and for every verse in
it;[83] otherwise, Christians are left with a book that
abounds in absurdities, contradictions, and matters too
lowly for religious concern.[84] Origen's allegorical
reading of the text thus appears directed against threats
from several quarters.

However we weigh the relative degree to which
Origen's exegesis reflects his own struggles against Jews
(or Judaizers) and Marcionites, Gribomont's claim that
the exegesis of the first three centuries was carried out
between the poles of Judaism and Gnosticism[85] is apt for
Origen. By the end of the fourth century, the Gnostic
world[86] and Judaism[87] posed fewer problems for Christians
in many, if not all, areas of the Empire; by then, the
debate centered on different theological, ethical, and
ecclesiological issues *within* the Christian camp.[88] The
interpretation of the Song of Songs in the third and
fourth centuries follows the pattern Gribomont posits:
in Origen's exegesis, the themes of Jewish-Gentile union
in Christianity and the goodness of the Old Testament

address problems occasioned by a Jewish and a Gnostic
presence. By the later fourth century, however, new
problems prompted Christians to exploit the Song of Songs
for quite different purposes. First we must turn to
Origen's project.

II

Throughout his exposition of the Song of Songs,
Origen argues for the superiority of the Gospel to the
Law,[89] yet strongly underscores the worth of the Hebrew
tradition. When heretics proclaim that the Old Testament
deity is inferior to the God of the New, they only manifest their own blindness, their inability to see the
Trinity therein.[90] Origen's comments on the Septuagint
reading of Song of Songs 1:2 ("Your breasts are better
than wine") demonstrate his appreciation of the Old
Covenant. He concedes that the Groom's "breasts" (i.e.,
Christ's wisdom and knowledge) are better than the "wine"
of the Law and the Prophets, but affirms that the latter
are nonetheless *good*. By drinking the Old Testament
"wine," the Bride readied herself to receive the even
better drink offered by Christ.[91]

Origen also affirms that the Law and the Prophets
were "most fitting" betrothal gifts for the Bride,[92] but
the veil that covers them must be taken away if they are
to be correctly (i.e., Christianly) understood.[93] Christians should always remember that the "lily" (2:1) of the
Church sprang up in a field that had been well-cultivated
by the Law and the Prophets.[94] Origen even styles the
Synagogue the "brother" or "sister" of the Church: since
Christ in his human aspect was a son of the Synagogue,
the text (1:13) rightly calls him the "nephew" of the
Bride.[95] To reach the mystic perfection of the Song of
Songs, Christians must rehearse the experience of the

ancient Israelites by marching through the sea upon dry
land, escaping from the hands of the Egyptians, and so
on.[96] Such themes accord well with Origen's view that
the "heretics" unjustly deprecate the Old Testament--and
that the Jews deserve censure for their failure to
appreciate the New.

If we closely plot Origen's path through the opening
verses of the Song of Songs, we see that it parallels
Paul's movement in the Epistle to the Romans. The key
lies in Origen's identification of the Bride: sometimes
she represents Judaism, but elsewhere she symbolizes the
Gentiles. The Bridegroom's wooing of her signifies
Christ's desire to bring both Jews and Gentiles into his
household. Throughout Book I of the *Commentary*, the
Bride signifies Judaism. Thus Origen writes that the
angels gave her the Law as a betrothal gift[97] and that
she prepared herself for the "breasts" of Christ through
imbibing the Law and the Prophets.[98] Near the end of
Book II, the Bride again is identified with the Jews:
she is the child who had the Law as her pedagogue before
the coming of Christ her Groom.[99] Yet most of Book II
depicts the Bride otherwise, as the Gentiles now being
drawn to Christianity.[100] Appropriating and adapting
Paul's image in Galatians 4, Origen contrasts the Bride
as the (Gentile) daughter of the "heavenly Jerusalem"[101]
with the Daughters of Jerusalem, that is, the "earthly
Jerusalem" of the Jews.[102]

Most instructive is Origen's discussion of Song of
Songs 1:5, "I am dark but comely, O Daughters of Jerusalem." The Daughters of Jerusalem (the Jews) have
called the Bride "dark" because she as a Gentile was not
enlightened by the Patriarchs' teachings. Acknowledging
their charge, the Bride pleads that she nonetheless was
beautified by the Image of God at creation. Now she

draws further adornment from the Logos,[103] who chants to
her Song of Songs 2:11, "Lo, the winter is past," meaning
the "winter" of her Gentile unbelief.[104] Furthermore,
the Daughters of Jerusalem who mocked the Gentile Bride
as "dark" are reminded that when Miriam criticized the
marriage of Moses (a type of Christ) to a black Ethiopian
woman, she was struck with leprosy.[105] The story stands
as a warning to the Daughters of Jerusalem (the Jews),
for what is Miriam but a type of the Synagogue?[106]

The former "darkness" of the Gentiles and the Jews'
present unbelief are understood by Origen to mean that
Jew and Gentile share a heritage of disobedience.[107]
Nonetheless, the Bride testifies that Christ her Groom
shall return her light to her and she shall be judged
worthy to be called "the light of the world."[108] Not
only the Gentiles shall be restored to God's favor
through Christ; Origen, following Paul, asserts that when
the fullness of the Gentiles has come in, Israel shall
receive a second call.[109]

Such examples indicate the extent to which Origen in
his *Commentary on the Song of Songs* was much occupied
with the theme of Judaism's relation to Christianity, a
theme that helped him counter both Jewish rejection of
Christianity and Marcionite rejection of the Old Testament. This theme, however, was apparently irrelevant to
later Christian concerns. Future generations were
attracted instead to Origen's exposition of the
individual soul in relation to Christ: this was a
"transportable" theme, suited to times when competition
with Jewish and Gnostic beliefs no longer occupied the
center stage of Christian debate.

To be sure, the soul's relation with Christ *is* a
prominent motif in Origen's *Homilies* and *Commentary* on
the Song of Songs. Thus Origen complements his

description of the betrothal gifts the Bride as Church
receives with a corresponding description of the gifts
received by the individual soul, namely, natural law and
reason.[110] When the Groom in Song of Songs 1:8 warns the
Bride, "Unless you know yourself, O fair one among women,
go forth...," Origen imagines that Christ here encourages
the soul to self-knowledge, as Greek and Hebrew sages had
earlier counseled.[111] Parallel to the progress of salvation history that will culminate in the churchly union of
Jew and Gentile is the soul's progress: although she was
a small child needing tutelage, not fed on the strong
meat of the Word but instructed only through "likenesses
and patterns," she will grow sufficiently to receive "the
King reclining at his table" (1:12).[112] As scholars have
previously noted, the theme of the soul's relation to
Christ becomes increasingly dominant as Origen proceeds
through his *Commentary*.[113] Later patristic commentators
upon the Song of Songs, however, exhibit further concerns, peculiar to their day and situation, and to them
we now turn.

III

Of Latin patristic commentators on the Song of Songs,
only one manifests as much interest in Judaism as Origen:
Aponius, who wrote a *Commentary* on the book between A.D.
405-415.[114] The leading scholar of Aponius' work posits
that Aponius was a convert from Judaism, since (he
claims) it would be unprecedented in the year 400 for a
Gentile Christian to treat the history of Judaism so
sympathetically.[115] Familiar with Origen's writings on
the Song of Songs[116] and furthering his interpretations
of Church and soul in relation to Christ,[117] Aponius
outstrips Origen in his positive evaluation of ancient
Israel. Whereas Origen cast the Daughters of Jerusalem

as earthly Jews who despised the Gentiles, Aponius
describes them as great-souled Israelites who pleased
God by observing the Law before Christ's Incarnation.[118]
Expunged from Aponius' interpretation is the unflattering
picture of unbelieving, disobedient Jews.[119] The
"fairest among women" (1:8) who to Origen signifies the
Gentile Bride, is identified by Aponius as the Hebrew
people, the most beautiful among the nations.[120] The
Bride represents not the Gentiles, but Israel who comes
to Christianity.[121] Similarly, the "chosen dove" (6:9)
is for Aponius the people of the synagogue.[122] Like
Origen before him, Aponius hopes that when the full
complement of Gentiles has been ushered into the Church,
the Jews will come to believe;[123] they will even desire
the crown of martyrdom,[124] the highest of all Christian
virtues.[125] Aponius, however, is the only Latin patristic interpreter of the Song of Songs to wax so
enthusiastic over the Israelites.

   More typical in this respect is Gregory of Elvira's
Commentary on the Song of Songs. Writing late in the
fourth century, Gregory probably knew both Origen's and
Hippolytus' works.[126] He accepts the now-traditional
explanation of the Song's cast of characters[127] as given
in Origen's first *Homily.*[128] Yet far from praising the
Jews as does Aponius, Gregory of Elvira calls the people
of the synagogue "old and foolish"; they live according
to the "old man," unlike the maidens who represent the
"new man" from among the Gentiles.[129] Whereas for Origen
the "sons of the mother who fought against me" (1:6) are
the apostles who fought in the Gentile Church to overcome
unbelief, pride, and disobedience,[130] for Gregory those
"fighting sons" are the Jews who persecuted the Church
and crucified Christ.[131] Thus Gregory's appreciation of
ancient Judaism is considerably dimmer than either
Origen's or Aponius'.

More striking, however, is the way in which fourth
and early fifth-century Christian writers interpreted the
Song of Songs to meet the very different demands of
church polity and theological struggle posed by their own
era. To what extent these interpreters of the Song of
Songs were inspired by Origen's *Commentary* and *Homilies*
is difficult to judge. In part, the difficulty arises
because Hippolytus' *Commentary* developed similar themes
to Origen's,[132] and since we know that fourth-century
Fathers such as Ambrose knew Hippolytus' *Commentary*[133] as
well as Origen's works,[134] it is imprudent to press the
argument that they depended upon Origen's interpretation
alone. Nonetheless, Origen's view that the Song of Songs
speaks of spiritual, not carnal, love,[135] and teaches
Jesus' love for the Church and the Christian's soul,
shaped the framework within which the fourth and fifth-
century interpreters wrote. In three ways the later
patristic writers expanded upon earlier readings of the
Song of Songs: first, they understood the Song of Songs
as an exhortation to Christian asceticism; second, they
developed a Mariological interpretation of the book; and
third, they exploited the Song to address contemporary
controversies on the nature of the Church.

Whereas Origen bypassed discussion of ascetic issues
in his work on the Song of Songs, Jerome and Ambrose con-
centrate heavily on an ascetic interpretation of the
book. Origen himself, of course, was a committed
ascetic[136] and included much moral exhortation in his
comments on the Song of Songs,[137] yet his hermeneutic
here is not governed by ascetic concerns. He even avoids
ascetic interpretations of passages that might suggest
them. For example, in his explication of the "turtledove" (the Septuagint reading of Song of Songs 1:10),
Origen notes the allegedly monogamous nature of the

bird,[138] but provides an ecclesiological rather than an
ascetic interpretation: turtledoves remind us that the
Church wants no union other than that with Christ.[139]
Moreover, a check of references to Biblical texts in
Henri Crouzel's *Virginité et mariage selon Origène*, per-
haps the most detailed exploration of ascetic themes in
Origen's writings, confirms the absence of ascetic argu-
ment in Origen's works on the Song of Songs.[140]

Although ascetic interpretation surfaces in the commentaries of Gregory of Elvira[141] and Aponius,[142] it is
Jerome and Ambrose, the great ascetic teachers of the
fourth-century Latin West, who exploit the Song of Songs
most fully as ascetic propaganda. Even though neither
composed a commentary *per se* on the Biblical book,[143]
their other writings abound in citations from the Song of
Songs.

In his famous *Epistle* 22 to the virgin Eustochium,
for example, Jerome cites the Song of Songs twenty-five
times. The girl (like Eustochium) who devotes herself to
virginity has Christ as her Spouse. Christ will lead her
into the bedchamber (1:4);[144] he is the one she will seek
upon her bed at night (3:1).[145] Although she, like all
humans, is "black" with sin, she may still claim to be
"comely" (cf. 1:5). Besides, the Bridegroom is not
haughty: he married an Ethiopian woman (Jerome's
exegesis here reveals his knowledge of Origen's exposition of this passage). Christ will impart his wisdom
to her and will miraculously lighten her complexion so
that others will inquire, in the words of the Septuagint
reading of Song of Songs 8:5, "Who is this that goes up
and has been made all white?"[146] At the time of her
death, Eustochium's spouse will call to her, "Arise, my
love, my fair one" (2:10).[147] As she ascends to heaven,
the angels will wonder, "Who is this that looks like the
dawn, fair as the moon, light as the sun?" (6:10).[148]

According to Jerome, the Song of Songs contains
practical as well as spiritual advice for the virgin.
The book teaches her not to roam outside, as did the
Bride in Song of Songs 3:2, or she may suffer the same
fate, to be wounded and stripped (5:7).[149] Besides,
Jesus is a jealous mate who will not take lightly his
fiancée's public expeditions.[150] She must remember that
she is "a garden enclosed, a fountain sealed"--an
interesting early use of Song of Songs 4:12 to counsel
ascetic seclusion.[151] If she but stay at home, Jesus
will knock at her door, whispering, "Open to me, my sister, my love, my dove, my perfect one" (5:2).[152] It
comes as no surprise that *Epistle* 22 was composed in
about the same year (383-384) that Jerome translated
Origen's *Homilies on the Song of Songs*.

Other letters of Jerome counseling ascetic renunciation also press the Song of Songs into service. He
deemed the book applicable to female Christians at all
stages of life. Thus he advises that the infant daughter
of Laeta be reared in the ascetic seclusion he thinks
Song of Songs 1:4, 5:3, 5:7, and 8:10 suggest.[153] The
adolescent virgin Demetrias, as a Bride of Christ, should
be encouraged in her devotion by Song of Songs 1:4, 1:7,
and 3:1;[154] she should recall that the "lilies" among
which the Bridegroom pastures his flocks (2:16) and with
which he identifies himself (2:1) signify his
virginity.[155] The widow Furia is promised that if she
continue in chastity, the King will say to her, "Thou art
all fair, my love; there is no spot in thee" (4:7).[156]
And at the death of his friend, the widow Paula, Jerome
cites Song of Songs 2:10-12 and 5:10 in her commemora-
tion.[157] Thus Christian ascetics of all ages and
"grades" could take encouragement and consolation from
the Song of Songs.

In addition to his use of the Song of Songs in his
letters, Jerome employs an ascetic interpretation of the
book in his debate with Jovinian. Jovinian had denounced
Jerome's ascetic views and claimed that the Song of
Songs' exaltation of marriage supported his case; Jerome
argued in reply that the Song of Songs counsels
virginity, not marriage.[158] In the *Adversus Jovinianum*,
Jerome interprets the passing of winter and arrival of
spring (2:11-13) to mean not just the passage from the
Old to the New Law, a meaning suggested earlier by
Origen;[159] for Jerome, the New Law specifically brings
with it the advent of virginity.[160] Likewise, according
to Jerome, the voice of the turtledove (2:12) heralds
chastity and reminds us that "even dumb birds reject
second marriage."[161] The swords that Solomon's mighty
men carry in Song of Songs 3:7-8 were to cut away the
pleasure of the flesh.[162] Further, Jerome provides an
explanation for why the "silver ornaments" of the Bride
(1:11) come in three varieties: they symbolize the
widows, the continent, and the married.[163] So heavily
does Jerome rely on the Song of Songs in *Against
Jovinian* I, 30-31 that he finally abandons his exegesis
for fear that scornful readers may already have spurned
his interpretation.[164]

Ambrose as well as Jerome uses the Song of Songs to
counsel ascetic living: well over fifty references to
the Song of Songs in his ascetic treatises testify to
this fact. Of special interest is Ambrose's use of the
Song of Songs 4:12 ("a garden enclosed, fountain sealed")
to counsel the virgin to remain "enclosed and sealed"[165]
so that she "preserves her fruit."[166] That this verse
was a favorite with him is suggested by his frequent use
of it to advocate virginity.[167] Ambrose thinks the verse
gives additional advice for the virgin: she is to keep

"closed" her modesty and her mouth, but "open" her ears,
her mind, and her hand in generosity to the poor.[168]
     A second line of later patristic interpretation on
Song of Songs 4:12 focused on the Virgin Mary as "enclosed and sealed." Early commentators did not much
concern themselves with Mary. For example, Hippolytus'
Commentary contains only two brief references to the
mother of Jesus.[169] The interest in Mariology, however,
had dramatically escalated by the late fourth century.
If the Song of Songs was now read as a hymn of praise to
virginity, Mary might fittingly be singled out for
special attention. Thus "the voice of the turtledove"
(2:12) reminds Aponius that chastity was first proclaimed
in the land when Mary asked the angel how she chould conceive, since she had not known a man:[170] Aponius leaps
with astounding alacrity from the turtledove's cry to
Mary's virginal conception. And throughout Aponius' *Commentary*, Mary serves as exemplar of the virginal life.
     Yet more could be done, and was done, to extol Mary's
virginity through an exegesis of the Song of Songs.
Indeed, Song of Songs 4:12 ("a garden enclosed, fountain
sealed") became the definitive Biblical verse by which
the notion of Mary's virginity *in partu* was argued. To
be sure, Origen himself was innocent of any such interpretation; in the fourteenth *Homily on Luke*, he even
writes that Mary's womb was opened by the birth of Christ
as it had not been by sexual intercourse.[172] But
Origen's understanding of Jesus' birth was too lowly for
later patristic writers, especially after Mary's virginal
childbearing had come under attack by Jovinian and
Bonosus.[173]
     Jerome himself did not take a definitive stand on
Mary's virginity *in partu*. Citing Song of Songs 4:12 in
Adversus Jovinianum I, 31, he notes that the verse

reminds us of Mary, who was simultaneously a mother and
a virgin. Although he interprets John 19:41 (that no one
was laid in Jesus' rock tomb "after him")[174] to mean the
perpetual virginity of Mary, a teaching he had championed
for at least a decade,[175] he does not here definitely
affirm Mary's virginity *in partu.* In *Epistle* 48, however, written within a year after the *Adversus Jovinianum*
as a defense of the book, Jerome returns to Song of Songs
4:12 and John 19:41, and adds two verses that tilt his
meaning toward an affirmation of Mary's virginity *in
partu*: John 20:19 (that Jesus entered through "closed
doors")[176] and Ezekiel 44:2-3 (that the east gate of the
Temple remains "always shut").[177]

    Although Jerome may have wavered on Mary's virginity
in partu, Ambrose reached a firmer conclusion. The very
birth of Jesus was "immaculate," he claims.[178] He states
the matter plainly: the closed womb of Mary was "not
loosed" (*non solvit*) by the birth; although Jesus passed
through her, he did not "open" (*aperuit*) her.[179] To Mary
should be applied Song of Songs 4:12 "a garden enclosed,
fountain sealed."[180] In *Epistle* 42 to Pope Siricius,
reporting on the Synod of Milan's condemnation of
Jovinian, Ambrose defends the *in partu* virginity of Mary
by reference to the *porta clausa* of Ezekiel 44:2, and
more circuitously, to the Apostles' Creed ("conceived by
the Virgin Mary" reminds Ambrose of Isaiah 7:14, the
Latin text of which--*Ecce virgo in utero accipiet, et
pariet filium*--he interprets to mean that Mary was a virgin not only when she conceived, but also when she
brought forth).[181] On this point, it is interesting to
have Augustine's notice that it was Ambrose's defense of
Mary's virginity *in partu* that gave Jovinian his opportunity to accuse the Catholics of "Manicheanism."[182]

Aponius, writing a few decades after Ambrose, is similarly convinced of Mary's *in partu* virginity. Since he mentions Bonosus by name in his *Commentary*,[183] Aponius' affirmation is probably directed against this detractor of the *in partu* virginity. His comments on the theme are found exactly where we would expect: at Song of Songs 4:12. Here Aponius writes that Mary's womb did not suffer "damage" through Christ's birth,[184] for the body of the baby Jesus "abandoned the intact womb of the Virgin."[185] The medieval Mariological interpretation of the Song of Songs thus owes much to these later Latin Fathers--but little to Origen himself.

A third and final use of the Song of Songs by the fourth and fifth-century Latin Fathers centered on ecclesiology. Although Origen had commented extensively on the Church in interpreting the Song of Songs,[186] he could not have foreseen the new service the book would provide in the Donatist controversy. Earlier Latin-writing Christians had already used the "closed garden" passage to defend the purity of the Church,[187] had cited the "dove" as a symbol of the Church's purity,[188] and had appropriated "I am black but comely" to prove how the Church could be simultaneously sinful and redeemed.[189] For example, in the midst of the Novatian dispute, Cyprian had cited both the "one dove" and the "garden enclosed" passages to champion the unity and the purity of the Church.[190] That a century and a half later both Donatists and Catholics might claim the Song of Songs (and Cyprian) for themselves opened a new chapter in the book's interpretation.[191]

The Donatists cited the "sealed fountain" to argue that the Church must be kept pure,[192] should expel sinners and *traditores* from its midst.[193] The Donatists often coupled the "sealed fountain" with Ephesians 5:27,

that the Church should be "without spot or wrinkle."[194]
In addition, the Donatists quoted Song of Songs 1:17
(the Groom pastures his flock at midday) to claim that
they were the true Church: "midday," *meridies*, is a
symbol of Africa, which exists *in meridiana orbis*.[195]
For the Donatists, the verse proved that Christ intended
to found his true Church, not that of the "spotted and
wrinkled" Catholics, in North Africa.

Against such arguments, Augustine developed an anti-
Donatist interpretation of the Song of Songs. His
attempt to enlist the Canticles for the Catholic cause is
notable, for Augustine, unlike Jerome and Ambrose, had
little interest in the book[196] if we judge correctly from
the paucity of references to the Song of Songs in his
voluminous writings. Nonetheless, since the schismatics
could not be allowed to co-opt the Song of Songs for
their sect, Augustine took up the argument. The "garden
enclosed, fountain sealed" (4:12), he claims, does not
refer to the whole Church, but only to the holy and
righteous Christians called by God. Yet who these may
be, only God knows for sure--and we must not rush
precipitously to pre-judge the matter. By asserting that
the "garden" and the "fountain" do not include sinners,
even if they are baptized members of the Church,[197]
Augustine attempts to ward off Donatist criticism of
Catholicism's tolerance of sinners within the pure Bride
of Christ.

Augustine also offers a second and different interpretation of the passage: in Song of Songs 4:12, we must
distinguish between the "garden" and the "fountain." The
"garden" signifies outward baptism, which even wicked
people receive; the "fountain," by contrast, denotes only
those to whom God gives the Holy Spirit and inducts as
"citizens of the angelic commonwealth." Although Simon

Magus in Acts 8:13 received outward baptism (the "garden"), he did not receive the "sealed fountain" that God
reserves for his beloved elect.[198]   By such ingenious
exegesis, Augustine in the face of Donatist attacks
explained why the Catholic Church tolerated sinners in
its ranks.

Augustine also responded to the Donatist challenge
with other verses from the Song of Songs. For him, the
"dove who is one" (6:9) represents the Catholic Church;
schismatics who split the Church (the Donatists) have no
share in that "one dove."[199]   If, however, they can be
persuaded to return to the "one dove" of Catholicism,
they need not be rebaptized.[200]   Although the "dove" of
the Church sighs and groans amid the rapacity of hawks[201]
and the wickedness of crows,[202] her present lot requires
her to endure these trials. Why else would Jesus have
taught us to pray, "Forgive us our debts," if already
on earth the Church were pure, as the Donatists insist?
Purity will not be found in the Church as a whole until
the future life.[203]   For the present, Augustine avers,
the Church is like the "lily among the brambles" (2:2),
the good mixed with the evil.[204]

Last, Augustine wished to correct the Donatist interpretation of Song of Songs 1:7, that Christ had pastured
his flock especially in North Africa, that is, in the
Donatist Church. The Church was not meant to thrive in
just one place, Augustine retorts, but in all the corners
of the earth; the "pastures" in which we are to feed
Christ's sheep exist everywhere.[205]   Besides, he adds in
a quaint astronomical aside, the midday sun is not at
its height over Africa, in any case, but over Egypt, the
country in which thousands of God's servants fulfill the
counsel of angelic perfection to sell their goods for
the sake of the poor (Matthew 19:21).   Moreover,

Augustine reminds his readers, "pastures" customarily
betoken quiet spots where Christians can find repose in
the Son of God, undisturbed by the "tumultuous unrest of
the raging *circumcelliones*."[206] Thus could the Song of
Songs, a favorite with the Donatists, be turned against
them by Augustine's skillful exegesis.

That the Song of Songs could have been employed in
these polemics might have surprised Origen, yet it was
his exegesis of the Church and the soul as Christ's Bride
that had opened the way to such novel interpretations of
the ancient Hebrew love poem. By interpreting the Song
of Songs as a saga of Judaism's and paganism's progress
to Christianity--a progress from the children's milk and
the weak man's vegetables to the solid food of Christ's
athletes[207]--Origen had furnished an exegesis relevant
to his own time and situation. In the same way, fourth
and fifth-century Latin commentators addressed the
religious problems of their own day by an appeal to the
Song of Songs.

NOTES

[1]See, for example, Charles Bigg, *The Christian Platonists of Alexandria*, 2nd ed. (Oxford: Clarendon Press, 1913); Jean Daniélou, *Origène* (Paris: La Table ronde, 1948); Hal Koch, *Pronoia und Paideusis: Studien über Origenes und sein Verhältnis zum Platonismus* Arbeiten zur Kirchengeschichte 22 (Berlin/Leipzig: W. deGruyter & Co., 1932); Walter Völker, *Das Volkommenheitsideal des Origenes*. Beiträge zur historischen Theologie 7 (Tübingen: J.C.B. Mohr [Paul Siebeck] 1931).

[2]Also commented on by N.R.M. deLange, *Origen and the Jews: Studies in Jewish-Christian Relations in Third-Century Palestine* (Cambridge: Cambridge University Press, 1976), p. 3.

[3]Jerome, *Origenes, Homiliae in Canticum Canticorum*, prologus (GCS 33, 26): "While in his other books, Origen surpassed everyone else, in his Song of Songs, he surpassed himself." The comment is repeated by Rufinus in a letter to Macarius (=Jerome, *Ep*. 80, 1 [CSEL 56, 102-103]) and by medieval commentators such as Peter of Riga (*Aurora Petri Rigae Biblia Versificata. A Verse Commentary on the Bible*, ed. Paul E. Beichner, The University of Notre Dame Publications in Mediaeval Studies 19 [Notre Dame, Ind.: University of Notre Dame Press, 1965], II, 703). I thank Ann Matter for the latter reference. For a brief overview of Origen's work on the Song of Songs, see Joseph W. Trigg, *Origen: The Bible and Philosophy in the Third-Century Church* (Atlanta: John Knox Press, 1983), pp. 201-205.

[4]G. Nathanael Bonwetsch, *Studien zu den Kommentaren Hippolyts zum Büche Daniel und Hohen Liede*, TU 16, 2 (Leipzig: J.C. Hinrichs, 1897), pp. 1-2, 7-8, 81-85; Bonwetsch provides a German translation of the Georgian text in *Hippolyts Kommentar zum Hohenlied auf Grund des Grusinischen Textes*. TU 23, 2 (Leipzig: J.C. Hinrichs, 1903); also see Gertrud Chappuzeau, "Die Auslegung des Hohenliedes durch Hippolyt von Rom," *Jahrbuch für Antike und Christentum* 19 (1976), 81.

[5]Olivier Rousseau, *Origène, Homélies sur le Cantique des Cantiques.* SC 37 (Paris: Les Editions du Cerf, 1954), p. 16.

[6]See Pietro Meloni, "Ippolito e il Cantico dei Cantici," *Ricerche su Ippolito. Studia Ephemeridis "Augustinianum"* 13 (1977), 98-100; Bonwetsch, *Studien,* pp. 53-56.

[7]Ernst Dassmann, "Ecclesia vel Anima. Die Kirche und ihre Glieder in der Hohenliederklärung bei Hippolyt, Origenes und Ambrosius von Mailand," *Römische Quartalschrift* 61 (1966), pp. 124-129 (p. 129: Hippolytus gives only a few interpretations pertaining to the individual soul).

[8]"Of the 574 known homilies only 21 have survived in Greek, and 388 no longer exist even in Latin translation": R.P. Lawson, "Introduction," *Origen. The Song of Songs. Commentary and Homily.* Ancient Christian Writers 26 (New York/Ramsey, N.J.: Newman Press, 1957), p. 16. Of the New Testament Commentaries, we have in Greek only eight books of the *Commentary on Matthew* and nine books of the *Commentary on John.* Epiphanius of Salamis claimed that he was read 6000 books of Origen (Rufinus, *De Adulteratione Librorum Origenis* 15 [CCL 20, 16]; also Jerome, *Apologia contra Rufinum* III, 23 [PL 23, 496]). Rufinus mocked Epiphanius' claim, and said he doubted that there were 2000 books of Origen to be read (Jerome, *Apologiam contra Rufinum* II, 22 [PL 23, 466]).

[9]Texts in GCS 33, 26-241. The *Homilies* were better known in the Middle Ages than the *Commentary:* see Helmut Riedlinger, *Die Makellosigkeit der Kirche in den Lateinischen Hohenliedkommentaren des Mittelalters.* Beiträge zur Geschichte der Philosophie und Theologie des Mittelalters 38, 3 (Münster Westf.: Aschendorff, 1958), pp. 24-25; Baehrens, "Einleitung," GCS 33, xxvii.

[10]E.g., Eugène de Faye, *Origène: sa vie, son oeuvre, sa pensée.* Bibliothèque de l'Ecole des Hautes Etudes, Sciences Religieuse 37 (Paris: Librairie Ernest Leroux, 1923), I, 63.

[11]E.g., Jacques Chênevert, *L'Eglise dans le Commentaire d'Origène sur les Cantique des Cantiques.* Studia. Travaux de recherche 24, (Bruxelles/Paris: Desclée de Brouwer, 1969), p. 8; Henri Crouzel, et al., *Origène. Homélies sur S. Luc.* SC 87 (Paris: Les Editions du Cerf, 1962), pp. 85, 87; Friedhelm Winkelmann, "Einige Bermerkungen zu

den Aussagen des Rufinus von Aquileia und des Heironymus
über ihre Ubersetzungstheorie und-Methode," *Kyriakon.
Festschrift Johannes Quasten*, ed. P. Granfield and J.A.
Jungmann (Münster Westf.: Aschendorff, 1970), II, 532-
547.

[12]Lawson, "Introduction," p. 19.

[13]Rufinus' translation of the *Commentary* was done in
ca. 410 in Sicily, where he had retired to escape the
Gothic invasion of Italy (see Lawson, "Introduction,"
pp. 4-5).

[14]Jerome, *Ep.* 33, 4 (CSEL 54, 256): the *Commentary*
was a ten-book work.

[15]Jerome mentions a *Commentary on the Song of Songs*
by Reticius of Autun (which he faults) in *Ep.* 37, 1
(CSEL 54, 286-287); In *De Viris Illustribus*, Jerome
reports the following Latin commentaries on the Song of
Songs, which he either knows first-hand or has heard of:
Hilary of Poitiers (100 [PL 23, 739]); Reticius (82 [PL
23, 727]); Victorinus of Pettau (74 [PL 23, 722]), in
addition to some Greek ones. Also see Friedrich Ohly,
*Hohenlied-Studien. Grundzüge einer Geschichte der Hohen-
liedauslegung des Abendlandes bis um 1200.* Schriften
der Wissenschaftlichen Gesellschaft an der Johann Wolfgang Goethe-Universität Frankfurt am Main, Geisteswissen-
schaftliche Reihe 1 (Wiesbaden: Frank Steiner, 1958),
27.

[16]Although Gregory of Elvira's *Commentary* may date to
the same decade: see Ohly, *Hohenlied-Studien*, pp. 28-
30. For a discussion of the literary background of
Gregory's work that helps establish its date, see André
Wilmart, "Les 'Tractatus' sur le Cantique attribués à
Grégoire d'Elvire," *Bulletin de Littérature Ecclésiastique* 3, 8 (1906), 233-299.

[17]Pierre Nautin, *Origène. Sa vie et son oeuvre.*
Christianisme antique 1 (Paris: Beauchesne, 1977), pp.
380-381, 403, 411; Eusebius, *Historia Ecclesiastica* VI,
32, 2 (GCS 9, 2, 586); Rousseau, *Origène*, pp. 8-9.

[18]Nautin, *Origène*, p. 238; W.A. Baehrens, *Uber-
lieferung und Textgeschichte der Lateinisch Erhaltenen
Origeneshomilien zum Alten Testament.* TU 42, 1 (Leipzig:
J.C. Hinrichs, 1916), pp. 233-234; Wilhelm Riedel, *Die
Auslegung des Hohenliedes in der jüdischen Gemeinde und
der griechischen Kirche* (Leipzig: A. Deichert, 1898),
pp. 52-53. Also see Jerome, *Ep.* 33, 4 (CSEL 54, 256).

[19]Noted especially by Riedel, *Die Auslegung*, p. 55.

[20]Jerome, *Origenes, Homiliae in Canticum Canticorum*, Prologus (GCS 33, 26).

[21]See especially Völker, *Die Volkommenheitsideal*, chp. 2.

[22]Origen, *Comm. Cant.* prologus, 1 (GCS 33, 61); *Hom. Cant.* I, 1 (GCS 33, 29). Section numbers for the *Commentary* are provided in the English translation, not in the Latin text.

[23]See Ohly, *Hohenlied-Studien*, p. 19, and D. de Bruyne, "Les Anciennes Versions latines du Cantique des Cantiques," *Revue Bénédictine* 38 (1926), 97-122, esp. pp. 120, 122.

[24]Origen, *Comm. Cant.* I, 1 (GCS 33, 89-90).

[25]Origen, *Comm. Cant.* III (IV), 15 (GCS 33, 229).

[26]Origen, *Comm. Cant.* prologus, 1 (GCS 33, 61); *Hom. Cant.* I, 1 (GCS 33, 29).

[27]Origen, *Comm. Cant.* I, 1 (GCS 33, 89); also see Riedl, *Die Auslegung*, p. 61.

[28]Origen, *Comm. Cant.* prologus, 3 (GCS 33, 75); *Hom. Cant.* I, 1 (GCS 33, 29).

[29]Origen, *Comm. Cant.* I, 3 (GCS 33, 100).

[30]Origen, *Comm. Cant.* II, 2 (GCS 33, 128-129); cf. *Hom. Cant.* I, 6 (GCS 33, 36).

[31]Origen, *Hom. Cant.* I, 1; 5 (GCS 33, 29, 34).

[32]Origen, *Comm. Cant.* I, 5 (GCS 33, 110-111).

[33]Origen, *Comm. Cant.* I, 2; 5 (GCS 33, 94, 111).

[34]Origen, *Comm. Cant.* I, 5 (GCS 33, 111).

[35]The theme of Koch's *Pronoia und Paideusis*, esp. pp. 32-36 and Pt. 1, chp. 5; also see Henry Chadwick's comments on Origen in *Early Christian Thought and the Classical Tradition: Studies in Justin, Clement, and Origen* (New York: Oxford University Press, 1966), chp. 3.

[36]Origen, *Comm. Cant.* II, 8 (GCS 33, 160-161).

[37]Origen, *Comm. Cant.* III, 12 (GCS 33, 208); Genesis 1:26.

[38]Origen, *Comm. Cant.* prologus, 2 (GCS 33, 63) (cf. Plato's *Symposium*).

[39]See Peter Gorday, *Principles of Patristic Exegesis: Romans 9-11 in Origen, John Chrysostom, and Augustine* (New York/Toronto: The Edwin Mellen Press, 1983), chp. 3; for Origen's understanding of Romans 11, see Hans Bietenhard, *Caesarea, Origenes und die Juden* (Stuttgart/ Berlin/Köln/Mainz: Verlag W. Kohlhammer, 1974), chp. 8.

[40]Nautin, *Origène*, pp. 346-347.

[41]Nautin, *Origène*, p. 347. Nautin's comments are made concerning the writing of the *Hexapla*; he opposes the view advanced by S.P. Brock, "Origen's Aims as a Textual Critic of the Old Testament," *Studia Patristica* 10 (1970), 215-218.

[42]Nautin, *Origène*, p. 347.

[43]See Origen's testimony in *De Principiis* I, 3, 4 (GCS 22, 53); *Sel. in Ezech.* 9, 2 (PG 13, 800); but note deLange's reservations about this individual (*Origen*, pp. 23-28).

[44]E.g., *De Principiis* IV, 3, 14 (GCS 22, 346); *Ep. ad Africanum* 6 (PG 11, 61); *Contra Celsum* I, 45; 55; II, 31 (GCS 2, 95, 106, 159).

[45]Jerome, *Apologia contra Rufinum* I, 13 (PL 23, 408), probably referring to a *Commentary on Psalms* now extant only in fragments (PG 12, 1056); see Nautin, *Origène*, pp. 277-278; deLange, *Origen*, p. 27 (the only Jewish teacher Origen mentions by name).

[46]DeLange, *Origen*, pp. 58, 22-23. For an argument that Origen's critical textual work was in part motivated by his desire that Christians be better armed for discussion and debate with Jews, see Dominique Barthélemy, "Origène et le texte de l'Ancien Testament," in *Epektasis. Mélanges patristiques offerts au Cardinal Jean Daniélou*, ed. J. Fontaine and C. Kannengiesser (Paris: Beauchesne, 1972), pp. 247-261, esp. pp. 248-249.

[47]David J. Halperin, "Origen, Ezekiel's Merkabah, and the Ascension of Moses," *Church History* 50 (1981), 261-275 (arguing for Origen's knowledge and use of Jewish homiletic expositions employed at Pentecost in third-century Caesarean synagogues); Reuven Kimelman, "Rabbi Yohanan and Origen on the Song of Songs: A Third-Century Jewish-Christian Disputation," *Harvard Theological Review* 73 (1980), 567-595 (arguing for Origen's use of Jewish commentary and for probable rabbinic knowledge of Origen's arguments).

[48]Full bibliographical data in n. 2 above.

[49]See evidence in deLange, *Origen*, pp. 86-87; also see S. Krauss, "The Jews in the Works of the Church Fathers," *The Jewish Quarterly Review* 5 (1893), 146-147, and Bietenhard, *Caesarea*, pp. 50-51.

[50]Origen, *Hom. in Lev.* X, 2 (GCS 29, 442-445).

[51]Origen, *Hom. in Jerem.* XII, 13 (GCS 6, 99-100).

[52]Lee I. Levine, *Caesarea Under Roman Rule* (Leiden: E.J. Brill, 1975), chp. 5; also see Bietenhard, *Caesarea*, pp. 8-11.

[53]Levine, *Caesarea*, p. 88.

[54]E.g., Y.F. Baer, "Israel, the Christian Church, and the Roman Empire from the Time of Septimius Severus to the Edict of Toleration of A.D. 313," *Scripta Hierosolymitana* 7 (1961), 100-105; Raphael Loewe, "Apologetic Motifs in the Targum to the Song of Songs," in *Biblical Motifs: Origins and Transformations*, ed. A. Altmann. Studies and Texts 3 (Cambridge, Mass.: Harvard University Press, 1966), pp. 161-162: Ephraim E. Urbach, "The Homiletical Interpretation of the Sages and the Exposition of Origen on Canticles, and the Jewish-Christian Disputation," *Scripta Hierosolymitana* 22 (1971), 247-252, 255, 257. Roland Murphy warns, however, that there is little or no evidence regarding the earliest interpretations of the book, either within Judaism or Christianity: "Patristic and Medieval Exegesis--Help or Hindrance?," *Catholic Biblical Quarterly* 43 (1981), 506-507.

[55]E.g., Baer, "Israel," p. 100; Urbach, "Homiletical," pp. 255, 263-265.

[56]Akiba, *m. Yadaim* 3, 5; cited and discussed in deLange, *Origen*, p. 60.

[57]Adolf Harnack, *Die kirchengeschichtliche Ertrag der exegetischen Arbeiten des Origenes. Teil I: Hexateuch und Richterbuch.* TU 42, 3 (Leipzig: J.C. Hinrichs, 1918), pp. 22-30, 47-52; *Teil II: Die Beiden Testamente mit Ausschluss des Hexateuchs und des Richterbuchs.* TU 42, 4 (Leipzig: J.C. Hinrichs, 1919), pp. 81-87.

[58]Gustave Bardy, "Les Traditions juives dans l'oeuvre d'Origène," *Revue Biblique* 34 (1925), 217-252.

[59]E.g., Krauss, "The Jews," pp. 139-157; A. Marmorstein, "Deux Renseignements d'Origène concernant les juifs," *Revue des Etudes Juives* 71 (1920), 190-199; A. Marmorstein, "Judaism and Christianity in the Middle of the Third Century," *Hebrew Union College Annual* 10 (1935), 223-261.

[60]Especially Books III and IV; see discussion in Alain Le Boulluec, "La Place de la polémique antignostique dans le *Peri Archôn*," in *Origeniana. Premier colloque international des études origéniennes,* ed. H. Crouzel, et al. Quaderni di Vetera Christianorum 12 (Bari: Istituto di Letteratura Cristiana Antica, Universita' di Bari, 1975), pp. 47-61; also Josep Ruis-Camps, "Orígenes y Marción. Carácter preferentemente antimarcionita del Peri Archôn," in *Origeniana*, pp. 297-312.

[61]Le Boulluec, "La Place," pp. 55, 58-61; also see Marguerite Harl, "Pointes antignostiques d'Origène: le questionnement impie des Ecritures," in *Studies in Gnosticism and Hellenistic Religions, Presented to Gilles Quispel on the Occasion of His 65th Birthday,* ed. R. Van den Broek and M.J. Vermaseren. Etudes Préliminaires aux Religions Orientales dans l'Empire Romain 91 (Leiden: E.J. Brill, 1981), 203.

[62]Le Boulluec, "La Place," p. 60.

[63]Eusebius, *Historia Ecclesiastica* VI, 18, 1-2 (GCS 9, 2, 556).

[64]Jerome, *Apologia contra Rufinum* II, 19 (PL 23, 462-463).

[65]Eusebius, *Historia Ecclesiastica* VII, 12 (GCS 9, 2, 666).

[66]Eusebius, *De Martyribus Palaestinae* X, 3 (GCS 9, 2, 931); the bishop dies in the company of someone

explicitly identified as coming from Caesarea (X, 2).
See Levine, *Caesarea*, p. 131.

[67] E.g., Origen, *Hom. in Ex.* III, 2 (GCS 29, 164);
Hom. in Num. IX, 1; XII, 2 (GCS 30, 54-55, 98); *Hom. in
Lev.* VIII, 9 (GCS 29, 407); *Hom. in Jesu Nave* VII, 7;
XII, 3 (GCS 30, 335, 370); *Hom. in Matt.* XII, 23 (GCS 40,
122).

[68] Harnack, "*Die kirchengeschichtliche Ertag,*" Teil I,
p. 38; Harl, "Pointes," p. 216.

[69] Origen, *Hom. in Gen.* II, 2 (GCS 29, 27-30); cf.
Contra Celsum V, 54 (GCS 3, 58).

[70] Origen, *Hom. in Num.* VII, 1 (GCS 30, 38); cf. *Contra
Celsum* III, 12 (GCS 2, 212).

[71] Origen, *Hom. in Num.* XXVII, 2 (GCS 30, 258).

[72] Origen, *Hom. in Jesu Nave* X, 2 (GCS 30, 359);
Joshua 9:27.

[73] Origen, *Hom. in Jesu Nave* XI, 6 (GCS 30, 366);
Joshua 10:26.

[74] Origen, *Hom. in Jerem.* XII, 5 (GCS 6, 91).

[75] Origen, *Hom. in Luc.* XVII (4) (GCS 35, 115).

[76] Origen, *Hom. in Matt.* XIV, 13 (GCS 40, 313-314).

[77] Origen, *Hom. in Luc.* XXV (5) (GCS 35, 162).

[78] Origen, *Comm. in Joan.* X, 26-27 (17-18); 40-41 (24-
25) (GCS 10, 198-201, 217-219); *Hom. in Gen.* II, 2-5
(GCS 29, 27-36).

[79] E.g., Origen, *Hom. in Num.* VII, 1 (GCS 30, 38);
Hom. in Jesu Nave X, 2; XI, 6 (GCS 30, 359, 366).

[80] E.g., Origen, *Hom. in Gen.* IV, 6 (GCS 29, 56-57);
Hom. in Num. IX, 4; XIX, 2 (GCS 30, 58-59, 181); *Hom. in
Lev.* V, 1; XI, 2 (GCS 29, 333-334, 451); *Hom. in Jesu
Nave* XII, 3 (GCS 30, 370); *Hom. in Ezech.* I, 1 (PG 13,
667).

[81] E.g., Origen, *Hom. in Num.* IX, 1; 4; XII, 2; XXVII,
2 (GCS 30, 55-58, 59, 98, 258); *Hom. in Lev.* XIII, 4 (GCS
29, 473-474); *Hom. in Ezech.* VII, 3-4; II, 5 (PG 13,

721-723, 686-687); *Hom. in Jerem.* X, 5; XVII, 2 (GCS 6, 75-76, 144-145); *Hom. in Luc.* XVII (4-5); XVIII (5) (GCS 35, 115-116, 125); *Comm. in Joan.* I, 13(14); VI, 3-6(2-3); X, 5-6(4) (GCS 10, 108-115, 175-176). Origen's *Commentary on John* was composed (at least in part) to refute the earlier commentary by the Gnostic Heracleon: see Elaine H. Pagels, *The Johannine Gospel in Gnostic Exegesis: Heracleon's Commentary on John*. SBL Monograph Series 17 (Nashville/New York: Abingdon, 1973). Also now see Jean-Michel Poffet, *La Méthode exégetique d'Heracléon et d'Origène. Commentateurs de Jn 4: Jésus, la Samaritaine et les Samaritains*. Paradosis 28 (Fribourg: Editions Universitaires, 1985).

[82]At least the questions the Gnostics posed were still a threat to Catholic Christianity: Harnack, *Die kirchengeschichtliche Ertrag*, Teil I, p. 38; Harl, "Pointes," p. 216. The fact that Origen chose to write a *Commentary on John* opposing Heracleon, at least a half-century after Heracleon's work, suggests that Gnostic interpretations still needed combating (in Alexandria, in this case).

[83]Origen, *Hom. in Num.* IX, 4 (GCS 30, 59): It is an "old" Testament only for those who take it in the fleshly sense; if we take it spiritually, it is always "new." Hence both testaments are "New Testaments." See Harl, "Pointes," pp. 216-27; LeBoulluec, "La Place," p. 49. DeLange calls "remarkable" Origen's failure to credit the Jews with the spiritual and allegorical interpretations he knew they held (*Origen*, pp. 82, 83, 105-106).

[84]See Origen's comments, for example, in *Hom. in Gen.* II, 2-5; III, 5; VI, 1-3; XI, 1; 2 (GCS 29, 27-36, 44-46, 65-70, 100-104); *Hom. in Ex.* II, 1-4; X, 2-4; XI, 2 (GCS 29, 154-161, 246-252, 253-254); *Hom. in Num.* VII, 1-2; XII, 1-2; XXVI, 3 (GCS 30, 37-41, 93-101); *Hom. in Lev.* IV, 7; X, 1; XVI, 2 (GCS 29, 326-327, 440-442, 246-249); *Hom. in Jesu Nave* XV, 1 (GCS 30, 381-382); *Comm. in Joan.* X, 26-32(17-18); 40-41(24-25) (GCS 10, 198-206, 217-219).

[85]J. Gribomont, "Nouvelles Perspectives sur l'exégèse de l'Ancien Testament à la fin du IIIe siècle," *Augustianianum* 22 (1982), 358; also see Hermann Josef Vogt, *Das Kirchenverständnis des Origenes*. Bonner Beiträge zur Kirchengeschichte 4. (Köln/Wien: Böhlau Verlag, 1974), p. 193.

420 *Ascetic Piety and Women's Faith*

[86]Gribomont, "Nouvelles Perspectives," p. 359: exceptions are Evagrius Ponticus and perhaps Gregory of Nyssa.

[87]Gribomont, "Nouvelles Perspectives," p. 359: exceptions for Syria and for some intellectuals like Jerome and Ambrosiaster.

[88]Gribomont, "Nouvelles Perspectives," p. 359.

[89]E.g., Origen, *Comm. in Cant.* III, 11; 13 (GCS 33, 205, 220).

[90]Origen, *Comm. in Cant.* II, 8 (GCS 33, 158).

[91]Origen, *Comm. in Cant.* I, 2 (GCS 33, 94, 96-97).

[92]Origen, *Comm. in Cant.* I, 1 (GCS 33, 89, 91).

[93]Origen, *Comm. in Cant.* III, 11 (GCS 33, 204-205).

[94]Origen, *Comm. in Cant.* III, 4 (GCS 33, 177-178).

[95]Origen, *Comm. in Cant.* II, 10 (GCS 33, 168-169); *Hom. in Cant.* II, 3 (GCS 33, 45): in the *Homilies*, "fratruelis" for the LXX's "adelphidos." For Jerome's translation, see Albertus Vaccari, ed., *Cantici Canticorum. Vetus Latina Translatio a S. Hieronymo ad Graecum Textum Hexaplarem Emenda* (Roma: Edizioni di Storia e Letteratura, 1959), p. 13 (Old Latin versions read "frater").

[96]Origen, *Comm. in Cant.* prologus, 4 (GCS 33, 80-81).

[97]Origen, *Comm. in Cant.* I, 1 (GCS 33, 91).

[98]Origen, *Comm. in Cant.* I, 1 (GCS 33, 96).

[99]Origen, *Comm. in Cant.* II, 8 (GCS 33, 157).

[100]Origen, *Comm. in Cant.* II, 1 (GCS 33, 113).

[101]Origen, *Comm. in Cant.* II, 3 (GCS 33, 131).

[102]Origen, *Comm. in Cant.* II, 1 (GCS 33, 114).

[103]*Ibid.*

[104]Origen, *Comm. in Cant.* III(IV), 14 (GCS 33, 226).

[105] Origen, *Comm. in Cant.* II, 1 (GCS 33, 114).

[106] Origen, *Comm. in Cant.* II, 1 (GCS 33, 118). The story is also told in *Hom. in Cant.* I, 6 (GCS 33, 36-37).

[107] Romans 1-3, 9-11.

[108] Origen, *Comm. in Cant.* II, 2 (GCS 33, 127).

[109] Origen, *Comm. in Cant.* III(IV), 15 (GCS 33, 233-234).

[110] Origen, *Comm. in Cant.* I, 1 (GCS 33, 91).

[111] Origen, *Comm. in Cant.* II, 5 (GCS 33, 141, 143).

[112] Origen, *Comm. in Cant.* II, 8 (GCS 33, 164-165).

[113] E.g., by Riedl, *Die Auslegung*, p. 60.

[114] Johannes Witte, *Der Kommentar des Aponius zum Hohenliede* (Erlangen: Von Junge & Sohn, 1903), pp. 77, 21-22, 34, 39-46, 69.

[115] Witte, *Der Kommentar*, pp. 67, 69.

[116] Witte, *Der Kommentar*, pp. 90-92.

[117] Witte explicates, *Der Kommentar*, pp. 80-81.

[118] Aponius, *In Canticum Canticorum Explanatio* I (PL Supp. 1, 818).

[119] *Ibid.*

[120] Aponius, *In Cant.* II (PL Supp. 1, 831).

[121] *Ibid.*

[122] Aponius, *In Cant.* IX (PL Supp. 1, 962).

[123] Aponius, *In Cant.* XII (PL Supp. 1, 1011).

[124] Aponius, *In Cant.* XII (PL Supp. 1, 1024).

[125] Aponius, *In Cant.* I; III (PL Supp. 1, 805, 856).

[126] See Ohly, *Hohenlied-Studien*, pp. 28-30, for a discussion of Gregory of Elvira and his work on the Song of Songs.

[127]Gregory of Elvira, *Commentarium in Cantica Canti-corum*, praefatio (*Bibliotheca Anecdotorum. Pars I: Monumenta Regni Gothorum et Arabum in Hispaniis*, ed. Gotth. Heine [Leipzig: T.O. Weigel, 1848]), p. 134.

[128]Origen, *Hom. in Cant.* I, 1 (GCS 33, 29).

[129]Gregory of Elvira, *Comm. in Cant.* I (Heine, pp. 138-139).

[130]Origen, *Comm. in Cant.* II, 3 (GCS 33, 131).

[131]Gregory of Elvira, *Comm. in Cant.* II (Heine, pp. 141-142).

[132]See Bonwetsch, *Hippolyts Kommentar*, p. 89.

[133]See Bonwetsch, *Hippolyts Kommentar*, pp. 13, 28, 37, 49, 56, 60 for passages apparently borrowed by Ambrose; also see Riedlinger, *Die Makellosigkeit*, pp. 20-21.

[134]In the opinion of F. Homes Dudden, Ambrose probably knew the following works of Origen: the *Commentary* and *Homilies on Genesis*, the *Homily on Psalms 36-38*, the *Commentary on Psalm 1*, *Homily XIII on Numbers*, the *Homilies on Luke* and the *Commentary on the Song of Songs* (*The Life and Times of St. Ambrose* [Oxford: Clarendon Press, 1935], I, 113 n. 3). On Augustine's very limited knowledge of Origen see Pierre Courcelle, *Les Lettres grecques en occident de Macrobe à Cassiodorus*. Bibliothèque des Ecoles Françaises d'Athénes et de Rome 159. 2nd ed., rev. (Paris: E. de Boccard, 1948), pp. 185-187.

[135]Origen, *Comm. in Cant.* prologus, 1 (GCS 33, 62).

[136]Eusebius, *Historia Ecclesiastica* VI, 3, 9-12; 8, 1-2 (GCS 9, 2, 526, 528, 534).

[137]E.g., Origen, *Comm. in Cant.* prologus, 2; II, 3; 5; 7 (GCS 33, 70-73, 134, 143, 187-188).

[138]Origen, *Comm. in Cant.* II, 7 (GCS 33, 155); see *Physiologus* (28, 2).

[139]Origen, *Comm. in Cant.* II, 7 (GCS 33, 155). Origen's other interpretation of the turtledove in *Comm. in Cant.* III(IV), 14 (GCS 33, 224) (the bird shuns crowds) is also taken from the *Physiologus* (28, 1).

140Henri Crouzel, *Virginité et mariage selon Origène*. Museum Lessianum, section théologique 58 (Paris/Bruges: Desclée de Brouwer, 1963): the Song of Songs is not much exploited by Origen for this purpose, according to the index of Biblical texts.

141Gregory of Elvira, *Comm. in Cant.* I (Heine, p. 141): the curtains of Solomon (Song of Songs 1:5) are red from the blood of Christ's passion and white to show the splendor of consecrated virgins; II (Heine, p. 149): the "neck" (Song of Songs 1:10) of the Church is decorated with martyrs and virgins.

142E.g., Aponius, *In Cant.* I; III; IV; VI; VIII; XI (PL Supp. 1, 802, 816, 860; 850; 868-869; 896-897; 943-944; 989).

143Ambrose's *De Isaac et Anima*, however, nearly constitutes a running commentary on the Song of Songs; also see his peculiar use of the Song of Songs to describe Valentinian II's qualities (mostly spiritual) in *De Obitu Valentiniani Consolatio* 58-77 (PL 16, 1437-1442).

144Jerome, *Ep.* 22, 1 (CSEL 54, 145).

145Jerome, *Ep.* 22, 17 (CSEL 54, 166).

146Jerome, *Ep.* 22, 1 (CSEL 54, 145).

147Jerome, *Ep.* 22, 41 (CSEL 54, 209).

148*Ibid.*

149Jerome, *Ep.* 22, 25 (CSEL 54, 178-180).

150*Ibid.*

151*Ibid.*

152Jerome, *Ep.* 22, 26 (CSEL 54, 181).

153Jerome, *Ep.* 107, 7 (CSEL 55, 298).

154Jerome, *Ep.* 130, 2; 7 (CSEL 56, 177, 186).

155Jerome, *Ep.* 130, 8 (CSEL 56, 187).

156Jerome, *Ep.* 54, 3 (CSEL 54, 463).

424 *Ascetic Piety and Women's Faith*

[157] Jerome, *Ep.* 108, 28; 31 (CSEL 55, 347, 349).

[158] Jerome, *Adversus Jovinianum* I, 30 (PL 23, 263).

[159] Origen, *Comm. in Cant.* III(IV), 14 (GCS 33, 226).

[160] Jerome, *Adversus Jovinianum* I, 30 (PL 23, 263).

[161] Jerome, *Adversus Jovinianum* I, 30 (PL 23, 263), reading "mutis avis" rather than "multis avis."

[162] Jerome, *Adversus Jovinianum* I, 30 (PL 23, 264).

[163] Jerome, *Adversus Jovinianum* I, 30 (PL 23, 263).

[164] Jerome, *Adversus Jovinianum* I, 31 (PL 23, 266).

[165] Ambrose, *De Institutione Virginis* 9, 58; 61 (PL 16, 335).

[166] Ambrose, *De Institutione Virginis* 9, 60 (PL 16, 335).

[167] See also Ambrose, *Ep.* 63, 36 (PL 16, 1250); *Exhortatio Virginitatis* 5, 29 (PL 16, 359); *Expositio Evangelii secundam Lucam* IV, 13 (PL 15, 1700).

[168] Ambrose, *De Institutione Virginis* 9, 58 (PL 16, 335).

[169] Hippolytus, *Comm. in Cant.* 2; 21 (Bonwetsch, pp. 33, 56).

[170] Aponius, *In Cant.* IV (PL Supp. 1, 868-869).

[171] Aponius, *In Cant.* III; IV; VI; XI (PL Supp. 1, 850, 869, 897, 988).

[172] Origen, *Hom. in Luc.* XIV (7-8) (GCS 35, 100-101). For Origen's Mariology, see H. Crouzel, "Introduction," *Origène, Homélies sur S. Luc.* SC 87 (Paris: Les Editions du Cerf, 1962), pp. 11-64.

[173] Bonosus is specifically mentioned by Aponius as a detractor of Mary's perpetual virginity (*In Cant.* II [PL Supp. 1, 830]). Ambrose against Jovinian on this point: *Ep.* 42, 12-13 (PL 16, 1176). Augustine also testifies to Jovinian's attack upon Ambrose in *De Nuptiis et Concupiscentia* II, 5, 15 (PL 44, 445).

[174]Jerome, *Adversus Jovinianum* I, 31 (PL 23, 265).

[175]Since his treatise *Adversus Helvidium*, dated to 383 A.D.

[176]Jerome, *Ep.* 49(48), 21 (CSEL 54, 386).

[177]*Ibid.*

[178]Ambrose, *Expositio Evangelii secundum Lucam* II, 56 (PL 15, 1654). For Ambrose's views, see Dudden, *Life*, II, 393-395, 599; also see Charles W. Neumann, *The Virgin Mary in the Works of Saint Ambrose.* Paradosis 17 (Fribourg: Editions Universitaires, 1962).

[179]Ambrose, *De Institutione Virginis* 8, 52-53 (PL 16, 334).

[180]Ambrose, *De Institutione Virginis* 17, 111 (PL 16, 347). Ambrose also applied the *porta clausa* of Ez. 44:2 to Mary: see *Ep.* 42, 5-6 (PL 16, 1174) and *De Institutione Virginis* 8, 52 (PL 16, 334).

[181]Ambrose, *Ep.* 42, 5-6 (PL 16, 1174).

[182]Augustine, *Contra Julianum* I, 2, 4 (PL 44, 643); also *De Haeresibus* 82 (PL 42, 45-46: "Virginitatem Mariae destruebat, dicens eam pariendo fuisse corruptam.")

[183]Aponius, *In Cant.* II (PL Supp. 1, 830).

[184]Aponius, *In Cant.* VII (PL Supp. 1, 918: "nulla fraude corruptionis reserato utero").

[185]Aponius, *In Cant.* IX (PL Supp. 1, 963: "...intactum uterum Virginis derelinquens...").

[186]See Chênevert, *L'Eglise*, for numerous references; also his "L'Eglise et les parfaits chez Origène," *Sciences Ecclésiastiques* 18 (1966), 253-282.

[187]E.g., by Jerome, *Ep.* 15, 1 (CSEL 54, 62-63).

[188]E.g., by Ambrose, *De Mysteriis* 7, 37 (PL 16, 418).

[189]E.g., Ambrose *De Santu Spiritu* II, 10, 112 (PL 16, 799); *De Mysteriis* 7, 35 (PL 16, 417).

[190] Cyprian, *Ep.* 69 (=76), 2 (PL 3, 1186).

[191] For Cyprian's influence on the Donatists, see W.H.C. Frend, *The Donatist Church. A Movement of Protest in Roman North Africa* (Oxford: Clarendon Press, 1952), pp. 131, 136-138, 140, 238, 316, 318-320; for Cyprian's influence on Augustine, see pp. 130, 134, 237 n. 1.

[192] Felix of Ammacura in Augustine, *De Baptismo* VI, 40, 77, (PL 43, 221); Fulgentius, *Libellus de Baptismo* 5; 7; 8 (Paul Monceaux, *Histoire littéraire de l'Afrique chrétienne depuis les origines jusqu'à l'invasion arabe* [Paris: E. Leroux, 1901-1923], V. 336-337); Fulgentius in Augustine, *Contra Fulgentium Donatistam* 6 (PL 43, 765-766).

[193] Fulgentius, *Libellus de Baptismo* 5; 16 (Monceaux, V, 337; 339); Augustine, *De Correctione Donatistarum* 9, 38 (PL 33, 809-810).

[194] Fulgentius, *Libellus de Baptismo* 15 (Monceaux, V, 339); Augustine, *Contra Fulgentium Donatistam* 21 (PL 43, 772); also used by Donatists at the Council of Carthage in 411 (*Gesta Collationis Catharginensis* 249 [PL 11, 1406-1407]).

[195] Augustine, *De Unitate Ecclesiae* 16, 40; 24, 69 (PL 43, 421-422, 441).

[196] See Ohly, *Hohenlied-Studien*, pp. 46-47.

[197] Augustine, *De Baptismo* V, 27, 38; VI, 3, 5; VII, 51, 99 (PL 43, 195, 199, 241).

[198] Augustine, *Contra Cresconium* II, 15, 18 (PL 43, 477).

[199] Augustine, *De Baptismo* I, 11, 15; III, 17, 22-18, 23; IV, 3, 5; V, 16, 21 (PL 43, 118, 149-151, 157, 187).

[200] Augustine, *De Baptismo* III, 18, 23 (PL 43, 150).

[201] Augustine, *De Baptismo* III, 17, 22 (PL 43, 149-150).

[202] Augustine, *De Baptismo* V, 16, 21 (PL 43, 187).

[203] Augustine, *De Correctione Donatistarum* 9, 38-39 (PL 33, 809-810).

[204]Augustine, *De Unitate Ecclesiae* 14, 35; 21, 60 (PL 43, 417-418, 436).

[205]Augustine, *De Unitate Ecclesiae* 16, 40; 19, 51 (PL 43, 422, 430-431), alluding to John 21:17.

[206]Augustine, *De Unitate Ecclesiae* 16, 41 (PL 43, 423).

[207]Origen, *Hom. in Lev.* I, 4 (GCS 29, 286).

STUDIES IN WOMEN AND RELIGION

Books by
Elizabeth A. Clark

Ascetic Piety and Women's Faith
Essays in Late Ancient Christianity

Clement's Use of Aristotle
*The Aristotelian Contribution to Clement of Alexandria's
Refutation of Gnosticism*

Jerome, Chrysostom, and Friends
Essays and Translations

John Chrysostom
On Virginity; Against Remarriage
translated by Sally Rieger Shore
(with introduction by Elizabeth A. Clark)

The Golden Bough, The Oaken Cross
The Virgilian Cento of Faltonia Betitia Proba
(with Diane Hatch)

The Life of Melania the Younger
Introduction, Translation, and Commentary

Women and Religion
A Feminist Sourcebook of Christian Thought
(with Herbert Richardson)

Women in the Early Church